TRENDS IN PHYSIOLOGICAL SCIENCES

CELLS TO SYSTEMS

Editor

Mohammad Fahim

SERIALS PUBLICATIONS
NEW DELHI

First Published in 2002

ISBN 81-86771-04-2

Published by : **Serials Publications**
4, B.S.S. Hall,
Khyber Pass Market
Civil Lines, Delhi-110054 (India)
Phone : 0091-11-3931659
Fax : 0091-11-3932678
Email : serials@satyam.net.in

Printed at : Shivam Offset Press
A-12/1, Naraina Ind. Area-I
New Delhi-110 028

PRINTED IN INDIA

CONTENTS

PREFACE

The proceedings of the symposia on Cellular and Molecular Physiology, Environment and Pollution and Drug Development and Toxicity comprise papers presented by eminent scientists invited from India and abroad who are globally known for their contributions in these important areas of life sciences. The symposia were jointly organized by Vallabhbhai Patel Chest Institute, University of Delhi, Delhi and the Physiological Society of India.

Only recently in depth knowledge in these areas has been possible with the availability of new techniques for learning cellular and molecular physiology which integrates the functions of various types of cells into a whole system of human and animal body. Human life relies upon the functions of the total system and not on functions of any part in isolation. However, at cellular and molecular level, physiology provides precise information regarding the mechanisms involved in the normal and abnormal functioning of the specific organs of the body by keeping a balance through a vast network of feedback controls. This internal balance (homeostasis) is essential for normal life which is generally disturbed in disease. With the accelerating rate of biomedical advances, it is necessary to update the knowledge of the subject in a comprehensive manner with emphasis on recent developments and controversial issues.

This book encompasses latest developments in the fields of cellular, molecular and systemic physiology with contributions from acknowledged authorities in these disciplines. It covers a wide range of topics in Life Sciences including oxidants, environment, molecular cardiology and cancer. This book can be used as a guidebook by graduate and post-graduate stdents who want to pursue a career in Life Sciences and as a reference book by senior researchers who are interested in some of the current problems in the emerging areas of Life Sciences.

Acknowledgment is due to all scientists who have contributed to the scientific content of the book, my colleagues and students for helping me at various stages in the preparation of this book and Shivam Offset Press, New Delhi for its publication. The financial assistance from, Department of Biotechnology (DBT), Department of Science & Technology (DST), Council of Scientific & Industrial Research (CSIR), National Acadmy of Medical Sciences (NAMS), Defence Research & Development Organisation (DRDO) and Indian Council of Medical Research (ICMR) is thankfully acknowledged.

Mohammad Fahim

SIDE EFFECTS OF LITHIUM ON VARIOUS TISSUES : USE OF COLLAGEN AS A MODEL SYSTEM

MARGARET TZAPHLIDOU

Medical Physics Laboratory, Medical School, Ioannina University, 45110 Ioannina, Greece

Summary

Lithium is widely used in medicine as an antidepressive drug and for myelosuppression attenuation during chemotherapy. In spite of abundant literature, questions on the effects of lithium on collagen which is one of the major components of tissues and organs are far from being answered. We have examined the effects of lithium (1.5 meq/Kg of body weight) on mouse and rabbit skin, mouse bone, rabbit liver as well as rat cranial arachnoid and dura mater collagen fibrils by electron microscopy and image analysis. Animals were sacrificed 1 day, 2 and 6 months after the end of a 30 consecutive days experimental period. In all cases investigated although there were areas with normal collagen fibrils there were also regions where the characteristic parallel packing of fibrils was lost completely or it was preserved for a part of the area. Lithium treated collagen fibrils had a significant decrease in mean diameter and showed a higher degree of variability in width and shape than collagen fibrils from controls. In skin as well as in cranial arachnoid and dura mater many clusters of abnormal fibrils were found with a highly irregular outline when viewed in cross-sections.

INTRODUCTION

Lithium is being widely used in the treatment of

mental diseases (Foster, 1992; Emilien et al., 1995) and in the attenuation of myelosuppression during chemotherapy (Cass et al., 1981; Lyman et al., 1981). Since its introduction numerous studies have been published on its possible side effects on various tissues or organs while the effects of lithium on the cellular level only recently started to be extensively investigated (Tyobeka and Becker, 1990; Matthopoulos et al., 1995; Spiegel and Soares, 1999). Studies on side effects concern the haemopietic tissues (Barthelmebs et al., 1993), kidneys (Ottosen et al., 1987), bone metabolism (Holak and Raisz, 1979) and skin (Deandrea et al., 1982; Kounadi et al., 1994; Tzaphlidou and Kounadi, 1998). To our knowledge, however, the effects of lithium on collagen, which is one of the major components of tissues and organs have not extensively been reported in the literature. This paper reports the appearance of structural abnormalities of skin, bone, liver as well as cranial arachnoid and dura mater collagen fibrils due to treatment with lithium chloride.

MATERIALS AND METHODS

Male, Swiss Albino mice 5 weeks and 1 year of age, Wistar rats 5 weeks old as well as rabbits 7 months old were used throughout. Animals were injected (intraperitonealy) with lithium chloride (LiCl) solution once a day for 30 consecutive days in a way that each injection corresponds to a dose of 1.5 meq Li/Kg of body weight (meq=milliequivalent). This dose was chosen for study as this is a common dose for the treatment of manic depression (Wissocq et al., 1979). After treatment, the animals were kept in groups of four. They were sacrificed 1 day, 2 and 6 months after the last injection. The same number of animals that were given no injections served as controls. These animals, in groups of four, were age-matched with the LiCl-treated animals. Killing of animals was performed under light ether anesthesia. All studies were approved by the Ioannina University Institutional

Animal Care and Use Committee.

Skin pieces of 1 mm^2 were obtained from the left shoulder area from each mouse and rabbit. Such sized pieces from rabbit liver and rat cranial arachnoid and dura mater were also obtained. Samples were fixed overnight at 4°C in 2.5% glutaraldehyde buffered to a pH of 7.4 with 0.1 mol/L sodium cacodylate. Then they washed in 0.1 mol/L sodium cacodylate buffer and postosmicated for 2 h at 4°C in 1% osmium tetroxide in cacodylate buffer (0.1 mol/L, pH 7.4), followed by washing in the same buffer, and finally rinsed in distilled water. The specimens were then dehydrated in a graded alcohol series and infiltrated overnight with a 1:1 mixture of propylene oxide, and the resin used for embedding. Final embedding was performed in capsules with agar resin. Polymerization was completed in 48 h at 60° C.

In addition, the right tibia from each mouse was removed, carefully freed from the soft tissue, and prepared for electron microscopy. The tissue was fixed in a solution containing 4 mL of 0.05 mol/L phosphate buffer (pH 7.2), 0.5 mL of 25% glutaraldehyde, and 0.5 mL of 12.5 % ethylene-diamine tetraacetic acid (EDTA) disodium salt. After 2 h the bone was administered changes of 2 mL of EDTA in 3 mL of phosphate buffer until decalcified. These bone samples were trimmed into approximately 0.5 mm^3 cubes and fixed in 2.5% glutaraldehyde in 0.05 mol/L phosphate buffer (pH 7.2). The specimens were washed in the same buffer before and after fixation and rinsed in distilled water. Finally, specimens were dehydrated and processed for embedding in agar resin as other samples.

Ultrathin sections were stained positively with 2% aqueous solution of phosphotungstic acid (PTA; pH 3.3) for 1 h and then with 2% aqueous solution of uranyl acetate (UA; pH 4.3) for 30 min and then washed briefly in distilled water before and after UA staining.

Electron microscopy was performed on a JEOL JEM-100 CX-II electron microscope and micrographs were taken at X8,000-X20,000. Grating replicas were used for magnification calibration.

For measurements of the diameter of collagen fibrils, areas of cross-sectional collagen were photographed. At least 400 collagen fibrils from at least four micrographs were analyzed for each animal. Thus, as in each group four animals were involved, the diameters of at least 1600 fibrils from 16 micrographs were averaged for each group. Measurements were carried out by the use of an appropriate algorithm developed in the laboratory. The mean and standard deviation, as well as data from an unpaired t-test, were calculated with a laboratory computer according to Snedecor and Cochran (1967) and Hays (1988). The significance of the difference between the two samples compared was estimated by using a p value following the statistical methods described by Snedecor and Cochran (1967).

RESULTS

With a lithium dose of 1.5 meq Li/Kg , after 30 days of treatment, severe alterations in mouse and rabbit skin collagen fibrils were detected at the ultrastructural level. Abnormalities were observed from the first stage, i.e. when animals were sacrificed 1 day after the last lithium injection. In mouse skin, areas with normal collagen fibrils were seen to contain fibrils in marked disarray (Figure 1a,b). In some regions the characteristic parallel packing of normal fibrils (Figure 1d) was lost completely, whereas in others it was preserved for a part of the area. In addition, Figure 1(a) demonstrates how some of the fibrils in a bundle, instead of being in register with the rest of the fibrils, form a 'hairpin' loop. Helical twisting is also apparent and in some regions this is very pronounced (Figure 1c). Although results shown in Figure 1 come from mouse skin collagen similar abnormalities

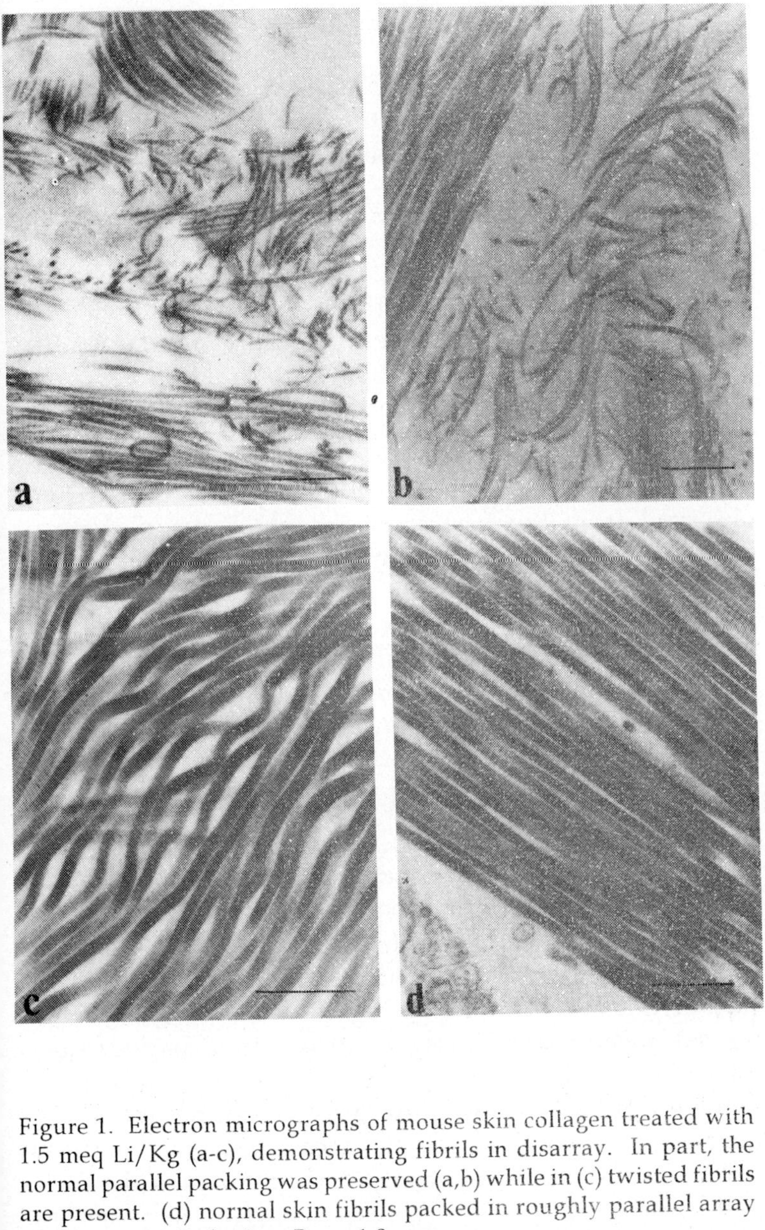

Figure 1. Electron micrographs of mouse skin collagen treated with 1.5 meq Li/Kg (a-c), demonstrating fibrils in disarray. In part, the normal parallel packing was preserved (a,b) while in (c) twisted fibrils are present. (d) normal skin fibrils packed in roughly parallel array from age-matched mice. Bar = 1.0 μm

were observed in skin collagen from other animals, such as rabbits. In Figure 2 results are presented from rabbit skin collagen fibrils treated with lithium chloride. In some cases the organization of the fibrils in the whole area is very anarchic (Figure 2a,c) and the formation of the 'hairpin' loop is highly abnormal (Figure 2b,d).

Collagen from other tissues was also examined. The overall collagen fibril architecture from rabbit liver and rat cranial arachnoid and dura mater was disturbed from the first stage. In both tissues, in most areas the arrangements of fibrils is very anarchic, similar to that shown in Figure 3b-d. Although there are some areas where the normal parallel packing (Figure 3a) of fibrils remains this is usually replaced by a random arrangement.

In mouse bone collagen the abnormalities were not observed from the first stage, in which the packing of lithium treated fibrils resembles to normal. In the other two cases, i.e. when the animals were sacrificed 2 and 6 months after treatment, areas with normal collagen fibrils were seen to contain fibrils in marked disarray. In some regions, even in the areas where the characteristic parallel packing remained there were fibrils showing a marked twisting (Tzaphlidou et al., 2000).

Lithium treatment had a dramatic effect on collagen fibril diameter. Mouse skin collagen fibrils treated with 1.5 meq Li/kg revealed a marked decrease ($p<0$) in their diameter compared to normal with a high variability in width (Figure 4a-d). Table 1, in the first column of figures, summarizes the mean diameter values (with standard deviation) of collagen fibrils from lithium-treated mice (5 weeks of age) and sacrificed various times after the last injection. A comparison has been made between these values and those obtained from age-matched, normal mice. In all cases, there is a significant difference ($p<0$) in the mean diameter between the index and control subjects. In the last two cases, i.e. when the animals were sacrificed 2 and 6 months after the last

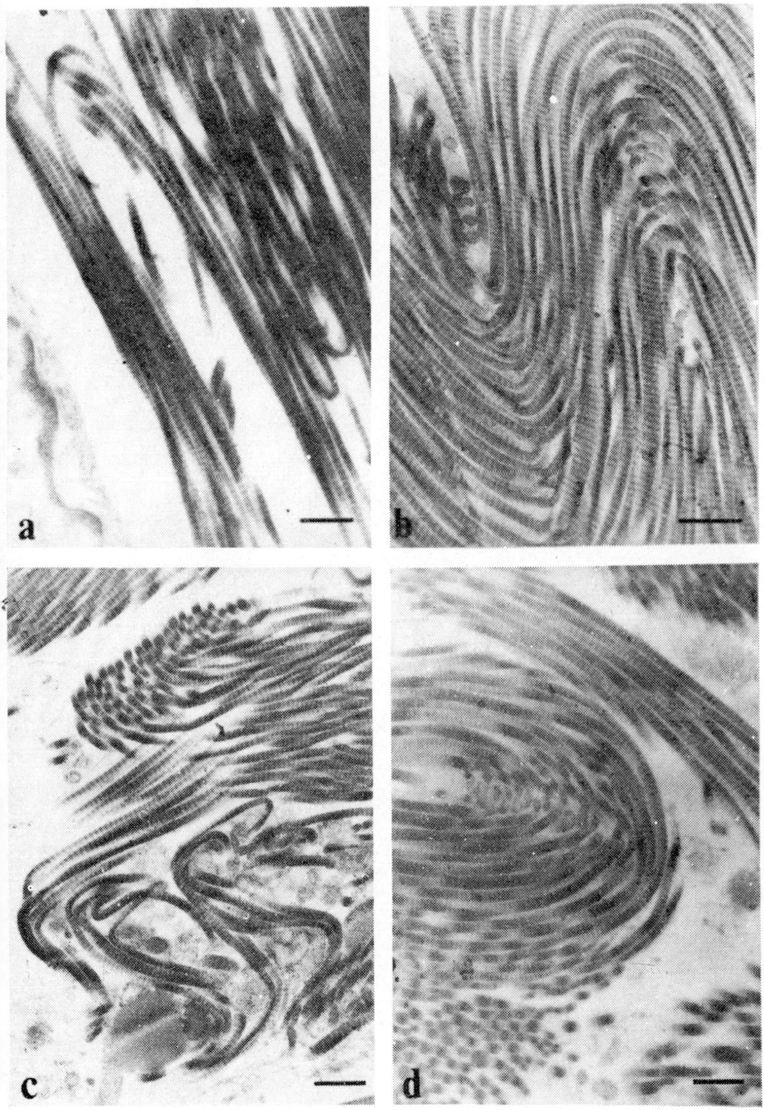

Figure 2. Rabbit skin collagen fibrils treated with 1.5 meq Li/Kg. The parallel packing of fibrils is interrupted by fibrils forming a 'hairpin' loop (a, d). In some areas this feature is very prominent (b, c). Bar = 0.5 μm

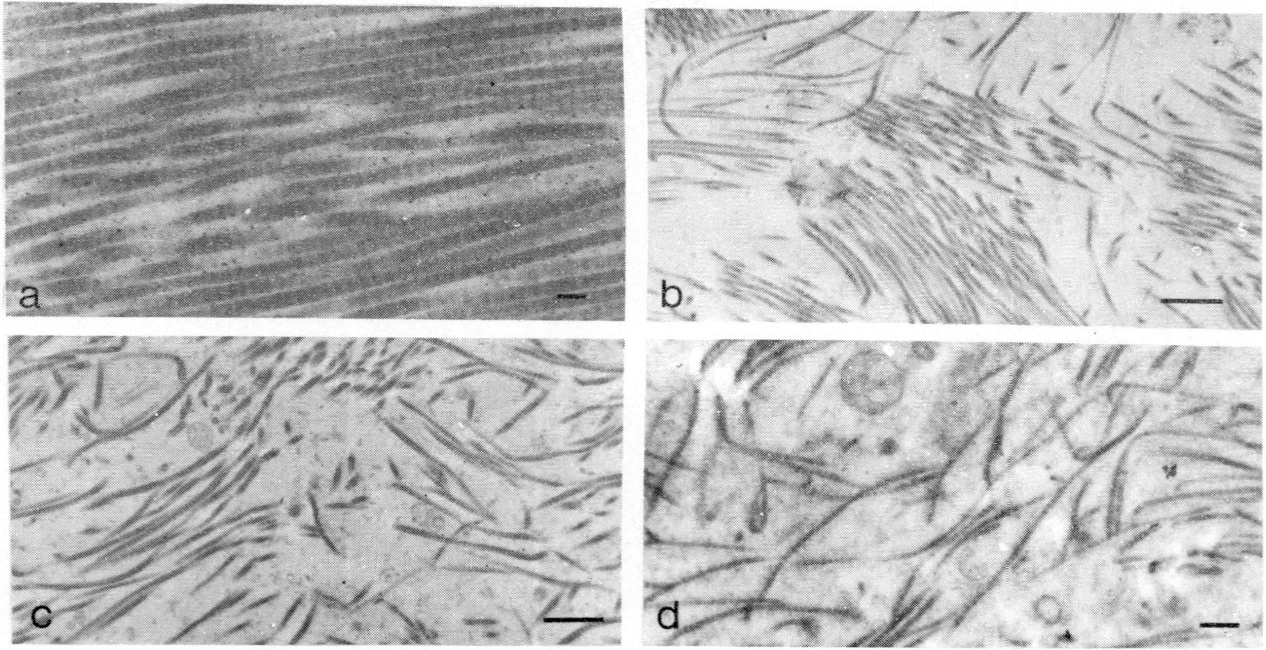

Figure 3. Electron micrographs of rat dura mater collagen treated with 1.5 meq Li/Kg (b-d) demonstrating fibrils in disarray. In some regions the characteristic parallel packing of normal fibrils (a) was lost completely (c,d), whereas in others it was preserved for a part of the area (b). Bar = 0.8 μm

TABLE 1

The effect of 1.5 meq Li/kg on mouse skin collagen fibrils: mean diameter of fibrils from lithium treated mice and sacrificed various times after the last injection compared with those from age-matched normal fibrils.

	Mean diameter values and standard deviation (nm)			
Time of sacrificing	Animals five weeks of age treated with Li	Animals one year of age treated with Li	Normal age-matched animals with the fist group	Normal age-matched animals with the second group
1 day	95.2±11.6	94.4±13.1	110.9±9.1	109.3±11.2
2 months	96.1±10.7	-	110.9±12.9	-
6 months	95.5±10.4	95.8±12.6	109.1±11.5	109.4±12.9

lithium injection, many clusters of abnormal fibrils were found, with a diameter of 187.9 ± 25.2 nm and an irregular outline (Figure 4c,d) deviated from an ideal circular or elliptical profile. These abnormal large fibrils constituted approximately 15% of the whole population and were not taken into account for the calculation of the mean diameter.

Lithium treated rabbit skin fibrils were smaller than those found in the control with a high variability in width similar to that seen in Figure 4a-d. Many clusters of abnormal fibrils were also detected here even from the first stage with a diameter of 131.8 ± 9.6 nm and an irregular outline.

The effect of age was also studied. Skin collagen fibrils from adult mice (1 year old) treated with LiCl at the same experimental period with the same dose as the young ones (5 weeks old) do not assembly normally. When studied at the ultrastructural level, fibrils in marked disarray were seen. In some regions, the parallel packing

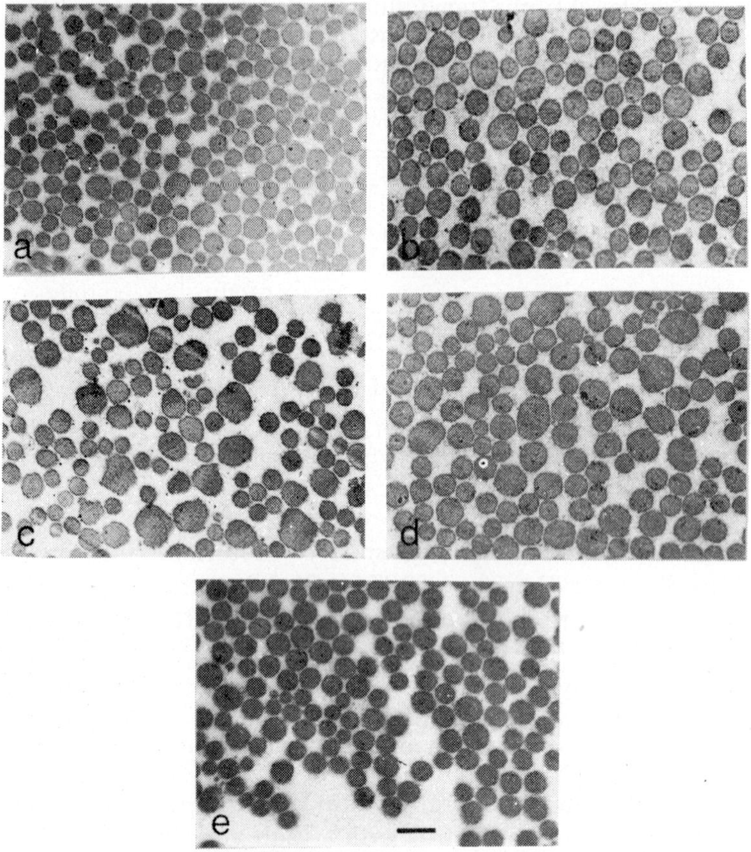

Figure 4. Ultrastructure of collagen fibrils seen in cross sections. In (a-d) the animals were injected for 30 consecutive days with 1.5 meq Li/Kg and were sacrificed 1 day (a,b), 2 months (c) and 6 months (d) after the last injection. These are compared with control fibril diameters (e). Bar = 0.2 μm

of fibrils was preserved for a part of the area. However, even in those areas there were fibrils which showed a twisting which is absent in normal fibrils. When viewed in cross-sections, lithium fibrils had a high variability in width, in contrast to normal. Many clusters of abnormal fibrils were found throughout even from the first stage. Some of them were very large having an externally lobulated cross-sectional profile. The second column of figures of Table 1 shows mean diameter values (and standard deviation) obtained from 1 year old lithium treated animals and sacrificed 1 day and 6 months after the last injection. These values are compared with those from age-matched normal control animals shown in the last right-hand column of the table. The results point to a significant decrease in mean value of treated subjects ($p<0$).

Similar results were obtained in mouse skin collagen using lower or higher doses than the one used (1.5 meq Li/Kg) in these studies, i.e. 0.3, 0.7 or 6 meq Li/Kg (Kounadi et al., 1995; Tzaphlidou and Kounadi, 1998), with the same experimental period, i.e. 30 consecutive days. The effects are more pronounced when the dosage is higher. For doses 0.7 and 6 meq Li/Kg, the arrangement of fibrils is disorganized in most areas. Fibrils were significantly ($p<0$) smaller in their diameter compared to normal with a high variability in width. In addition, abnormally large fibrils constituting about 10-22% of the whole population, depending on the dose, were found. With the lowest dose (0.3 meq Li/Kg), the normal parallel packing of fibrils is preserved in most areas. However, there are areas where the twisting of fibrils seen in other doses is apparent. The effect on fibril diameter is slighter ($p<0.13$) than the other doses.

The length of the duration of treatment was also investigated. Treatment for 7 days at doses of 0.7 and 1.5 meq Li/Kg had an effect on mouse skin collagen fibril organization (Kounadi et al., 1995). Clusters with abnormal fibrils found at longer duration of treatments are not apparent here. However, fibrils are smaller than the control ($p<0$). This decrease in mean diameter is more pronounced at prolonged times after treatment.' An interesting feature is that fibril diameter becomes altered progressively with time. As the time of treatment increases mouse skin collagen fibrils become smaller ($p<0$).

Mouse bone collagen fibrils at later stages, i.e. 2 and 6 months after treatment, were significantly smaller ($p<10^{-3}$) than those found in the control. Table 2, in the first column of figures, summarizes the mean diameter values (with standard deviation) of lithium-treated fibrils sacrificed various times after the last injection compared with age-matched normal mice (second column). In the first case, i.e. when the animals were sacrificed 1 day after the end of the experimental period, the mean diameter value is close to normal. Fibril diameter becomes altered at prolonged times after treatment where there is a significant difference ($p<10^{-3}$) in the mean diameter between the index and control subjects. In these two last cases, occasionally, clusters of abnormal fibrils were

TABLE 2

The effect of 1.5 meq Li/kg on mouse bone collagen fibrils: mean diameter of fibrils from lithium treated mice and sacrificed various times after the last injection compared with those from age-matched normal fibrils.

	Mean diameter values and standard deviation (nm)	
Time of sacrificing	Animals treated with Li	Normal age-matched animals
1 day	44.2±10.7	44.0±7.4
2 months	42.6±9.8	45.0±6.3
6 months	41.2±10.8	46.3±7.8

found similar to those detected in skin. Here these abnormal large fibrils constitute a very small percentage of the whole population, i.e. not as high as in skin.

Such clusters of abnormal fibrils with a highly irregular outline also appeared in rat cranial arachnoid and dura mater collagen fibrils treated with 1.5 meq Li/Kg. These cross-sections which occur at later stages, i.e. 6 months after treatment, have a mean diameter of 130.8 + 32.6 nm and constitute about 14 % of the whole population. All fibrils, were significantly ($p<10^{3}$) smaller than those found in the control.

Aggregates of abnormal fibrils were not observed in rabbit liver collagen fibrils treated with lithium as well as variations in fibril thickness. However, fibrils are smaller than the control.

DISCUSSION

This study demonstrates that lithium treatment leads to severe abnormalities on collagenous tissues. These abnormalities consist of decreased mean diameter and irregularity of shape of collagen fibrils (when viewed in cross-sections) as well as marked disorganization in the packing of the fibrils. It is important to recognize that these abnormal structures are present in mice, rats and rabbits tissues after a relatively short period of lithium treatment (30 days), even though the dose is maintained within the therapeutic limits used in the treatment of manic patients. This was also observed by McAuliffe and Olesen (1983) who pointed out that short periods (7 weeks) of oral lithium therapy can cause significant changes in the structure of various portions of the nephron in rats.

The pathogenic mechanism responsible for these abnormalities is still obscure. Alterations could occur at any level of collagen biosynthesis and extracellular processing. According to Holak and Raisz (1979) who studied the effect of lithium on bone metabolism in organ culture, lithium does not inhibit the incorporation of labeled proline in collagen and non-collagen proteins.

The abnormal appearance of bundles of collagen fibrils after lithium treatment may not be due to changes in the collagen molecule itself but could arise from alterations occurring in other components of the extracellular matrix. Smaller proteoglycans are known to play an important interfibrillar role and lithium-induced alterations to these proteoglycans could have a profound effect on the morphology of collagen fibril bundles. Waterhouse et al. (1986) reported that non-collagenous components in murine bone marrow cell culture media showed changes in response to lithium treatment.

A point worth noting is that even at prolonged times after lithium treatment, i.e. 6 months, collagen abnormalities are more severe than at earlier stages, e.g. 1 day after the end of treatment. This occurs at all tissues examined. It is not clear why lithium effects become more dramatic after a prolonged time after treatment. Among other factors, the interactions of collagen types that constitute the collagen molecules in the tissues and organs examined may be important for regulation of fibril structure. The predominance of type III collagen in skin during development suggests that this collagen by itself may play an important role in the organization of fibrils in this case. Waterhouse et al. (1986) pointed out that lithium does not affect the types of collagen synthesized by murine bone marrow cells, although the relative proportions of collagen types may differ from controls. Whether or not this also happens here requires detailed biochemical and immunohistochemical studies.

In conclusion, our results show that lithium under the present experimental conditions can induce permanent structural collagen alterations. Since collagen is one of the main components of living organs and tissues, it could be the means through which lithium induces side-effects.

REFERENCES

Barthelmebs, M., Ehrhardt, J.D., Schweitzer-Ehret, A., Danion, J.M. and Imbs, J.L. (1993). Le rapport erythroplasmatique du lithium. Methode de mesure et stabilitee individuelle. Encephale 19 : 321-327.

Cass, E., Turner, A.R., Selner, M., Allalunis, M.J. and Tan, T.H. (1981). Effect of lithium on the myelosuppressive and chemotherapeutic activities of vinblastine. Cancer Research 41: 1000-1005.

Deandrea, D., Walker, N., Mehlmauer, M. and White, K. (1982). Dermatological reactions to lithium: a critical review of the literature. *Journal Clinical Psychopharmacology* 2: 199-204.

Emilien, G., Maloteaux, J.M., Seghers, A. and Charles, G. (1995). Lithium therapy in the treatment of manic-depressive illness. Present status and future perspectives. A critical review. Archives Internationales Pharmacodynamie et de Therapie 330: 251-278.

Foster, J.R. (1992) Use of lithium in elderly psychiatric patients : a review of the literature. Lithium 3: 77-93.

Hays, W.L. (1988) Statistics, 4th ed. New York: Holt, Rinehart and Winston.

Holak, H.M. and Raisz, L.G. (1979). Effect of lithium on bone metabolism in organ culture. Endocrinology 104: 908-911.

Kounadi, E., Tzaphlidou, M. and Glaros, D. (1994). An electron microscopic study of collagen fibril after lithium treatment -I. The effect of different lithium doses on mouse skin collagen. Micron 25: 233-240.

Kounadi, E., Tzaphlidou, M., Fountos, G. and Glaros, D. (1995). An electron microscopic study of collagen fibril after lithium treatment -II. The effects of low lithium dose and short treatment on mouse skin collagen. Micron 26: 113-120.

Lyman, G.H., Williams, C.C., Preston, D., Goldman, A., Dinwoodie, W.R., Saba, H., Hartmann, R., Jensen, R. and Shukovsky, L. (1981). Lithium carbonate in patients with small cell lung cancer receiving combination chemotherapy. American Journal Medicine 70: 1222-1229.

Matthopoulos, D., Tzaphlidou, M. and Leontiou, I. (1995). Morphological alterations caused by lithium in various cell lines. Cell Biology International 19: 499-506.

McAuliffe, W.G. and Olesen, O.V. (1983). Effects of lithium on the structure of the rat kidney. Nephron 34: 114-124.

Ottosen, P.D., Nyengard, J.R., Jacobsen, N.O. and Christensen, S. (1987). A morphometric and ultrastructural study of lithium induced changes in the medulary collecting ducts of the rat kidney. Cell Tissue Research 249: 311-315.

Snedecor, G.W. and Cochran, W.G. (1967) Statistical Methods, 6th ed., Ames, IA: Iowa State University

Spiegel, C.N. and Soares, M.J. (1999). Biological effects of lithium chloride on Herpetomonas muscarum and Blastocrithidia culicis (Kinetoplastida:trypanosomatidae). Journal Parasitology 85: 729-733.

Tyobeka, E.M. and Becker, R.W. (1990). Growth and morphological changes induced by lithium chloride treatment of HL-60 cells. Cell Biology International Reports 14: 667-679.

Tzaphlidou, M. and Kounadi, E. (1998). The effect of lithium treatment on collagenous tissues: an electron microscope study. Micron 29: 235-248.

Tzaphlidou, M., Kounadi, E. and Kafantari, H. (2000). Influence of lithium on mouse bone collagen fibrils. Journal Trace and Microprobe Techniques 18: 321-326.

Waterhouse, E.J., Quesenberry, P.J. and Ballian, G. (1986). Collagen synthesis by murine bone marrow cell culture. Journal Cell Physiology 127: 397-402.

Wissocq, J.C., Stelz, T., Heurteaux, C., Biscont, J.C. and Thellier, M. (1979). Application of A(n,á) nuclear reaction to the microlocalization of lithium in the mouse brains. Journal histochemistry and Cytochemistry 27: 1462-1470.

NEUTROPHIL SIGNALING AND SUPEROXIDE FREE RADICAL PRODUCTION: PATHOPHYSIOLOGIC MODULATIONS

MOHAMMED M. SAYEED, AM, Ph.D., FCCM

Professor of Surgery and Physiology Director of Trauma/ Critical Care Research, Loyola University Chicago Medical Center, Maywood, Illinois 60153, USA

I. INTRODUCTION

While the enucleated red blood cells carry out vital oxygen transport functions under both physiological and pathophysiological conditions, the mononuclear (namely, monocytes and lymphocytes) and polymorphonuclear (namely, neutrophils) white blood cells conduct vital host defense functions under pathophysiologic and pathologic conditions. The white blood cells play the host defense role by virtue of certain peptide, protein and lipid mediators they produce under pathophysiologic/ pathologic conditions. These mediators may also serve as regulatory molecules under physiological conditions. However, at present there is inadequate knowledge of the physiologic roles of such mediator substances. In the face of pathophysiologic/pathologic challenges such as bacterial infections, the monocytes and polymorphpnuclear neutrophils serve as "front line" of defense against the pathogen; their actions constitute the Innate Immune Response. Subsequent to the innate immune response, there occurs the activation of lymphocytes, T and B cells, which is referred to as the Adaptive Immune Response.

Innate Responses followed by the generation of adaptive responses provide for the total immune defense by the host organism against the invading organism (Janeway & Travers, 1996). Recent studies have indicated that the innate immune responses are initiated not only with the host invasion by a pathogenic microbial organism but also after a variety of bodily injuries in the mammalian host. For example, trauma or thermal injury, which are understandably non-infectious challenges, results in an activation of the innate immune response. Other forms of injuries such as tissue hypoxia/ischemia or tissue ischemia followed by reperusion also lead to elicitation of the innate immune responses. This article presents a summary of recent studies which have evaluated neutrophil's functions and their relations to the intracellular signaling mechanisms responsible for the neutrophil functional responses elicited in an animal model of a full thickness skin burn injury.

The neutrophil response under ordinary pathophysiologic conditions leads to phagocytosis of either the invading organisms or the tissue debris resulting from a thermal, mechanical or a chemical (toxic) damage to the tissue. The phagocytised material is then degraded via neutrophils' intracellular release of the superoxide free radicals and proteolytic enzymes and their actions on the phagocytised material. The aforementioned responses by neutrophil are beneficial to the host as they eliminate from host's body the invading organisms or the injured tissue debris. This article emphasizes that although neutrophil responses are capable of providing for host defense with an outcome that is beneficial for the host, the same neutrophil responses, under pathophysiologic/pathologic conditions, are harmful to the host tissues in that they cause disruption of the host tissues' structural/functional integrity.

The studies to be reviewed have shown that in an early period after a burn injury to animals, the neutrophils produce superoxide free radicals in inappropriately excessive quantities. Such excess superoxide production can cause damage to an otherwise functional host tissue and/or organ rather than causing destruction or lysis of invading microbes and/or the potentially harmful tissue debris. The production of excessive quantities of the superoxide anion ($\bar{O}_2$) presumably results from an injury-related "hyperactivation" of neutrophils. Such neutrophil hyperactivation could arise from either the release in the host organism of excessive quantities of neutrophil activating agents or from an increased susceptibility of the neutrophil intracellular mechanisms to these activating agents. The latter increase in neutrophil sensitivity could be related to an inappropriate upregulation of neutrophils' intracellular signaling pathway (s). A main thrust of the present article is to present experimental studies, which have evaluated the thermal injury caused modulations of neutrophils' signaling mechanisms responsible for their hyperactivation. Aberration in intracellular signaling mechanisms could be fundamental causes of the aberrant responses produced by the neutrophils under the injury conditions.

II. NEUTROPHIL RESPONSES AND THEIR SIGNALING MECHANISM

The neutrophils' functional responses could be initiated by the actions of extracellular signal molecules directly derived from bacteria, such as lipopolysaccharide (LPS) and formylated di-and tripeptides (e.g. /-MP and / -MLP), or serum complement proteins activated subsequent to bacterial product generation (e.g. C5a). The substances produced by monocytes and macrophages could also initiate activation of neutrophils' functions when microbial products such as LPS, lipoleichoic acid, peptidoglycans, or zymosam (ZY) stimulate these leukocytes. The monocycte and macrophage products that have been shown to modulate neutrophil functions are: bioactive lipids, leukotriene B4 (LTB4), platelet activating factor (PAF), or cytokines, tumor necrosis factor

(TNF-"), interleukin 1 (IL-1) and granulocyte-macrophage colony stimulating factor (GMCSF).

Upon stimulation/activation, the neutrophils migrate from blood (chemotaxis), cross the lining of the blood vessels (diapedesis), reach the site of tissue inflammation caused by tissue damage or tissue invasion of the pathogen (see Figure 1). At the site of inflammation/infection, the neurtophils engage in engulfing of the invading organisms and/or tissue debris (phagocytosis), and cause their degradation. The degradation of engulfed material is accomplished through lytic agents produced by neurtophils such as superoxide free radicals (0^{-}_{2}) and proteolytic enzymes. While the superoxide radicals cause oxidative/peroxidative damage to the bacterial membrane phospholipid, the proteolytic enzymes promote bacterial protein breakdown (Figure 1).

The above mentioned neutrophil functional responses, namely chemotaxis, diapedesis, phagocytosis, superoxide radical and enzyme release are sequentially generated

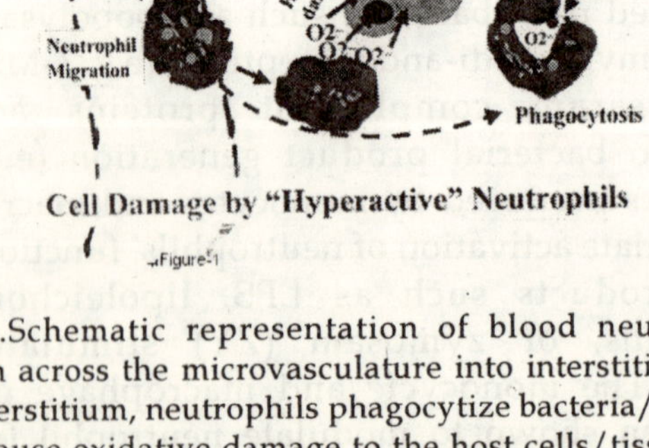

Figure 1.Schematic representation of blood neutrophils, their migration across the microvasculature into interstitial space. In the tissue interstitium, neutrophils phagocytize bacteria/bacterial debris and/or cause oxidative damage to the host cells/tissue via their0_2G release.

with continual stimulation of the neutrophils by the inflammatory mediators (LPS, C5a, /-MP//-MLP, TNF-", LTB4, PAF, IL-8, GMCSF) through the neutrophil receptor systems for these ligands. /-MP//-MLP, LTB4, PAF, IL-8 and C5a are known to bind to a seven-transmembrane domain receptor system on the neutrophil surface membrane (Witko-Sarsat et al., 2000); these agonists are referred to as "Activating " agonists. On the other hand, TNF-" and GM-CSF, which bind to their specific receptors, are called "Priming" agonists (see Figure 2). The sequence of events leading to activation of circulating neutrophils and their migration into the inflamed/infected tissue is shown in Figure 1. Also shown in this figure is the production of 0^-_2 by the neutrophils after their migration into the site of inflamed tissue. Whereas the intracellular production of 0^-_2 by neutrophils subsequent to their engulfing of bacteria leads to bacterial destruction, an excessive extracellular rather than intracellular production of 0^-_2 before the engulfing of bacteria can cause oxidative/ peroxidative damage to host's own cellular elements and extracellular matrix within the tissue interstitium.

The neutrophil activating agonists which bind to the seven-transmembrance receptor system initiate a series of intracellular signaling events (Figure 2). The most proximal events in the activation of neutrophil via such receptors is activation within the neutrophil plasma membrane of the G_i protein (pertussis toxin-sensitive GTP binding protein) which in turn dissociates into an" and a $(subunits (Thelen, DeWald & Baggiolini, 1993). The $(unit of the G_i protein is known to activate the membrane enzyme phospholipase C (PLC). PLC in turn hydrolyses the membrane phosphoinositide lipids to lead to generation of inositol triphosphate (IP_3) and diaceylglycerol (DAG). IP_3 is the intracellular messenger known to trigger the release of Ca^{2+} from the intracellular Ca^{2+} stores such that intracellular Ca^{2+} concentration is elevated. The elevation of the Ca^{2+} concentration (Ca^{2+}) *per se* serves as a signal to trigger subsequent distal

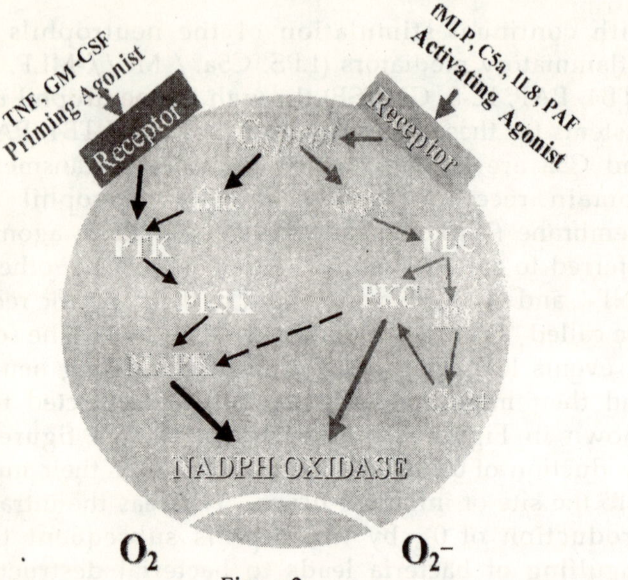

Figure-2

Figure 2.Diagram showing neutrophil activating agents binding to neutrophil receptors and triggering intracellular signaling pathways leading to 0_2G production.

signaling events leading to production of 0_2 by the neutrophils. DAG is a known to be the activator of the enzyme protein kinase C (PKC), which is intimately involved in the phosphorylation of neutrophil cytosolic proteins p47 and p67, which in turn play vital roles in the assembly and stimulation of the plasma membrane enzyme NADPH oxidase. The latter enzyme catalyzes the reduction of molecular oxygen in the cellular environment to result in the formation of the superoxide free radical, 0^-_2. The PKC stimulation can be potentiated by the Ca^{2+} signal. Thus, both Ca^{2+} and PKC signals can jointly cause an 0^-_2 production response by the neutrophils (Sayeed, 2000). The NADH oxidase can also be stimulated without an actual production of significant quantities of0^-_2 radicals. Such stimulation of the enzyme is referred to as the priming of the enzyme system, and occurs via actions of neutrophil stimulating agents such as TNF-″ and GM-CSF. The latter agonists, the so-called "Priming" agonists, activate their own specific receptors on the neutrophil cell membrane (see Figure 2). The actions of the "Priming" agonists result in the activation of protein tyrosine kinases (PTK) and the subsequent signaling pathway including activation of phosphatidyl inositol 3-kinase (PI-3k) and mitogen-activated protein kinases (MAPK). This signaling pathway operates independently of the generation of the Ca^{2+} signal, and is therefore also referred to as the Ca^{2+}-independent pathway. As mentioned above, this signaling pathway is responsible for the stimulation of the enzyme NADPH oxidase without an actual generation of the 0^{-}_{2} radical. However, priming of neutrophils with TNF-″ or GM-CSF followed by stimulation with an "Activating" agonist can lead to generation of 0^{-}_{2} radicals in greater quantities than that resulting from the actions of an "Activating" agonist alone. Thus, a prior "priming" of neutrophil NADPH oxidase can lead to a potentiation of production superoxide by agonists such as /-MLP, IL-8, PAF or C5a.

III. ROLE OF NEUTROPHILS IN ACUTE INJURY AND SEPSIS SYNDROME

A number of investigators have studied the functional capabilities of neutrophils harvested from acutely injured humans and from animal models of such injury conditions. These injuries, including thermal (burn) or mechanical (trauma) damage to the host body, result in a disruption of cellular structural/functional integrity in the host organs systems away from the site of the injury. For example, bodily injury in the extremities (limbs) causing critical cell/tissue damage can lead to functional derangements in lungs, kidney, liver and/or intestine. The spread of the injuries to remote organs might provoke association with a post-injury invasion of the host by microbial pathogens, which are found on the body surface or in the environment. The invading microbial may additionally be the body's own indigenous bacteria, which reside in the intestine. With the spread of the injury to the intestinal tissue, there might occur a breakdown of the intestinal mucosal barriers, which could allow for gut luminal bacteria to cross the intestinal mucosa and gain entrance into other extra-intestinal tissues/organisms. The airborne microbes found at body surface enter into the host via damaged body surfaces or via catheters implanted into patients under medical care. The response of the body to acute injury with or without the invasion of the microbe is activation of cells of the immune defense system (namely, neutrophils, macrophages/monocytes, and lymphocytes) within the injured tissue site(s) as well as in the entire vascular compartment. Thus, an activation of the immune system cells locally and systemically occurs initially which may lead to a second wave of such activation occurring with the invasion of the injured host's body by the microbes.

In either the initial activation with acute injury, or with the subsequent microbial invasion, the activation of the leukocytes resulting in the release of their products (the inflammatory mediators) leads to the so called "systemic inflammatory response syndrome (SIRS)." The various inflammatory mediators released during SIRS (TNF", IL-1, IL-6, IL-8, prostaglandin E_2 (PGE_2), Thromboxane, PAF, etc.) are responsible for the different signs and symptoms that are observed in the acutely injured hosts. These signs include, fever, leukocytosis, increased heart and respiratory rates, metabolic acidosis, and possible hypotension and modulations in the cardiac output. The latter signs and symptoms mark the onset of a typical sepsis episode. Thus, SIRS following acute injuries can also be referred to as a sepsis syndrome. The aforementioned signs and symptoms can be ascribed to the actions of the various inflammatory mediators released principally by the leukocytes. It should be pointed out that the inflammatory mediators contributing to sepsis syndrome signs and symptoms can also be derived from non-immune system cells when the latter are stimulated by the mediators released from the leukocytes.

As described in the previous sections of this article, neutrophils elicit their responses under the influence of several of the inflammatory mediators. While the neutrophil responses may in general serve host-defense roles, certain of these responses are presumably elicited at inappropriate levels and are detrimental to the host cell/tissue function. The latter non-adaptive injurious responses contribute to host morbidity and eventual mortality following the acute injury conditions. One of the rationales for the study of the neutrophils' superoxide free radical production response has been to evaluate its detrimental effect in the injured hosts. Several previous studies have supported this role of neutrophil (Witko-Sarsat et al., 2001). However, there is little knowledge of the molelcular /cellular mechanism of neutrophil response modulations causing production of inappropriately high levels of the superoxide free radical. An investigation of the mechanism of the production of inappropriate quantities of the superoxide free radicals by the neutrophils under acute injury conditions has the prospects of elucidating potential causes of pathogenesis of the sepsis syndrome following such injuries. As discussed in the previous section of this article, the neutrophil's intracellular signaling might be critically affected under the injury conditions such that inappropriate superoxide production might ensure during the course of injury.

IV. NEUTROPHILS' SUPEROXIDE PRODUCTION AND ITS RELATIONSHIP TO CA^{2+} SIGNALING FOLLOWING THERMAL INJURY

Several previous studies have established the dependency of neutrophil's 0_2^- production on Ca^{2+} signaling through experiments which were carried out in neutrophils harvested from healthy human volunteer or control animal blood (Downy et al., 1995). A blockade of Ca^{2+} signaling in isolated healthy subject blood neutrophils, *in vitro*, resulted in cessation of 0_2^- production by the neutrophils. Although a role of the Ca^{2+}-independent signaling pathways has been implicated in the priming of the neutrophil's NADPH oxidase enzyme system, actual 0_2^- generation, *in vivo*, is regulated with the involvement of both the Ca^{2+}- dependent and Ca^{2+} - independent-signaling pathways. Our research group has evaluated both the 0_2^- production response and the Ca^{2+} signal generation capabilities in neutrophils derived from burn-injured rats. In these studies, anesthetized rats were subjected to a thermal injury protocol, which resulted in a full-skin thickness scald over approximately 30% of rat's total body surface. To scald the skin, animals' backs were shaved and then exposed to 98°C water for 10 seconds. Details of the burn injury protocols have been described in several previous publications (Sabeh, Hockberger & Sayeed, 1998). An exposure of 30% of rat's body surface to 37°C served as a sham procedure in the study.

The rats were sacrificed using an anesthetic overdose at day 1, 3, 7, or 10 post-burn/sham procedure. Immediately after anesthetizing rats with the high anesthetic dose, rat blood was obtained through cardiac puncture into heparinized tubes. Neutrophils were then isolated using the histopaque gradient centrifugation technique. Isolated neutrophils were stimulated with |MLP (1Fm) for a 3-5 minute period. Superoxide free radical (0_2^-) production by the stimulated neutrophils was assayed by following the oxidation of ferricytochrome C in the presence of a ferricytochrome C reductase. The resulting change in absorbency of the cytochrome C quantitated nmoles of 0_2^- produced.

For the assessment of the Ca^{2+} signal generation, isolated neutrophils were labeled with the Ca^{2+} chelating fluorescent dye Fura 2. Fluorescent signals from the Fura

2 loaded cells were quantitated using dual excitation wavelengths, 340 and 380 nM, and monitoring intensity of emitted fluorescent at 510 nM. The emitted fluorescent signals at the two-excitation wavelengths yielded values of neutrophils' cytosolic Ca^{2+} concentration. Such fluorescent signals were recorded in neutrophils before and after their stimulation with ¦MLP. The measurements before stimulation reflected basal or resting cytosolic Ca^{2+} concentrations while an elevation in Ca^{2+} concentrations after stimulation with ¦MLP reflected the generation of the Ca^{2+} signal. The subtraction of the basal cytosolic Ca^{2+} concentration from the elevated Ca^{2+} concentration value, obtained after ¦MLP stimulation, yielded an approximation of the size of the Ca^{2+} signal generated by the neutrophils.

Figure 3 shows the superoxide generation response by neutrophils harvested on day 1, 3, 7, and 10 after the burn injury in rats. The figure also shows 0_2^- generation value obtained in the sham group of animals. The 0_2^- values shown are responses in ¦MLP stimulated neutrophils. The response on day 1 after burn was significantly higher (p<. 05) then in the sham group. On day 3-post-burn, the 0_2^- response was approximately 5 times higher than that observed in the sham group. The 0_2^- production on day 7 and day 10 after burn was significantly lower than on day 3, and on day 10 seemed to return to levels observed in the sham group. These observations established a heightening of the neutrophil superoxide production in the early stages after burn (day 3-post-injury). Our previous studies have shown that the occurrence of such heightened neutrophil 0_2^- production response was temporally related to increased infiltration of the neutrophils into the hosts of intestinal tissue (Fazal et al., 1999). Furthermore, the increased 0_2^- response appears to be temporally related to derangements in the intestinal wall permeability to solutes as well as to intestinal bacterial transport from the intestinal lumen to the mesenteric lymph nodes. The occurrence of these

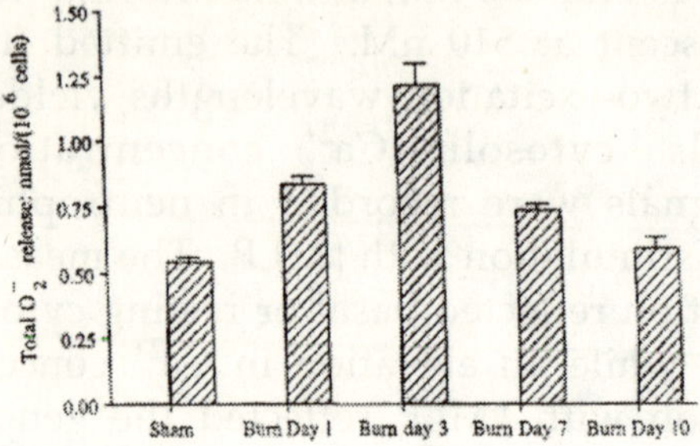

Figure 3.Oxygen free radical (0_2G) production by neutrophils harvested from sham or burn rats. 0_2G measurements were made on days 1 to 10 after a 30% total body surface area burn in rats.

intestinal function derangements with burn injury would be potentially due to overactivation of neutrophils' superoxide production. This is supported by the findings that such derangements do not occur when burn injury is produced in rats which are depleted of circulating neutrophils (Fazal et al., 2000). Thus, our studies have linked an organ dysfunction (namely intestinal dysfunction) occurring after burn injury probably due to the heightened superoxide production responses of the neutrophils.

The measurements of the Ca^{2+} signal generation in the neutrophils harvested from burn injured rats assessed whether the Ca^{2+} signal modulation could be related to the heightened 0_{2-} production and the intestinal functional derangements. The data on Ca^{2+} signal size recorded in neutrophils from sham and burn-injured rats are shown in Figure 4. The Ca^{2+} signal generated in response to ¦MLP stimulation on day 1 post-burn is nearly 2 times the Ca^{2+} response in the sham group. The Ca^{2+} response appeared to remain heightened on day 3 and day 7 post-injury. On day 10-post-injury, it tended to return to the level found in the sham group. This data indicate that an over activation of the neutrophil Ca^{2+} signaling capacity also occurs early after the burn-injury. It perhaps occurs even prior to the observed heightening in the neutrophil O_2^- response, which occurred at 3 day-post-injury. A heightening of the burn-induced Ca^{2+} signaling response prior to the observed heightening of the neutrophils' O_2^- response could be the trigger mechanism for the heightening of O_2^- response with burn injury. We prevented the elevation in the signal generation capacity in neutrophils of the burn-injured rats by treating such injured rats with a calcium antagonist, namely diltiazem. Diltiazem treatment of the burn-injured rats attenuated not only the Ca^{2+} signal generation but also the O_2^- production response by the neutrophils (Sabeh, Hockberger & Sayeed, 1998). Such data supported a potential role of neutrophils Ca^{2+} signaling modulation with burn-injury as a primary event, which could contribute to the neutrophils heightened O_2^- production. The mechanism which initially causes the modulation of neutrophil's Ca^{2+} signaling after burn, and subsequently contributes to excessive inappropriate O_2^- production by the neutrophils is not fully elucidated. However, it is pausible that the initial increase in the levels of the neutrophil activating inflammatory mediators, both

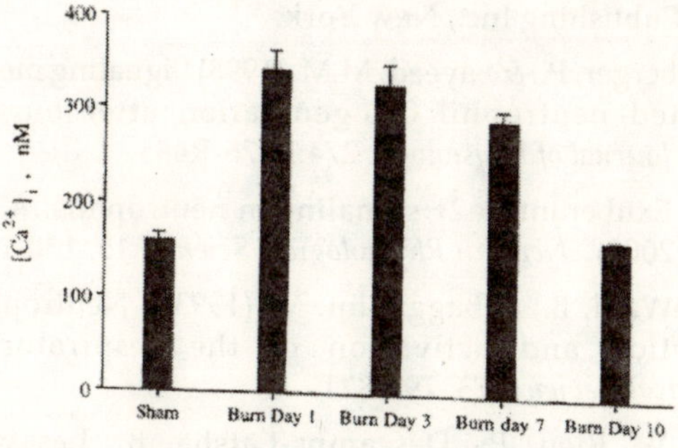

Figure 4. Ca^{2+} signaling response in neutrophils harvested from sham and burn rats. Burn rat neutrophils were studied days 1 to 10 post-burn.

"priming" and "activating" agonists, in circulation in burn-injured rats primarily affect the neutrophil signaling pathways such that there occurs an excessive/inappropriate release of 0_2^- by the neutrophils. In other words, the inflammatory mediators release during burn-injury seem to hypersensitize the neutrophils' signaling pathways of 0_2^- production.

ACKNOWLEDGEMENT

At the time of this writing, research in the author's laboratory was supported by U.S. NIH grants GM56865, and GM53235.

REFERENCES

Dawny, G.P., Fukushima, T., Fialkow, L., & Waddell, T.K. Intracellulalr signling in neutrophil priming and activation. (1995). *Seminars in Cell Biology*. 6, 345, 345-356.

Fazal, N., Knaus, U.G., Sabeh, F., Gamelli, R.L., & Sayeed, M.M. (1998). Enhanced expression of neutrophil NADPH oxidase components in intestines of rats after burn injury. *Shock*. 12, 438-441.

Fazal, N., Shamim, M., Khan, S., Gamelli, R., & Sayeed, M.M. (2000). Neutrophil depletion in rats reduces burn-injury induced intestinal bacterial translocation. *Critical Care Medicine*. 28, 1550-1555.

Janeway, C.A., & Travers, P. (1996) Immunobiology. pp. 1:11-13. Garland Publishing Inc., New York.

Sabeh, F., Hockberger, P., & Sayeed, M.M. (1998) Signaling mechanisms of elevated neutrophil 0_2G generation after burn injury. *American Journal of Physiology*. 274:R476-R485.

Sayeed, M.M. Exuberant Ca2+ signaling in neutrophils: A cause for concern (2000). *News in Physiological Science*. 15, 130-136.

Thelen, M., DeWald, B., & Baggiolini, M. (1993). Neutrophil signal transduction and activation of the respiratory burst. *Physiological Reviews*. 73, 797-821.

Witko-Sarsat, V., Rieu, P., Descamps-Latsha, B., Lesavre, P., & Halbwachs-Mecarelli, L. Neutrophils: molecules, functions and pathophysiological aspects. (2000). *Laboratory Investigations*. 80, 617-653.

CROSS-TALK BETWEEN Ca^{2+} AND cAMP SIGNALLING PATHWAYS IN THE REGULATION OF CARDIAC MUSCLE CALMODULIN-DEPENDENT CYCLIC NUCLEOTIDE PHOSPHODIESTERASE

RAJENDRA K. SHARMA

Department of Pathology, College of Medicine, Saskatoon Cancer Centre, University of Saskatchewan, 20 Campus Drive, Saskatoon, Saskatchewan S7N 4H4 Canada

INTRODUCTION

The response of living cells to changes in cell environment depends on the production and actions of second messenger molecules. The two most extensively studied second messengers are Ca^{2+} and cAMP, each of which has been demonstrated to regulate unique metabolic reactions and pathways. Examination of these regulatory reactions suggests that the two second messenger systems also undergo complex interactions during cell activation that serve to modulate the overall cell response. Interactions between these systems can occur on two levels: a metabolic level where the actions of one second messenger affects the cellular concentration of the other, and a functional level where the actions of one second messenger modulates the effects of the other second messenger. Furthermore, these actions can occur at multiple points in a reaction pathway to provide feedback inhibition or stimulation of previous, future, or ongoing reactions.

Calcium ions regulate many cellular processes that are usually achieved through their interaction by binding to receptor proteins such as calmodulin (CaM), troponin C, S-100 proteins and calcyclin to transmit the Ca^{2+} signal[1-3]. CaM was originally described as an activator of cyclic nucleotide phosphodiesterase (PDE) by Cheung[4,5]. CaM is a heat-stable, acidic protein with a molecular mass of approximately 17 kDa intracellular protein and it was established that the stimulation of PDE required a physiological concentration of Ca^{2+} and CaM[6]. Later, CaM was found to regulate many other enzymes and proteins. CaM-regulated processes in many cases are summarized in Figure 1.

A general mechanism for the activation of PDE by CaM was proposed by Wang et al[6], as represented below:

$$Ca^{2+} + CaM \rightleftharpoons Ca^{2+} - CaM \rightleftharpoons Ca^{2+} - CaM^*$$

$$Ca^{2+} - CaM^* + PDE \rightleftharpoons Ca^{2+} - CaM^* - PDE \rightleftharpoons Ca^{2+} - CaM^* - PDE^*$$

where CaM and PDE stand for calmodulin and calmodulin-dependent cyclic nucleotide phosphodiesterase respectively, and the superscript * denotes the activated state for the proteins. The PDE activation is initiated by the binding of Ca^{2+} to CaM. As a result, an active form of the CaM (Ca^{2+} – CaM*) is formed and this activated Ca^{2+} – CaM* then associates with the enzyme (PDE) to convert the enzyme to an activated state Ca^{2+} – CaM* – PDE*.

In general, the concentration of intracellular second messengers such as cyclic adenosine monophosphate (cAMP) and guanosine monophosphate (cGMP) are

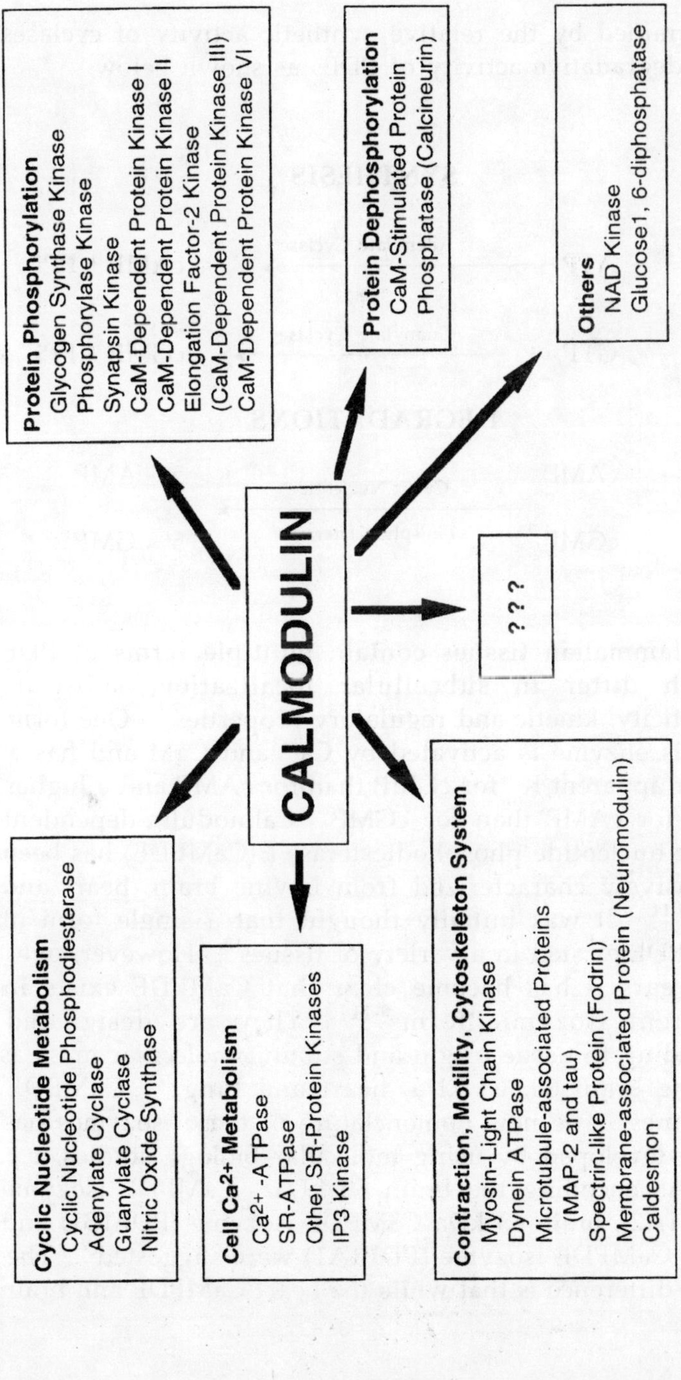

Figure 1. CaM-regulated processes and CaM-dependent proteins.

determined by the relative synthetic activity of cyclases and degradative activity of PDEs as shown below:

SYNTHESIS

$$ATP \xrightarrow{\text{Adenylate Cyclase}} cAMP + PPi$$

$$GTP \xrightarrow{\text{Guanylate Cyclase}} cGMP + PPi$$

DEGRADATIONS

$$\begin{matrix} cAMP \\ cGMP \end{matrix} \xrightarrow[\text{Phosphodiesterases}]{\text{Cyclic Nucleotide}} \begin{matrix} 5' - AMP \\ 5' - GMP \end{matrix}$$

Mammalian tissues contain multiple forms of PDE which differ in subcellular localization, substrate specificity, kinetic and regulatory properties[7,8]. One form of this enzyme is activated by Ca^{2+} and CaM and has a lower apparent K_m for cGMP than for cAMP and a higher V_{max} for cAMP than for cGMP. Calmodulin-dependent cyclic nucleotide phosphodiesterase ((CaMPDE) has been extensively characterized from bovine brain, heart and lung[9-11]. It was initially thought that a single form of CaMPDE existed in a variety of tissues[12]. However, over the years it has become clear that CaMPDE exists in different isozymic foɪms[9-11]. They are designated according to tissue origin and subunit molecular mass as bovine brain 60, 63 kDa, heart and lung[13-16] CaMPDE isozymes. The new nomenclature of these isozymes has been developed by using molecular biology studies, e.g. cDNAs encoding the brain 60 kDa. CaMPDE isozyme (PDE1A2), brain 63 kDa CaMPDE isozyme (PDE1B1) and heart CaMPDE isozyme (PDE1A1) were suggested[17]. The main difference is that while the heart CaMPDE and brain

60 kDa isozyme[14,18] are substrates of the cAMP-dependent protein kinase, the brain 63 kDa isozyme is phosphorylated by CaM-dependent protein kinase in a Ca^{2+}-CaM-dependent reaction[19]. Moreover, the brain 63 kDa isozyme is kinetically different from the brain 60 kDa, heart and lung CaMPDE isozymes[20]. Although brain 60 kDa, heart and lung CaMPDE isozymes are almost identical in terms of immunological properties they are differentially regulated by CaM[20]. We have also observed that, at identical CaM concentrations, the bovine heart CaMPDE isozyme is stimulated at much lower Ca^{2+} concentrations than the bovine brain 60 and 63 kDa isozymes[20]. Similarly, the porcine brain CaMPDE has been shown to have a lower affinity for CaM than the isozyme from porcine artery[21]. Examination of the regulatory properties of the heart CaMPDE has revealed distinct and complex control mechanisms. This article reviews the cross-talk between Ca^{2+} and cAMP in the regulation of cardiac muscle CaMPDE.

1. Regulation by cAMP and Ca^{2+}: Many metabolic processes are regulated by one of the second messengers; a brief schematic overview is presented in Figure 2. The interactions of extracellular factors with specific cell membrane receptors can activate membrane-bound acetylate cyclase to catalyze the production of cAMP, or elevate intracellular [Ca] by stimulation of the entry of extracellular Ca^{2+} or release of Ca^{2+} ions from intracellular stores. In both cases, the sequence of events following an elevation in cellular second messenger concentration involves: (i) the binding of the second messenger to its specific target protein, (ii) activation of that protein, and (iii) subsequent modification of other cellular proteins resulting in changes in the activities of these latter proteins. In the case of the cAMP system, cAMP-dependent protein kinase(s) is the only established target protein in eukaryotic cells[22]. Prior to the binding of cAMP, the enzyme exists as an inactive protein complex of

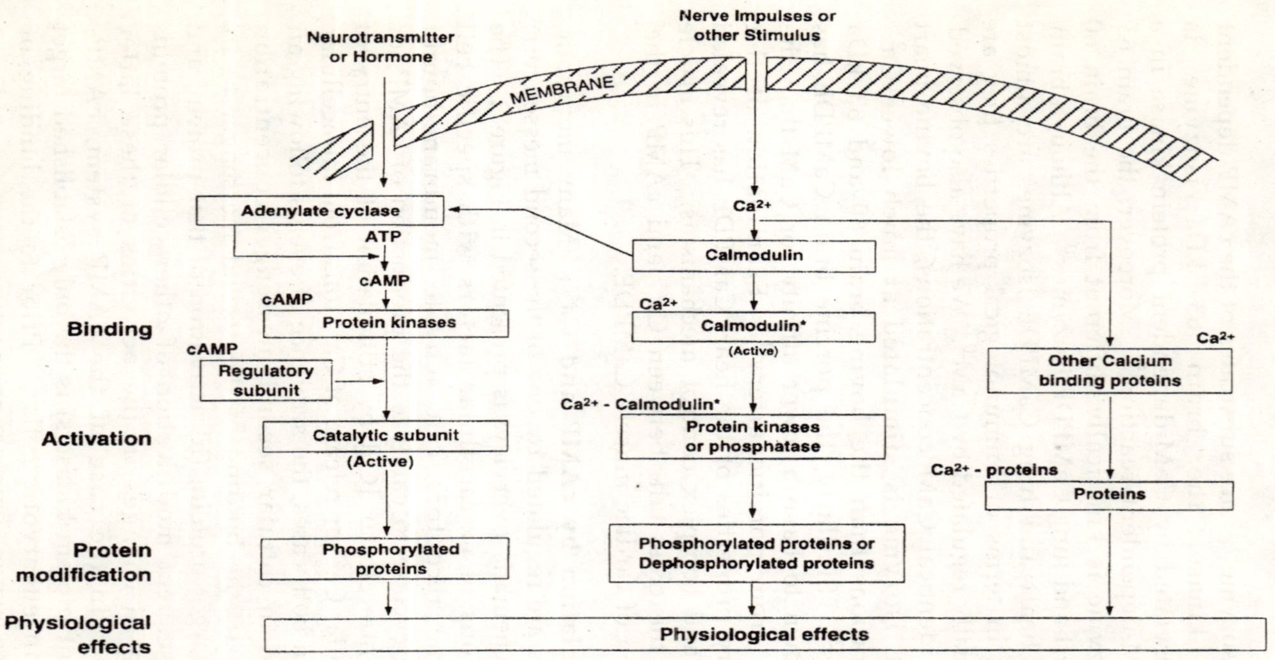

Figure 2. A general interactions between the cAMP and Ca^{2+} second messenger molecules.

two distinct subunits (R_2C_2), one of a catalytic (C) and one of a regulatory (R) nature. Upon binding of cAMP to the regulatory subunit, the subunits dissociate and two catalytically active subunits are released. This catalytic subunits catalyze the phosphorylation of specific proteins.

Although there is more than one type of cAMP-dependent protein kinase, all appear to phosphorylate common protein substrates, with a resultant change in specific activity and induction of a physiological event. Regulation of metabolic processes by Ca^{2+} resembles that by cAMP, but has unique features as shown in Figure 2. The Ca^{2+} regulatory pathway is mediated by the Ca^{2+}-binding protein, CaM, and involves a Ca^{2+}-dependent, reversible association of CaM with its target protein(s), resulting in changes in target protein activity (3, 23). CaM-dependent enzymes participate in various physiological processes either directly, or indirectly, through regulating the activity of other cellular proteins by phosphorylation or dephosphorylation. This cascade is common to all tissues, yet results in a tissue specific response to a given stimulus. This implies that the CaM regulated proteins of each tissue are different and mediate this specificity of response.

2. Concerted Regulation by Both Second Messengers: It has become apparent that in many systems, both second messengers (Ca^{2+} and cAMP) act in a concerted fashion to control the regulatory process (Figure 3). One example at the metabolic level which has been encountered: cyclic nucleotide phosphodiesterase represents the intracellular mechanism for the degradation of cAMP and is regulated by Ca^{2+}-CaM[23]. On the functional level, there are at least three mechanisms by which the two messenger systems exert their mutual effects. Firstly, a CaM-stimulated enzyme may be a substrate of cAMP-dependent protein kinase. Examples of this are phosphorylase kinase (24-26) and smooth muscle myosin light chain kinase (27,28), enzymes involved in glycogenolysis and smooth muscle

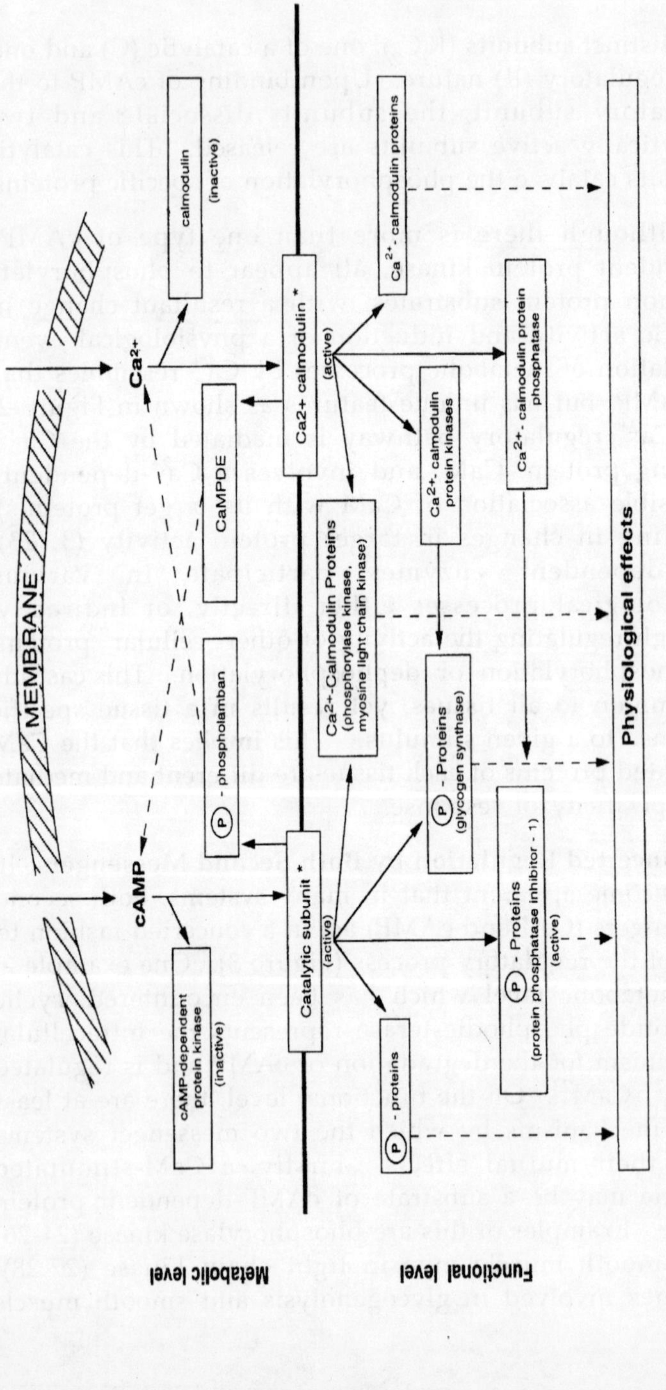

Figure 3. A complex interactions between the cAMP and Ca^{2+} second messenger molecules.

contraction, respectively.

A second mechanism of cAMP and Ca^{2+}-CaM interaction involves phosphorylation of common protein substrates by cAMP and Ca^{2+}-CaM-stimulated protein kinases. Glycogen synthase can be phosphorylated by cAMP-dependent protein kinase and by the CaM-dependent glycogen synthase kinase and phosphorylase kinase, as well as by at least four other kinases[29-30]. With one exception, these phosphorylations inactivate both muscle and liver glycogen synthase; the exception is that phosphorylation of the liver enzyme by CaM-dependent glycogen synthase kinase has no effect on enzyme activity (30). A third mode of interaction between the Ca^{2+} and cAMP signal systems involves the dephosphorylation (and thus inactivation) of several enzymes which are phosphorylated by cAMP-dependent protein kinase. The dephosphorylation of phosphoprotein phosphatase inhibitor 1[31] is a good example. When cAMP levels rise in the cell, cAMP-dependent protein kinase phosphorylates many proteins, among them inhibitor-1. When phosphorylated, inhibitor-1 is active and can inhibit the activity of protein phosphatase-1[32]. When inhibitor-1 is dephosphorylated and inactivated by CaM-dependent phosphatase, protein phosphatase 1 is reactivated. Thus, by modulating the activity of inhibitor 1, CaM-dependent phosphatase indirectly can control the activity of protein phosphatase 1.

PURIFICATION AND PURITY OF HEART CAMPDE

CaMPDE was purified to apparent homogeneity from the total CaM-binding fraction of bovine heart in a single step by C1, a mono-clonal immunoaffinity chromatography[14]. C1, a monoclonal antibody specific for the 60 kDa CaMPDE isozyme from bovine brain, was shown to cross-react with the heart CaMPDE. The

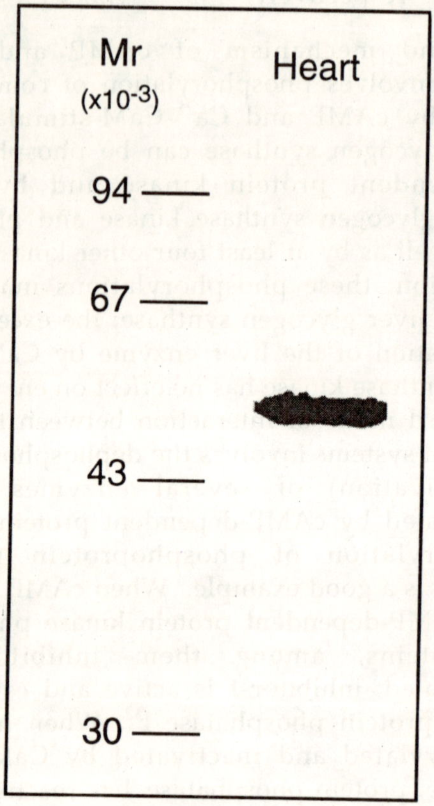

Fugure 4. Analysis of purified CaMPDE by SDS-polyacrylamide gel electrophoresis.

recovery of the CaMPDE activity in this step was always greater than 90%. The specific activity of the purified heart CaMPDE ranged from 265 to 300 units/mg. Under native conditions, the purified CaMPDE exhibited an apparent molecular mass of 120 kDa, whereas under denaturing conditions the enzyme represented an apparent molecular mass of approximately 59 kDa (Figure 4), suggesting that heart CaMPDE is composed of two subunits of identical weight.

PHOSPHORYLATION AND DEPHOSPHORYLATION OF HEART CaMPDE

Incubation of heart CaMPDE with the catalytic subunit of cAMP-dependent protein kinase and [Y-^{32}P] ATP, followed by SDS-polyacrylamide gel electrophoresis and autoradiography, revealed that the heart CaMPDE was phosphorylated (Figure 5, lane 9). The inclusion of Ca^{2+} and CaM in the incubation reaction completely abolished the CaMPDE phosphorylation (Fig 5, lane 14), suggesting that CaM exerts its effects on the phosphorylation through binding to the CaMPDE rather than by acting directly on the kinase. The phosphorylation of CaMPDE by cAMP-dependent protein kinase could be markedly increased by the use of histidine buffer, pH 7.0, instead of Tris-HCl buffer, pH 7.0 (Figure 5, lane 12).

The rate of the CaMPDE phosphorylation in histidine buffer was compared with that in Tris-HCl buffer, pH 7.0 (Fig 6). The initial rate of phosphorylation was about 4-fold higher in histidine buffer than in Tris-HCl buffer with an increased level of CaMPDE phosphorylation. A maximal incorporation of approximately 1 mole of phosphate was achieved per mole of CaMPDE subunit after 60 min in histidine buffer, whereas in Tris-HCl buffer, the reaction was slow. A number of other buffers were therefore tested for their effect on phosphorylation of heart CaMPDE. Table 1 shows that histidine buffer appears to be the best buffer for the phosphorylation reaction. The rates of CaMPDE phosphorylation with other buffers were similar to that observed with Tris-HCl.

Phosphorylation of CaMPDE by cAMP-dependent protein kinase was accompanied by a decrease in the affinity of the enzyme for CaM (Figure 7A). These findings were confirmed by comparing the dose-dependent activation of the non-phosphorylated CaMPDE with that

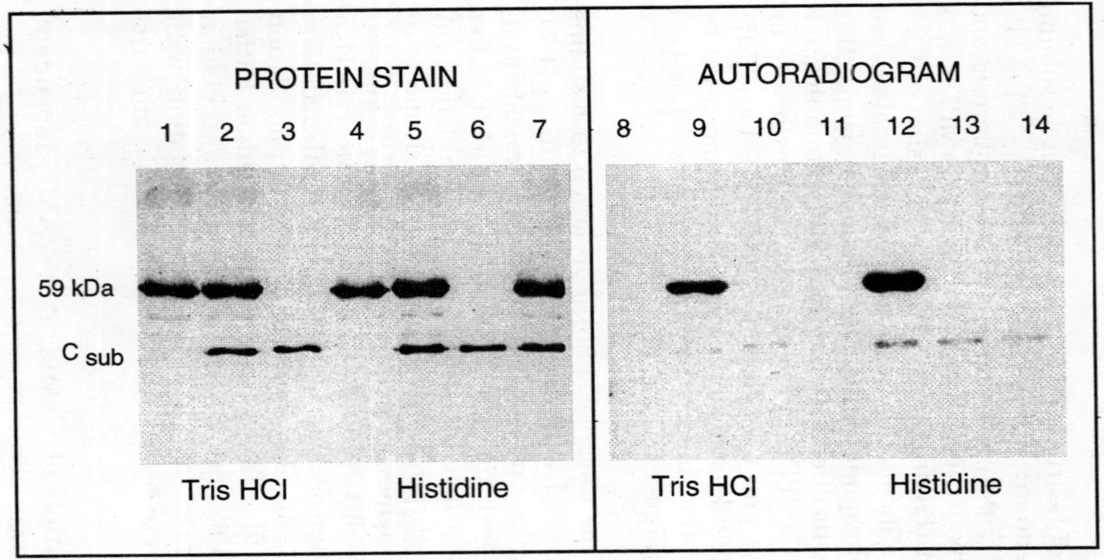

Figure 5. Phosphorylation of bovine heart CaMPDE by cAMP-dependent protein kinase. Purified phosphodiesterase was phosphorylated by cAMP-dependent protein kinase for 40 min. Phosphorylation was carried out in Tris-HCl buffer, pH 7.0 (lanes 1-3), and histidine buffer, pH 7.0 (lanes 4-7). Reaction was also carried out in the presence of Ca^{2+} and CaM (lane 7). Lanes 1 and 4, purified CaMPDE; lanes 2 and 5, purified CaMPDE and cAMP-dependent protein kinase; lanes 3 and 6, cAMP-dependent protein kinase alone; lane 7, same as lane 5 with Ca^{2+} and CaM; lanes 8-14, respective autoradiographs of lanes 1-7.

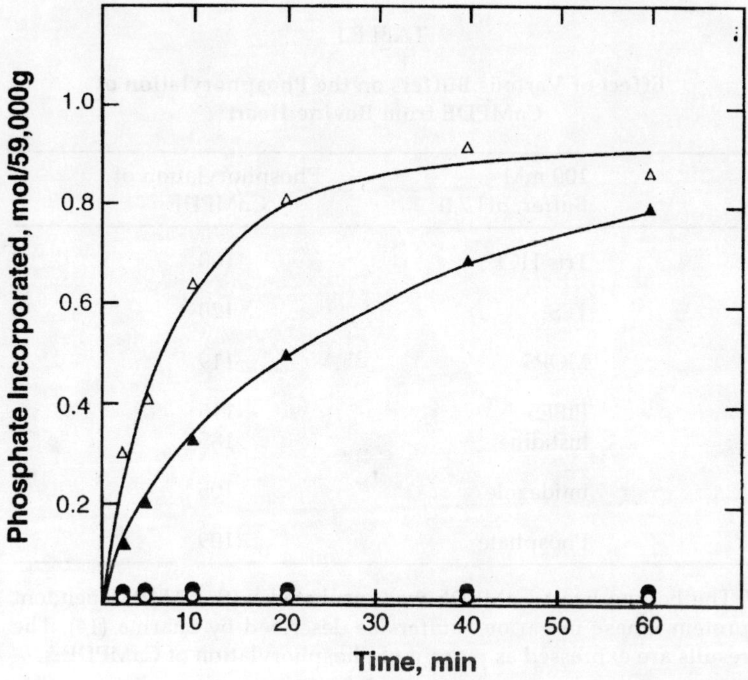

Figure 6. Time course of phosphorylation of CaMPDE by cAMP-dependent protein kinase. Purified CaMPDE was phosphorylated by cAMP-dependent protein kinase in Tris-HCl buffer, pH 7.0 (▲ – ▲); or histidine buffer, pH 7.0 (Δ – Δ); CaMPDE alone in Tris-HCl buffer, pH 7.0 (● – ●) or histidine buffer, pH 7.0 (O – O).

of the phosphorylated enzyme. The concentration of CaM required for half-maximal activation of the phosphorylated CaMPDE was approximately 10-fold higher than that of the non-phosphorylated enzyme. Phosphorylation also results in a difference in Ca^{2+} concentration required for activation of CaMPDE at a constant concentration of CaM. At saturating levels of CaM, the non-phosphorylated CaMPDE was half-maximally activated by 0.8 M Ca^{2+}, whereas the phosphorylated enzyme required 20.0 M Ca^{2+} (Figure

TABLE 1

Effect of Various Buffers on the Phosphorylation of CaMPDE from Bovine Heart[α]

100 mM Buffer, pH 7.0	Phosphorylation of CaMPDE
Tris-HCl	100
TES	120
MOPS	119
PIPES	115
histidine	185
imidazole	105
Phosphate	109

[α] The bovine heart CaMPDE was incubated with cAMP-dependent protein kinase in various buffers as described by Sharma (14). The results are expressed as percent of phosphorylation of CaMPDE.

5B), suggesting that phosphorylation of heart CaMPDE may modulate the Ca^{2+} sensitivity of the enzyme *in vivo*. The phosphorylated CaMPDE can be dephosphorylated by a CaM-dependent phosphatase (calcineurin) in the presence of Ni^{2+} and CaM (Figure 8). The dephosphorylation is accompanied by an increase in the affinity of the CaMPDE for CaM (Fig 8). The various second-messenger effects on the CaMPDE are summarized in Table 2.

PHYSIOLOGICAL SIGNIFICANCE OF HEART CaMPDE IN THE REGULATION OF [cAMP]

The activation of phosphodiesterase by Ca^{2+} and CaM represents a key reaction in the complex interaction between the Ca^{2+} and cAMP second messenger systems. In many cases of cell activation, both Ca^{2+} and cAMP

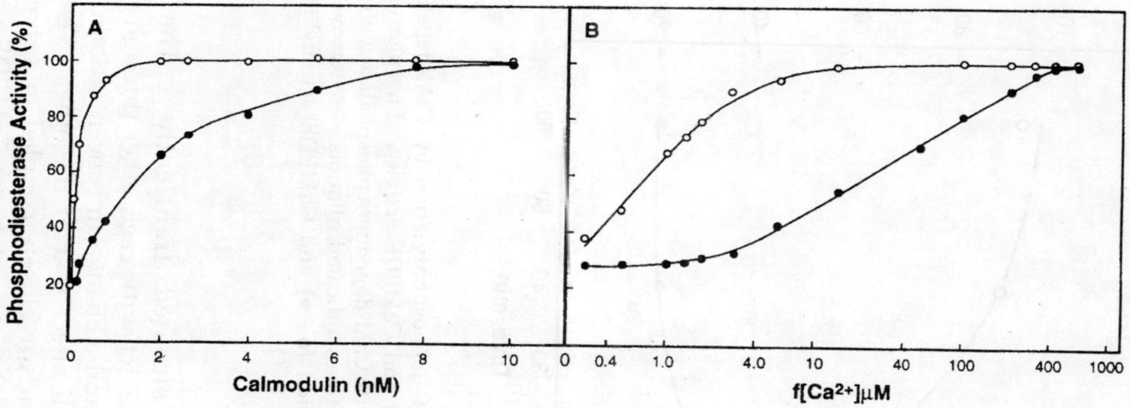

Figure 7. Effect of phosphorylation on the CaM and Ca^{2+} concentration dependence of CaMPDE activation. The CaMPDE was phosphorylated by cAMP-dependent protein kinase. Control reaction was carried out under identical conditions except buffer was substituted for [^{32}P] ATP. A, the non-phosphorylated (O – O) and the phosphorylated (● – ●) CaMPDE were analyzed for activity with various concentrations of CaM in the presence of 0.1 mM Ca^{2+}. B, the non phosphorylated (O – O) and phosphorylated enzyme (● – ●) were assayed for CaMPDE activity with various concentrations of Ca^{2+}, in the presence of 1.0 M CaM.

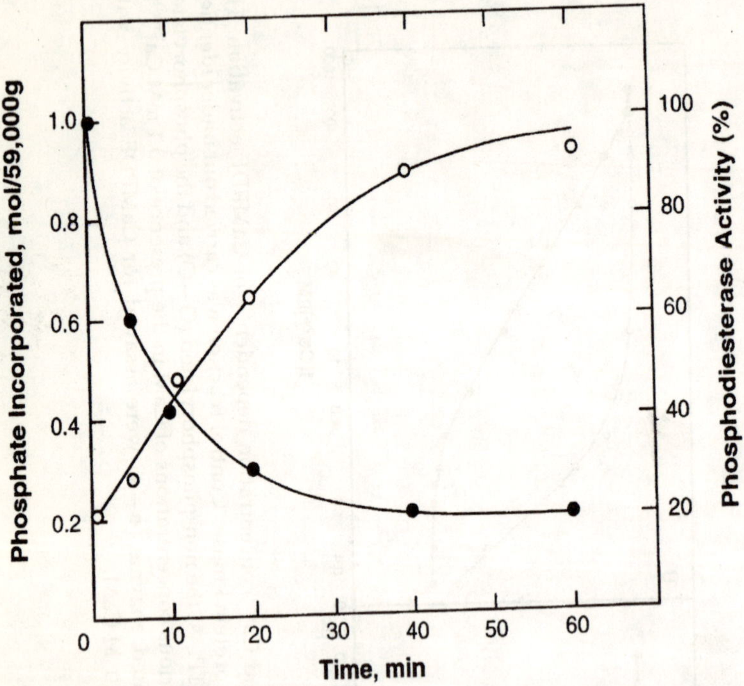

Figure 8. Time course of dephosphorylation by CaM-dependent phosphatase (calcineurin) and CaMPDE activity. Phosphorylated CaMPDE was incubated with CaM-dependent phosphatase with CaM in the presence of Ni^{2+}. At times indicated, aliquots were removed for assay of dephosphorylation (●–●) and CaMPDE activity in the presence of 0.1 mM Ca^{2+} (O–O).

concentrations are elevated transiently. The two signalling systems interact with each other through many regulatory reactions, and a change in concentration of one second messenger will affect that of the other. The two signal fluxes, therefore, are closely coupled in a dynamic fashion. Analysis of the role of heart CaMPDE in this signal-coupling phenomenon has shed light on the mechanism(s) of this coupling.

TABLE 2

Regulation of Bovine Heart CaMPDE by Ca^{2+} and cAMP

1.	Activation by Ca^{2+} and CaM
2.	Phosphorylation by cAMP-dependent protein kinase with reduction of phosphodiesterase affinity towards CaM
3.	Blockage of CaMPDE phosphorylation by Ca^{2+} and CaM
4.	Reversal of CaMPDE phosphorylation by CaM-dependent phosphatase (calcineurin)

A working hypothesis, describing the role of CaMPDE in the coupling between the two messenger fluxes, is presented in Figure 9. At least four possible modes of action exist by which Ca^{2+} and CaM may affect CaMPDE activity. Firstly, the enzyme is directly stimulated by Ca^{2+}-CaM. Secondly, the CaMPDE is phosphorylated by cAMP-dependent protein kinase and the phosphorylated enzyme requires higher concentrations of Ca^{2+} for activity. Thirdly, Ca^{2+} and CaM, by binding to the CaMPDE, block phosphorylation. Fourthly, phosphorylation of the CaMPDE is reversed through the action of the CaM-dependent phosphatase (calcineurin). It is conceivable that such complex regulation of the CaMPDE confers greater versatility on the interaction between the Ca^{2+} and cAMP systems. In most cases, cell activation involves transitory increases in both cAMP and cell Ca^{2+}. The operation of the different regulatory mechanisms on the CaMPDE may be temporally separated during the signal fluxes. This temporal separation of the regulatory reactions is a result of the Ca^{2+} and cAMP signal fluxes on the one hand, and contributes to determining the intensity and duration of the fluxes on the other hand. Thus, an initial increase in cAMP concentration during cell activation may bring about phosphorylation of CaMPDE and thereby prevent the enzyme from being activated by the low concentrations of Ca^{2+} existing at the early stages of cell activation. The hydrolysis of cAMP, therefore, is

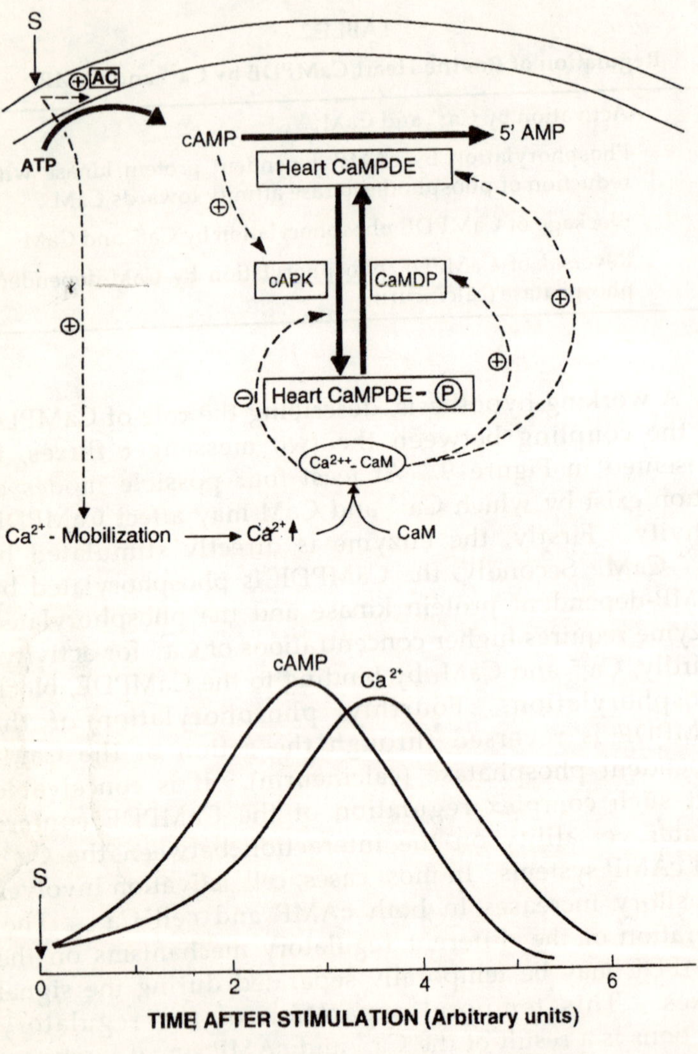

Figure 9. Hypothesis of the temporally-separated regulation of bovine heart CaMPDE by Ca^{2+} and cAMP (upper panel) and the CaMPDE mediated coupling between Ca^{2+} and cAMP fluxes (lower panel). AC, adenylate cyclase; cAPK, cAMP-dependent protein kinase; CaMDP, CaM-dependent phosphatase; p, phosphorylated; +, activation; −, inhibition; S, stimulus.

inhibited coordinately with the stimulation of adenylate cyclase by external signals. This ensures a rapid and sharp rise in intracellular [cAMP]. At later stages of cell activation, when intracellular free Ca^{2+} concentration is increased, the phosphatase reaction is activated to reverse phosphorylation of the CaMPDE. The CaMPDE then becomes fully activated by Ca^{2+} and CaM. Since Ca^{2+}-CaM can block the CaMPDE phosphorylation, the dephosphorylated state of the enzyme will be maintained, even though the cAMP concentration may still be high in the cell. The concerted actions of these regulatory mechanisms on the CaMPDE, namely the phosphatase reaction, Ca^{2+}-CaM stimulation of the phosphodiesterase, and Ca^{2+}-CaM inhibition of phosphorylation, bring about a rapid decline in cAMP concentration.

CONCLUSIONS

The main feature of the working hypothesis (Figure 9) for the regulation of the CaMPDE is that the multiple regulatory actions exerted by the second messengers on the CaMPDE are temporally separated. This is possible because the concentrations of both cAMP and Ca^{2+} undergo continuous change during cell activation. When the cell Ca^{2+} flux changes, the cAMP flux will change accordingly. The transitory elevations of the two messengers during cell activation are coupled to each other, with the CaMPDE playing key roles in the signal-coupling phenomenon. The exact physiological functions of CaMPDE are not clear, because most of regulatory studies have been carried out *in vitro*; therefore, it is essential that further research be directed to *in vivo* studies.

REFERENCES

1. Clapham, D.E. (1995) *Cell* 80, 259-268
2. Berridge, M.J. Bootman, M.D. and Lipp, P. (1998) *Nature* 395, 645-649

3. Klee, CB. (1988) In Molecular Aspects of Cell Regulation, vol 5, P. Cohen and C.B. Klee, editors, New York: Elsevier Science Publishing Co. 35-36
4. Cheung, W.Y. (1967) *Biochem. Biophys. Res. Commun.* 29, 478-482
5. Cheung, W.Y. (1976) *Biochem. Biophys. Res. Commun.* 38, 533-538
6. Wang, J.H., Teo, T.S., Ho, H.C. and Stevens, F.C. (1975) *Adv. Cyclic Nucleotide Res.* 5, 179-194
7. Appleman, M.M., Thompson, W.J. and Russell, T.R. (1973) *Adv. Cyclic Nucleotide Res.* 3, 65-98
8. Beavo, J.A., Hansen, R.S., Harrison, S.A., Hurwitz, R.L., Martins, T.J. and Mumby, M.C. (1982) *Mol. Cell. Endocrinol.* 28, 387-410
9. Kakkar, R., Raju, R.V.S. and Sharma, R.K. (1999) *Cell. Mol. Life Sci.* 55, 1164-1186
10. Sharma, R.K. and Hickie, (1996) *In phosphodiesterase inhibitors.* G. Dent, K. Rabe and C. Schudt, editors. New York: Academic Press
11. Beavo, J.A. (1995) *Physiol. Rev.* 75, 725-743
12. Wells, J.N. and Hardman, J.G. (1977) *Adv. Cyclic Nucleotide Res.* 8, 119-143
13. Hansen, R.S., and Beavo J.A. (1982) *Proc. Natl. Acad. Sci.* USA 79, 2788-2792
14. Sharma R.K. (1991) *Biochemistry* 30, 5963-5968
15. Sharma, R.K., Adachi, A.M., Adachi, K., and Wang, J.H. (1984) *J. Biol. Chem.* 259, 9248-9254
16. Sharma, R.K., and Wang, J.H. (1986) *J. Biol. Chem* 261, 14160-14166
17. Beavo, J.S., Conti, M. and Heaslip, R.J. (1994) *Mol. Pharmacol.* 75, 399-405
18. Sharma, R.K., and Wang, J.H. (1985) *Proc. Natl. Acad. Sci. USA* 82, 2603-2607
19. Sharma, R.K., and Wang, J.H. (1986) *J. Biol. Chem.* 261, 1322-1328
20. Sharma, R.K., and Kalra, J. (1994) *Biochem. J.* 299, 97-100
21. Keravis, T.M., Duemler, B.M., and Wells, J.M. (1986) *J. Cyclic Nucleotide Protein Phospho. Res.* 11, 365-372
22. Krebs, E.G. and Beavo, J.A. (1979) *Annu.Rev.Biochem.* 48, 923-959
23. Cheung, W.Y. (1980) *Science* 207, 19-27
24. Cohen, P., Burchel,l A., Foulkes, J.G., Cohen, P.T.W., Vanaman, T.C. and Mairn, A.C. (1981) *FEBS Lett.* 92, 287-293

25. Tam, S.W., Sharma, R.K. and Wang, J.H. (1982) *J.Biol.Chem.* 257, 14907-14913

26. Hayakawa, T., Perkins, J-P. and Krebs, E.G. (1973) *Biochem.* 12, 574-579

27. Walsh, M. and Hartshorne, D.J. (1982) *Calcium and Cell Function* 3, 223-260

28. Adelstein, R.S., Conti, M.A., Hathaway, D.A. and Klee, C.B. (1978) *J.Biol.Chem.* 253, 8347-8350

29. Soderling, T.R., Jett, M.F., Hutson, N.J. and Khatra, B.S. (1977) *J.Biol.Chem.* 252, 7517-7524

30. Camici, M., Ahmad, Z., and Depaoli-Roach, P.J. (1984) *J.Biol.Chem.* 259, 2466-2473

31. Stewart, A.A., Ingebritsen, T.S., Manalan, A., Klee, C.B., and Cohen, P. (1982) *FEBS Lett.* 137, 80-84

32. Huang, F.L. and Glinsmann, W.H. (1976) *Eur.J.Biochem.* 70, 419-426

Proceedings of 11th Annual Conference of the Physiological Society of India

POST-NATAL DEVELOPMENTAL CHANGES IN THE REGULATION OF L-TYPE CALCIUM CHANNELS IN RABBIT HEART CELLS

RAJIV KUMAR AND RONALD W. JOYNER

The Todd Franklin Cardiac Research Laboratory, The Children's Heart Center, Department of Pediatrics, Emory University School of Medicine,2040 Ridgewood Dr. NE. Atlanta, GA 30322

Summary

1. The whole cell patch clamp technique was used to examine the developmental changes in the regulation of L-type calcium current (Ica) by cGMP in freshly isolated adult and newborn rabbit ventricular cells.
2. To elucidate the mechanism responsible for the developmental decline and the significance of PKG in the regulation of cardiac calcium channels, full length rabbit heart PKG I cDNA was isolated, its sequence was determined and then expressed in mammalian cells. The expressed mRNA and protein levels of PKG were also determined in adult and newborn heart cells.
3. In adult ventricular cells, neither inhibitors of G-cyclase (methylene blue and LY-83583 which inhibit G-cyclase and thus lower cGMP levels), nor the internal application of 8BrcGMP produced any significant effect on basal I_{Ca}.
4. In newborn ventricular cells, the application of methylene blue or LY-83583 produced an irreversible inhibition of basal I_{Ca}, while intracellular perfusion of 8BrcGMP or 8CPT-cGMP significantly and reversibly increased basal I_{Ca}. The extracellular application of methylene blue during

the intracellular perfusion of 8BrcGMP was unable to inhibit I_{Ca}.

5. The NO donor GSNO produced a significant and reversible increase of basal I_{Ca} in newborn ventricular cells but not in adult.
6. The PKG inhibitor KT-5823 produced an irreversible significant inhibition of basal I_{Ca} in newborn ventricular cells but not in adult. KT-5823 completely blocked the stimulatory effect of GSNO.
7. In newborn ventricular cells, inhibition of cAMP dependent protein kinase blocked the stimulatory effect of cAMP but not of 8CPT-cGMP.
8. The stimulatory effect of GSNO on Ica was not blocked by the phosphodiesterase inhibitor IBMX, with GSNO producing an additive effect on Ica stimulated by IBMX.
9. The effect of Isoproterenol was substantially potentiated by the presence of 8BrcGMP or GSNO in newborn cells.
10. The coding region of rabbit PKG type Iα showed 94% homology to published sequences of human and bovine PKG type Iα.
11. The deduced amino acid sequence showed major substitutions in two CGMP binding site domains.
12. The expressed recombinant PKG was catalytically active, stimulated by cGMP, and showed the same immunoreactivity as the native PKG.
13. Expressed mRNA and protein levels for PKG type I were much higher in newborn compared to adult.
14. We propose that, for newborn rabbit ventricular cells, CGMP plays a crucial role in maintaining basal I_{Ca} by a mechanism mediated via Protein Kinase G dependent phosphorylation of calcium channels or some associated protein.
15. The greater expression of PKG in newborn cells could be responsible for differences in the significance of cGMP in adult and newborn rabbit cells.

INTRODUCTION

During fetal and early postnatal life, several changes are known to occur in the cardiac contractility, metabolic sensitivity, and autonomic innervation. Understanding the developmental changes in ion channel regulation is required for proper treatment of cardiac dysfunction in neonatal human. cGMP has been shown to exert a variety of generally inhibitory actions on adult heart cells, including a negative inotropic effect (Nawrath, 1977) and inhibition (Hartzell & Fischmeister, 1986; Levi*et al.*, 1989; Wahler *et al.*, 1990) as well as stimulation (Ono & Trautwein, 1991; Wahler & Dollinger, 1995; Kirstein*et aL*, 1995) of L-type calcium current, particularly in the presence of adrenergic stimulation or elevated cAMP levels. However, the physiological role of EGMP in regulation of cardiac activity is still controversial. Various studies on the effects of cGMP on I_{Ca} in different species have shown dissimilar findings and have failed to observe consistent effects of CGMP on electrical activity of cardiac muscle (Hartzell, 1988; Sperelakis, 1988). cGMP activates a specific cGMP dependent protein kinase (PKG) which can phosphorylate a number of proteins and can also stimulate or inhibit specific phospodiesterases (PDES) to produce either antagonistic or synergistic effects with cAMP elevating agents. Three pathways for the modulation of I_{Ca} by cGMP have been demonstrated: (i) activation of an endogenous PKG, which leads to inhibition of I_{Ca} in guinea pig (Levi *et al.*, 1989; Ono & Trautwein, 1991) or rat (Mery *et al.*, 1991) ventricular cells; (ii) activation of cGMP-stimulated PDE that leads to the inhibition of I_{Ca} (Hartzell & Fisclimelster, 1986) (Rivet-Bastide *et al.*, 1997); and (iii) inhibition of cGMP inhibited PDE which results In an increase of I_{Ca} (Kirstein et *al.*, 1995; Ono & Trautwein, 1991). In mammalian heart, both potentiation and inhibition by cGMP (or cGMP analogs) of β-adrenergic- or cAMP- effects on I_{Ca}, were shown in guinea pig ventricular cells by different groups of investigators, but none of these studies showed any significant effects on basal Ica.

PKG is selectively activated by CGMP and regulates cytoplasmic Ca^{2+} concentration by several pathways

(Komalavilas & Lincoln, 1994; Ruth *et al.*, 1990). There are two types of PKG present in eukaryotic cells: type I and type II (Lincoln & Cornwell, 1993). PKG type I is a dimer of identical subunits, each with a mass of approximately 78 kDa. PKG II also exists as a dimer whose subunit mass is approximately 86 kDa. PKG type I has two subtypes, α, and β (Lincoln *et al.*, 1988). Both PKG type Iα and type Iβ have been cloned (Wemet *et al.*, 1989; Sandberg et al., 1989; Tamura *et al.*, 1996) and shown to be present in mammalian cells (Lincoln & Cornwell, 1993). The tissue specific expression of PKG is highly variable and appears to be under physiological control. Very little information is available concerning the expression of PKG in cardiovascular tissues. Although PKG was found in adult cardiac muscle (Lincoln & Keely, 1981), but it was most abundant in cardiac vasculature.

No previous studies on the developmental differences in the effect of CGMP on I_{Ca} have appeared. CGMP may be more important in the regulation of basal Ica and β-adrenergic-stimulated I_{Ca} in newborn ventricular cells than in adult cells. We have shown that basal levels of CGMP (per mg protein) in isolated ventricular cells were significantly higher in newborn (1-4 days old) (272±33 fmol/mg protein) compared to adult (55±7 fmol/mg protein) (Kumar *et al.*, 1994) cells. We examined the effects of CGMP by elevating its levels either by intracellular application of CGMP analogs by a pipette perfusion system or by stimulating G-cyclase by NO using NO donor nitrosoglutathione (GSNO) or lowering its levels by inhibiting G-cyclase by methylene blue and LY-83583 on L-type Ca^{2+} current in adult and newborn rabbit ventricular cells. We have also examined the effects of cAMP dependent protein kinase inhibitor (PKI, 5-22), cGMP dependent protein kinase inhibitor (KT5823) and phosphodiesterase inhibitor (3-isobutyl-l-methylxanthine, IBMX). To elucidate the mechanism responsible for the developmental decline and the significance of PKG in the regulation of cardiac calcium channels, we isolated the full-length rabbit heart PKG type Iα cDNA, determined the sequence to examine species-specific sequence heterogeneity, and expressed the construct in mammalian cells to verify that the cloned cDNA encodes PKG. We also analyzed expressed levels of PKG type I mRNA by Northern blotting and PKG type I protein levels by Western immunoblotting to investigate the regulation of PKG expression during postnatal development of rabbit heart.

METHODS

1. Preparation of isolated cells: New Zealand White adult (1.5-2 kg) and newborn (1-4 days old) rabbits of either sex were used. Adult rabbits were heparinized (heparin, 1000 units, iv) and anesthetized with sodium pentobarbital (50 mg/kg, i.v.). For newborn rabbits the same drugs were given intraperitoneally. Hearts were rapidly removed via thoracotomy with artificial ventilation and the aorta was cannulated. Single ventricular cells were obtained by enzymatic dissociation as we previously described (Kumar *et aL,* 1996).

2. Recording of whole cell calcium current: Voltage-clamp experiments were performed as we described earlier {808} in the whole cell configuration of the patch-clamp method by use of an Axopatch-200 patch-clamp amplifier (Axon Instruments, Foster City, CA), using fire-polished borosilicate glass pipettes with resistance of 1-2 MΩ for adult cells and 2-4 MΩ for newborn cells when filled with the normal pipette solution. A tight seal (3-5 GΩ) is established in normal Tyrode solution. After breaking the membrane by applying a quick suction to the pipette, the external solution is changed to the test solution. The complete change in the bath solution is obtained within 1 min.

For routine monitoring of I_{Ca}, the ventricular cells were depolarized every 10 see from a holding potential of

-40 mV to a test potential of +15 mV for 270 msec. No leakage correction was required. The elicited Ica was filtered at a corner frequency of 2 kHz, digitized at 200-μsec intervals, and stored and analyzed on IBM compatible computer with pCLAMP6 software (Axon Instruments). I_{Ca} was measured as the peak inward current. All experiments were performed at room temperature (21-23°C). Membrane capacitance was measured using the calibrated capacity compensation circuit of the Axopatch voltage clamp amplifier using 5 mv-hyperpolarizing pulses. We expressed all the current data as current density (pA/pF) by normalizing the peak Ica for each cell to the cell capacitance. Cells which showed rundown were excluded from the analysis by only accepting the data from cells in which I_{Ca} was stable in the control condition and reached a stable effect with the tested drugs.

3. Solutions and Drugs. The compositions of standard solutions used were as follows (mM). *Normal Tyrode* : NaCl 148.8, KCl 4.0, $CaCl_2$ 1.8, $MgCl_2$ 0.53, NaH_2PO_4 O.33. HEPES 5.0, glucose 5.0, pH 7.4 with NaOH. Ca^{2+} *-free solution*: NaCl 100, KCl 10, KH_2PO_4 1.2, $MgSO_4$ 5, Taurine 50, glucose 20, HEPES 10, pH 7.1 with NaOH. *Storage solution*: K glutamate 140, Taurine 20, $MgCl_2$ 5, EGTA 1, glucose 10, HEPES 10, pH 7.4 with KOH. I_{Ca}. *Test solution:* NaCl 130, CaCI2 1.8, CsCl 20, $MgCl_2$ 0.53, HEPES 5, glucose 5, pH 7.4 with NaOH. *Normal pipette solution*: CSOH 110, Aspartic acid 90, CsCl 20, Tetraethylammonium CI (TEACI) 10, HEPES 5, EGTA 10, MGATP 5, Na_2 Creatine Phosphate 5, GTP(Tris) 0.4, leupeptin 0. 1, pH 7.2 with CSOH. Modifications to these solutions are described below as appropriate for specific protocols. For perfusion of different internal solutions in the patch pipette in whole cell voltage clamp mode, we use a pipette perfusion system (2PK+, Adams and List, NY) as described earlier (Kumar *et al.,* 1997).

4. Preparation of RNA: For mRNA isolation, hearts were rapidly excised from anesthetized adult and newborn rabbits and plunged into cold Trizol solution (Gibco-BRL). Ventricles were carefully separated and homogenized with a polytron homogenizer. The total RNA was isolated by one step isolation using phenol-guanidinium isothiocyanate solution developed by Chomczynski and Sacchl (1987). We used an oligo(dT)-cellulose column to isolate mRNA from total RNA for cDNA cloning and for Northern blot analysis.

5.Cloning and Expression of rabbit PKG type Iα cDNA: To construct PCR mediated PKG type Iα cDNA, the coding sequence from bovine lung cDNA was divided in different regions (Kumar *et al.*, 1999), each corresponding to the published sequence for the cDNA encoding bovine lung PKG type Iα. (Wemet *et aL*, 1989). Poly (A+) selected RNA (mRNA) was purified from total RNA isolated from newborn rabbit heart. The mRNA was converted to first strand of cDNA using avian malony virus reverse transcriptase. The cDNA derived from reverse transcription reactions was amplified with PKG specific primers using standard PCR protocol. The three amplified cDNA fragments (Al-A2, BI-B2, and C1-C2) were sequentially ligated (Rapid DNA ligation, Boehringer Mannheim Corpn., Indianapolis, IN) into pcDNA 3.1 (+) vector (Invitrogen, Carlsbed, CA) to yield the entire cDNA sequence.

6. Expression of PKG and assay of PKG activity: COS-7 cells (monkey fibroblasts) were grown to 80% confluency in 60 mm culture dishes and then transiently transfected with 5 μg of pcDNA3.1/PKG using TFX[TM] transfection reagent as described earlier (Kumar *et al.*, 1999). Aliquots of extract were analyzed for PKG activity and also for Western blotting using an affinity purified polyclonal rabbit anti-PKG antibody as described later. PKG activity was assayed as described earlier (Boerth & Lincoln, 1994) using a peptide substrate (BPDEtide, RKISASEFDRPL) selective for PKG. All assays were performed in the presence of 1 μM cAMP dependent protein kinase inhibitor peptide (5-24), 0.1 mM 3-isobutyl-l-methylxanthine (IBMX), and in the presence or absence of 1 μM cGMP. The difference in the phosphorylation of substrate in the presence and absence of cGMP was taken as PKG activity and expressed as pmoles/min/mg protein.

7. Northern Blot Analysis: Northern blot analysis was carried out using a standard method (Bloch *et al.,* 1991). To identify PKG type I mRNA, we used bovine PKG type Iα cDNA, rabbit cardiac PKG type Iα containing 999-2016 nucleotides (C1-C2 fragment), and rabbit cardiac PKG type Iα containing 456-1,663 nucleotides (B1-CB2 fragment) which can identify both type Iα and Iβ. Equal loading of the RNA samples was initially verified by using cDNA probe for mRNA of GAPDH, since expression of GAPDH mRNA is not developmentally regulated. Relative amounts of specific mRNAs in adult and newborn ventricular mRNA preparations were quantified by 2 dimensional gel imaging by using an Alpha Imager 2000 documentation and Analysis system (Alpha Innotech Corp., USA) for multiple adult and newborn preparations from different hearts.

8. Preparation of total homogenates from isolated cells and Western Blot analysis: To prepare total homogenates from isolated ventricular cells (Kumar *et al.,* 1994), cells were homogenized in hypotonic membrane buffer (containing in mM, Tris/HCI (pH 7.5) 50, MgCI2 5, EDTA 1, dithiothreitol 1, Pepstatin A 0.001, Phenylmethylsul fonyl fluoride 0.4, Phenanthroline I and lodoacetamide 1) by sonication. The homogenate was then centrifuged at 100xg for 15 min to separate the unbroken cells, and the supernatant (total homogenate) was stored at -70 °C in small aliquots. Protein was determined by a dye method (BioRad, Hercules, CA). Immunological characterization and quantification of the amounts of PKG type I in homogenates prepared from enzymatically dissociated ventricular cells, or from whole ventricles was performed by as described in our publications (Kumar *et al.*, 1994; Kumar *et aL,* 1999).

9. Immunofluorescence Microscopy: Adult and newborn rabbit ventricular cells were fixed at room temperature in 2% formaldehyde in low Ca-Tyrode solution. The Cells were washed twice with phosphate buffered saline (PBS) and then permeabilized with 0.3% Tritonx 100 in PBS. The permeabilized cells, after blocking with 5% rabbit serum in PBS were incubated with rabbit anti-PKG antibody at 4 °C overnight. The cells were then washed several times with PBS and stained with FITC-conjugated goat anti-rabbit IgG for 30 min. Finally, cells were washed in PBS, mounted in gelmount, and viewed on Noran Confocal Laser Scanning Microscope coupled to an Olympus IX-70 Inverted Microscope with x60 water immersion objective.

10. Statistics: All values are presented as mean ± SEM. Statistical analysis were performed using SigmaStat for windows with paired t test. P value less than 0.05 was defined as significant.

RESULTS

Increasing intracellular cGMP levels increase I_{Ca}. in newborn but not in AD ventricular cells

To investigate the effect of increasing levels of cGMP on basal ICa, we applied 8BrcGMP intracellularly by perfusing the patch pipette with a solution containing 8BrcGMP for adult and newborn ventricular cells. We used 8BrcGMP, which is a nonhydrolyzable analog of cGMP. For a newborn ventricular cell the time course of I_{Ca} peak current is shown in Figure IA. For this cell, we switched the internal solution to one containing 30 μM 8BrcGMP after achieving a steady state basal I_{Ca} and this concentration produced an increase in I_{Ca} of 80-100% over

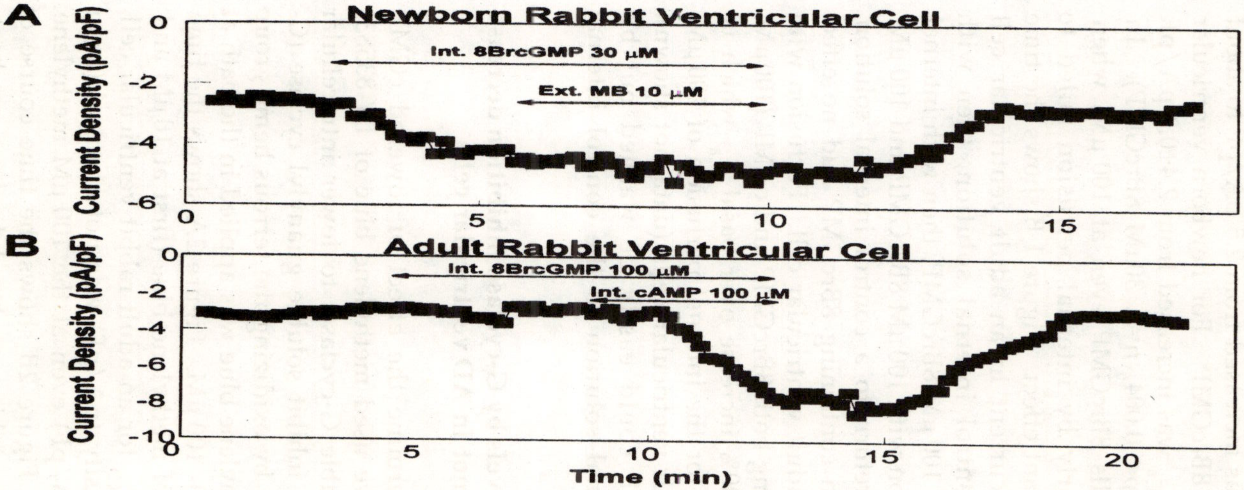

Figure 1. **(A)** Time course of L-type Calcium Current (pA/pF) for a newborn rabbit ventricular cell with intracellular exposure to 30 μM 8BrcGMP in the internal (Int.) perfusion solution and then the addition of 10 μM methylene blue (MB) to the external (ext.) solution while maintaining the 8BrcGMP in the internal perfusion solution. To washout 8BrcGMP, cell was perfused with normal internal solution. **(B)** Time course of L-type Calcium Current (pA/pF) for an adult rabbit ventricular cell with intracellular (int.) exposure to 100 μM 8BrcGMP and then the combination of 100 μM cAMP and 100 μM 8BrcGMP in the internal perfusion solution. To washout cAMP and 8BrcGMP, cell was perfused with normal internal solution. The time period of exposure is indicated by horizontal arrows. (from (Kumar *et al.*, 1997))

basal I_{Ca}. Basal I_{Ca} was increased from 2.5 pA/pF to about 5 pA/pF by 30 μM 8BrcGMP. For newborn ventricular cells, average basal I_{Ca} was increased from 2.4±0.2 pA/pF to 4.3±0.3) pA/pF ($p < 0.004$, n=5, 30μM 8BrcGMP). In adult ventricular cells 8BrcGMP even at 100 μM, when applied intracellularly by internal perfusion failed to produce any significant effect. Figure I B shows the time course of I_{Ca} peak current in an adult ventricular cell recorded with a control internal solution, then with internal perfusion of 100 μM 8BrcGMP, then with internal perfusion of a solution with 100 μM 8BrcGMP and 100 μM cAMP, and then a return to a control internal solution. The internal solution containing 8BrcGMP had no effect on basal I_{Ca} of this adult ventricular cell. Perfusion with the solution containing both 8BrcGMP and cAMP (100 μM each) produced a 200% increase over basal I_{Ca}, which is similar to the effect for the internal perfusion of 100 μM cAMP alone for adult ventricular cells (data not shown). The effect of cAMP could easily be washed out by switching the internal solution to the control internal solution.

Decreasing cGMP levels by G-cyclase inhibition decrease I_{Ca} in newborn but not in AD ventricular cells

In order to determine the effect of lowered cGMP levels on basal I_{Ca} we used methylene blue or LY-83583, as inhibitors of soluble G-cyclase, to lower intracellular cGMP levels. They inhibit soluble guanylyl cyclase (G-cyclase), presumably by oxidizing the ferrous heme group of the enzyme. Methylene blue was applied in the bath at a concentration of 10- 100 μM. Figure 2A shows the time course of the effect of methylene blue (first at 10 μM and then at 100 μM) on I_{Ca} for an adult rabbit ventricular cell. For this cell, I_{Ca} density (pA/pF) was not changed (from 5.3 pA/pF to 5.4 pA/pF) even at the 100 μM methylene blue concentration. Figure 2B shows the time course of the effect of methylene blue on basal I_{Ca} in a newborn rabbit ventricular cell. After a period of control solution, for which the basal I_{Ca} was 2.8 pA/pF, the application of 10 μM methylene blue inhibited I_{Ca}, over a 5 min period to a level of 0.9 pA/pF. The inhibitory effect of methylene blue was not reversed even after extended washout of the drug. In newborn cells, methylene blue (10-100 μM) produced a significant inhibitory effect on average basal I_{Ca} from 2.4±0.2 pA/pF to 0.85±0.2 pA/pF ($p<0.005$, $n=5$, 10 μM methylene blue) and to 0.55±0.08 pA/pF ($p<0.003$, $n=3$, 100 μM methylene blue). In further experiments, we used 10 μM methylene blue to avoid any possible non-specific effects. We also applied methylene blue intracellularly by adding it to the internal solution and found similar results. If methylene blue produces its inhibitory effect on I_{Ca} by lowering cGMP levels through inhibition of Gcyclase, then under conditions of an excess of cGMP, methylene blue would not be able to produce inhibition. To examine whether the inhibitory effect of methylene blue on Ica is mediated by lowering the cGMP levels or if it produces an inhibitory effect nonspecifically, we added 10 μM methylene blue to the external solution during the continued internal perfusion of 30μM 8BrcGMP (Figure IA). Figure IA shows that the addition of methylene blue to the external solution during the internal perfusion of 8BrcGMP had no inhibitory effect on I_{Ca} stimulated by 8BrcGMP. Fig. 2C shows the time course of the effect of 10 μM LY-83583 on basal I_{Ca} in a newborn ventricular cell. For this cell, control I_{Ca} of 3.2 pA/pF was decreased to about 1.8 pA/pF by external application of 10 μM LY-83583 and this effect was not reversible on wash out of LY-83583. In newborn ventricular cells, LY-83583 at a concentration of 10 μM produced a 35% inhibition in average basal I_{Ca} (from 2.39±0.3 2 pA/pF to 1.53±0.15 pA/pF, $p<0.03$, $n=4$). In adult ventricular cells LY-83583 at a concentration of 10 μM produced no significant effect on basal I_{Ca} (data not shown).

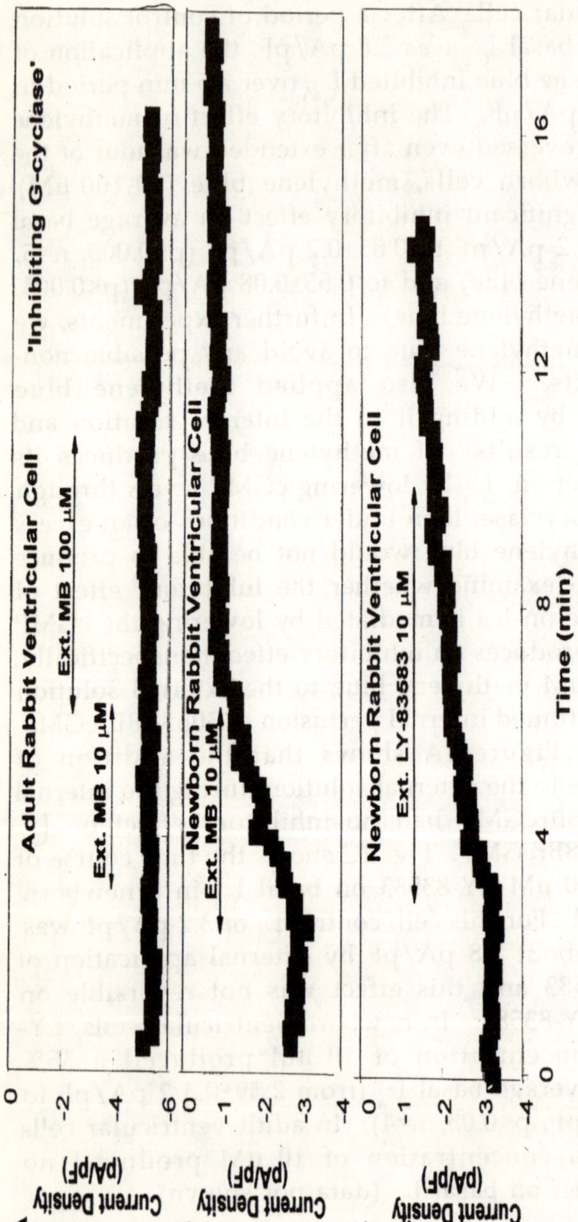

Figure 2. Time course of L-type Calcium Current (pA/pF) for the effects of external (ext.) application of 10 μM methylene blue (MB) and then 100 μM methylene blue in an adult ventricular cell (A), of 10μM methylene blue in a newborn rabbit ventricular cell (B), and of 10 μM LY 83583 in a newborn rabbit ventricular cell (C). The time periods of exposure is indicated by horizontal arrows. (From (Kumar *et al.*, 1997))

Stimulating PKG increases I_{Ca} while inhibiting PKG decreases I_{Ca} in newborn ventricular cells

To evaluate more directly the involvement of cGMP-dependent protein kinase in the maintenance of basal I_{Ca}, we used a potent activator of PKG, 8Chlorophenylthio-cGMP (8CPT-cGMP), to stimulate PKG by intracellular perfusion. As with the 8BrcGMP, we perfused the cells with 30 μM 8CPT-cGMP after achieving a steady state basal I_{Ca}. In a newborn ventricular cell, the time course of I_{Ca} peak current is shown in Figure 3A, showing that the intracellular perfusion of 8CPT-cGMP resulted in an increase of basal I_{Ca} by about 100%. I_{Ca} was increased from a basal level of 1.6 PA/PF to 3.5 PA/PF by 8CPT-cGMP, an increase very similar to the one observed in the presence of 8BrcGMP. We also used KT-5823, an inhibitor of PKG, extracellularly at a sufficiently low concentration of 0.2 μM to inhibit PKG much more specifically than PKA. The Ki of KT-5823 for PKG is 0.234 μM and for PKA is more than 10 μM (Kase *et al.*, 1987). Figure 3B shows the time course of the effect of KT-5823 on basal I_{Ca} in a newborn ventricular cell. After a period of control solution, for which the basal Ica was 1.6 pA/pF, the application of 0.2 μM KT-5823 inhibited I_{Ca} to a level of 0.9 pA/pF. The inhibitory effect of KT-5823 was not reversed after washout of the drug. Average basal I_{Ca} in newborn ventricular cells was decreased by 0.2 μM KT-5 823 from 2.36±0.27 pA/pF to 1.3±0.17 pA/pF ($p<0.01$, $n=5$). In adult ventricular cells, 0.2 μM KT-5823 had no effect on basal I_{Ca} (data not shown).

Stimulating G-cyclase by NO donor increases I_{Ca}

Nitric oxide is well known as a stimulator of soluble G-cyclase and produces its effects by increasing intracellular cGMP concentrations. We used a relatively stable nitric oxide donor GSNO which has a half life of 150 hrs and does not involve the formation of oxygen free radicals (Barnett *et al.*, 1994). To determine whether an

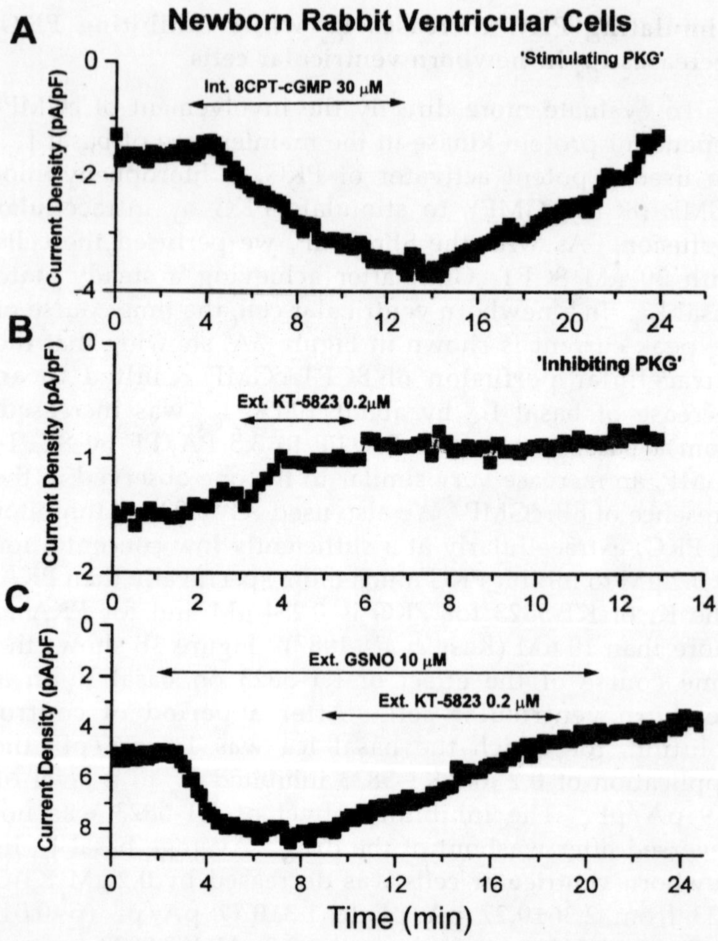

Figure 3. **(A)** Time course of L-type Calcium Current (pA/pF) for a newborn rabbit ventricular cell with intracellular (Int.) exposure to 30 μM 8CPT-cGMP in the internal perfusion solution. To washout 8CPT-cGMP, cell was perfused with normal internal solution. **(B)** Time course of L-type Calcium Current (pA/pF) for newborn rabbit ventricular cells with exposure to 0.2 μM KT-5823 in the external solution (ext.). **(C)** Time course of L-type Calcium Current (pA/pF) for newborn rabbit ventricular cells with exposure to 10 μM GSNO in the external solution and then the additional exposure to 0.2 μM KT-5823 in the presence of 10 μM GSNO. The time periods of exposure is indicated by horizontal arrows.

increase in intracellular cGMP concentration produces effects similar to intracellular application of 8BrcGMP, we applied GSNO at a concentration of 10 μM extracellularly to newborn ventricular cells. In a newborn ventricular cell, the time course of I_{Ca} peak current is shown in Figure 3C, showing that the extracellular application of GSNO resulted in an increase of basal Ica by about 50%. Ica was increased from a basal level of 5.0 pA/pF to 8.5 pA/pF by GSNO. We then applied 0.2 μM KT-5823 in the continuing presence of GSNO. The application of KT-5 823 completely blocked the stimulatory effect of GSNO on I_{Ca}. Application of 10 μM GSNO did not produce any effect in adult ventricular cells. We also used reduced glutathione (GSH) to rule out the possible stimulation of I_{Ca} by GSH which is one of the product during the formation of NO from GSNO. GSH (10 μM) did not produce any effect on basal I_{Ca} in newborn ventricular cells (data not shown).

Does cAMP dependent protein kinase mediate the effect of cGMP on basal I_{Ca}?

The above results suggested that changes in cGMP levels in newborn cells play a crucial role in determining basal I_{Ca} and that the PKG inhibitor KT-5823 inhibits basal I_{Ca} and blocked the stimulatory effect of GSNO. It remained unclear whether these effects are exclusively mediated by actions of cGMP (or its derivatives) on PKG or resulted from actions of cGMP on cAMP dependent protein kinase (PKA). To evaluate this possibility, we examined the effects of 8CPT-cGMP under conditions in which PKA had been inhibited. Figure 4A illustrates results for a newborn ventricular cell for which we used a pipette solution which included 1 μM of PKA inhibitor (5-22, PKI). The presence of PKI produced a gradual decline in the value of basal I_{Ca} to about 40% of the initial value. The subsequent perfusion of internal solution containing 30 μM cAMP and 1μM PKI failed to produce any increase in the value of Ica inhibited by PKI. We specifically used 30 μM cAMP to compare the effect of 30

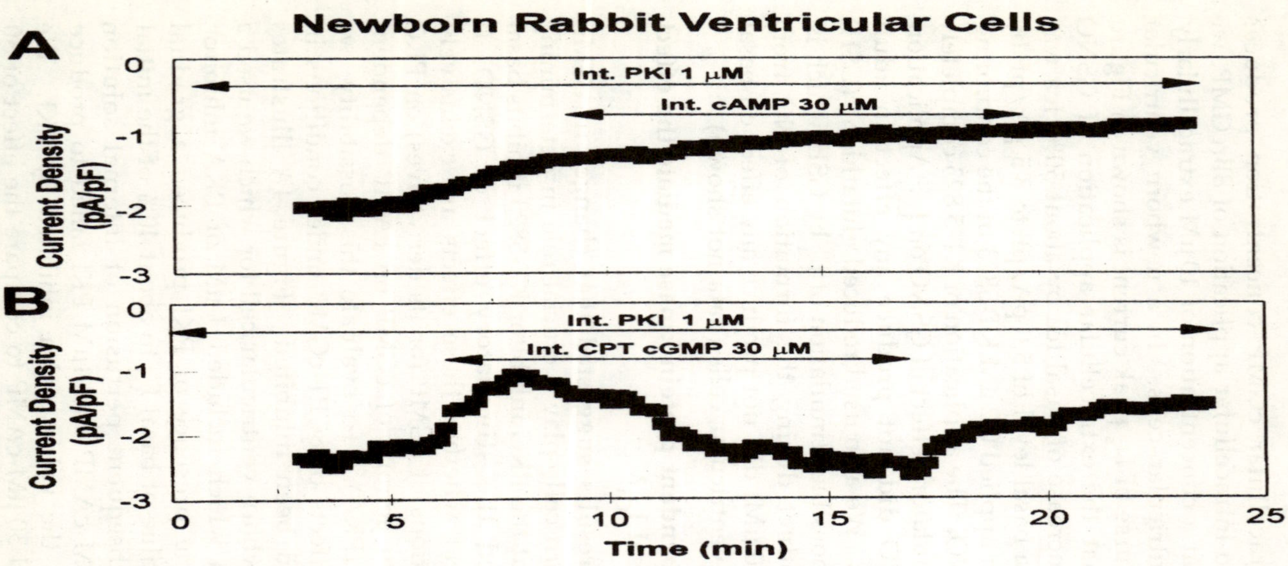

Figure 4. **(A)** Time course of L-type Calcium Current (pA/ pF) for a newborn rabbit ventricular cell with intracellular exposure to 1 μM PKI (included in the pipette filling solution) and then the additional exposure to 30 μM cAMP and 1 μM PKI in the internal (Int.) perfusion solution. **(B)** Time course of peak value of L-type Calcium Current (pA/ pF) for a newborn rabbit ventricular cell with intracellular exposure to 1 μM PKI (included in the pipette filling solution) and then the additional exposure to 30 μM 8CPT-cGMP and 1 μM PKI in the internal (Int.) perfusion solution. The time periods of exposure is indicated by horizontal arrows. (From (Kumar *et al.*, 1997))

μM cAMP with a 30 μM concentration of the cGMP analog. 30 μM cAMP itself produces about a 100% increase in I_{Ca} when applied intracellularly. Figure 4B shows a similar experiment for a newborn ventricular cell in which we again included 1 μM PKI in the pipette solution, producing a decline in the value of basal I_{Ca}, but the addition of 30μM 8CPT-cGMP (to stimulate PKG) to the internal solution with PKI substantially increased the level of I_{Ca} inhibited by PKI. After washout of the 8CPT-cGMP from the internal solution (but retention of PKI in the internal solution) the level of basal I_{Ca} again declined. Intracellular application of 1 μM PKI reduced the average I_{Ca} from 2.16 ± 0.07 to 1.45 ± 0.09 pA/pF ($p<0.05$, n=6), a decrease of 33%. Intracellular application of 10 μM PKI produced a similar decrease of 31% of basal I_{Ca} (from 2.40 ± 0.06 to 1.66 ± 0.05 pA/pF; $p<0.05$, n=7). When we applied 30 μM 8CPTcGMP intracellularly in the presence of 1 μM PKI, the average I_{Ca} increased from 1.64 ± 0.05 to 2.49 ± 0.06 pA/pF ($p<0.05$, n=3), an increase of 52%. The average increase in I_{Ca} by 8CPTcGMP was somewhat decreased from 100% under control condition to 52% under the inhibitory influence of PKI.

Do phosphodiesterases mediate the stimulatory effect of cGMP?

To exclude the possible involvement of PDE's in the stimulatory effect of cGMP, we used IBMX, a nonspecific inhibitor of PDE's near the concentration required for half maximal stimulation of I_{Ca} (EC_{50} 64 ± 20 μM) in newborn ventricular cells, as we reported earlier (Akita) (*et al.*, 1994). We first exposed newborn ventricular cells to 50 μM IBMX and then added 10 μM GSNO (which increases cGMP levels inside the cell and consistently produces about a 50% increase in basal I_{Ca}) in the presence of 50 μM IBMX. Figure 5A shows current recordings and time course of I_{Ca} peak current (inset) for a newborn cell before and after application of 50 μM IBMX and then the application of 10 μM GSNO plus 50 μM IBMX after reaching

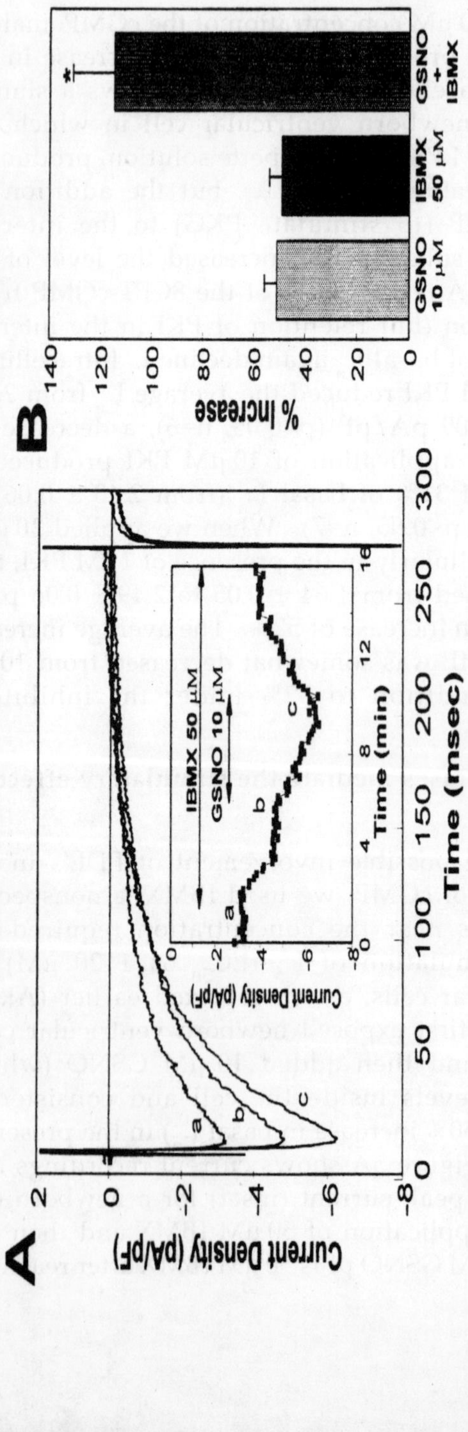

Figure 5. **(A)** The superimposed I_{Ca} recordings and time course (inset) of L-type Calcium Current (pA/pF) for a newborn rabbit ventricular cell with the addition of 50 μM IBMX to external solution and then the addition of 10 μM GSNO with 50 μM IBMX to external solution. The I_{Ca} current traces labeled as 'a', 'b' and 'c' were obtained at the times marked by the corresponding letters in the inset. The three traces 'a', 'b' and 'c' correspond to the control solution, 50 μM IBMX and to the 10 μM GSNO plus 50μM IBMX, respectively. **(B)** Bar graph showing average mean values of percent increase in I_{Ca} by treatment with 10 μM GSNO (n=5), 50 μM IBMX (n=4), or 10 μM GSNO plus 50 μM IBMX (n=4) over control. Error bars indicate SEM.* indicates the percent increase by 10 μM GSNO plus 50 μM IBMX is significantly different than the percent increase by GSNO or IBMX alone. (From (Kumar *et al.*, 1997))

the steady state of I_{Ca} with 50 μM IBMX. I_{Ca} increased from 3.2 to 4.8 pA/pF with the application of 50μM IBMX and this current was further increased by the presence of 10 μM GSNO to 6.2 pA/pF. Figure 5B summarizes the effects of 10 μM GSNO alone, 50 μM IBMX alone, and the combination of 10 μM GSNO and 50 μM IBMX. GSNO (10 μM) alone, as we presented above for a separate group of cells, increased basal I_{Ca}, by 51 ± 5% ($p<0.05$, n=5). Extracellular application of 50 μM IBMX produced an increase of 49 ± 7.2 % (from 2.83 ± 0.23 to 4.2 ± 0.41 pA/pF; $p<0.05$, n=4), which is close to the value we published earlier {2424}. When we applied 10 μM GSNO in the presence of 50 μM IBMX, the average I_{Ca} was further increased from 4.2 ± 0.41 to 6.05 ± 0.66 pA/pF ($p<0.05$, n=4), an additional increase of 66% over IBMX alone and an overall increase of 115 ± 17% over control.

cGMP is not antagonistic to cAMP in newborn ventricular cells

We have also done experiments on the modulation of β-adrenergic stimulation of I_{Ca} by elevated cGMP levels. To elevate cGMP levels, we applied 8BrcGMP inside the cell or applied GSNO extracellularly to stimulate G-cyclase. Figure 6A shows the time course of I_{Ca} with the application of 0.1 μM ISO (which by itself produces only a 70% increase in basal I_{Ca} in newborn cells (Osaka & Joyner, 1992)) in the presence of 30 μM 8BrcGMP in the patch pipette. The steady state I_{Ca} was about 3.5 pA/pF in the presence 8BrcGMP. ISO (0.1 μM), in the presence of 8BrcGMP, resulted in a further increase in Ica to 10.5 pA/pF (an increase of 200%) , a much greater effect than the application of ISO alone. We also used GSNO, which by itself produces about a 50% in basal I_{Ca} as shown earlier. Figure 6B shows the time course of I_{Ca} with the application of 0.1 μM ISO and then with the addition of 10μM GSNO+ 0.1 μM ISO, showing a substantial further increase in I_{Ca} in response to GSNO after the treatment by ISO. These results show that the effect of ISO on I_{Ca} was substantially

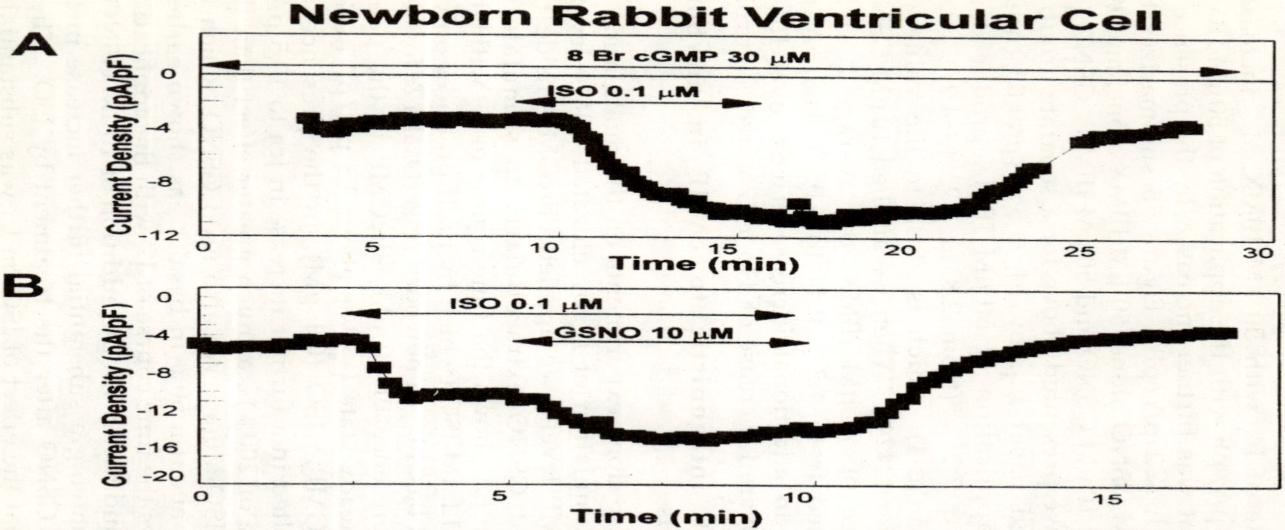

Figure 6. **(A)** Time course of peak value of L-type Calcium Current (pA/pF) for a newborn rabbit ventricular cell with intracellular exposure to 30 μM 8BrcGMP (included in the pipette filling solution) and then the additional exposure to 0.1 μM Isoproterenol in the continuing presence of 30 μM 8BrcGMP. **(B)** Time course of peak value of L-type Calcium Current (pA/pF) for newborn rabbit ventricular cells with exposure to 0.1 μM Isoproterenol in the external solution and then the additional exposure to 10 μM GSNO in the presence of 0.1 μM Isoproterenol. The time periods of exposure is indicated by horizontal arrows.

potentiated by 8BrcGMP or GSNO and suggests that the effects of cAMP and cGMP on I_{Ca} are at least not antagonistic and may be additive or synergistic in newborn cells.

Cloning and Expression of Rabbit PKG type Iα cDNA: We obtained cDNA fragments of PKG type Iα from rabbit cardiac MRNA using RT PCR technique. The composed nucleotide sequence of rabbit cardiac PKG type Iα cDNA (GenBank Accession Number AF076969) consisted of 2095 bp (1-2095) and contains an open reading frame of 2013 bp (Kumar *et al.*, 1999). The coding region of rabbit cardiac PKG type Iα has 94% homology to published sequences of human and bovine PKG type Iα (Tamura *et al.*, 1996; Wemet *et al.*, 1989), and consisted of 671 amino acids with a molecular mass of 76,452 Da. There were seven amino acid substitutions between human (Tamura *et al.*, 1996) or bovine (Wernet *et al.*, 1989) and rabbit PKG type la, these substitutions are shown in figure 7. The "LeucineIsoleucine zipper" responsible for dimerization of subunits and the autophosphorylation sites in the Iα specific N-tenninal region (1-89 amino acids) were conserved between human, bovine and rabbit PKG type Iα. The major substitutions were found in the cGMP binding domains (AA 102-341). These substitutions were Val^{140} to Ala^{140} in the cGMP2 binding site domain and Gly^{245} to Glu^{245}, Ile^{248} to Ser^{248}, Val^{279} to Ile^{279} (human and bovine to rabbit) in the cGMP 1 binding site domain. The amino acid at position 265 (Lys^{265}) in rabbit was the same as for the bovine form but different from Thr^{265} in human PKG type Iα. Similarly, the amino acid at position 275 (Ser^{275}) was the same as in the human form but different from Asn^{275} in bovine PKG type Iα.

We have expressed PKG Iα cDNA in COS7 cells and immunoreactivity and enzyme activity of recombinant PKG was measured (Kumar *et al.*, 1999). Polyclonal antibodies to PKG recognized a band at 79 kDa in extracts of PKG transfected cells (Data not shown). The extracts

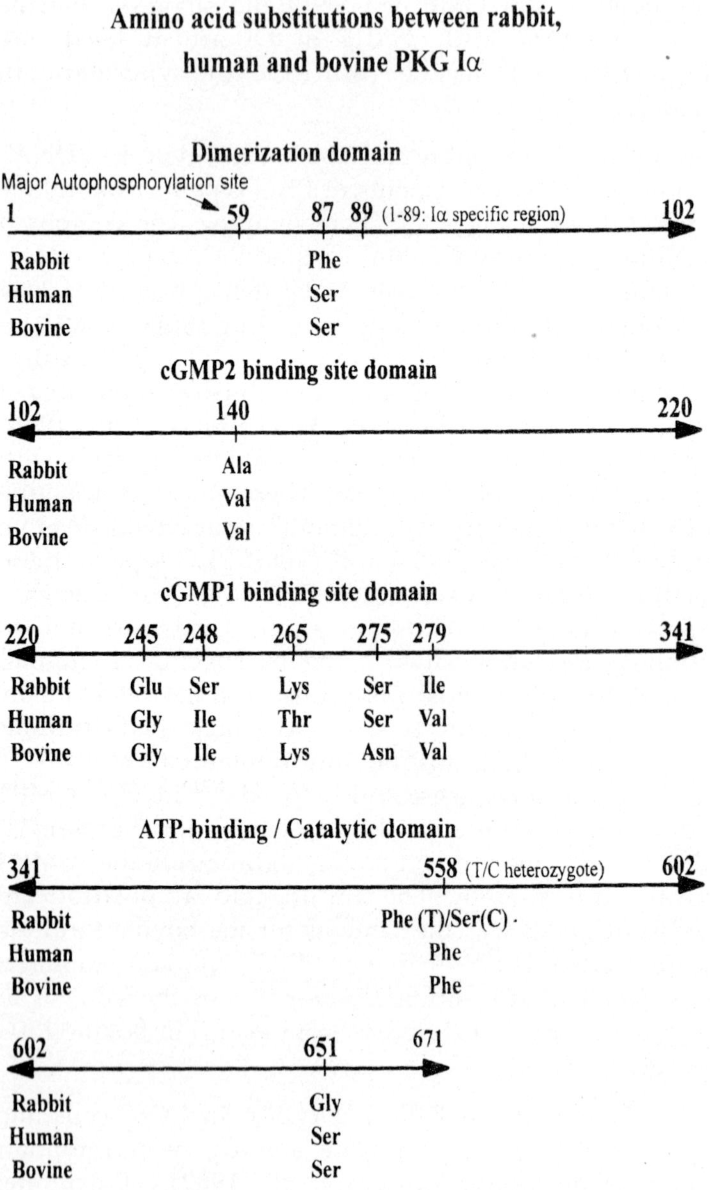

Figure 7. Specific amino acid substitutions in different regions between human, bovine and rabbit PKG type Iα. (From (Kumar *et al.*, 1999))

of cells transfected with pcDNA3.1 with no insert and of cells without any transfection displayed no immunoreactive PKG at 79 kDa. The cells transfected with PKG Iα cDNA demonstrated very high cGMP stimulated kinase activity. The activity was increased 3 fold from 24 h to 48 h of transfection (from 662±53 pmoles/min/mg protein after 24 h of transfection to 2084±90 pmoles/min/mg protein after 48 hrs of transfection, n=3). As expected (Vaandrager & De Jonge, 1996), no activity was detected in extracts of cells - transfected with pcDNA 3.1 without any insert (Control). These results on PKG expression clearly demonstrate that cloned PKG Iα cDNA encodes an immunologically and enzymatically active form of PKG (Kumar *et al.*, 1999).

Northern Blot Analysis in adult and newborn heart To determine if PKG type I mRNA levels are different in adult and newborn heart, we analyzed PKG expression by Northern blot analysis of cardiac PKG using mRNA isolated from adult and newborn rabbit ventricles. Figure 8 shows representative blots in which lanes marked as newborn and AD contained 5 μg of mRNA from newborn and adult rabbit ventricles, respectively. The blot shown in Figure 8A was probed with the bp 456-1663 region of rabbit PKG type Iα cDNA which was expected to detect both types Iα and Iβ mRNA, as expressed by other species. We detected only one band at 6.8 kb with this probe, the same message was identified with cDNA probes for bovine PKG type Ia and rabbit cardiac PKG type Iα (containing C1 - C2 fragment) (data not shown). The results confirm the expression of only one mRNA species of PKG type I in adult and newborn rabbit ventricles. However, the relative abundance of PKG type I mRNA appears to be age dependent with significantly more abundance in the newborn ventricles than in adult. Figure 8C shows the relative amounts of PKG type I mRNA in adult and newborn rabbit ventricles calculated by comparing the peak area of band from multiple adult and newborn animals by densitometric analysis. PKG type I mRNA levels were 3.5 times higher in newborn compared to adult (4851±817 arbitrary units for newborn and 1389±389 arbitrary units for adult, n=4, $p<0.05$). In order to eliminate the possibility of unequal loading of adult and newborn mRNA, the same membranes were re-probed (after stripping the PKG probe) with a cDNA probe for Glyceraldehyde 3-phosphate dehydrogenase (GAPDH) as shown in Figure 8B. No significant differences were observed (4408±290 arbitrary units for newborn and 3910±718 arbitrary units for adult, n=4, $p>0.5$) in the density of adult and newborn bands probed with GAPDH as evident from densitometric analysis in figure 8D.

Western Blot Analysis in adult and newborn heart: We assessed the levels of PKG type I protein by Western blot analysis in homogenates prepared from whole ventricles (Data not shown), as well as from isolated ventricular cells (Figure 9) of adult and newborn rabbit heart, using a PKG type I specific antibody. Figure 9 shows a representative immunoblot in which lanes labeled as NB (newborn) and lanes labeled as AD (adult) each contained 60 μg of homogenate protein prepared from ventricular cells isolated from different adult and newborn rabbit hearts. We loaded 3 ng of purified bovine lung PKG type Iα in lanes labeled as PKG as positive control. The results indicate an immunoreactive protein at an apparent molecular weight of 79 kDa in newborn and adult preparations that was aligned with the positive control of PKG. The PKG levels were much higher in newborn (n=6) compared to adult (n=6), from which PKG levels were too low to be detected in some adult preparations. Figure 9B shows the relative amount of PKG in adult and newborn rabbit ventricular cells calculated by normalizing the adult and newborn band density to PKG positive control. The relative amount of PKG resent in newborn rabbit ventricular cells (39.4±7.6 ng/mg protein, n=6) was much greater ($p < 0.05$) than the PKG present in adult rabbit ventricular cells (1.25±0.53 ng/mg protein, n=6). On comparing the Western blotting results in preparations

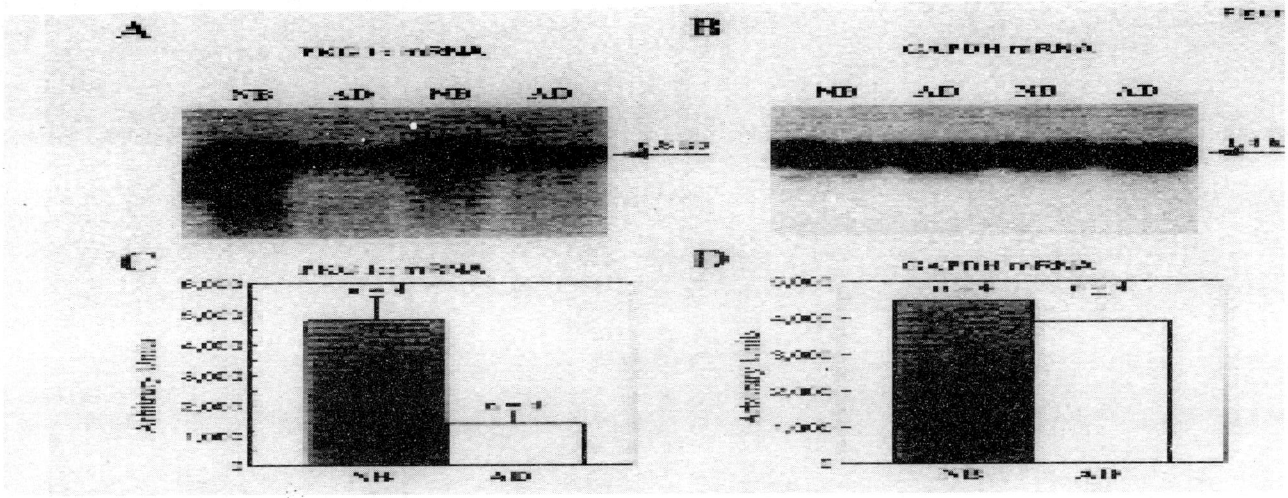

Figure 8. Northern blot analysis of PKG type Iα and GAPDH mRNAs using poly(A^+) RNA from adult and newborn rabbit ventricles. 5 μg Poly (A^+) RNA isolated from adult (AD) and newborn (NB) ventricles was loaded in each lane. The replicate lanes represent samples from different animals. Panel **A**, shows a blot hybridized with a cDNA fragment generated by RT-PCR from rabbit mRNA. The probe detected a message of ~6.8 kb corresponding to PKG type Iα mRNA in newborn and adult rabbit heart. Panel **B** shows a Northern blot analysis of the same blot hybridized with a cDNA probe encoding GAPDH as an internal control. Panel C shows the changes in PKG mRNA levels (arbitrary units of peak area) from newborn to adult rabbit ventricles. Panel D shows changes in GAPDH levels (arbitrary units of peak area) from newborn to adult. (From (Kumar *el al.*. 1999))

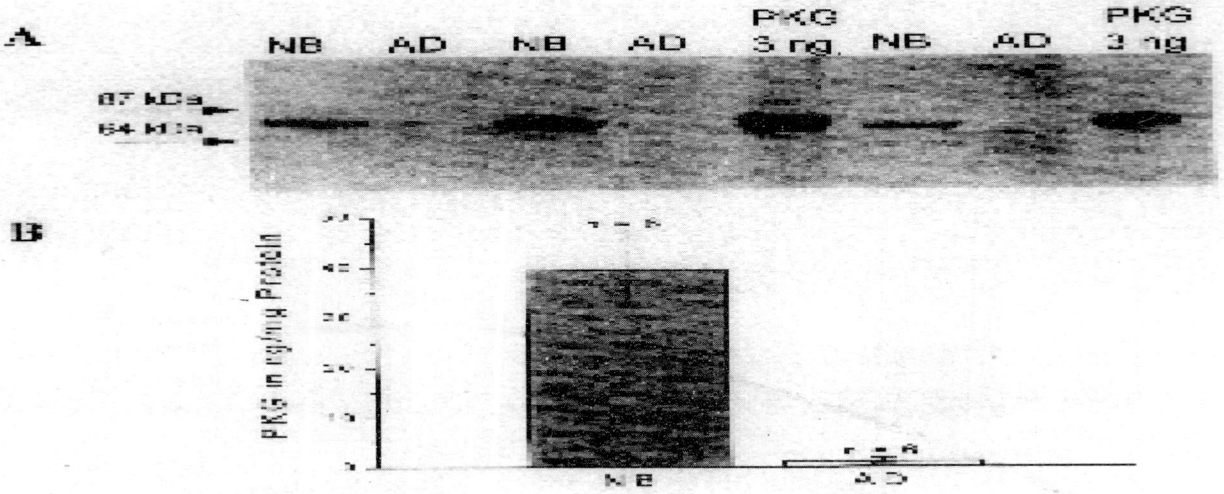

Figure 9. **(A)** Immunoblot analysis of PKG in total homogenates prepared from isolated ventricular cells of adult and newborn rabbit hearts. Lanes marked as NB (newborn) and AD (adult) contained 60 μg homogenate protein from adult and newborn ventricular cells respectively. The replicate lanes represent samples from different animals. The lanes marked as PKG contained 3 ng purified bovine lung PKG. The blots were probed with an affinity-purified goat PKG antibody at 1: 1000 dilution and immunostained bands were visualized by enhanced chemiluminescence. **(B)** Changes in PKG levels (ng/mg protein) from newborn to adult in isolated ventricular cells. Bands visualized by enhanced chemiluminescence were quantified by measuring density and normalized to the value for purified bovine lung PKG. (From (Kumar *et al.*, 1999))

from whole ventricles (Data not shown) with preparations from isolated ventricular cells, we found PKG levels in isolated ventricular cells were much greater (30-fold) compared to whole ventricles (2.35-fold).

Immunofluorescence staining for PKG

In freshly isolated rabbit ventricular cells, Immunofluorescence staining using PKG specific antibody as shown in figure 10, demonstrated that PKG was widely distributed in cytoplasm, prominent on myofilaments and in the nucleus in newborn cells. The intensity of PKG staining was much greater in newborn cells as compared to AD cells. This further confirmed that PKG is highly expressed in newborn ventricular cells and its expression declines during post-natal development.

Discussion

The present study was focused on the differences in the modulation of L-type I_{Ca} by cGMP in adult and newborn ventricular cells and cDNA cloning, and expression of PKG type Iα, and the postnatal changes in the expressed mRNA and protein levels of PKG type I in rabbit ventricles. The salient findings of this study are summarized as follows:

(1) In adult ventricular cells, neither inhibitors of G-cyclase (methylene blue and LY-83583 which inhibit G-cyclase and thus lower cGMP levels), nor the internal application of 8BrcGMP produced any significant effect on basal I_{Ca}.

(2) In newborn ventricular cells, the application of methylene blue or LY-83 583 produced an irreversible inhibition of basal Ica, while intracellular perfusion of 8BrcGMP or 8CPT-cGMP significantly and reversibly increased basal I_{Ca}.

(3) In newborn ventricular cells, extracellular application of methylene blue during the intracellular perfusion of 8BrcGMP was unable to inhibit I_{Ca}.

Adult Rabbit Ventricular cell

NB Rabbit Ventricular Cells

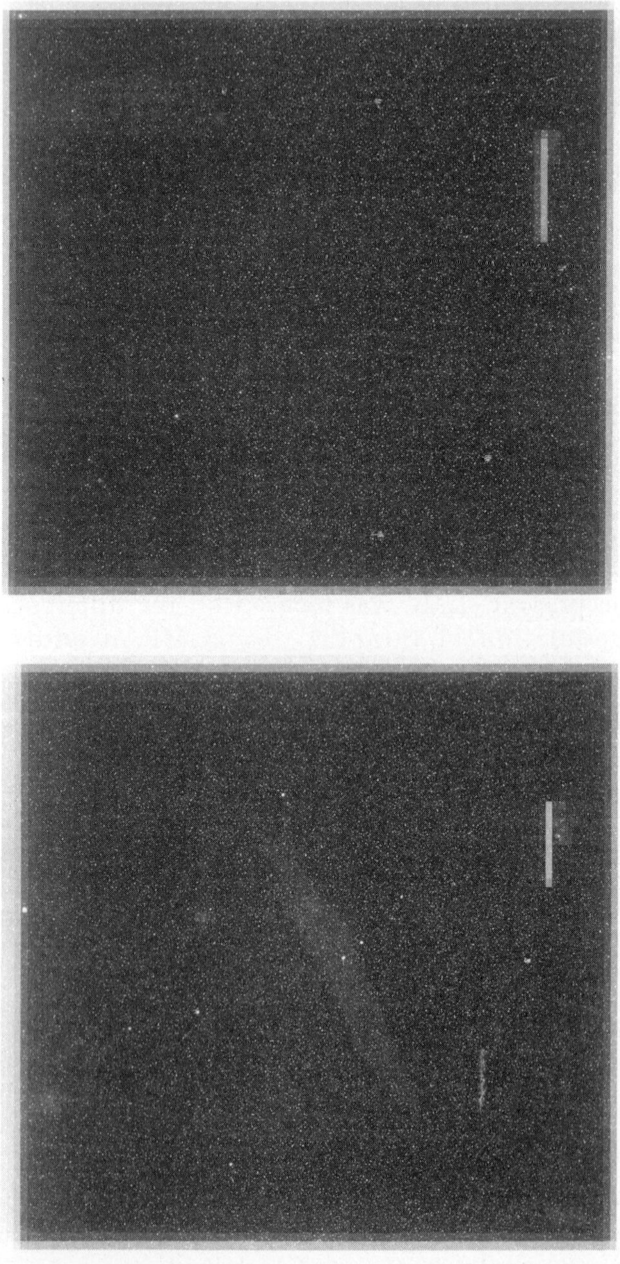

Figure 10. Immunofluorescene staining for PKg in isolated nowborn and adult rabbit ventricular cells. Bar, 20 μm for newborn cell and 25 μm for adult cell

(4) The-NO donor GSNO produced a significant and reversible increase in basal I_{Ca} in newborn ventricular cells but not in adult.

(5) The PKG inhibitor KT-5823 produced an irreversible significant inhibition of basal I_{Ca} in newborn ventricular cells but not in adult, and blocked the stimulatory effect of GSNO.

(6) In newborn ventricular cells, the stimulatory effects of GSNO or 8CPT-cGMP were not blocked by phosphodiesterase inhibitor IBMX or PKA blocker (5-22), respectively.

(7) In newborn ventricular cells, the stimulatory effect of Isoproterenol was potentiated by 8BrcGMP or GSNO.

(8) The coding region of rabbit PKG type Iα showed 94% homology to published sequences of human and bovine PKG type Iα.

(9) The deduced amino acid sequence showed major substitutions in two cGMP binding site domains.

(10) The expressed recombinant PKG was catalytically active, stimulated by cGMP, and showed the same immunoreactivity as the native PKG.

(11) Expressed mRNA and protein levels for PKG type I were much higher in newborn compared to adult.

Regulation of I_{Ca} by cGMP in adult and newborn rabbit Ventricular cells

The lack of any effect of extracellular application of methylene blue or of intracellular perfusion of 8BrcGMP in adult ventricular cells basically supports the earlier findings of several investigators in different species (Ono & Trautwein, 1991; Hartzell & Fischmeister, 1986; Mery *et al.*, 1993; Levi et *al.*, 1994), in which they did not observe any effect of cGMP or methylene blue on basal I_{Ca}. Ono and Trautwein (1991) have shown no effect of intracellular perfusion of cGMP on basal I_{Ca} and the stimulatory effect of intracellular perfusion of cGMP was present only when the I_{Ca} was first stimulated by Isoproterenol in guinea pig ventricular cells. In contrast to our findings on adult rabbit ventricular cells, Tohse *et al.* (1995) have shown a relatively small inhibitory effect of extracellular application of 300 μM 8BrcGMP and of Atrial Natriuretic peptide on basal I_{Ba}. Our findings in newborn cells in which intracellular perfusion of 8BrcGMP or 8CPT-cGMP raised basal I_{Ca} are certainly surprising and entirely different from the earlier findings in adult cells or in cultured avian embryonic heart cells. We have also shown that the nitric oxide donor GSNO produced a stimulatory effect similar to 8BrcGMP or 8CPT-cGMP in newborn ventricular cells but no effect in adult ventricular cells. SIN- 1, which is a nitric oxide donor and has been shown to increase intracellular cGMP by G-cyclase stimulation, had no effect on basal I_{Ca} and had both inhibitory or stimulatory effects on Isoproterenol-stimulated I_{Ca} (Wahler & Dollinger, 1995) in guinea pig ventricular cells. In a recent study on 2-21 days old rat ventricular cells, Sumii and Sperelakis (1995) have shown that 8BrcGMP itself did not produce any effect on basal I_{Ca} but exogenous PKG with 8BrcGMP, when applied intracellularly, produced inhibition of basal I_{Ca}. This could be because the type of PKG isoform present in newborn rabbit heart may be different from the one present in rat heart or there may be species differences in the regulatory sites for kinases modulating the calcium channel. Moreover, in newborn rabbit ventricular cells, we found that the PKG inhibitor KT-5823 inhibits basal I_{Ca} which further strengthens our proposal that PKG is not inhibitory but is stimulatory in newborn rabbit ventricular cells.

We used methylene blue, which has been widely used as an inhibitor of soluble G-cyclase, in our experiments to lower the intracellular cGMP concentration. Methylene blue had no effect in adult cells but significantly inhibited the basal I_{Ca} in newborn cells. A similar inhibitory effect on I_{Ca} was observed with another G-cyclase inhibitor LY-83583, which confirms the involvement of G-cyclase in the regulation of I_{Ca}. Methylene blue mediated inhibition was irreversible on washout of the methylene blue, but inhibition of I_{Ca} by methylene blue could be prevented by the prior internal perfusion of the cell by a cGMP analog. This further confirms that the lowering of cGMP levels in newborn cells inhibits basal I_{Ca} and that increases in cGMP levels increase basal I_{Ca}. A recent study of Levi *et al.* (1994) on adult guinea pig ventricular cells showed no effect of methylene blue on basal I_{ca}. In contrast to the results of Levi *et aL* (1994), Wahler and Dollinger (1995) used guinea pig ventricular cells and showed an increase in basal Ica when LY-83583 (at 10 and 100 μM) was added to the pipette solution. They also showed that 0.1 μM KT5823, an inhibitor of PKG, had no effect on basal I_{Ca} (Wahler & Dollinger, 1995). Our results also showed that KT-5823 had no effect in adult rabbit ventricular cells, but inhibited basal I_{Ca} in newborn rabbit ventricular cells. It is important to note that the inhibitory effects of methylene blue and LY-83583, both of which presumably inhibit PKG by lowering cGMP concentration, and of PKG inhibitor KT-5823, were irreversible. The lack of reversibility of methylene blue and LY-83583 could be because of irreversible inhibition of G-cyclase due to the oxidation of the ferrous heme moiety of enzyme.

In our studies, the stimulatory effect of 8CPT-cGMP was not blocked by PKI, but somewhat attenuated. The stimulatory effect of GSNO was present even after I_{Ca} was increased by either the inhibition of phosphodiesterases by exposure to IBMX or by Isoproterenol. Similarly, the effect of Isoproterenol was potentiated by the increased levels of intracellular 8BrcGMP. These findings clearly suggest that the stimulation of I_{Ca} by 8BrcGMP, 8CPT-cGMP, or GSNO is probably not mediated via the activation of cAMP dependent protein kinase or by inhibition of cGMP inhibited phosphodiesterases. The observed stimulatory effects of 8BrcGMP, 8CPT-cGMP, or GSNO are more likely due to the activation of protein Kinase G. The attenuation of the stimulatory effect of 8CPTcGMP in the presence of PKI could presumably be due to the interactions between regulatory sites of PKA and PKG. It seems that cGMP and cAMP are not antagonistic and the role of cGMP in the regulation of I_{Ca} stimulated by elevated cAMP may be synergistic or additive in newborn heart cells.

Cloning and Analysis of Rabbit PKG Iα:

We identified only one distinct species of mRNA by Northern blotting of PKG type I in mRNA preparations of adult and newborn rabbit ventricles. Based on this, we performed cDNA cloning of rabbit PKG type Iα from ventricular tissue of newborn rabbit. The composed nucleotide sequence and deduced amino acid sequence of rabbit cardiac PKG type Iα. cDNA showed some significant differences from published human and bovine PKG type Iα. sequences (Tamura *et al.*, 1996; Wernet el *al.*, 1989). Most amino acid substitutions were found in the cGMP binding domains. The two cGMP binding sites are different on the basis of their affinities for various cGMP analogs and are responsible for the cooperative nature of cGMP binding and activation. In the case of the PKG type Iα form, 8-substituted analogs of cGMP (e.g., 8Bromo-cGMP and 8Chlorophenylthio-cGMP) are much more potent activators of enzyme than the native nucleotide (Wolfe *et al.*, 1989). The substitutions in cGMP binding domains might be important in determining the affinity of PKG for cGMP binding. The cloning of human PKG type Iα has shown two amino acid substitutions from bovine PKG type Iα to human PKG type Iα (Lys^{265} to Thr^{265} and Asn^{275} to Ser^{275}) (Tamura *et al.*, 1996). It is interesting to note that Lys^{265} in rabbit was the same as in bovine but different from human (Thr^{265}) and Ser^{275} in rabbit was same as in human but different from bovine (Asn^{275}). In addition to these substitutions, we also found amino acid substitutions in the amino terminal Iα specific region and C-terminal region. The four different autophosphorylation sites (Ser^{51}, Thr^{59}, Ser^{73} and Thr^{85}) observed by Aitkin *et al.* (1981) and the Leucine-Isoleucine zipper were conserved. The substitutions we found in type Iα specific region (Ser^{87} to Phe^{87}) and in C-terminal region (Ser^{651} to GIY^{651}) may be due to species differences.

To verify that the isolated cDNA encodes PKG, we transfected COS cells using our cDNA clone. The PKG holoenzyme has been successfully expressed in COS cells. Western blotting experiments using homogenates of PKG transfected COS cells confirmed that expressed PKG is immunoreactive and has the same molecular mass as the native PKG. The extracts of PKG transfected cells also showed PKG enzyme activity that was stimulated by cGMP. This confirmed that expressed PKG is not only immunoactive but also catalytically active. The availability of this recombinant cardiac PKG may help to define the roles of specific cGMP-dependent phosphorylation in cardiac cells.

Northern Blot analysis showed PKG type I mRNA message as a single band at 6.8 kb in both adult and newborn rabbit ventricular mRNA preparations. The message size for type I isoform in newborn and adult rabbit ventricles exceeds that of coding region by more than 2-fold which shows that PKG type I mRNA contains a large noncoding region. Similar results were obtained by other investigators (Wernet *et aL*, 1989; Sandberg *et al.*, 1989-, Cornwell *et al.*, 1994). Our studies could be interpreted that PKG type I isoform is highly expressed in newborn heart but expressed at a very low level in adult heart. A developmental decrease in PKG type I mRNA was also shown during postnatal development of rat heart by Sandberg *et al.* (I 989). however, they found two PKG type I mRNA species in rat heart at 7.5 and 6.5 kb and showed a faster and more complete decrease for 6.5 kb than for 7.5 kb species during development.

Western immunoblotting experiments with homogenates prepared from isolated ventricular cells and immunofluorescence staining of isolated cells also showed that PKG is present in appreciable amounts in newborn heart cells. The apparent molecular weight of PKG present in ventricular cells is similar to that of bovine lung PKG (79 kDa). The immunodetectable levels of PKG type I protein were 30-fold higher in newborn compared to adult ventricular cells. Similarly, the immunostaining in newborn cells was much greater than adult cells. This 30-fold difference in PKG levels between adult and newborn ventricular cells was diminished to 2.35-fold when PKG levels were measured in preparations from intact ventricles of adult and newborn heart (Data not shown). The developmental decline in PKG protein levels (2.3 5 -fold) from newborn to adult ventricles was comparable to the decline in PKG mRNA levels (3.5-fold) from newborn to adult ventricles. However, the developmental decline in PKG type I protein levels from newborn and adult ventricular cells (30-fold) was much higher than was revealed by decline of protein or mRNA levels in newborn and adult intact ventricles. This discrepancy in the levels of PKG in intact ventricles and isolated ventricular cells could be due to the fact that PKG mRNA and protein levels detected in adult ventricles may have been derived largely from cardiac vascular tissue. The expressed mRNA levels or protein levels in whole ventricles may not represent the specific expression in cardiac cells because other cell types are included within the heart tissue. Ecker *et aL* (1989) have shown that cardiac vasculature is particularly rich in PKG. In contrast to our findings by Northern and Western analyses, Sandberg *el al.* (I 989) have shown no postnatal decrease in rat cardiac PKG protein during development, although they showed a sharp decrease in PKG mRNA levels. The differences in

PKG levels between adult and newborn may be of physiological and pathological significance. Previous studies on aorta and heart have shown that PKG levels were affected by experimental hypertension (Ecker *et al.*. 1989) but these changes were mainly associated with the change in vascular PKG.

In conclusion, Our findings suggest that intracellular cGMP levels may be of great significance in regulating basal I_{Ca} in newborn, but not in adult, rabbit ventricular cells. This difference between adult and newborn may also be due to a different mechanism of action of cGMP in heart cells in early post-natal life. We suggest that newborn rabbit ventricular cells may have a phosphorylation site associated with the calcium channel which can be phosphorylated by one or both types of PKG and that this site, when phosphorylated, increases the availability of L-type Ca-channels and is involved in maintaining basal I_{Ca}. Our findings on cDNA cloning and analysis of expression of PKG suggest that PKG is developmentally regulated in rabbit heart and its expressed levels are much higher in newborn as compared to adult ventricular cells. Rabbit PKG type Iα shows considerable homology to bovine and human PKG type Iα. However, several amino acid substitutions in rabbit PKG type Iα compared to bovine and human may perhaps change some of the catalytic properties of PKG in rabbit heart by changing the cGMP binding affinity. The greater expression of PKG in newborn cells compared to adult cells could be responsible for differences in the effects of cGMP on L-type calcium current in adult and newborn rabbit ventricular cells.

REFERENCES

AITKIN, A., BILHAM, T., COHEN, P., ASWAD, D. & GREENGARD, P. (1981). A specific substrate from rabbit cerebellum for guanosine-3': 5' - monophosphate-dependent protein kinase. *Journal of biological Chemistry* 256, 3501-3506.

AKITA, T., JOYNER, R.W., LU, C., KUMAR, R. & HARTZELL, H.C. (1994). Developmental Changes in Modulation on Calcium Currents of Rabbit Ventricular Cells by Phosphodiesterase Inhibitors. *Circulation* 90, 469-478.

BARNETT, D.J., MCANINLY, J. & WILLIAMS, D.L.H. (1994). Transnitrosation between nitrosothiols and thiols. *J Chem. Soc., Perkin Trans.* 2, 1131-1133.

BLOCH, K.D., STRUHL, K., TABOR, S., SEHARF, S.J., GELFAND, D.H. & BOYLE, A. (1991). Current Protocols in Molecular Biology. In eds. AUSUBEL, F.M., BRENT, R., KINGSTON, R.E., MOORE, D.D., SEIDMAN, J.G., SMITH, J.A. & STRUHL, K., pp. 3.0.1-3.18.7New York, NY: John Wiley & Sons Inc.

BOERTH, N.J. & LINCOLN, T.M. (1994). Expression of the catalytic domain of cyclic GMPdependent protein kinase in a baculovirus system. *FEBS. Lett.* 342, 255-260.

CHOMCZYNSKI, P. & SACCHI, N. (1987). Single step method of RNA isolation by acid guanidium thiocyanate-phenol-chloroform extraction. *Anal.Biochem.* 162, 156-159.

CORNWELL, T.L., SOFF, G.A., TRAYNOR, A.E. & LINCOLN, I-.M. (I 994). Regulation of the expression of cyclic GMP-dependent protein kinase by cell density in vascular smooth muscle cells. *Journal of Vascular Research* 31, 330-337.

ECKER, T., GOBEL, C., HULLIN, R., RETTIG, R., SEITZ, G. & HOFMANN, F. (1989). Decreased cardiac concentration of cGMP kinase in hypertensive animals. An index for cardiac vascularization? *Circ.Res.* 65, 1361-1369.

HARTZELL, H.C. (1988). Regulation of cardiac ion channels by catecholamines, acetylcholine and second messenger systems. *Progress in Biophysics & Molecular Biolo* 52, 165-247.

HARTZELL, H.C. & FISCHMEISTER, R. (1986). Opposite effects of cyclic GMP and cyclic AMP on Ca^{2+} current in single heart cells. *Nature* 323, 273-275.

KASE, H., IWAHASHI, K., NAKANISHI, S., MATSUDA, Y., YAMADA, K., TAKAHASHI, M., MURAKATA, C., SATO, A. & KANEKO, M. (1987). K-252 Compounds, Novel and Potent Inhibitors of Protein Kinase C and cyclic Nucleotide-dependent Protein Kinase. *Biochem Biophys Res Commun* 142, 436-440.

KIRSTEIN, M., RIVET-BASTIDE, M., HATEM, S.. BERNARDEAU, A., MERCADIER, J. & FISCHMEISTER, R. (1995). Nitric oxide regulates the calcium current in isolated human atrial myocytes. *JClin.Invest.* 95, 794-802.

KOMALAVILAS, P. & LINCOLN, T.M. (1994). Phosphorylation of the Inositol 1,4,5-Trisphosphate Receptor by Cyclic GMP-dependent Protein Kinase. *Journal o Biological Chemistry* 269, 8701 8707.

KUMAR, R., AKITA, T. & JOYNER, R.W. (1996). Adenosine and carbachol are not equivalent in their effects on L-type calcium current in rabbit ventricular cells. *Journal of Molecular & Cellular Cardiology* 28, 403-415.

KUMAR, R., JOYNER, R.W., HARTZELL, H.C., ELLINGSEN, D., RISHI, F., EATON, D.C., LU, C. & AKITA, T. (I 994). Postnatal changes in the G-proteins, cyclic nucleotides and adenylyl cyclase activity in rabbit heart cells. *J. Mol. Cell. Cardiol.* 26, 1537-1550.

KUMAR, R., JOYNER, R.W., KOMALAVILAS, P. & LINCOLN,'I'.M. (1999). Analysis of expression of cGMP-dependent protein kinase in rabbit heart cells. *J. Pharm. Exp. Ther.* 291, 967-975.

KUMAR, R., NAMIKI, T. & JOYNER, R.W. (1997). Effects of cGMP on L-type calcium current of adult and newborn rabbit ventricular cells. *Cardiovascular Reseurch* 33, 573-582.

LEVI, R.C., ALLOATTI, G. & FISCHMEISTER, R. (1989). Cyclic GMP regulates the Ca-channel current in guinea pig ventricular myocytes. *Pflugers.Arch.* 413, 685-687.

LEVI, R.C., ALLOATTI, G., PENNA, C. & GALT,O, M.P. (1994). Guanylate-cyclase-mediated inhibition of cardiac Ica by carbachol and sodium nitroprusside. *Pflugers Archiv - European Journal of Physiology* 426, 419-426.

LINCOLN, T.M. & CORNWELL, T.L. (1993). Intracellular cvclic GMP receptor proteins. *FASEB Journal* 7, 328-338.

LINCOLN, T.M. & KEELY, S.L. (1981). Regulation of cardiac cyclic GMP-dependent protein kinase. *Biochim Biophys Acta* 676, 230-244.

LINCOLN, T.M., THOMPSON, M. & CORNWELL, T.L. (1988). Purification and characterization of two forms of cyclic GMP-dependent protein kinase from bovine aorta. *Journal of Biological Chemistry* 263, 17632-17637.

MERY, P.F., LOHMANN, S.M., WALTER, U. & FISCHMEISTER, R. (1991). Ca^{2+} current is regulated by cyclic GMP-dependent protein kinase in mammalian cardiac myocytes. *Proceedings of the National Academy of Sciences of the United States o America* 88, 1197-1201.

MERY, P.F., PAVOINE, C., BELHASSEN, L., PECKER, F. & FISCHMEISTER, R. (1993). Nitric oxide regulates cardiac Ca^{2+}

current. *Journal of Biological Chemistry* 268, 26286-26295.

NAWRATH, H. (1977). Does cyclic GMP mediate the negative inotropic effect of acetylcholine in the heart? *Nature* 267, 72-74.

ONO, K. & TRAUTWEIN, W. (1991). Potentiation by cyclic GMP of β-adrenergic effect of Ca^{2+} current in guinea-pig ventricular cells. *J. PhysioL (London)* 443, 387-404.

OSAKA, T. & JOYNER, R.W. (1992). Developmental changes in the beta-adrenergic modulation of calcium currents in rabbit ventricular cells. *Circulation Research* 70, 104-115.

RIVET-BASTIDE, M., VANDECASTEELE, G., HATEM, S., VERDE, I., BENARDEAU, A., MERCADIER, J.J. & FISCHMEISTER, R. (I 997). cGMP-stimulated cyclic nucleotide phosphodiesterase regulates the basal calcium current in human atrial myocytes. *J. Clin. Invest.* 99, 2710-2718.

RUTH, P., WANG, G.R., BOEKHOFF, I., MAY, B., PFEIFER, A., PENNER, R., KORTH, M., BREER, H. & HOFMANN, F. (1 990). Transfected cGMP-dependent protein kinase suppresses calcium transients by inhibition of inositol 1,4,5-triphosphate production. *Proc Natl Acad Sci U S A* 90, 2623-2627.

SANDBERG, M., NATARAJAN, V., RONANDER, I., KALDERON, D., WALTER, U., LOHMANN, S.J. & JAHNSEN, T. (1989). Molecular cloning and predicted full length amino acid sequence of the type l beta isozyme of cGMP-dependent protein kinase from human placenta. *FEBS Letters* 255, 321-329.

SPERELAKIS, N. (1988). Regulation of calcium slow channels of cardiac muscle by cyclic nucleotides and phosphorylation. *J. Mol. Cell. Cardiol.* 20, 75 -105.

SUMII, K. & SPERELAKIS, N. (I 995). cGMP-dependent protein kinase regulation of the L-type calcium current in rat ventricular myocytes. *Circ.Res.* 77, 803-812.

TAMURA, N., ITOH, H., OGAWA, Y., NAKAGAWA, O., HARADA, M., CHUN, T., SUGA, S., YOSHIMASA, T. & NAKAO, K. (I 996). CDNA cloning and gene expression of Human type Iα. cGMP-dependent protein kinase. *Hypertension* 27, 552-557.

TOHSE, N., NAKAYA, H., TAKEDA, Y. & KANNO, M. (I 995). Cyclic GMP-mediated inhibition of L-type Ca^{2+} channel activity by human natriuretic peptide in rabbit heart cells. *British Journal of' Pharmacolo,gy* 114, 1076-1082.

VAANDRAGER, A.B. & DE JONGE, H.R. (I 996). Signalling by cGMP-dependent protein kinases. [Review] [67 refs]. *Molecular & Cellular Biochemistry* 157, 23-30.

WAHLER, G. & DOLLINGER, S.J. (1995). Nitric oxide donor SIN-I inhibits mammalian cardiac calcium current through cGMP-dependent protein kinase. *Am.J.Physiol.* 268, C-45-C-54

WAHLER, G.M., RUSCH, N.J. & SPERELAKIS, N. (1990). 8-Bromo-cyclic GMP inhibits the calcium channel current in embryonic chick ventricular myocytes, *Canadian Journal of Physiology & Pharmacology* 68, 531-534.

WERNET, W., FLOCKERZI, V. & HOFMANN, F. (1989). The cDNA of the two isoforms of bovine cGMP-dependent protein kinase. *FEBS Letters* 251, 191-196.

WOLFE, L., CORBIN, J.D. & FRANCIS, S.H. (1989). Characterization of a novel isozyme of cGMP-dependent protein kinase from bovine aorta. *Journal of Biological Chemistry* 264, 7734-7741.

ISCHEMIC PRECONDITIONING ATTENUATES PROTEIN KINASE C MEDIATED INCREASE IN CORONARY VASOCONSTRICTOR TONE

S. JAMAL MUSTAFA, RAVI B. MARALA, ROBERT M. LUST*
AND MOHAMMED A. NAYEEM

*Departments of Pharmacology and *Physiology, Brody School of Medicine, East Carolina University, Greenville, NC 27858*

Abstract

Background : The protective effects of ischemic preconditioning (IPC) on myocytes are well established, but little is known about the effects of IPC directly on the coronary arteries serving those myocytes. This study examined the effect of IPC on coronary arteries and the role of protein kinase C (PKC) in their responsiveness. **Methods:** Regional ischemia was produced in canines by ligating the left circumflex artery (Ischemia : Occlude 1 hr., reperfuse 3 hrs.; IPC : similar to ischemia, but preceded by a single 5 min. occlusion, 10 min. reperfusion). Left circumflex arteries were harvested and endothelium removed to study changes in the smooth muscle component of the vessels. Concentration-dependent contractile responses to PKC activators phorbol ester (PDBu) and endothelin-1 (ET-1) were recorded. PKC activity in these arteries was determined and changes in PKC isoformes were determined by western blotting. **Results** : Both PDBu and ET-1 produced tension responses that were significantly enhanced after ischemia compared to controls. However, IPC responses were attenuated significantly compared to unmodified ischemia. PKC assay indicated that ischemia caused a marked increase in PKC activity compared to control, whereas, in IPC the activity was significantly less than control. Western blot analysis using PKC isoforms antibodies indicated the presence of α, γ, δ, ε and ι isoforms in canine circumflex artery. Isoforms λ and μ were not tested. Isoforms α, ε and ι were upregulated by ischemia, isoform γ was not significantly altered, whereas, data for δ isoform were inconclusive. **Conclusions** : Ischemia/IPC responses in vasoconstrictor tone could be mediated through PKC mechanisms. Another interesting observation was that even though the left circumflex artery was ligated to produce ischemia/IPC, similar effects (contractility and PKC activity) were observed in left anterior descending (LAD) and right coronary arteries, which perfuse adjacent and remote non-ischemic myocardium, respectively. Though preliminary, these data suggest that the protective effects of IPC is global even if the ischemia is regional. The mechanism(s) remains to be elucidated.

INTRODUCTION

A brief period of myocardial ischemia has been shown to render the heart resistant to damage caused by subsequent prolonged ischemic insult, a phenomenon commonly termed "preconditioning"[1]. Cardioprotective effects of preconditioning have been demonstrated in various animal models including rat[2], dog[1,3,4], pig[5] and rabbit[6,7]. Even though the exact mechanism(s) for such cardioprotection remains vague, some possible mechanisms have been proposed. Pharmacological stimulation of adenosine A_1 receptors have implicated an adenosine-mediated mechanism in some models, but not all[8-10]. Improved post-ischemic myocyte viability also has been demonstrated experimentally by blocking the loss of adenosine by the myocyte[11]. Therefore, both loss of adenosine with subsequent stimulation of A_1 receptors, and blockade of adenosine loss are protective. Interestingly, most pharmacologic interventions are not as effective as the biological effect of brief occlusion and reperfusion. Ischemia/reperfusion involves and integrates responses of both the myocyte as well as the nutrient vasculature, but the potential involvement of the vasculature during myocardial IPC response remains largely unstudied.

Protein kinase C (PKC) is believed to be an important component in the maintenance of vascular smooth muscle tone and various other cellular signal pathways[12,13]. Activation of PKC (resulting in the contraction of smooth muscle) is the result of a cascade of events initiated at the receptor level. Activation of receptors like endothelin-1 (ET-1) receptor activates phospholipase C (PLC) which catalyzes the hydrolysis of phosphatidylinositol 4,5-bisphosphate forming IP_3 and diacyl glycerol (DAG). IP_3 mobilizes Ca^{2+} from intracellular stores. The accumulation of DAG and Ca^{2+} activates PKC, which results in the contraction of smooth muscle by mechanisms not yet clearly understood[13,14]. ET-1, a 21 amino acid peptide released by vascular endothelial cells, is the most potent vasoconstrictor known to date[15-17]. ET-1 is known to interact with its cell surface receptor causing the activation of PKC via PLC activation[18-21]. In contrast to the receptor mediated activation of PKC by ET-1, phorbol 12, 13-dibutyrate (PDBu) activates PKC directly, independent of any receptors.

Recent studies indicate that PKC could be involved in cardioprotection phenomenon. Short period (2.5 to 10 min.) of myocardial ischemia caused an activation (translocation) of protein kinase C in rat heart, whereas, prolonged ischemia (15 to 60 min.) caused an upregulation of the cytosolic protein kinase C [22]. This is further supported by the fact that protein kinase C inhibitors prevent the preconditioning phenomenon in isolated rat heart [23]. Activators of protein kinase C like endothelin-1 have been shown to be cytotoxic to cultured neonatal rat myocytes during ischemia[24] and this cytotoxic effect could be blocked by protein kinase C inhibitor, staurosporine, once again emphasizing the role of protein kinase C.

Therefore, the objective of the present study was to determine the changes in the protein kinase C, and responsiveness of the coronary arteries serving the myocytes that have undergone ischemic or preconditioning treatment. We show that coronary arteries serving the ischemic myocardium are more responsive to activators of PKC (PDBu and ET-1), indicating an upregulation of PKC. This inference is further supported by the quantitation of PKC and by western blot analysis. Furthermore, these changes in vascular PKC were attenuated during myocardial preconditioning. Additionally, the vascular effects of myocardial ischemia and preconditioning seems to be global and not restricted to the area at risk.

MATERIALS AND METHODS

Instrumentation for acute study

Thirty mongrel dogs of either sex, weighing 17.2 to 23.6 kg (mean 21.5 ± 0.7 kg), were anesthetized (pentobarbital, 30 mg/kg), intubated and ventilated using room air. Anesthesia was maintained by supplemental intravenous infusions of pentobarbital. The thorax was entered through the left fifth interspace. The pericardium was incised, and the heart was suspended in a pericardial cradle. The left atrial appendage was snared, and two catheters were inserted. A fluid-filled catheter was positioned in the left atrium for subsequent injection of microspheres. The second catheter, a pressure-tipped micromanometer (Millar Instruments, Houston, TX) was advanced into the left ventricle. The proximal circumflex coronary artery, between the bifurcation with the left anterior descending and the origin of the large obtuse marginal, was dissected carefully from surrounding tissue in the atrioventricular groove. A pair of ultrasonic transit time crystals was placed in the circumflex perfusion (ischemic) region, and a second pair of crystals was placed in the perfusion territory of the anterior descending coronary artery (non-ischemic), to monitor regional wall motion. Arterial pressure was monitored using a fluid-filled catheter placed in a femoral artery. This line was also used for periodic reference blood sampling during microsphere procedures, and blood gas determinations. Subcutaneous leads were placed to monitor the scalar electrocardiogram. Where applicable, analog tracings of all parameters were recorded continuously for subsequent analysis. Wall motion was analyzed by calculating the shortening or thickening fraction, using the end-diastolic and end-systolic segment lengths, gated according to the onset of the QRS complex, and the end of peak left ventricular systolic pressure development, respectively.

Animals were subjected to ischemia, or ischemia preceded by a single preconditioning episode. The standard ischemic insult was one hour of regional ischemia (circumflex occlusion), followed by three hours of reperfusion. Animals were randomly assigned to receive either the standard ischemic insult, or the standard insult preceded by a single preconditioning episode (five minute occlusion, ten minute reperfusion). A third group of animals received a thoractomy and were instrumented, but were not subjected to any occlusive regimens. These animals served as time controls for the surgical/anesthetic effects. Regional blood flow (15 μm radioactive microspheres, New England Nuclear, Boston, MA) was determined under baseline conditions, after thirty minutes of ischemia, and at the end of reperfusion. In the preconditioning group, additional flow determinations were made during the ischemia and reperfusion phases of the preconditioning period.

At the end of the experiments, the hearts were removed and weighed. In some animals, infarct size was established using simultaneous perfusion of the left main coronary artery with evans blue dye, and the circumflex artery distal to the occlusion site using triphenyltetrazolium chloride. These stains provided demarcation of the area at risk for infarction, and the actual area of infarction, with definitive staining of the non-risk regions. Once stained, the hearts were divided into five millimeter transmural cross-sectional rings along the long axis of the ventricle. In the remaining animals from each group (n=4), perfusion staining was not performed. Instead, the hearts were immediately transferred to ice-cold Krebs solution for subsequent removal of coronary vessels. After the vessels had been removed, the hearts were divided in rings as with the perfusion staining technique. These rings were incubated for twenty minutes in 1% triphenyltetrazolium chloride solution to demarcate the margin of the infarction. Rings from either staining technique were then fixed in formalin, and anatomic tracings of stained margins were transferred onto acetate, and quantitated using planimetry. This incubation method was chosen in addition to pressure perfusion, since many dyes affect subsequent responsiveness of vessel rings. Once stained margins had been transferred to acetate for analysis, a midpapillary ring was selected and divided into seven wedges. Anterior regions, perfused by the left anterior descending artery, were designated as normal, or non-ischemic and posterior regions, perfused by the circumflex artery, were designated as ischemic. Each sample was weighed and analyzed for gamma activity (Packard Instrument Co., Sterling, VA). By computer analysis, counts were corrected for overlap between emission spectra, translated to flow values and normalized for tissue weight to yield final blood flow determinations in millimeter per minute per gram. These flow determinations were used to establish ischemia during occlusive periods, collateral flow control for differences in infarct size, and reflow during reperfusion episodes. Infarct size, regional wall motion, and global hemodynamic parameters were compared using analysis of variance, followed by Duncan's multiple range test when indicated. Data are reported as mean ± SD, and were considered significant when $p < 0.05$. All experiments were conducted in accordance with the Guide for the Care of Laboratory Animals (DHHS Publication

No. 85-23, revised 1985) and were approved by our Institutional Animal Care and Use Committee.

Arterial ring preparation : Canine hearts (from three treatment groups : control; ischemic preconditioned and ischemic) from either sex were immediately collected in ice-cold Krebs-Henseleit (118 mM NaCl, 4.7 mM KCl, 2.5 mM $CaCl_2$, 1.2 $MgSO_4$, 1.2 mM KH_2PO_4, 25 mM $NaHCO_3$ and 10 mM glucose, pH 7.4) oxygenated with 95% O_2+5% CO_2. The left circumflex coronary artery was dissected from each heart and cleaned of the adherent fat and connective tissue. Arterial rings (~4 mm wide) were cut and the endothelium denuded (the endothelium was removed by rubbing the intimal surface gently with forceps). In certain experiments, left anterior descending (LAD) and right coronary arteries were also dissected and processed in identical fashion.

Isometric tension measurement : Arterial rings were equilibrated for 2 hrs at an initial resting tension of 2 gm between two stainless steel hooks in a 10 ml organ chamber filled with Krebs-Henseleit (pH 7.4) at 37°C with constant oxygenation (95% O_2+5% CO_2). During the equilibration period, the buffer was changed at 15 min. intervals. Changes in isometric tension were measured with a force transducer (Grass FT.03C) connected to a Sensormedics dynograph (R611). Following equilibration, the arterial rings were challenged with 35 mM KCl until reproducible contractions were achieved. The absence of a functional endothelium was confirmed by the inability of bradykinin (10^{-7} M) to relax the arterial rings precontracted with 35 mM KCl. Cumulative concentration-response contraction for PDBu (10^{-10} - 10^{-6} M) and ET-1 (10^{-11} - 10^{-7} M) were generated.

The data are presented as mean ± S.E. Data were analyzed by Students t-test and values were considered significant when $P < 0.05$. Vessel rings were weighed after each experiment and the data are expressed as grams of tension produced per gram wet weight of the tissue.

Estimation of PKC activity : For estimation of PKC activity, the arteries (left circumflex or right coronary) were cut longitudinally and the endothelium scraped gently with a scalpel blade. The following steps were carried out at 4°C except where mentioned. The arteries were rinsed twice with homogenizing buffer (50 mM Tris-HCl, pH 7.5, 5 mM EDTA, 10 mM EGTA, 0.3% w/v ß-mercaptoethanol, 10 mM benzamidine and 50 µg/ml phenylmethylsulphonyl fluoride) followed by homogenization in 6 volumes of the same buffer using a Polytron (4 x 30 sec at a setting of 6). The homogenate was centrifuged at 2000 rpm for 10 min., and the supernatant centrifuged at 105,000 x g for 1 hr. The supernatant was used as the cytosol for PKC assay. There were no drugs present during the PKC assay.

PKC activity in the cytosol was estimated using RPN 77 kit (Amersham) according to the manufacturer's instructions. The RPN 77 kit provides a simple, reliable and reproducible method of estimating PKC without extensive purification of the samples. The system is based upon the PKC catalyzed transfer of the γ-phosphate group of adenine-5'-triphosphate to a peptide which is specific for PKC (RPN-77 product literature). The RPN-77 kit is quite selective for PKC. Activities (% of PKC activity) demonstrated by other kinases for the substrate peptide used in the kit are : cAMP dependent protein kinase (catalytic subunit) (8%); phosphorylase kinase (13%); hexokinase (0%) and myosine light chain kinase (0%) (RPN-77 product literature). The protein concentrations were determined using Bio-Rad method. The PKC activity was expressed as pmoles phosphate transferred per minute per mg protein. The data are presented as mean ± S.E. Data were analyzed by Students t-test and values were considered significant when $P < 0.05$.

Western blot analysis of PKC isoforms : Western blot analyses were performed (in left circumflex arteries only) using monoclonal antibodies to PKC isoforms as described by the manufacturer (Transduction Laboratories, Lexington, KY). The cytosolic fraction (25 μg) from left circumflex arteries from three groups : 1) control, 2) IPC and 3) ischemia, were subjected to 10% sodium dodecyl sulfate-polyacrylamide gel electrophoresis (SDS-PAGE)[25] followed by electroblotting to an Immobilon membrane (Amicon). The membranes were blocked with PBS (10 mM Tris-HCl, pH 7.5, 150 mM NaCl and 0.1% Tween 20) containing 5% skimmed milk (TBS-milk) at 4°C overnight. The membranes were then incubated for 1 hr at room temperature with TBS-milk containing PKC isoform antibody. The membranes were washed 6 x 5 min. with TBS containing 0.1% Tween 20. The membrane was incubated with goat anti-mouse IgG-HRP for 1 hr at room temperature. The membranes were washed 6 x 5 min. with TBS containing 0.1% Tween 20, and visualized by chemiluminiscense followed by autoradiography. The manufacturer of the PKC isoform specific monoclonal antibodies (Transduction Laboratories, Lexington, KY) provided limited information in product literature indicating some cross-reactivity exhibited by the antibodies. Briefly, PKCa antibody exhibits some cross-reactivity with PKCb, PKCg antibody exhibits some cross-reactivity with PKCa and finally PKCi and PKCl antibodies exhibit some cross-reactivities with PKCl and PKCi, respectively.

Materials

PDBu was purchased from Sigma Chemical Co. (St. Louis, MO). ET-1 was purchased from Peninsula Laboratories Inc. (Belmont, CA). RPN 77 kit and (g-^{32}P)ATP were purchased from Amersham (Arlington heights, IL). PKC isoform specific monoclonal antibodies, goat anti-mouse-HRP, and chemiluminiscense substrate (WesternView^{R}) were purchased from Transduction Laboratories (Lexington, KY). All other reagents were of analytical grade and purchased commercially.

RESULTS

Cardioprotection by preconditioning

The ischemic preconditioning protocol produced typical and reproducible effects on myocardial necrosis and mechanical performance. Compared to unmodified ischemia, preconditioning significantly reduced the size of the infarction (34.6 ± 7.1% vs. 9.3 ± 4.5% infarct size/ risk area, $p < 0.01$). Both groups demonstrated similar shortening fractions under baseline (preischemic) conditions (27.3 ± 1.3% vs. 27.7 ± 1.4%, control and IPC, respectively), which was impaired to a similar extent in both groups during the occlusion phase. The end-diastolic segment lengths increased in the ischemic regions of both groups (15.7 ± 0.8 vs. 13.9 ± 0.5 mm and 14.7 ± 0.7 vs. 12.9 ± 0.6 mm, occlusion vs. pre-ischemia time points, control and IPC respectively) and active shortening was replaced with systolic expansion, (27.3 ± 1.3% vs. -7.6 ± 0.9% and 27.7 ± 1.4% vs. -7.5 ± 0.8%, occlusion vs. pre-ischemia time points, control and IPC, respectively, $p < 0.05$ between time points within both groups). Changes during the occlusion phase of the protocol were not different between preconditioning and control groups. Although wall motion in the ischemic region remained impaired in both groups following three hours of reperfusion, recovery was improved significantly in the preconditioning group compared to control (unmodified) ischemia (27.3 ± 1.3% vs. 5.4 ± 0.3% and 27.7 ± 1.4% vs. 12.8 ± 0.5%, preischemia vs. end reperfusion, control and preconditioning, $p < 0.05$ time points within both groups, respectively, $p < 0.05$, between groups). Preconditioned segments recovered approximately half of basal shortening, while control ischemic segments recovered only about one fourth of preischemic shortening (55.2 ± 7% vs. 26 ± 4% of baseline, preconditioned vs. control, $p < 0.05$). These and other cardiovascular changes data are summarized in Table 1.

TABLE 1

Summary of Cardiovascular Changes Following Regional Ischemia and Reperfusion With and Without Preconditioning

Group	Variable		Ischemia			Reperfusion		
		Baseline	5 min	15 min	60 min	30 min	60 min	180 min
Ischemia only (n=11)								
Global	Sys BP (mm Hg)	136 ±12	109 ± 10	95 ± 8	95±8	110±11	115±11	15±12
	Dias BP (mm Hg)	86± 5	72± 8	64±6	53±5	69±7	72± 8	70±6
	Mean BP (mm Hg)	97± 7	84±9	74±6	67 ± 7	83±7	86±9	85± 8
	LV +dP/Dt (mmHg/Sec)	2150± 120	1300 ± 125	1225 ± 95	1095 ± 50	1150± 70	1225 ± 80	1365±85
	LV -dP/Dt (mmHg/Sec)	1975±135	1295 ± 75	950 ±70	1075 ± 50	1075 ± 75	1135±75	1180±90
Ischemic region	ESL (mm)	10.1± 0.5	14.3± 0.5	15.8 ± 0.8	16.9± 0.7	14.5± 0.9	14.0± 0.6	14.0±0.7
	EDL (mm)	13.9± 0.5	14.5± 0.6	14.8±0.8	15.7± 0.8	14.9± 0.8	14.9± 0.5	14.8± 0.6
	Shortening (%)	27.3±1.3	1.4± 0.1	-6.8±0.5	-7.6± 0.9	2.7± 0.4	6.0± 0.4	5.4± 0.3
	Flow (ml/g/min)	1.15 ±0.16	0.08 ± 0.02		0.09± 0.0	21.45±0.20		0.89 ± 0.12
Nonischemic region	ESL (mm)	10.5±0.6	11.1± 0.5	10.8±0.7	11.4± 0.7	12.0± 0.8	11.6± 0.5	11.8± 0.7
	EDL (mm)	14.4±0.7	16.3± 0.5	17.4±0.7	17.7± 0.8	16.6± 0.7	15.8± 0.6	15.5± 0.6

TABLE 1 (CONTD...)

Group	Variable	Ischemia				Reperfusion		
		Baseline	5 min	15 min	60 min	30 min	60 min	180 min
	Shortening (%)	27.1±1.6	31.9± 2.7	37.9±2.4	35.6± 2.9	27.7± 1.9	26.6± 1.8	23.9± 1.5
	Flow (ml/g/min)	1.09±0.1	1.32 ± 0.15		1.37 ± 0.13	1.30 ± 0.12		1.25 ± 0.14
Infarct size	% LV							14.5± 4.3
	% Risk Area							34.6± 7.1
Ischemia + IPC (n=11)								
global	Sys BP (mm Hg)	139± 10	104±11	90±7	92±7	115± 13	117± 14	122±15
	Dias BP (mm Hg)	84±7	70±8	69±5	55± 6	73± 7	70±7	74±9
	Mean BP (mm Hg)	99±8	81± 8	76±5	67± 6	87± 9	86±9	90±11
	LV +dP/Dt (mmHg/Sec)	2270±140	1370±105	1215± 70	1190±80	1250±85	1445± 90	1500±100
	LV -dP/Dt (mmHg/Sec)	2005±135	1020±60	1050± 65	1030±65	1170±70	1170± 95	1290±95
Ischemic region	ESL (mm)	9.3±0.6	13.6± 0.6	14.5±0.8	15.8± 0.8	14.0± 0.7	13.3±0.5	12.4± 0.5
	EDL (mm)	12.9±0.6	13.5± 0.5	13.8±0.8	14.7± 0.7	14.7± 0.9	14.2±0.5	13.9± 0.9
	Shortening (%)	27.7±1.4	-0.7± 0.1	-5.1±0.5	-7.5± 0.8	5.4± 0.5	8.3±0.6	12.8 ± 0.5*
	Flow (ml/g/min)	1.11±0.1	0.09 ± 0.01		0.10 ± 0.03	1.55 ± 0.20		0.94 ± 0.09

TABLE 1 (CONTD...)

Group	Variable	Baseline	Ischemia			Reperfusion		
			5 min	15 min	60 min	30 min	60 min	180 min
Nonischemic region	ESL (mm)	9.2±0.5	9.7± 0.6	10.0±0.7	10.6± 0.8	12.0± 0.7	11.1±0.7	11.2± 0.8
	EDL (mm)	12.7±0.8	14.8± 0.7	15.7±0.7	16.3± 0.8	16.6± 0.9	15.7±0.5	15.1± 0.7
	Shortening (%)	27.5±1.9	34.5± 2.8	36.3±2.4	35.0± 2.5	27.7± 2.9	29.3±2.4	25.8± 2.5
	Flow (ml/g/min)	1.05 ±0.11	1.41 ± 0.16		1.39 ± 0.18	1.32 ± 0.17		1.27±0.17
Infarct size	% LV							4.1±2.8*
	% Risk Area							9.3±4.5*

All values mean ± SD. *$p<0.05$ vs comparable value in ischemia only group. Sys, systolic; Dias, diastolic; BP, blood pressure; LV, left ventricle; ESL, end-systolic segment length; EDL, end-diastolic segment length; Shortening, (EDL-ESL)/EDL x 100.

Effect of preconditioning on PDBu-induced contractions

Concentration-dependent contractile responses to PDBu (10^{-10} to 10^{-6} M) were recorded in arterial rings harvested from ischemic, IPC and control hearts. Rings from control hearts produced maximal tension of 218 ± 5.2 g/g tissue at 10^{-6} M PDBu (Fig. 1). However, the contractile tension did not reach a plateau even at the highest concentration of PDBu used in this study (10^{6} M) (Fig. 1). The tension responses of rings from ischemia group were significantly enhanced compared to controls, whereas, from IPC were attenuated significantly compared to unmodified ischemia group. PDBu produced concentration-dependent contractions in arterial rings from ischemic and IPC treated hearts. The maximum tensions produced at 10^{6} M PDBu were : ischemia, 546 ± 37 and IPC, 332 ± 8.3 g/g tissue, even though plateau contractions were not achieved at the highest concentration of PDBu used (10^{-6} M) (Fig. 1). At concentrations ≥ 10^{-7} M, vascular rings from both IPC and ischemic groups developed tensions significantly greater than control vessels, while the IPC responses were significantly attenuated compared to unmodified ischemia. The EC_{50} (concentration of PDBu that produced 50% contraction) of the three groups were in the same range, about 10^{-7} M (EC_{50} was calculated considering the contraction produced by the highest PDBu concentration used (10^{-6} M) even though plateau were not achieved at this concentration in any group). Similar results were observed when LAD arterial rings were contracted with increasing concentrations of PDBu (10^{-9} to 10^{-6} M) (data not shown). The PDBu induced tension responses of LAD arterial rings from ischemic hearts were significantly greater compared to control, whereas, IPC responses were attenuated significantly compared to unmodified ischemia (data not shown).

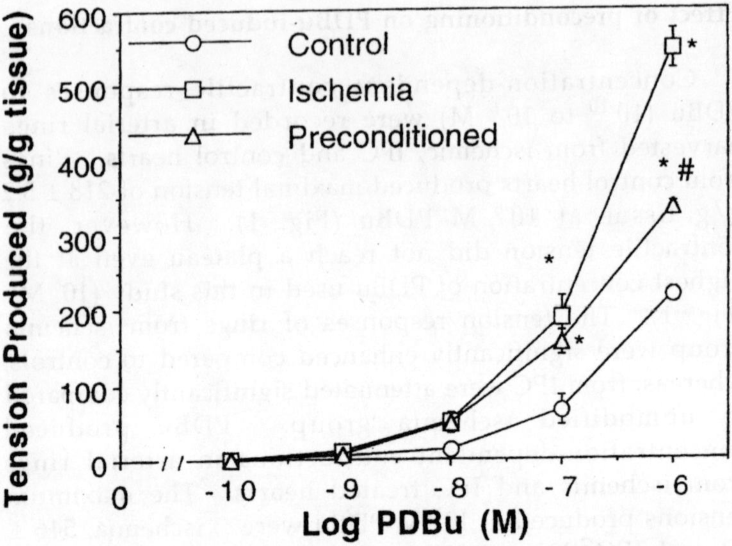

Figure 1. Effect of preconditioning on PDBu-induced contractions. Canine circumflex arterial rings from three groups of animals: control (no treatment); regional ischemic; and IPC, were contracted with increasing concentrations of PDBu. Data are means ± SE for 12 vascular rings from at least 4 hearts. * Values significantly different from control ($p<0.01$). [#] Value significantly different from ischemic group ($p<0.01$).

Effect of preconditioning on ET-1-induced contractions

Similar concentration-dependent results were obtained with endothelin-stimulated PKC. ET-1 produced concentration-dependent (10^{-11} to 10^{-7} M) contraction in arterial rings from all three animal groups (Fig. 2). ET-1 (10^{-7} M) produced tensions 1.75 fold higher in coronary arteries from hearts subjected to unmodified ischemia, while arteries from IPC pretreated group contracted similar to controls. ET-1 (10^{-7} M) produced the following tensions, in g/g tissue : Control, 202.7 ± 9.7; Ischemia, 351.72 ± 26.5; IPC, 241.77 ± 9.57 (Fig. 2). Tensions

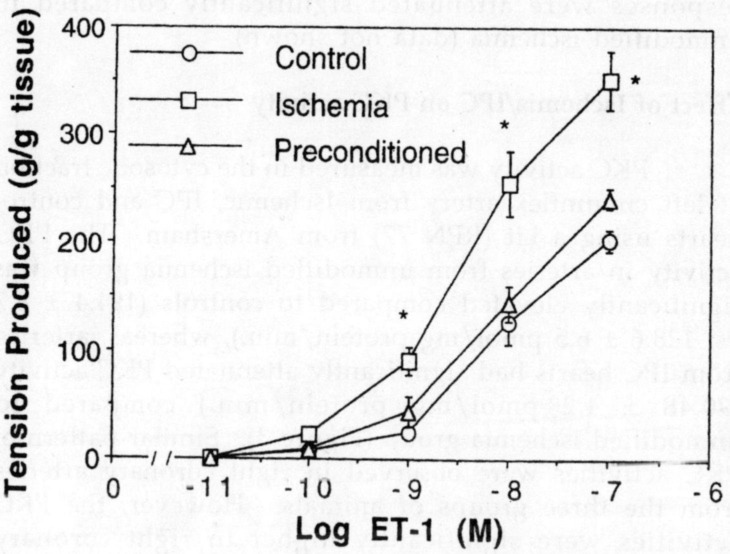

Figure 2. Effect of preconditioning on ET-1-induced contractions. Canine circumflex arterial rings from three groups of animals: control (no treatment); regional ischemic; and IPC, were contracted with increasing concentrations of ET-1. Data are means ± SE for 12 vascular rings from at least 4 hearts. * Values significantly different from control ($p<0.01$).

developed were significantly greater at all doses $\geq 10^{-9}$ M, in vessels from ischemia group, compared to both control and IPC. The EC_{50} (concentration of ET-1 that produced 50% contraction) of the three groups were in the same range, about 5×10^{-9} M (EC_{50} was calculated considering the contraction produced by the highest ET-1 concentration used (10^{-7} M) even though plateau was not achieved at this concentration in any group). Similar results were observed when LAD arterial rings were contracted with increasing concentrations of ET-1 (10^{-11} to 10^{-7} M) (data not shown). The ET-1 induced tension responses of LAD arterial rings from ischemic hearts were significantly greater compared to control, whereas, IPC responses were attenuated significantly compared to unmodified ischemia (data not shown).

Effect of Ischemia/IPC on PKC activity

PKC activity was measured in the cytosolic fraction of left circumflex artery from Ischemic, IPC and control hearts using a kit (RPN 77) from Amersham. The PKC activity in arteries from unmodified ischemia group was significantly elevated compared to controls (194.4 ± 8.7 vs. 128.6 ± 6.5 pmol/mg protein/min.), whereas, arteries from IPC hearts had significantly attenuated PKC activity (90.48 ± 4.2 pmol/mg protein/min.) compared to unmodified ischemia group (Figure 3). Similar pattern of PKC activities were observed in right coronary arteries from the three groups of animals. However, the PKC activities were significantly higher in right coronary arteries when compared to left circumflex (Figure 3, inset). The PKC activity in right coronary arteries from ischemic hearts was significantly higher when compared to control group (365.1 ± 7.4 vs. 281.55 ± 8.65 pmol/mg protein/min.), whereas, IPC attenuated significantly (127.5 ± 4.3 pmol/mg protein/min.) compared to ischemia (Figure 3, inset).

Effect of Ischemia/IPC on PKC isoforms

Western blot analysis using specific antibodies to PKC isoforms indicate the presence of the α, γ, δ and ι isoforms in canine left circumflex artery. PKC isoforms β, ε, ζ and θ could not be detected. Canine brain homogenate was used as a positive control. However, different isoform was differentially modulated in arteries from ischemia group. These changes were estimated by densitometry. PKCα, with a molecular weight of 80 kDa, was upregulated about four fold in arteries from ischemia group when compared to control, and IPC protects against ischemia induced upregulation (Figure 4 A and B). PKCγ,

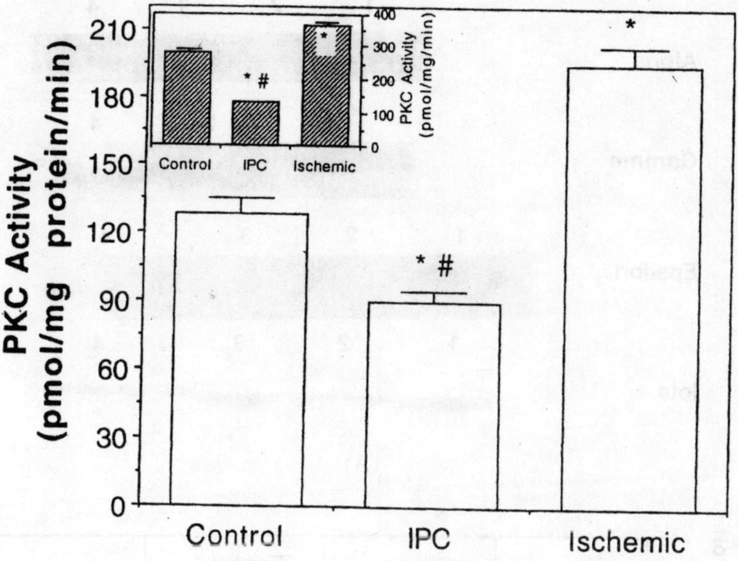

Figure 3. Effect of Ischemia/IPC on PKC activities. PKC activity in the cytosolic fractions from canine left circumflex arteries from three groups of animals : control (no treatment); regional ischemic; and IPC, were estimated using RPN 77 kit (Amersham) as described in "Materials and Methods" section. Data are means ± SE from 6 hearts. * Values significantly different from control (p<0.01). # Value significantly different from ischemic group (p<0.01). Inset: PKC activity in the cytosolic fractions from canine right circumflex arteries from the three groups of animals. Data are means ± SE from 6 hearts. * Values significantly different from control (p<0.01). # Value significantly different from ischemic group (p<0.01).

migrating at 80 kDa, was unaltered in arteries from both ischemia and IPC groups when compared to control (Figure 4 A and B). However, PKCi, migrating at 70 kDa was upregulated by about three fold in arteries from ischemia group, and IPC seems to partially restore these isoforms (Figure 4 A and B). The data for PKCδ are inconclusive at this time. Interestingly, PKCε, migrating at 90 kDa, could not be readily detected in arteries from control group but appears as a significant immunoreactive

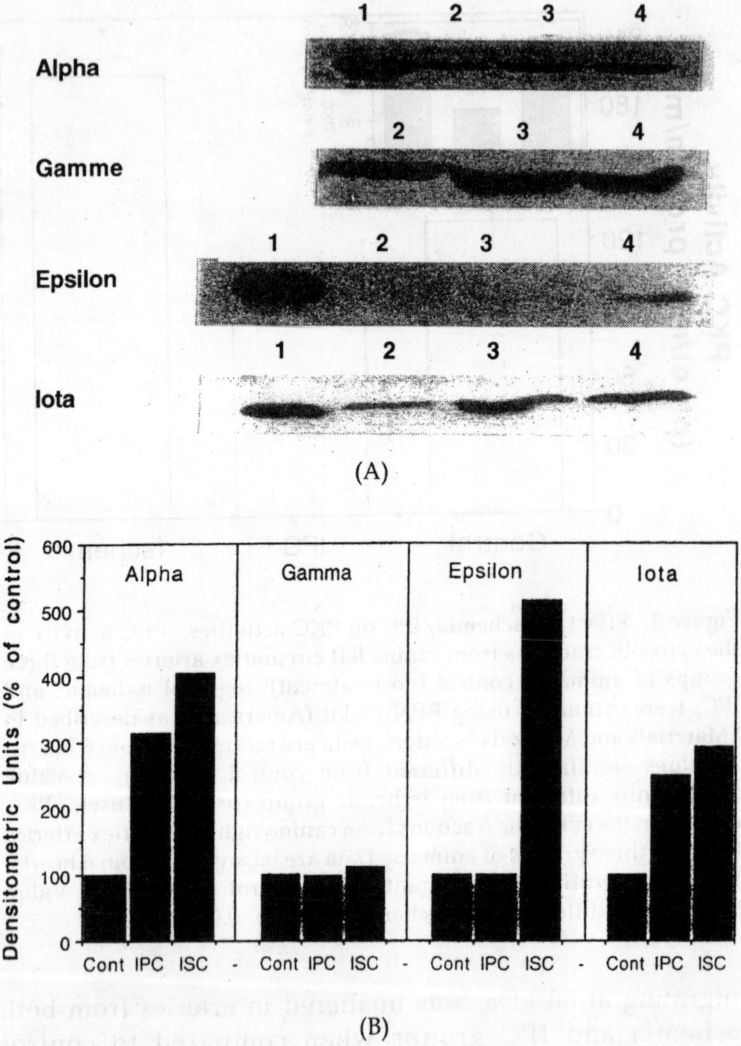

Figure 4. Effect of Ischemia/IPC on PKC isoforms. Cytosolic fractions (25 μg protein) from canine left circumflex arteries from three groups of animals : control (no treatment); regional ischemic; and IPC, were analyzed by 10% SDS-PAGE followed by western blotting using PKC isoform specific antibodies. Immunogenic bands were visualized by chemiluminiscense (Panel A) and quantitated by densitometry (Panel B). Lane 1 = Canine brain homogenate positive control; Lane 2 = control; Lane 3 = IPC; and Lane 4 = ischemic.

band (about five fold increase) in the ischemic group (Figure 4 A and B). In IPC group the PKCε isoform is barely visible.

DISCUSSION

In this study we have investigated the effects of myocardial ischemic preconditioning directly on the coronary arteries serving the myocytes that have undergone ischemic/IPC treatment. It is likely that the coronary arteries themselves are not ischemic due to occlusion, since collateral blood flow provides sufficient oxygen to these arteries. Our data demonstrate that 1) myocardial IPC has effects directly on the coronary artery, 2) myocardial ischemia enhances the vasoconstrictor responsiveness of the coronary artery, 3) the myocardial ischemia-induced increase in vasoconstrictor tone is, at least in part, mediated by upregulation of PKC-dependent mechanisms, 4) IPC attenuates the myocardial ischemia induced alteration of PKC (activity and upregulation of a, e and i isoforms) in the coronary artery, and 5) regional myocardial ischemia/preconditioning can produce global vascular changes.

Recently, the cardioprotective effects of ischemic preconditioning have received considerable attention[1-7]. Preconditioning of the myocardium with brief period of ischemia renders it resistant to many consequences of ischemia, including necrosis[1,5], arrhythmia[26], and postischemic mechanical dysfunction[27]. The exact mechanism(s) involved in such a cardioprotective phenomenon of preconditioning is still vague, but more recently, adenosine has been proposed to play a key role in preconditioning. Adenosine, a natural nucleoside, is produced from cardiac myocytes by the breakdown of adenine nucleotides and produces a variety of responses including bradycardia, hypotension, coronary vasodilation[28,29]. Adenosine has been shown to produce cardioprotection and to be equipotent with ischemic preconditioning[30]. Using more selective adenosine analogs, the same authors have demonstrated that the cardioprotective effects of adenosine are mediated through the adenosine A_1 receptor.

The effects of ischemia and preconditioning on cardiac myocytes have been demonstrated by several investigators. However, there are limited reports describing the effects of such treatments on the responsiveness of the coronary arteries serving these myocytes. Coronary vascular endothelium dysfunction has been reported by several investigators. Global ischemia and reperfusion has been shown to impair endothelium-dependent relaxations to aggregating platelets in canine coronary artery[31,32,33]. G-protein dysfunction has been proposed as the underlying mechanism for the endothelium-dependent changes[34]. Acute, as well as, long-term impairment of endothelium-dependent relaxations to aggregating platelets following reperfusion injury has been reported in canine coronary artery[35,36]. However, not much information is available regarding the changes in smooth muscle component of coronary artery following ischemia reperfusion. The present study was therefore, undertaken to evaluate the changes that occur in coronary artery due to myocardial ischemia and preconditioning. We studied one aspect of these arteries : PKC-mediated contractility.

In this study, we demonstrated that endothelium denuded circumflex arterial rings from control (no treatment), ischemic and IPC treated canine hearts could be contracted in a concentration-dependent fashion with PKC activators : PDBu and ET-1. The contractions produced by maximal concentrations used for PDBu (10^{-6} M) and ET-1 (10^{-7} M) were comparable. Arterial rings from ischemic hearts produced significantly greater tension compared to control arterial rings, indicating that the increase in the vasoconstrictor tone was, at least in part, mediated by upregulation of PKC-dependent mechanisms. Our data are in agreement with other reports in rat heart[22], that prolonged ischemia (15 to 60 min.) causes an upregulation of cytosolic PKC. However, arterial rings from IPC canine hearts showed a protective effect. Contractions produced in IPC arterial rings in response to PKC activators, PDBu and ET-1, were comparable to control rings. These data presents an intriguing question. Does these changes in the vascular reactivity play a role in cardioprotective effect of preconditioning? We do not have an answer at this time, however, it will be interesting aspect for future research.

The exact mechanism(s) by which preconditioning block the ischemia-induced increase in contractile responsiveness of the coronary artery is not yet clearly understood. However, an extrapolation from the report by Strasser *et al.*[22], which demonstrated that prolonged ischemia (15 to 60 min.) causes an upregulation of cytosolic PKC to the present study, permits speculation regarding one possible mechanism. In this hypothesis, the ischemic insult causes an upregulation of PKC, whereas, preconditioning protects against this upregulation. Protein kinase C plays an important role in the maintenance and contraction of vascular smooth muscle[12-14,37,] and upregulation of PKC due to ischemia produces elevated contractile response in the arteries to activators of PKC (ET-1 and PDBu). Preconditioning, however, protects against the ischemia-induced upregulation of PKC thus producing lower contractile responses when compared with ischemia alone, indicating that IPC attenuates the ischemia-induced upregulation of PKC in coronary artery. In an attempt to prove this hypothesis, PKC was measured by assay and western blotting in arteries from the three groups (control, ischemia and IPC). Ischemia caused a modest elevation of PKC activity by about 1.5 fold. Preconditioning attenuated the ischemia-induced upregulation of PKC to even lower than the control activity. This decrease of the activity below the control due to preconditioning is not yet clearly understood. Ischemia caused PKC isoforms a, e, and i to be upregulated. The upregulation of the isoforms were inhibited by preconditioning. Since phorbol ester has been shown to activate the a and e isoforms (among others) in cardiac myocytes [38], could be one explanation for the greater contractile response of ischemic arteries by PDBu when compared to ET-1, which is believed to activate the e and not a isoform[38].

It is well accepted that the first window of IPC protection vanishes within 2 hours based on the infarct size limitation data[39]. Other effects of IPC not immediately measurable as a change in infarct size, may take more or less than 2 hours. For example, the induction of cardiac stress protein begins with a single IPC episode, but the effect of that induction on infarct size limitation can not be observed in less than 24 hours (second window of protection)[40]. In our study, the hearts were collected immediately after experimental protocol and arteries were isolated without any delay. It is worth noting that the three groups (control, IPC and ischemia) were handled under identical conditions.

This study also provides preliminary evidence that ischemia/preconditioning phenomenon is not restricted to the area at risk but is global. In this study, left circumflex artery was occluded to produce ischemia or preconditioning and the same artery was used for the experiments. However, right circumflex artery, which is distal to the ligation site or area at risk, demonstrates contractile responses and PKC activities very similar to those of left circumflex artery. Though an interesting observation, the reason and mechanism(s) for such response is not yet clearly understood.

There is an abundance of evidence that PKC plays a key role in preconditioning of myocardium in several animal models including rat[41-43] and, rabbit[44,45]. Ten minutes of global ischemia was shown to cause the translocation of PKC from cytosol to membrane fraction in isolated perfused rat heart[41]. Activators of PKC (phorbol myristate acetate) has been shown to mimic preconditioning, whereas, inhibitors of PKC (staurosporine and polymixin B) were capable of blocking the cardioprotective effects of preconditioning in rabbit heart[44,45]. Inhibitors of PKC have also been shown to block cardioprotective effects of preconditioning in rat heart[42,43], Liu et al[44] have put forth an interesting theory for the role of PKC and adenosine in preconditioning. This two-step hypothesis proposes that during the brief ischemic period (preconditioning) adenosine initiates a cascade of events resulting in the activation of the membrane bound PKC, as well as, translocates the cytosolic PKC to membrane. This process results in minimal protein phosphorylation. With the onset of sustained ischemia, adenosine (via receptor occupation) immediately activates membrane bound PKC. This theory indicates the vital role of adenosine and PKC during both the preconditioning and sustained ischemia periods. However, data from canine model challenges the PKC translocation theory. Using fluorescence staining/confocal microscopy and biochemical quantification, Przyklenk et al[46] show that, in canine model, there was no difference in the amount or distribution of PKC with preconditioning. Although PKC may play a role in preconditioning, it appears there are several subtle differences between species.

In conclusion, this study provides us with information regarding the effects of ischemia and preconditioning on coronary arteries serving the cardiac myocytes affected by such treatments. We conclude that myocardial ischemia enhances the vasoconstrictor responsiveness of the coronary arteries, through PKC-mediated mechanisms, whereas, preconditioning protects such changes. Therefore, at least some of the protective effect observed with IPC may be attributable to better preservation of vasodilatory properties during reperfusion, secondary to direct effects of the coronary artery.

REFERENCES

1. Murry CE, Jennings RB, Reimer KA. Preconditioning with ischemia : a delay of lethal cell injury in ischemic myocardium. *Circulation*. 1986;74 : 1124-1136.

2. Liu Y, Downey JM. Ischemic preconditioning protects against infarction in rat heart. *Am J Physiol*. 1992;263 : H1107-H1112.

3. Li GC, Vasquez JA, Gallagher KP, Lucchesi BR. Myocardial protection with preconditioning. *Circulation*. 1990;82 : 609-619.

4. Gross GJ, Auchampach JA. Blockade of ATP-sensitive potassium channels prevents myocardial preconditioning in dogs. *Circ Res*. 1992; 70 : 223-233.

5. Schott RJ, Rohmann S, Braun ER, Schaper W. Ischemic preconditioning reduces infarct size in swine myocardium. *Circ Res*. 1990; 66 : 1133-1142.

6. Thornton JD, Liu GS, Downey JM. Pretreatment with pertussis toxin blocks the protective effects of preconditioning : evidence for a G-protein mechanism. *J Mol Cell Cardiol*. 1993; 25 : 311-320.

7. Iwamoto T, Miura T, Adachi T, Noto T, Ogawa T, Tsuchida A, Iimura O. Myocardial infarct size-limiting effect of ischemic preconditioning was not attenuated by oxygen free-radical scavengers in the rabbit. *Circulation*. 1991; 83 : 1015-1022.

8. Cave AC, Collis CS, Downey JM, Hearse DJ. Improved functional recovery by ischaemic preconditioning is not mediated by adenosine in the globally ischemic isolated rat heart. *Cardiovasc. Res*. 1993; 27 : 663-668.

9. Asimakis GK, Inners-McBride K, Conti VR. Attenuation of postischaemic dysfunction by ischaemic preconditioning is not mediated by adenosine in the isolated rat heart. *Cardiovasc. Res*. 1993; 27 : 1522-1530.

10. Li Y, Kloner RA. Adenosine deaminase inhibition is not cardioprotective in the rat. *Am. Heart J*. 1993; 126(6) : 1293-1298.

11. McClanahan TB, Martin BJ, Wolke LJ, Mertz TE, Klohs WD, Gallagher KP. Inhibition of adenosine deaminase with pentostatin reduces infarct size in rabbits [Abstract]. *Circulation*. 1992; 86(suppl I) : I-23.

12. Nishizuka Y. Studies and perspectives of protein kinase C. *Science* 1986; 233 : 305-312.

13. Singer HA. Phorbol ester-induced stress and myosin light chain phosphorylation in swine carotid medial smooth muscle. *J. Phar. Exp. Ther*. 1990; 252 : 1068-1074.

14. Ratz PH. Effect of kinase inhibitor, H-7, on stress, crossbridge phosphorylation, muscles shortening and inositol phosphate production in rabbit arteries. *J. Phar. Exp. Ther.* 1990; 252 : 253.

15. Yanagisawa M, Kurihara H, Kimura S, Tomobe Y, Kobayashi M, Mitsui Y, Yazaka Y, Goto K, Masaki T. A novel potent vasoconstrictor peptide produced by vascular endothelial cells. *Nature* 1988; 332 : 411-415.

16. Yanagisawa M, Masaki T. Endothelin, a novel endothelium-derived peptide. Pharmacological activities, regulation and posible roles in cardiovascular control. *Biochem. Pharmacol.* 1989; 38 : 1877-1883.

17. Kasuya, Y., Ishikawa T, Yanagisawa M, Kimura S, Goto K, Masaki T. Mechanism of contraction to endothelin in isolated porcine coronary artery. *Am. J. Physiol.* (Heart Circ. Physiol. 26). 1989; 257 : H1828-H1835.

18. Resink TJ, Scott-Burden T, Buhler FR. Endothelin stimulates phospholipase C in cultured vascular smooth muscle cells. Biochem. *Biophys. Res. Commun.* 1988; 157 : 1360-1368.

19. Muldoon LL, Rodland KD. Forsythe ML, Magun BE. Stimulation of phosphatidylinositol hydrolysis, diacylglycerol release, and gene expression in response to endothelin, a potent new agonist for fibroblasts and smooth muscle cells. *J. Biol. Chem.* 1989; 264 : 8529-8536.

20. Griendling KK, Tsuda T, Alexander RW. Endothelin stimulates diacylglycerol accumulation and activates protein kinase C in cultured vascular smooth muscle cells. *J. Biol. Chem.* 1989; 264 : 8237-8240.

21. Lee T-E., Thao T, Hu K-Q, King GL. Endothelin stimulates a sustained 1,2-diacylglycerol increase and protein kinase C activation in bovine aortic smooth muscle cells. *Biochem. Biophys. Res. Commun.* 1989; 162 : 381-386.

22. Strasser RH, Walendzik H, Marquetant R. Prolonged myocardial ischemia provokes an induction of protein kinase C activity. (Abstract) *Circulation* 1991; 84(suppl II) : II-620, #2463.

23. Mitchell MB, Parker CG, Meng X, Brew EC, Ao L, Brown JM, Harken, AH, Banerjee A. Protein kinase C mediates preconditioning in isolated rat heart. *Circulation*, 1993; 88 (#4, part 2) # 3405.

24. Stawski G, Olsen UB, Grande P. Cytotoxic effect of endothelin-1 during ischemia in cultured neonatal rat myocytes. (Abstract) *Circulation*. 1991; 84(suppl II) : II-616, #2450.

25. Laemmli, U. K. Cleavage of Structural proteins during the assembly of the head of bacteriophage T_4. *Nature* (Lond.) 1970; 227 : 680-685.

26. Shiki K, Hearse DJ. Preconditioning of ischemic myocardium : reperfusion-induced arrhythmia. *Am J Physiol*. 1987; 253 : H1470-H1476.

27. Cohen MV, Liu GS, Downey JM. Preconditioning causes improved wall motion as well as smaller infarcts after transient coronary occlusion in rabbits. *Circulation*. 1991; 84 : 341-349.

28. Kusachi S, Thompson RD, Olsson RA. Ligand selectivity of dog coronary adenosine receptor resembles that of adenylate cyclase stimulatory (Ra) receptors. *J. Pharmacol. Exp. Ther.* 1983; 227 : 316-321.

29. Mustafa SJ. Cellular and molecular mechanism(s) of coronary flow regulation by adenosine. *Mol. Cell. Biochem.* 1980; 31 : 61-87.

30. Downey JM, Liu GS, Thornton JD. Adenosine and anti-infarct effects of preconditioning. *Cardiovasc. Res.* 1993; 27 : 3-8.

31. Pearson PJ, Lin PJ, Schaff HV. Global myocardial ischemia and reperfusion impair endothelium-dependent relaxations to aggregating platelets in the canine coronary artery : a possible cause of vasospasm after cardiopulmonary bypass. *J Thorac Cardiovasc Surg* 1994; 57 : 1550-6.

32. Vanhoutte PM, Houston DS. Platelets, endothelium and vasospasm. *Circulation* 1985; 72 : 728-734.

33. Vanhoutte PM, Shimokawa H. Endothelium-derived relaxing factor and coronary vasospasm. *Circulation* 1989; 80 : 1-9.

34. Evora PRB, Pearson PJ, Schaff HV. Impaired endothelium-dependent relaxation after coronary reperfusion injury : evidence for G-protein dysfunction. *Ann Thorac Surg* 1994; 57 : 1550-1556.

35. Pearson PJ, Schaff HV, Vanhoutte PM. Acute impairment of endothelium-dependent relaxations to aggregating platelets following reperfusion injury in canine coronary artery. *Circ Res* 1990; 67 : 385-393.

36. Pearson PJ, Schaff HV, Vanhoutte PM. Long-term impairment of endothelium-dependent relaxations to aggregating platelets after reperfusion injury in canine coronary artery. *Circulation* 1990; 81 : 1921-1927.

37. Rasmussen H, Takuwa Y, Park S. Protein kinase C in the regulation of smooth muscle contraction. *FASEB J.* 1987; 1 : 177-185.

38. Sugden PH, Bogoyevitch MA. Endothelin-1-dependent signaling pathways in myocardium. *Trends Cardiovasc Med.* 1996; 6 : 87-94.

39. Murry CE, Richard VJ, Jennings RB, Reimer KA. Myocardial protection is lost before contractile function recovers from ischemic preconditioning. *Am J Physiol* (Heart Circ Physiol). 1991; 260 : H796-H804.

40. Marber MS, Latchman DS, Walker JM, Yellon DM. Cardiac stress protein elevation 24 hours after brief ischemia or heat stress is associated with resistance to myocardial infarction. *Circulation.* 1994; 1264 : 1272.

41. Strasser R, Braun-Dullaeus MR, Walendzik H, Marquetant R. a_1-Receptor-independent activation of protein kinase C in acute myocardial ischemia. *Circ Res.* 1992; 70 : 1304-1312.

42. Li Y, Kloner RA. Does protein kinase C play a role in ischemic preconditioning in rat hearts? *Am J Physiol.* 1995; 268 : H426-H431.

43. Mitchell MB, Meng X, Ao L, Brown JM, Harken AH, Banerjee A. Preconditioning of isolated rat heart is mediated by protein kinase C. *Circ Res.* 1995; 76 : 73-81.

44. Liu Y, Ytrehus K, Downey JM. Evidence that translocation of protein kinase C is a key event during ischemic preconditioning of rabbit myocardium. *J Mol Cell Cardiol.* 1994; 26 : 661-668.

45. Ytrehus K, Liu Y, Downey JM. Preconditioning protects rabbit heart by protein kinase C activation. *Am J Physiol.* 1994; 266 : H1145-H1152.

46. Przyklenk K, Sussman MA, Simkhovich BZ, Kloner RA. Does ischemic preconditioning trigger translocation of protein kinase C in canine model. *Circulation.* 1995; 92 : 1546-1557.

OXIDATIVE STRESS AND ANTIOXIDANTS IN HUMAN DISEASES

T Lazar Mathew, R Varshney, S Gupta and B S Dwarakanath

Institute of Nuclear Medicine and Allied Sciences, Brig S K Mazumdar Road, Delhi-110 054

Summary

The generation of free radicals or reactive oxygen species (ROS) is a normal, steady state event in cells with intact respiratory metabolism. Uncontrolled production of ROS often results in damage to cellular macromolecules like nucleic acids (DNA), proteins and lipids as well as other molecules in the cell. A number of cellular defense mechanisms exist that neutralize the damaging effects of these reactive species. This comprises of enzymatic systems functioning by direct or sequential removal of ROS through superoxide dismutase (SOD), catalase and glutathione peroxidases or non-enzymatic scavenging through endogenously produced glutathione (GSH), ubiquinols and uric acid or those derived from the diet *viz.* vitamin C & E, lipoic acid, carotenoids, riboflavin, selenium and zinc.

Under physiological conditions, a fine balance exists between the generation of free radicals and the capacity of detoxification systems. A persistent oxidative stress either due to enhanced generation of ROS or reduced efficiency of detoxifying mechanisms leads to reversible and irreversible sub-cellular changes resulting in a variety of patho-physiological conditions. Some of the diseases caused by oxidative stress include cancer, cardiovascular diseases, diabetes-related disorders, neurodegenerative disorders, pancreatitis, haemolytic anaemia and infertility.

The current approaches in the management of oxidative stress induced pathophysiological conditions include dietary supplementation of vitamins (E and C) and other antioxidants such as β-carotenoids besides essential trace elements like Selenium, Zinc etc. While, daily doses of alpha-tocopherol (Vitamin E), beta-carotene and selenium have been shown to reduce the incidence of lung and oral cancer, as well as mortality due to stomach cancer, a seleno-organic compound ebselen which has glutathione peroxidase activity and membrane permeable ascorbic acid derivative CV-3611 have been demonstrated to be effective against pancreatic edema. However, to date, controlled clinical studies have demonstrated only the prophylactic effects of antioxidants, while their therapeutic efficacy needs to be established. An in-depth knowledge about the sources of free radicals, mechanisms of injury and biochemical regulation of antioxidant defense mechanisms might facilitate the development of new therapeutic strategies for the management of stress related disorders.

INTRODUCTION

The intracellular milieu of unicellular and multicellular biological systems with intact respiratory metabolism generate highly reactive intermediates due to the incomplete reduction of oxygen resulting in superoxide radicals, hydrogen peroxide and hydroxyl radical (Mates and Sanchez-Jinenez, 2000: Halliwell, 1994: reviews). These and other related species generated in cells due to environmental or exogenous agents like ionizing radiation, UV and certain chemicals are often referred to as "Reactive Oxygen Metabolites" (ROM) or more commonly the "Reactive Oxygen Species" (ROS). Due to their highly reactive nature and ability to oxidize, they attack biomolecules of vital importance to the cell survival and various functions. Owing to their self-adoptive and regulatory nature, biological systems have evolved excellent cellular defense mechanisms which detoxify the destructive effects of ROS. These include the non-enzymatic reduction of ROS by a variety of molecules like glutathione, thioredoxin etc. and inactivation by several enzymes like superoxide dismutase, glutathione peroxidase, catalase etc. Both these defense mechanisms are together referred to as cellular antioxidants. In addition, antioxidants are also available as constituents of a number of plant products *viz.* fruits and vegetables, which are currently used to supplement the systemic antioxidant defenses against ROS.

An imbalance between the production of ROS and antioxidant defense systems, results in the generation and accumulation of excess ROS, which is referred to as the "Oxidative Stress". (Bandyopadhyay *et al.*, 1999; Halliwel, 2000; McCord, 2000 – Reviews). These conditions greatly enhance the interaction between ROS and biomolecules and structures resulting in lethal and non-lethal lesions (Gutteridge and Halliwell, 1990; Stadtman and Oliver, 1991; Dizadaroglu, 1992; Halliwell and Dizadaroglu, 1992; Imlay *et al.*, 1998) that lead to cell death, transformation and functional disturbances. These three events in target tissue are mainly responsible for the ROS mediated pathophysiology that includes ageing and diseases like cancer, neurodegenerative disorders, cardiovascular diseases, endocrine disorders etc. ROS has occupied a central role in a wide variety of diseases and several antioxidant mediated therapeutic strategies have been developed in the last couple of decades and successfully applied in atleast a few diseases (Mates *et al.*, 1999; Bandyopadhyay *et al.*, 1999; Carroll *et al*, 1987 - Reviews). A number of reviews on this important subject of biomedical sciences have appeared in the last few years and only a brief overview of our understanding and current scenario is presented here.

Reactive oxygen species and their site of generation

Molecular oxygen (O_2) behaves like a radical (a biradical) due to the presence of two unpaired electrons with parallel spin. The one electron reduction product of oxygen is superoxide radical ($O_2^{\cdot-}$). If two electrons are transferred, the product is hydrogen peroxide (H_2O_2), which still can receive two electrons making it to be a cytotoxic oxidant. Certain chelates of ferrous ion and cuprous ions are capable of transferring a third electron to hydrogen peroxide by the following Fenton reaction (Mates and Sanchez-Jinenez, 2000):

$$Fe^{2+} + H_2O_2 \rightarrow Fe^{3+} + {}^{\cdot}OH + OH^-$$

Traces of Fe^{3+} can react further with H_2O_2 to form the following product

$$Fe^{3+} + H_2O_2 \rightarrow Fe^{2+} + O^{\cdot-}_2 + H^+$$

The net result is:

$$O^{\cdot-}_2 + H_2O_2 \rightarrow O_2 + {}^{\cdot}OH + OH^-$$

Hydroxyl radical can further be reduced to water by accepting another electron. The overall reaction is

$$O_2 + 4H^+ + 4e^- \rightarrow 2\,H_2O$$

These free radicals are endogenously produced during normal metabolic reactions. The most important sources of superoxide radical in aerobic cells are the electron transport chains of mitochondria and endoplasmic reticulum.

Under normal conditions, univalent reduction of oxygen in respiring cells is restricted by cytochrome oxidase of mitochondrial electron transport chain, which reduces O_2 by four electrons to H_2O without releasing superoxide or H_2O_2 (Chance *et al*, 1979). However, superoxide radicals are invariably produced in respiring cells due to the probable leak of single electron at the specific site of the mitochondrial electron transport chain. The production of mitochondrial superoxide radicals occurs primarily at two discrete points in the electron transport chain, namely at complex I (NADPH dehydrogenase) and at complex III (ubiquinone – cytochrome c reductase). Complex III is the major source of mitochondrial superoxide production (Turrens, 1997). Electrons from complex I or II dehydrogenases are transferred to coenzyme Q, also called ubiquinone. The resulting reduced form (QH_2) of coenzyme subsequently undergoes two sequential one-electron reductions (the Q cycle) using oxidized and reduced form of cytochrome b and cytochrome c. The unstable intermediate in the Q cycle can lead to superoxide formation by transferring electrons directly to molecular oxygen (Finkel and Holbrook, 2000).

Similarly, cytochrome P-450 reductase and cytochrome b-5 reductase in the endoplasmic reticulum generate $O^{\cdot-}_2$ and H_2O_2 during their catalytic cycle (Koop, 1992; Gaeptar *et al*, 1995)

The phagocytic cells, such as neutrophils when activated during phagocytosis, generate $O^{\cdot-}_2$ and H_2O_2 through the activation of NADPH oxidase (Chanock *et al*, 1994; Moslen, 1994; Robinson and Badwey, 1994). Nitric oxide a nitrogen based free radical is synthesized endogenously by enzyme nitric oxide synthase (NOS) from its precursor L-arginine (Shinde *et al.*, 2000- a review).

In addition to these four sources of oxidants, there are other enzymes capable of generating oxidants under normal or pathological conditions. Oxidative deamination of dopamine by monoamine oxidase, an event that occurs in synaptic terminals of dopaminergic neurons, generates dopamine metabolites and H_2O_2 (Fahn and Cohen, 1992).

Exogenous factors like ultraviolet (UV) radiation ionizing radiation, chemotherapeutic agents etc. can generate high levels of ROS that can perturb the normal redox balance and shift cells into a state of oxidative stress (Feinendege *et al*, 1995).

Defense against ROS

The oxidizable substances, which are present at low concentrations and can significantly delay or inhibit oxidation of the substrates, are termed as antioxidants. Antioxidants can act at different levels in the oxidative sequence like

1. Decreasing localized O_2 concentrations.
2. Preventing chain initiation by scavenging initiating radicals.
3. Binding metal ions, thus inhibiting the generation of initiating species.
4. Decomposing peroxides by converting them to non-radical products.
5. Chain breaking.

Biological antioxidants may bc classified into two principal groups:

(a) Antioxidant enzymes (catalase, peroxidase and superoxide dismutase)

(b) Low molecular weight antioxidant compounds:

(i) Hydrophilic radical scavengers such as ascorbate, urate, and glutathione (GSH)

(ii) Lipophilic radical scavengers such as tocopherols, flavonoids (e.g. quercetin), carotenoids (β-carotene, lycopene) and ubiquinol.

Antioxidant enzymes: The first enzyme involved in the antioxidant defense is superoxide dismutase (SOD), a metalloprotein, found in both prokaryotic and eukaryotic cells (Fridovich, 1995). The iron containing and manganese containing SOD are characteristics of prokaryotes. In eukaryotic cells, the predominant forms are the copper - containing and zinc containing enzyme, located in the cytosol. The second type is manganese containing SOD found in the mitochondrial matrix. The SOD catalyzes the disproportionation reaction:

$$2O^{-}_2 + 2H^{+} \rightarrow H_2O_2 + O_2$$

This dismutation or disproportionation reaction makes use of the fact that superoxide is both an oxidant and a reductant. Catalase works in a similar way, because hydrogen peroxide can be a weak reductant as well as a fairly strong oxidant. The catalase reaction mechanism may be written as follows:

$$2H_2O_2 \rightarrow 2H_2O + O_2$$

Catalase, which is localized in peroxisomes, is a hemoprotein and catalyses the decomposition of H_2O_2 to water and oxygen (Aebi, 1980). Glutathione peroxidase catalyses the reaction of hydrogen peroxides with reduced glutathione (GSH) to form glutathione disulphide (GSSG) and the reduction product of the hydrogen peroxide. It is a seleno enzyme, which is present in cytosol and mitochondria (Sundstrom *et al.*, 1984).

$$ROOH + H_2O_2 + GSH \rightarrow ROH/H_2O + GSSG$$

Defense by low molecular weight antioxidants (LMWA): Secondary defense against ROS is offered by small molecules, which react with radicals to produce other radical species called scavengers. These scavengers further produce lesser harmful radical species, called antioxidants. For example, α-tocopherol, ascorbate, reduced glutathione (GSH), and uric acid may act as cellular antioxidants. Alpha- tocopherol, present in the cell membrane and plasma lipoproteins functions as a chain breaking antioxidant. Once the tocopherol radical is formed, it can migrate to the membrane surface and is reconverted to α- tocopherol by a reaction with ascorbate. The resulting ascorbate radical can regenerate ascorbate by reduction with GSH, which can also directly scavenge ROS. The oxidized product of glutathione (GSSG) can regenerate GSH through NADPH-glutathione reductase system. Ascorbate also acts as a prooxidant at lower concentrations in the presence of metal ions, generating H_2O_2 and ·OH radical (Cotgreave *et al.*, 1988).

Thiol (SH) groups are essential in the protection against the deleterious effects of ROS. The tripeptide GSH is the most important protective system (Mustafa *et al.*, 2000). Uric acid also acts as a powerful scavenger of peroxyl and ·OH radicals (Carrol *et al.*, 1987). Reaction of ·OH with uric acid produces a range of carbon-centered radicals that mostly react with O_2 to give urate peroxyl radical. These urate derived radicals are much less reactive.

Antioxidants of extracellular fluids

The extracellular fluids of human body, such as blood plasma, tissue fluid, cerebrospinal fluid (CSF), synovial fluid, or seminal plasma contain insignificant catalase activity and only low activities of superoxide dismutase and selenium glutathione peroxidase (Hunter, 1985). Reduced glutathione is also present at very low concentrations. It suggests that enzymes contribute little to the antioxidant activity of extracellular fluids. Blood lipoproteins contain only vitamin E as the chain breaking antioxidants. However, oxidants can still be generated in the plasma e.g. O^{-}_2 and H_2O_2 can arise from enzymes and activated phagocytic cells.

In blood, O^{-}_2 and H_2O_2 might interact with erythrocytes and can form highly toxic·OH radical (Lynch and Fridovich, 1978). In order to prevent the formation of ·OH, blood plasma has transferrin, a transition metal iron binding protein (Pacht and Davies, 1988). The protein lactoferrin secreted by phagocytic cells acts as an antioxidant in the same way. Hemoglobin can also act as a prooxidant both by its decomposition to release iron and by a direct interaction of peroxides with the protein. Plasma contains the hemoglobin-binding protein known as hepatoglobin, as well as haem binding protein (haemopexin). This binding results in the reduction of the effectiveness of these iron compounds in stimulating ROS induced oxidation. Similarly, plasma caeruloplasmin also acts as an antioxidant (Marklund, 1986; Pacht and Davies, 1988). Caeruloplasmin has a ferroxidase activity, ferroxidase action allows it to inhibit iron dependent ·OH formation from H_2O_2. Albumin can also bind copper ions, and inhibit copper dependent ·OH radical formation. Albumin is also a powerful scavenger of hypochlorous acid (HOCl), an oxidant produced by the enzyme myeloperoxidase in activated phagocytic cells.

Thus, the major antioxidant action of plasma is to prevent transition metal ions from accelerating free radical reactions.

An imbalance between ROS and antioxidants results in an oxidative stress, causing macromolecular and structural damage, leading to cell death and tissue damage, which is primarily responsible for the pathophysiology of ROS mediated diseases (Fig. 1). The major mode of ROS induced cell death in most multicellular organism appears to be apoptosis.

Reactive oxygen species and apoptosis

It is becoming apparent that the redox status of a cell plays an important role and can have complex effects during the induction and execution of apoptosis (Tores-Roca *et al.*, 1995; McGowan *et al.*, 1996). Most forms of aerobic apoptosis involve utilization of ROS as essential intermediate messengers (Slater *et al.*, 1995; Sugiyama *et al.*, 1996; Albright *et al.*, 1997). Increased ROS levels can lead to apoptosis and antioxidants can block apoptosis in a variety of systems (Slater *et al.*, 1996). Oxidative stress results in a variety of signals which include the detection

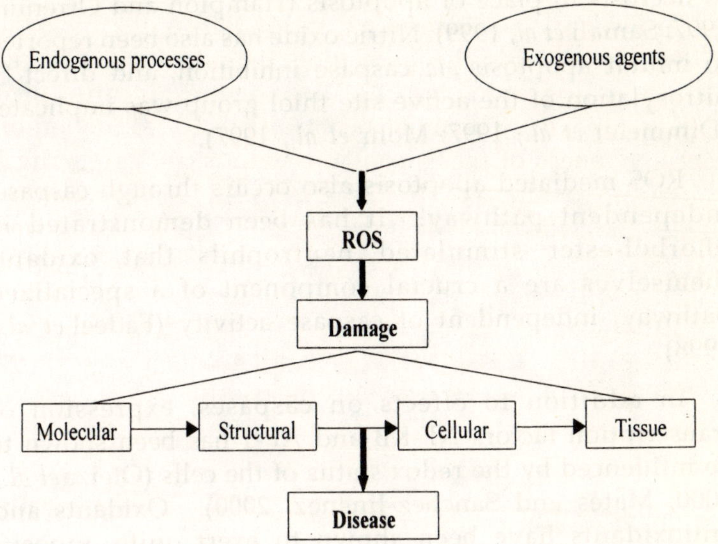

Fig 1. Development of ROS induced tissue damage and disease

of damage and activation of apoptotic machinery like the DNA damage and p53 or activation of specific signal pathways leading to apoptosis. Oxidative regulation of different protein kinase pathways and transcription factors has already been observed (Suzuki *et al.*, 1997; Hampton and Orrenius, 1997; Sen and Packer, 1991).

The extent of oxidative stress appears to determine the mode of cell death. A switch from apoptosis to necrosis is common with oxidants and redox active compounds (Dypbukt *et al.*, 1994). While a high degree of oxidative stress can cause necrosis, lower levels will trigger apoptosis (Lennon *et al.*, 1991; Dypbukt *et al.*, 1994). Indeed, caspases (central components of apoptotic program) are proposed to be inactivated due to the oxidation of thiol groups at the active site by the addition of H_2O_2 exogenously (under high oxidative stress) leading to necrosis in place of apoptosis (Hampton and Orrenius, 1997; Samali *et al*, 1999). Nitric oxide has also been reported to inhibit apoptosis *via* caspase inhibition, and direct S-nitrosylation of the active site thiol group was implicated (Dimmeler *et al.*, 1997; Mohr *et al.*, 1997).

ROS mediated apoptosis also occurs through caspase-independent pathway. It has been demonstrated in phorbol-ester stimulated neutrophils that oxidants themselves are a crucial component of a specialized pathway, independent of caspase activity (Fadeel *et al.*, 1998).

In addition to effects on caspases, expression of transcription factors NF-KB and AP-1 has been shown to be influenced by the redox status of the cells (Oteiza*et al.*, 2000; Mates and Sanchez-Jinenez, 2000). Oxidants and antioxidants have been shown to exert quite opposite effects on NF-KB and AP-1, with H_2O_2 and antioxidants activating and inhibiting NF-KB respectively, while the reverse is true for AP-1. This has led to the proposal that AP-1 is an antioxidant responsive factor whereas NF-KB responds to oxidants (Pahl and Baeurle, 1994). Also, Bcl $^{-2}$ (an anti-apoptotic protein) has been shown to protect against apoptosis by blocking cytochrome c release by influencing and modifying ROS production (Cai and Jones, 1998; Kane *et al.*, 1993). However, evidences are also available disputing the antioxidant ability of Bcl^{-2} (Zhong *et al.*, 1993; Shimizu *et al.*, 1995).

Inhibition of antioxidant enzymes (GPX, SOD, CAT) lead to a decrease in proliferation rates and increase in the apoptotic bodies in fibroblasts (Burdon*et al.*, 1996). Therefore, intracellular conditions that are more prooxidant than normal, appear to favor apoptosis over proliferation in fibroblasts.

Since, increased ROS can induce apoptosis, while antioxidants inhibit the process *in vitro*, systemic modulation of antioxidant levels may affect tumor cell apoptosis and thus, tumor growth rates. Indeed Salganik *et al.* (2000) have shown in choroid plexus tumor bearing mice that feeding an antioxidant-poor diet causes a significant increase in ROS and apoptosis resulting in a substantial reduction in tumor burden while sparing normal tissues. Since, many anticancer therapeutic agents function by apoptotic mechanism which involve ROS as essential mediators (McGovan *et al.*, 1998), it is possible that feeding an antioxidant-poor diet could even enhance the therapeutic effects of standard anticancer agents.

Since, ROS mediated apoptosis results in several pathophysiological conditions in normal tissues, elucidation of the signal transduction pathways of oxidant-induced apoptosis may provide alternate therapies for treatment of various diseases induced by ROS.

ROS and human diseases

Despite the existence of endogenous defense mechanisms against ROS, it has been observed that decrease in the level of the cellular antioxidants or increase in ROS levels results in oxidative damage to the cells, finally leading to several pathological conditions. A brief account of some of these ROS mediated disorders / diseases is presented in the following sections.

Ageing

There is sequence of events encoded into the genome for programmed ageing. However, with continuous oxidative insult these sequences are altered and accelerate the process of ageing (Finkel and Holbrook, 2000). This has been shown that animals with higher metabolic rate often have shorter life spans (Ku *et al.*, 1993) which could be due to more endogenous ROS production (Turrens, 1997). A rise in intracellular oxidant level has two potentially important effects: damage to various cell components and triggering of the activation of specific signaling pathways (Alder, 1999). Both of these effects can influence numerous cellular processes linked to ageing and development of age related diseases. In addition to generating oxidant mainly through mitochondrial electron transport chain, metabolism can produce other by products including glyoxal and methylglyoxal, which can contribute to advanced glycation end product (AGE) formation that, in turn, contribute to the ageing phenotype (Finkel and Holbrook, 2000).

It is now generally agreed that accelerated ageing results from ROS mediated oxidative damage of lipids, proteins and DNA molecules. Several studies have shown that ageing cells and organisms accumulate increased levels of oxidant-damaged lipid, protein and nuclear and mitochondrial DNA. Mitochondrial DNA is considered to be more sensitive to ROS induced damage because of its proximity and deficient repair machinery (Ames, 1989; Richter, 1992; Shigenaga *et al.*, 1994). Increasing damage to mitochondrial DNA inevitably leads to compromised mitochondrial function and integrity. Damaged mitochondria is thought to release more ROS and set in motion a vicious cycle of increasing DNA damage leading to increased ROS production that in turn leads to more DNA damage.

A number of stress response mechanisms have been evolved to help the cell and organism to adapt to acute stress. Among the main stress signaling pathways activated in response to oxidant injury are the extracellular signal-regulated kinase (ERK), c-jun amino-terminal kinase (JNK) and p38 mitogen activated protein kinase (MAPK) signaling cascade, the phosphoinositide 3-kinase (PI(3)K/ Akt pathway, the nuclear factor (NF)-KB signaling system, p53 activation (Wang *et al.*, 2000; Alder *et al.*, 2000; Gayton *et al.*, 1998; Supakar *et al.*, 1995). The degree to which a given pathway is activated is highly dependent on the nature and duration of the stress. A common effect of the activation of these pathways is a change in pattern of gene expression mediated largely through modulation of the activities of transcription factors. Accordingly, a large number of oxidative stress-responsive transcription factors and genes have been identified and implicated in ageing processes.

Attempts have been made to test directly the role of free radicals in the ageing process by supplying antioxidants, mainly in the form of thiol compounds, α-tocopherol and ascorbic acid. α-tocopherol prolongs the life span of several simple organisms (Mc Call and Frei, 1999). However, the effects of administered antioxidants on the life span of mammals are small. Restructuring the caloric intake has also shown to delay ageing process through i) decreased production of mitochondrial $O_2^{\cdot}$ and H_2O_2, and ii) increased production of antioxidant defenses by supplementation of antioxidants from outside (Masoro, 2000).

Cancer

Cancer is a disease that develops in a step-wise manner, where somatic cells accumulate mutations in specific classes of genes *viz.* protooncogenes, tumor suppressor genes, apoptosis regulating genes and DNA repair genes that collectively regulate genomic stability, cell proliferation and cell death. The mutated genes include the ones that code for growth factors and their receptors, transcription factors, signal transduction proteins, besides Bcl-1 & 2, p53, pRB etc. DNA damage is the major cause of genetic instability leading to the development of cancer and human diseases with DNA repair deficiency are often associated with a higher incidence of cancer (Caldecott *et al.*, 2000).

The three distinct stages involved in carcinogenesis have been identified as initiation, promotion and progression, each involving a set of identified molecular, structural and functional changes in the committed cell and tissue involved (Stanely *et al.*, 1995; Mates and Sanchez-Jinenez, 2000). Oxidative stress appears to be systemic in nature and there is enough evidence for its involvement in all three processes of carcinogenesis (Mates and Sanchez-Jinenez, 2000; Perchellet *et al.*, 1995; Dedon *et al.*, 1998; Kenedy *et al.*, 1998) as shown in fig. 2. Increase in oxidative stress has been found in cancer patients as well as in individuals at increased cancer risk (Fenkel *et al.*, 1988).

ROS mediated induction of DNA lesions (in the form of base damage and strand breaks) and inhibition of DNA repair (due to lipid peoxidation mediated membrane damage) contribute to the initiation and promotion, while, oxidation of proteins and inhibition of antiproteases, coupled with tissue injury facilitate the progression and metastasis of the disease (Mates and Sanchez-Jinenez, 2000; Hursting *et al.*, 1999). Further, the oxidative bursts releasing ROS during inflammation has been shown to facilitate tumor promotion (Desai *et al.*, 1996). At least two transcription factors (NF-KB & AP-1) are known to be regulated by the oxidative status of cells, whose binding sites are located on the genes directly involved in the pathogenesis of cancer (Mates and Sanchez-Jinenez, 2000). Tumors where imbalances between oxidants and antioxidants are strongly related to the pathogenesis include cancers of the bladder, blood, bowel, breast, lung, kidney, oesophagus, skin and prostate etc. Despite the currently available wealth of data and understanding, the mechanisms of ROS mediated initiation and progression of cancer is not completely understood.

Prevention of Cancer: Progress made particularly on the mechanisms of chemical and radiation induced cancer has identified several stages along the carcinogenesis pathway that are amenable to mechanism based prevention strategies (Hursting et al., 1999). Direct scavenging of DNA reactive intermediates with antioxidants or other agents that scavenge electrophiles is one of the strategies

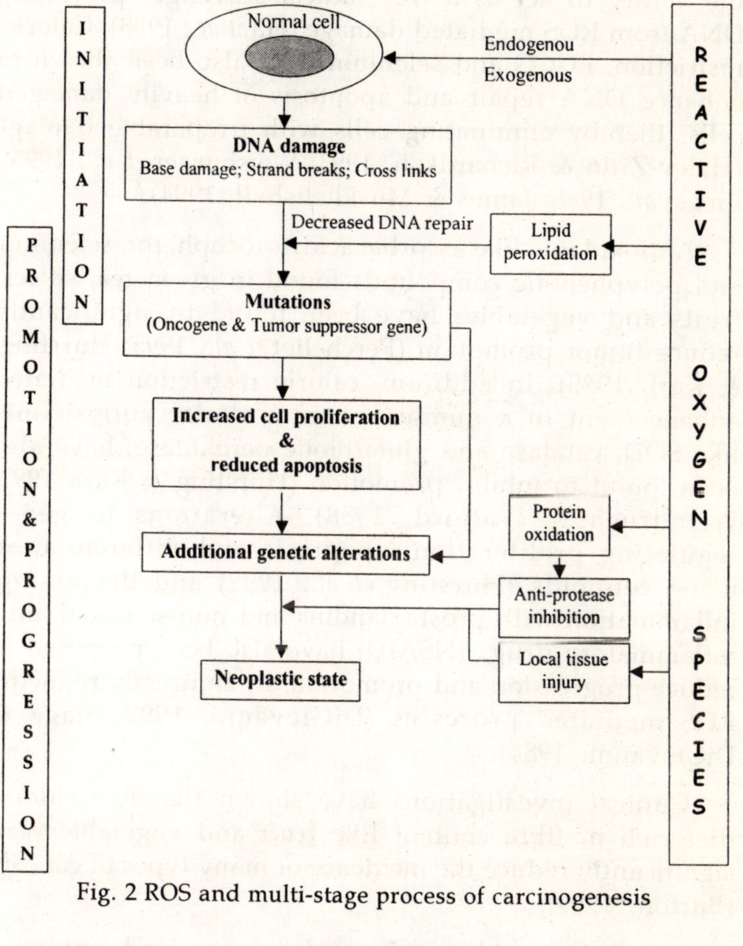

Fig. 2 ROS and multi-stage process of carcinogenesis

for reducing the induction of DNA damage and modulating the early initiation processes (Hursting*et al.*, 1999). Calorie restriction, diet supplementation with epigallocatechin (EGCG) and selenium and use of certain plant compounds like flavonoids, coumarins are among the alternative strategies for preventing initiation (James & Muskhelishvil, 1994; Salganik *et al.*, 2000). Naturally occurring polyamines like spermine/spermidine also have the ability to act as a free radical scavenger protecting DNA from ROS mediated damage (Ha *et al.*, 1998). Calorie restriction, EGCG and selenium have also been shown to enhance DNA repair and apoptosis of heavily damaged cells, thereby eliminating cells with irreparable damage (Haley-Zitin & Richardson, 1993; Weisburger *et al.*, 1995; Birt *et al.*, 1988; James & Muskhelishvil, 1994).

Antioxidants like ascorbic acid, α-tocopherol, selenium and polyphenolic compounds found in green tea, spices, fruits and vegetables have been found to significantly reduce tumor promotion (Perchellet *et al.*, 1995; Hursting & Kari, 1995). In addition, calorie restriction mediated enhancement in a number of intracellular antioxidants like SOD, catalase and glutathione peroxidase, have also been found to inhibit promotion (Hursting & Kari, 1995; Weindruch & Walford, 1988). Alterations in genes regulating proliferation, apoptosis and differentiation using retinoids (Hursting *et al.*, 1999) and decreasing inflammation with prostaglandins and non-steroidal anti-inflammatory drugs (NSAID) have also been proposed to reduce progression and promotion, by indirectly reducing ROS mediated processes (DiGiovanni, 1992; Slaga & DiGiovanni, 1984).

Clinical investigations have shown that low calorie diet rich in fibre content like fruit and vegetables can significantly reduce the incidence of many types of cancers (Burton, 1999).

Cancer therapy: Although, endogenous and environmentally produced ROS is responsible for the induction of cancer, anti-cancer therapy using ionizing radiation and many of the chemotherapeutic drugs rely on the ROS mediated tumor cell kill produced by these agents. Nearly 70% of the damage caused by low LET ionizing radiation (extensively used in the radiotherapy of tumors) are caused by free radicals and require molecular oxygen for its efficiency (Riley, 1994; Hall, 2000). Anti-cancer drugs such as bleomycin, mitomycin C, anthracyclins, quinone compounds etc. also require adequate amount of intracellular oxygen for their cytotoxic effects mediated through the induction of DNA damage (Kalyanaraman *et al.*, 1989; Khan *et al.*, 1992). The efficacy of current day tumor therapy is, therefore, limited by the presence of hypoxic tumor cells and susceptibility of oxic normal tissues, besides the risk of treatment induced secondary tumors. Therefore, there has been continued interest in developing approaches for selective radiosensitization of tumors using sensitizers of tumor cells and protectors of normal tissues in cancer therapy (Varshney and Kale, 1990, 1996; Hall, 2000). Hyperbaric oxygen, electron affinity compounds like imidazoles, modifiers of blood flow and oxygen like pentoxyfilin and carbogen are among some of the approaches developed for radiosensitization, while radical scavengers and antioxidants like aminothiols, glutathione, vitamins, antioxidant enzymes etc. have been used as radio- and chemo-protectors (Wadleigh *et al.*, 1992; Mills, 1988; Capizzi, 1999; Jaakkola *et al.*, 1992; Hardmeier, 1997; Petkau *et al.*, 1976; Nordenson, 1978; Wong, 1995). However, currently available radiomodifiers (sensitizers or protectors) are either ineffective at tolerable doses or lack a differential effect between tumor and normal tissues. An approach based on the energy linked modification of DNA and cellular repair processes using a glucose analog and inhibitor of glycolytic ATP production has been found to differentially enhance radiation damage of tumors *in vitro* and *in vivo* (Jain & Pohlit, 1973; Jain *et al.*, 1990; Dwarakanath and Jain, 1989; Dwarakanath *et al.*, 1999, 2001). Since, the oxidative status and energy status are tightly coupled in cells, it is likely that radiomodification by metabolic inhibitors such as 2-Deoxy-D-Glucose (2-DG), 6-aminonicotinamide (6-AN) etc., is due to the alterations in the oxidative status. Preliminary results have indeed shown 2-DG and 6-AN induced changes in the intracellular oxidative status in irradiated cells (Varshney *et al.*, unpublished results). Dietary antioxidant depletion have also been shown to enhance tumor regression by inducing apoptosis and inhibiting proliferation in mice (Salganik *et al.*, 2000).

Neurodegenerative diseases

Neurodegenerative diseases have been suggested to involve oxidative stress mechanism (Floyd, 1999). Brain is considered abnormally sensitive to oxidative stress because it is enriched in the more easily peroxidizable fatty acids, consume about 20% of the total oxygen consumption for its relatively small weight, and is not enriched in antioxidant defenses (Floyd and Carney, 1992). Additionally, human brain has higher levels of iron in certain region like substantia nigra and in general has high levels of ascorbate (Zaleska *et al.*, 1989). When brain is injured by trauma or by ischemia, cell death tends to occur, and this iron could be released and may stimulate free radical reactions. Parkinson's disease is caused by death of cells in the substantia nigra (Adams and Odunze, 1991; Halliwell, 1992; Yoshikawa, 1993; Gerlach *et al.*, 1995). Management of Parkinson's disease is not possible by supplying vitamin E (Shoulson *et al.*, 1993). However, clinical trial with vitamin E has shown a beneficial effect in Alzheimer disease (Sano *et al.*, 1997). Similarly, deprenyl (an antioxidant) was effective in improving cognitive function in a clinical trial of dementia (Klebutrz *et al.*, 1998). This suggests that more studies are needed to understand the success and failure of various antioxidant-based trials.

Cardiovascular diseases

Oxidative stress has been implicated as an important etiologic factor in atherosclerosis and vascular dysfunction (Abe and Berk, 1998; Frei, 1999). Atherosclerosis is a chronic disease of large and medium sized arteries with hardening and loss of elasticity of the arterial walls and narrowing of the arterial lumen. Atherosclerosis is the principal cause of cardiovascular diseases leading to angina pectoris, myocardial infraction, and ischemic stroke. The atherosclerotic lesion develops in several stages, initially fatty streaks are formed as a consequence of lipid peroxidation of lipoproteins, fatty streaks then may develop into fibrous plaque with deposition of extracellular cell debris, lipids and cholesterol crystal (Schwartz, 1994). Antioxidants may inhibit atherogenesis (Esterbauer *et al.*, 1992) and improve vascular function by two different mechanisms. First, lipid soluble antioxidants such as α-tocopherol, β-carotene and lycopene present in low density lipoprotein (LDL) (Esterbauer et al, 1991) and water soluble antioxidants present in the extracellular fluid of the arterial wall, including ascorbic acid inhibit oxidative modification of LDL through an LDL-specific antioxidant action (Retsky *et al.*, 1992; Frei, 1999). Second, antioxidants present in the cells of the vascular wall decrease cellular production and release of reactive oxygen species, inhibit endothelial activation i.e. expression of adhesion molecules and vascular chemoattractants. Recently, uric acid concentration was found to be high in a person prone to atherosclerosis. The higher serum uric acid concentration seemed associated with elevated total serum antioxidant capacity among individuals with atherosclerosis. Hyperuricemia may be a compensatory mechanism to counteract oxidative damage related to atherosclerosis (Nieto *et al.*, 2000).

Endocrine disorders

Diabetes: Type I diabetes or insulin dependent diabetes mellitus (IDDM) is a complex, multifactorial disease involving severe destruction of the insulin-producing β cells (Neurp *et al.*, 1998; Oberley, 1988; Ludvigsson, 1993; Rabinovitch and Suarez, 1998). Now, it has been suggested that ROS play an important role in the pathogenesis of the IDDM (Ho Ermley and Tammy, 1999).

Patients with IDDM appear to have significant defects in antioxidant protection system compared to healthy persons (Maxwell *et al.*, 1997). Several studies have demonstrated a significant reduction in total antioxidant status in both plasma and serum samples from IDDM. There is a significant decrease in erythrocyte total glutathione, glutathione peroxidase, plasma α-tocopherol, and β-carotene (Dominguez *et al.*, 1998). It means low antioxidant defenses enhance oxidative stress in diabetic patient that can activate the transcription factor NFKB (Sehreek et al, 1992). ROS mediated activation of NFKB may be the modulator in the pathway that begins with the triggering of ROS production by multiple factors that leads to the ultimate destruction of β cells and the development of IDDM. Disregulation or aberrant activation of NFKB could also initiate inappropriate autoimmune and inflammatory responses. After translocation of NFKB in the nucleus it binds with DNA and modulates the expression of several genes (Baldwin, 1996). Increase in ROS in hyperglycemia can be prevented by an inhibitor of electron transport chain complex II, uncoupling protein I (Nishikawa *et al.*, 2000). Normalizing levels of mitochondrial ROS with each of these agents prevent activation of NFKB, formation of advanced glycation product responsible for development of cataract and accumulation of sorbitol in eyes.

Thyroid disorders: High basal metabolic rate (BMR) in hyperthyroid patient causes an increased production of ROS through hyperactivity of mitochondria. Antioxidant status is also altered to a great extent (Binachi *et al.*, 1999; Komosinska *et al.*, 2000). A significant decrease in cellular glutathione, glutathione peroxidase and catalase activities were observed. However, SOD gene activity is upregulated to counteract the high generation of superoxide radicals. Inspite of upregulation of SOD activity, the overall production of ROS is more in hyperthyroid persons. High ROS caused a myopathy and other related disorders in hyperthyroid subjects.

Supplementation of vitamins E and vitamin C has shown to improve treatment of hyperthyroidism (Adalt *et al.*, 1999).

Ischemia-reperfusion

Ischemia-reperfusion injury is considered to play a major role in the organ dysfunction accompanying trauma, shock and sepsis, also in cardiovascular diseases. Interruption of blood flow (ischemia) to an organ results in cascade of biochemical events that cause increased production of ROS on reperfusion (Omer *et al.*, 1991; Pincemail, 1995). Sources of free radicals in the reperfused organ are activation of xanthine oxidase and phospholipase, alteration in the electron transport chain, increased metabolism of arachidonic acid by cyclooxygenase and lipooxygenase, hemoglobin oxidation and iron release from ferritin etc. The role of antioxidants in the management of ischemia-reperfusion is difficult to decide. This is due to difficulties in the delivery of the drug to the specific target and the timing of antioxidant administration. It is therefore, crucial to define a therapeutic window for antioxidants during ischemia-reperfusion.

Reproductive disorders

Spermatozoa and leukocytes generate reactive oxygen species (ROS). ROS are involved in the regulation of sperm function such as capacitation and the acrosome reaction (Lamirande and Gagnon, 1993). But, infections of male genital tract lead to excessive ROS production. It has been demonstrated that excess generation of ROS can impair the sperm function leading to male infertility (Oschsendorf and Fuches, 1993, 1997; Sharma and Aggarwal, 1996; Oschsendorf, 1999). Spermatozoa lose their motility more rapidly, this is due to a high content of polyunsaturated fatty acids mainly docosahexaenoic acid in its plasma membrane (Jones *et al.*, 1979; Storey, 1997; Zalata *et al.*, 1998). Recent studies showed that peroxidative damage was the major cause of defective sperm motility in semen.

In addition, excess ROS diminished intracellular ATP, which led to a reduction in axonenal protein phosphorylation and sperm mobilization (Lamirande and Gagnon, 1992 a, b). DNA oxidation was also found to occur in spermatozoa (Lopes *et al.*, 1998). The reason for increased ROS was increased activities of xanthine oxidase, NADPH oxidase that is located in the sperm plasma membrane and of NO synthetase (Leclerec *et al.*, 1997, 1998; Perera *et al.*, 1996). Various cytokines that are present in the human semen such as transforming growth factor (TGF)-α (Nocera and Chu, 1993; Yie *et al.*, 1994), epidermal growth factor (EGF) (Hirata *et al.*, 1987), tumor necrosis factor (TNF)-α (Hussenet *et al.*, 1993) also increased ROS production. During infections, IL-2 and IL-8 concentrations in seminal plasma were found to be significantly higher than those of fertile man, while IL-4 concentration were lowered under these conditions (Omu *et al.*, 1998). ROS produced during infections of testes and epididymis are more harmful to spermatozoa due to longer contact time and lack of antioxidant protection. An infectious injury involving ROS in the prostate gland, seminal vesicle or epididymis could impair sperm function indirectly. Drug therapies that interferes with the generation of ROS as well as that modify ROS induced damage have received some attention (Cash, 1997; Kang *et al.*, 1998). They may be grouped into antioxidant substances (as substitutive therapy) (SOD, thiol groups, vitamins E, C), chelating agents (desferroxamine), inhibitors of superoxide ions (allopurinol) and superoxide scavenger flavonoids etc. (Robak and Marcinkiewicz, 1995) to be employed as substitutive therapy . Antibiotic therapy is also shown to improve sperm parameters in men with seminal infection by increasing antioxidant activity and IL-4 and by reducing IL-2 and IL-8 (Levert *et al.*, 1998).

CONCLUDING REMARKS

It is increasingly becoming clear that biological systems are constantly under attack by ROS, but also possess a plethora of antioxidant defence mechanisms that facilitate the system to cope-up with the oxidative stress. However, the inherent antioxidant defenses do not appear to be adequate at all the time and needs to be supplemented by appropriate antioxidant rich diet, besides chemopreventive measures. Results of many preventive strategies evolved and evaluated so far have indeed shown the benefit of such an approach in reducing the incidence and/or progress of ROS mediated diseases such as ageing, cancer, neurodegenerative disorders etc. However, many mechanistic aspects of ROS mediated pathogenesis clearly needs further understanding, besides improvements in systemic and substitutive therapy to ensure long and disease-free existence in this oxygen rich biosphere.

REFERENCES

1. Abe J. & Berk B.C. (1998) Reactive oxygen species as mediators of signal transduction in cardiovascular disease. *Trends Cardiovasc. Med.* 87, 59-64.

2. Adalt M., Inal-Elden M., Akalin A. & Efe B. (1999) Effects of propylthiouracil, propranolol and vitamin E on lipid peroxidation and antioxidant status in hyperthyroid patients. *Clin. Biochem.* 32(5), 363-367.

3. Adams J.D. Jr. & Odunze I.N. (1991) Oxygen free radicals and Parkinson's disease. *Free radical Biol. Med.* 10, 161-169.

4. Adler V. (1999) Regulation of JNK signaling by GSTp. *EMBO J.* 18, 1321-1334.

5. Albright C. D., Liu R., Mar M. R., Shin O. H., Vrablic A. S., Salganik R. I. & Zeisel S. H. (1997) Diet apoptosis and carcinogenesis. *In AICR Dietary Fat and Cancer,* Plenum Press. New Yourk. 97-107.

6. Alder V., Yin Z., Tew K.D. & Ronai Z. (2000) Rold of redox potential and reactive oxygen species in stress signaling. *Oncogene.* 18, 6104-6111.

7. Ames B. (1989) Endogenous oxidative DNA damage, aging and cancer. *Free Radic. Res. Commun.* 7, 121-128.

8. Baldwin A.S. Jr. (1996) The NFkB and IkB proteins; new discoveries and insights. *Annu. Rev. Immunol.* 14, 649-683.

9. Bandyopadhyay U., Das D. & Banerjje R.K. (1999) Reactive oxygen species: oxidative damage and pathogenesis. *Current Sci.* 77 (5), 658-666.

10. Binachi G., Solaroli E., Zacchernoi V., Grossi G., Bargossi A.M., Melchinoda N. & Marchesini G. (1999) Oxidative stress and antioxidant metabolites in patients with hyperthyroidism: effect of treatment. *Harmo. Meta. Res.* 31 (11), 620-624.

11. Birt D.F., Julius A.D., Runice C.E., White L.T., Lawson T. & Pour P.M. (1988) Enhancement of BOP-induced pancreatic carcinogenesis in selenium-fed Syrian golden hamsters under specific directly conditions. *Nutr. Cancer.* 11, 21-33.

12. Burdon R.H., Gill V. & Alliangana D. (1996) Hydrogen peroxide in relation to proliferation and apoptosis inBHK-21 hamster fibroblasts. *Free Radical Res.* 24, 81-93.

13. Burton R.C. Cancer control in Australia. *XV Asia Pacific Cancer Conference December 12th -15th 1999.*

14. Cai J. & Jones D.P. (1998) Superoxide in apoptosis mitochondrial generation trigered by cytochrome c loss. *J. Biol. Chem.* 273, 11401-11404.

15. Caldecott K.W., Taylor R.M., Moore D.J. & Whitehouse J. (2000) XRCCI, A central regulation of single strands break repair and base excision repair. *91st Proceedings of the American Association for Cancer Research,* 41, 891.

16. Capizzi R.L. (1999) Recent developments and emerging options: the role of amifostine as a broad-spectrum cytoprotective agent. *Seminar in Oncology.* 26 (2) (Suppl. 7), 1-2.

17. Carroll E., Cross M.D., Halliwell B., Borish E.T., Pryor W.A., Ames B.N., Saul R.L., McCord J.M. & Harman D. (1987) Oxygen radicals and human disease. *Annals. of Internal Med.* 107, 526-545.

18. Cash C.D. (1997) Are the reactive oxygen-derived species (ROS) interactive properties of the many therapeutic drug form various categories pertinent to their beneficial effect?. *Gen. Pharmacol.,* 28, 169-175.

19. Chance B., Sies H. & Boveris A. (1979) Hydroperoxide metabolism in mammalian organs. *Physiol Rev.* 59, 527.

20. Chanock S.J., El B.J., Smith R.M. & Babior B.M. (1994) The respiratory burst oxidase. *J. Biol. Chem.* 269, 24519-24522.

21. Cotgreave I.A. (1987) N-acetylcysteine and glutathione-dependent protective effects of PZ51 (Ebselen) against diquat-induced cytotoxicity in isolated hepatocytes. *Biochem. Pharmacol.* 36, 2899.

22. Dedon P.C., Plastarns J.P., Rouzer C.A. & Marnett L.J. (1998) Indirect mutagenesis by oxidative damage: formation of the pyrimidopurihone adduct of deoxyguanosine by base propenal. *Proc. Natl. Acad. Sci.* 95, 11113-11116.

23. Desai K.N., Wci H. & Lamartinicre. (1996) The preventive and therapeutic potential of the squalene-containing compound. Roidex, on tumor promotion and regression. *Cancer Lett.* 101 93-96.

24. DiGovanni J. (1992) Multistage carcingenesis in mouse skin. *Pharmacol Therp.* 54, 63-128.

25. Dimmeler S., Haendeler J., Nehls M. & Zeiher A. M. (1997) Suppression of apoptosis by nitric oxide via inhibition of interleukin-1b-converting enzyme (ICE)-like and cysteine protease protein (CPP)-32-like protease's. *J. Exp. Mws.*, 185, 601-607.

26. Dizdaroglu M. (1992a) Measurement of radiation-induced damage to DNA at the molecular level. *Int. J. Radiat Biol.* 61, 175-183.

27. Dominguez C., Ruiz E., Gussinye M. & Carrascosa A. (1998) Oxidative stress at onset and in early stages of type I diabetes in children and adolescents. *Dibetes Care.* 21, 1736-1742.

28. Dwarakanath B.S. & Jain V.K. (1989) Energy linked modification of the radiation response in a human cerebral glioma cell line. *Int. J. Radiaion. Oncol. Biol. Phys.* 17, 1033-1040.

29. Dwarakanath, B.S., Adhikari J.S. & Jain V.K. (1999) Hematoporphyrin derivatives potentiate the radiosensitizing effects of 2-DG in cancer cells. *Int. J. Radion Oncol. Biol. Phys.* 43, 1125-1133.

30. Dwarakanath, B.S., Zolzer, F., Chandna, S., Bauch, T., Adhikari J.S. Muller, W. U., Streffer, C. & Jain V. (2001) Heterogeneity in 2-deoxy-D-glucose induced modifications in energetics and radiation responses of human tumor cell lines. *Int. J. Radion Oncol. Biol. Phys.*(In Press).

31. Dypbukt J. M., Ankarcrona M., Burkitt M., Sjoholm A., Strom K., Orrenius S. & Nico-Tera P. (1994) Different prooxidant levels stimulate growth, trigger apoptosis, or produce necrosis of insulin-

secreting RINm5F cells. *J. Biol. Chem.*, 269, 30553-30560.

32. Esterbauer H., Dieber-Rotheneder M., Striegl G. & Waeg G., (1991) Role of vitamin E in preventing the oxidation of low-density lipoprotein. *Am. J. Clin Nutr.* 53, 314S-321S.

33. Esterbauer H., Gebicki J., Puhl H. & Jurgens G. (1992) The role of lipid peroxidation and antioxidants in oxidative modification of LDL. *Free Radic. Biol. Med.* 13, 341-390.

34. Fadeek B., Ahlin A., Henter J-I, Orrenius S. & Hampton M.B. (1998) Involvement of caspases in neutrophil apoptosis: Regulation by reactive oxygen species. *Blood.* In press.

35. Fahn S. & Cohen G. (1992) The oxidant stress hypothesis in Parkinson's disease: Evidence supporting it. *Ann. Neurol* 32, 804-812.

36. Feinendegen L.E., Loken M., Booz J., Muehlensiepen H., Sondhaus C. A. & Bond V.P., (1995) Cellular mechanisms of protection and repair induced by radiation exposure and their consequences for cell systems responses. *Stem Cells,* 13, 7-20.

37. Finkel T. & Holbrook N.J. (2000) Oxidants, oxidative stress and the biology of ageing. *Nature.* 408, 239-245.

38. Floyd R.A. & Carney J.M. (1992) Free radical damage to protein and DNA: mechanisms involved relevant observations on brain undergoing oxidative stress. *Ann. Neurol.* 32, S22-S27.

39. Floyd R.A. (1999) Antioxidants, oxidative stress, and degenerative neruological disorders. *Pro. of Soc. Exp. Biol. Med.* 236-245.

40. Frei B. (1999) On the role of vitamin C and other antioxidants in atherogenesis and vascular dysfunction. *Pro. Of Soc. Exp. Biol. Med.* 196-204.

41. Frenkel K., Karkoszka J., Glassman T., Dubin N., Toniolo P., Taioli E., Mooney L. & Kato I., (1988) Serum autoantibodies recognizing 5-hydroxymethyl-2-deoxyuridine, an oxidized DNA base, as biomarkers of cancer risk in women. *Cancer Epidemiol Biomarkerrs Prev.* 7, 49-57.

42. Fridovich I. (1995) Superoxide radical and superoxide dismutases. *Annu. Rev. Biochem.* 64, 97-112.

43. Gaeptar A.R., Scheerens H. & Vermeulen N.P. (1995) Oxygen and xenobiotic reductase activities of cytochrome P450. *Crit. Rev. Taxicol.* 25, 25-65.

44. Gayton K.Z. et al. (1998) Activation of mitogen-activated protein kinase by hydrogen peroxide role in cell survival following

oxidants injury. *J. iol. Chem.* 271, 4138-4142.

45. Gerlach M., Reiderer P. & Youdim M.B.H. (1995) Neuroprotective therapeutic strategies: Comparsion of experimental and clinical results. *Biochem. Pharmacol.* 50, 10-16.

46. Gutteridge J.M., & Halliwell B. (1990) The measurement and mechanism of lipid peroxidation in biological systems. *Trends Biochem Sci.* 15, 129-135

47. Ha H.C., Sirisoma N.S., Kuppusamy P., Zweier J.L., Woster P.M. & Casero R.A. Jr. (1998) The nautral polyamine spermine functions directly as a free radical scavenger. *Proc. Natl. Acad. Sci.* 95, 1140-1145.

48. Haley-Zitlin V. & Richardson A. (1993) Effect of dietary restriction on DNA repair and DNA damage. *Mutat. Res.* 295, 237-45

49. Hall E. (2000) Radiobiology for the Radiologist, Lippincot Williams & Wilkins, Philadelphia.

50. Halliwell B. & Dizdaroglu M. (1992) The Measurment of oxidative damage to DNA by HPLC and GC/MS techniques. *Free Radical Res. Commun.* 16, 75-87.

51. Halliwell B. (1992) Reactive oxygen species and the central nervous system. *J. Neurochem.* 59, 1609-1623.

52. Halliwell B., (2000) Free radicals and antioxidants: a personal view. *Nutrition Reviews,* 52 (8), 253264.

53. Hampton M. B. & Orrenius S. (1997) Dual regulation of caspase activity by hydrogen peroxide: implications for apoptosis. *FEBS Lett.,* 414, 552-556.

54. Hardmeier R., Hoeger H., Fang-Kircher S., Khoschsorur A. & Lubec G. (1997) Transcription and activity of antioxidant enzymes after ionizing irradiation in radiation-resistant and radiation-sensitive mice. *Proceeding of the National Academy of Science,* USA, 94, 7572-7576.

55. Hirata Y., Uchichashi M. & Hazama M., (1987) Epidermal growth factor in human seminal plasma. *Horm. Metab. Res.* 19, 35-37.

56. Ho E. & Bray T.M. (1999) Antioxidants, NFkB activation, and diabetogenesis (44445). *The Society for Exp. Biol. And Med.* 205-213.

57. Hunter M.I.S. (1985) Lipid peroxidation products and antioxidant proteins in plasma and cerebrospinal fluid from multiple sclerosis patients. *Neurochem Res.* 10, 1645.

58. Hursting S.D. & Kari F.W. (1995) Inhibition of tumorigenesis by by clorie restriction. *Cancer Bull,* 47, 505-510.

59. Hursting S.D., Slaga T.J., Fisccher S.M., DiGiovanni J. & Phang J.M. (1999) Mechanism-based cancer prevention approaches: targets, examples, and the use of transgenic mice. *J. of the Nat. Can. Inst.* 91, 215-225.

60. Hussenet F., Dousset B., & Cordonnier J.L. (1993) Tumour necorosis factor alpha and interleukin 2 in normal and infected human seminnal fluid. *Hum. Reprod.* 8, 409-411.

61. Imlay J. A. & Linn S. (1988) DNA damage and oxygen radical toxicity. *Science,* 240, 1302-1309.

62. Jaakkola K., Lahteenmaki P., Laakso J., Haju E., Tykka H., & Mahlberg K. (1992) Treatment with antioxidant and other nutrients in combination with chemotherapy and irradiation in patients with small-cell lung cancer. *Anticancer Res.,* 12, 599-606.

63. Jain V. & Pohlit W. (1973) Influence of energy metabolism on the repair of X-ray damage in living cells. III. Effects of 2-deoxy-D-glucose on liquid holding reactivation in yeast. *Biophysik.* 10, 137-142.

64. Jain V., Kalia V., Dwarakanath B.S. & Singh S.P. (1990) Modification of repair processes for improving tumor radiotherapy. In: Jain, V.; Goel, H.; Pohlit, W.; *eds.* Recent advances in radiation oncology. Indian Council of Medical Research, New Delhi. 103-121.

65. James S.J. & Muskhelishvili L. (1994) Rates of apoptosis and proliferation vary with caloric intake and may influence incidence of spontaneous hepatoma in C57BL6XC3H F1 mice. *Cancer Res.* 54, 5508-10.

66. Jones R., Mann T. & Sherins R., (1979) Peroxidative breakdown of phospholipids in human spermatozoa. Spermicidal properties of fatty acid peroxides, and protective action of seminal plasma. Ifertil. Steril. 31, 531-537.

67. Kalyanaraman B., Memec J. & Sinha B.K. (1989) Characterization of free radicals produced during oxidation of etoposide (VP-16) and its catechol and quinone derivatives. An ESR study. *Biochemistry.* 28, 4839-4846.

68. Kane D.J., Sarafian T.A., Anton R., Kahn H., Butler-Gralla E., Selverstone-Valentine J., Ord T. & Bredesen D.E. (1993) *Science,* 262, 1274-1277.

69. Kang M.Y., Tsuchiya M. & Packer L. (1998) *In Vitro* study on antioxidant potential of various drugs used in the preoperative

period. *Acta Anaesthesiol. Scand.* 42, 40-12.

70. Kennedy C.H., Cueto R., Bellinsky S.A., Lechner J.F. & Pryor W.A. (1998) Overexpression of hMTHI mRNA: a molecular marker of oxidative stress in lung cancer cells. *FEBS Lett.*, 429, 17-20.

71. Khan S., Ramwani J.J. & O'Brien P.J. (1992) Hepatocyte toxicity of mechlorethamine and other alkylating anticancer drugs. *Biochem Pharmacol.* 34, 1962-1967.

72. Komosinska-Vassev K., Olczyk-K., Kucharz-E J, Marcisz-C, Winsz-Szczotka-K. & Kotubka- A (2000) Free radical activity and antioxidant defense mechanism in patient with hyperthyroidism due to graves disease: During therapy, *Clin Chim Acta*, 300 (1-2), 107-117.

73. Koop D.R. (1992) Oxidative and reductive metabolism by cytochrome P450 2E1. *FASEB J.* 6, 724-730.

74. Ku H.H., Brunk U. T. & Sohal R.S. (1993) Relationship between mitochondrial superoxide and hydrogen peroxide production and longevity of mammalian species. *Free Radical Biol. Med.* 15 621-627.

75. Lamirande E. & Gagnon C. (1992a) Reactive oxygen species and human spermatozoa I: Effects on the motility of intact spermatozoa and sperm axonemes. *J. Androl.*, 13, 368-378.

76. Lamirande E. & Gagnon C. (1993) A positive role for the superoxide anion in trigering hyperactivation and capacitation of human spermatozoa. *J. Androl.*, 16, 21-25.

77. Lamirande E. & Gagnon C., (1992b) Reactive oxygen species and human spermatozoa. II: Depletion of adenosine triphosphate. *J. Androl.* 13,379-286.

78. Leclerc P., de Lamirande E. & Gagnon C. (1997) Regulation of protein tyrosine phonphorylation and human sperm capacitation by reactive oxygen derivatives. *Free Rad. Biol. Med.* 22, 643-656.

79. Leclerc P., de Lamirande E. & Gagnon C. (1998) Interaction between Ca2+ cyclie 3'.5' adenosine monophosphate, the superoxide anion and tyrosine phosphorylation pathways in the regulation of human sperm capacitation. *J. ndrol.*, 19, 434-443.

80. Lenon S.V., Martin S.J. & Cotter T.G. (1991) Cell prolif., 24, 203-214.

81. Leonard Hayflick (2000) The future of ageing. *Nature,* 408, 267-269.

82. Levert H., Gressier B. & Moutard I. (1998) Azithromycin impact on neutrophil oxidative metabolism depends on exposure time. *Inflammation.* 22, 191-201.

83. Lopes S., Jurisicova A. & Sun J.G. (1998) Reactive oxygen species: potential cause for DNA fragmentation in human spermatozoa. *Hum. Reprod.* 13, 896-900.

84. Ludvigsson J. (1993) Intervention at diagnosis of type I diabetes using either antioxidants or photopheresis. *Diabetes Metab Rev.* 9, 329-336.

85. Lynch R.E. & Fridovich I. (1978) Permeation of the erythrocyte strom by superoxide radical. *J. Biol. Chem.* 253, 4697.

86. Marklund S.L. (1986) Ceruloplasmin, extracellular-superoxide dismutase, and scavenging of superoxide anion radical. *J. Free Radical Biol. Med.* 2, 255.

87. Masoro E.J. (2000) Caloric restriction and aging: an update. *Exp. Gerontol.* 35, 299-305 .

88. Mates J.M. & Sanchez-Jimenez F.M. (2000) Role of reactive oxygen species in apoptosis; implications for cancer therapy. *The Int. J. of Bioc.& Cell Biol.* 32, 157-170.

89. Mates J.M., Perez-Gomez C. & De-Castro I.M. (1999) Antioxidant enzymes and human diseases. *Clin. Biochem.* 32(8), 595-603.

90. Maxwell S.R., Thomason H., Sandler D., Leguen C., Baxter M.Z., Thorpe G.H., Jones A.F. & Barnett A.H. (1997) Antioxidant status in patients with uncomplicated insulin-dependent and non-insulin-dependent diabetes mellitus. *Eur. J. Clin. Invest.* 27, 484-490.

91. McCall MR. & Fei B. (1999) Can antioxidant vitamins maternally reduce oxidative damage in humans. *Free Radical Biol. Med.* 26, 1034-1053.

92. McCord J.M. (2000) The evolution of free radicals and oxidative stress. *The American J. of Med.* 108, 652-659.

93. McGovan A.J., Fernandes R.S., Samali A. & Cotter T.G. (1996) *Biochem. Soc. Trans.*, 24, 229-233.

94. Mills E. E. D. (1988) The modifying effect of betacarotene on radiation and chemotherapy- induced oral mucositis. *Br. J. Cancer,* 57, 416-417.

95. Mohr S., Zech B., Lapetina E. G. & Brune B. (1997) Inhibition of caspase-e by S-nitrosation and oxidation caused by nitric oxide. *Bicohem. Biophys. Res. Commun.*, 238, 387-391.

96. Moslen M.T. (1994) Reactive oxygen species in normal physiology, cell injury and phagocytosis. *Adv. Exp. Med. Biol.* 366, 17-27.

97. Mustafa G, Kutay F Z, Temocin S, Hanninen O (2000) Cellular and clinical implications of glutathione, *Ind.J. Exp. Biol.*, 38, 625-634.

98. Neurp J., Mandrup-poulsen T., Molvig J., Helqvist S., Wogensen L. & Egeber J. (1988) Mechanisms of pancreatic b-cell destruction in type I diabetes. *Diabetes Care.* 11 (suppl. 1), S16-S23.

99. Nieto F.J., Iribarren C., Dross M.D., Comstock G.W. & Cutler R.G. (2000) Uric acid and serum antioxidant capacity: a reaction to athersoclerosis?. *Atherosclerosis.* 148, 131-139.

100. Nishikawa T., Edelstein D., Di X. L., Yamagishi S-I., Matsumura T., Kaneda Y., Yorek M.A., Beebe D., Oates P.J., Hammest H-P., Giardino I. & Brownlee M. (2000) Normalizing mitochondrial superoxide production blocks three pathways of hyperglycaemic damage. *Nature.* 404 (13), 787-790.

101. Nocera M. & Chu M.T. (1993) Transforming growth factor beta as an immunosuppressive protein in human seminal plasma. *Am. J. Repord. Immunol.* 30, 1-8.

102. Nordenson I., (1978) Effects of superoxide dismutase and catalase on radiation-induced chromosome aberrations: dose and cell cycle dependence. *Hereditas.*, 89, 163-167.

103. Oberley L.W. (1988) Free radicals and diabetes. *Free Radic. Biol. Med.* 5, 113-124.

104. Ochsendorf E.R. & Fuchs J. (1993) Oxidative imbalance and male infertility In fuchs. J. and Packer L. (ed) *Oxidative stree on Dermatology.* Marcel Dekker Co. New York. Hong Kong. 481-529.

105. Ochsendorf F.R. (1999) Infections in the male genital tract and reactive oxygen species. *Human Reproduction Update.*, 5(5), 399-420.

106. Omar B., McCord J. & Downey J. (1991) Ischemia-reperfusion In: H. Sies (ed.): *Oxidative Stress. Oxidants and Antioxidants.* Academic Press, London, 494-527.

107. Onu. A.E., al-Othman S. & Mohamad A.S. (1998) Antibiotic therapy for seminal infection. Effect on antioxidant activity and T-yelper cytokines. *J. Repord. Med.* 43, 857-864.

108. Oteiza P. I., Clegg M. S., Zago M. P. & Keen C. L. (2000) Zinc deficiency induces oxidative stress and ap-1 activation in 3T3 cells. *Free Radical Biol. Med.*, 28 (7), 1091-1099.

109. Pacht E.R. & Davies W.B. (1988) Role of transferrin and cerulopasmin in antioxidant activity of lung epithelial lining fluid. *J. Appl. Qhysiol.* 64, 2092.

110. Pahl H.L & Baeurle P.A. (1994) *Bio. Essay*, 16, 497-502.

111. Perchellet J.P., Perchellet E.M., Gali H.U. & Gao X.M. (1995) Oxidant stress and multistage carcinogenesis. In: Mukhtar H. editor. Skin cancer mechanism and human relevance. *Boca Raton (FL): CRC Press,* 145-80.

112. Perera D.M.D., Katz M. & Heenbanda S.R. (1996) Nitric oxide synthase inhibitor N^G-monomethyl-L-areginine perserves sperm motility after swim-up. *Fertil Steril.* 66, 830-833.

113. Petkau A., Chelack W. S. & Pleskach S. D., (1976) Protection of post-irradiated mice by superoxide dismutase. *Int. J. of Rad. Biol.*, 29, 297-299.

114. Pincemail J. (1995) Free radicals and antioxidants in human diseases. *Analysis of Free Radical in Biol. System.* 83-97.

115. Rabinovitch A., & Suarez-Pinzon W.L., (1998) Cytokines and their roles in pancreatic islet b-cell destruction and insulin-dependent diabetes mellitus. *Bichoem. Pharmacol.* 55, 1139-1149.

116. Retsky K.L., Freeman M.W., & Frei B. (1993) Ascorbic acid oxidation product (s) protect human low-density lipoprotein against atherogenic modification: Anti-rather than pro-oxidant activity of vitamin C in the presence of transition metal ions. *J. Biol. Chem.* 268, 1304-1309.

117. Richter C. (1992) Reactive oxygen and DNA damage in mitochondria. *Mutat. Res.* 275, 249-255.

118. Riley PA. (1994) Free radicals in biology: oxidative stress and the effects of ionizing radiation. *Int. J. Radiat. Biol.* 65, 27-33.

119. Robak J. & Marcinkiewicz E. (1995) Scavenging of reactive oxygen species as the mechanism of drug action. *Pol. J. Pharmacol.* 47, 89-98.

120. Robinson J.M. & Badwey J.A. (1994) Production of active oxygen species by pahagocytic leukocytes. *Immunol. Ser.* 60, 159-178.

121. Salganik R. I., Albright C. D., Rodgers J., Kim J., Zeisel S. H., Sivashinskiy M. S. & Dyke T. A. V. (2000) Dietary antioxidant depletion: enhancement of tumor apoptosis and inhibition of brain tumor growth in transgenic mice. *Carcinognesis.*, 21 (5), 909-914.

122. Samali A., Nordgren H., Zhivotovsky B., Peterson E. & Orrenius S. (1999) A comparative study of apoptosis and necrosis in HipG2 cells: oxidant-induced caspase inactivation leads to necrosis. *Biochem. And Biophysi. Res. Communication.*, 255, 6-11.

123. Sano M., Ernesto M.S., Thomas R.G., Klauber MR., Schafer K.,

Grundman M., Woodbury P., Growdon J., Cotman C.W., Pfeiffer E. & Schneider L.S. (1997) A controlled trial of selegiline, a-tocopherol, or both as treatment of Alzheimer's disease. *N Engl. J. Med.* 336, 1216-1222.

124. Schwartz C.J. & Valente AJ. (1994) The pathogenesis of atherosclerosis. In: Frei B, Ed. Natural Antioxidants in Human Health and Disease. San Diego: *Academic Press,* 287-302.

125. Sehreek R., Albermann K. & Baeuorle P.A. (1992) Nuclear factor kappa B: An oxidative stress-responsive transcription factor of eukaryotic cells (a reivew). *Free Radic. Res.* 17, 221-237.

126. Sen C. K. & Packer L. (1991) Antioxidant and redox regulation of gene transcription. *FASEB J.*, 10, 2247-2258.

127. Sharma R.K. & Agarwal A. (1996) Role of reactive oxygen species in male infertility. *Urology*, 48, 835-850.

128. Shigenaga M.K., Hagen T.M. & Ames B.N. (1994) Oxidative damage and mitochondrial decay in ageing. *Proc. Natl. Acad. Sci.* 91, 10771-10778.

129. Shimizu S., Eguchl Y., Kosaka H., Kamiike W., Masuda H. & Tsujimoto Y. (1995) *Nature* 374, 811-813.

130. Shinde U.A., Mehta A.A. & Goyal R.K. (2000) Nitric oxide: a Molecule of the millennium. *Ind. J. of Exp. Biol.* 38, 201-210.

131. Shoulson I., Fahn S., Kieburtz K., Lang A., Langston J.W. & Olanow C.W. (1993) Effects of tocopherol and deprenyl on the progression of disability in early Parkinson's disease *N Engl. J. Med.* B328B, 176-183.

132. Slaga T.J. & DiGiovanni J. (1984) Inhibition of chemical carcinogenesis. In: searle CE, editor. American Chemical Society Monography 182. *Wash Ington (DC): American Chemical Society*, 2, 1279-94.

133. Slater A. F., Nobel C. S. & Orrenius S. (1995) The role of intracellular oxidants in apoptosis. *Biochim. Biophys. Acta,* 1271, 59-62.

134. Slater A.F.G., Nober C.S.I., van den Dobbelsteen D.J. & Orrenius S. (1996) *Cell Death Different.*, 3, 57-62.

135. Stadtman E.R. & Oliver C.N. (1991) Metal-catalyzed oxidation of proteins. Physiological consequences. *J. Biol. Chem.* 266, 2005-2008.

136. Stanley L.A.(1995) Molecular aspects of chemical carcinogenesis: the roles of oncogenes and tumour suppressor genes. *Toxicology,* 96, 173-194.

137. Storey B.T. (1997) Biochemistry of the induction and prevention of lipoperoxidative damage in human spermatozoa. *Mol. Hum. Reprod.*, 3, 203-213.

138. Sugiyama H., Kashihara N., Makino H., Yamasaki Y. & Ota Z. (1996) Reactive oxygen species induce apoptosis in cultured human mesangial cells. *J. Am Soc. Nephrol.*, 7, 2357-2363.

139. Sundstrom H.., Korpela H, Vinikka L. & Kauppila A. (1984) Serum selenium and glutathione peroxidase, and plasma lipid peroxides in uterine, ovarian or vulvar cancer, and their responses to antioxidant in patients with ovarian cancer. *Cancer Lett.* 24, 1-10.

140. Supakar P.C., Jung M.H., Song C.S., Chatterjee B. & Roy A.K. (1995) Nuclear factor kappa B functions as a negative regulator for the rat androgen receptor gene and NF-kappa B activity increases during the age-dependent desensitization of the liver. *J. Biol. Chem.* 270, 837-842.

141. Suzuki Y. J., Forman H. J. & Sevaninan A. (1997) Oxidant as stimulators of signal transduction. *Free Radical Biol. Med.*, 22, 269-285.

142. Tores-Roca J.F., Lecoeur H., Amatore C. & Gougeon M.I. (1995) *Cell Death Differ.*, 2, 309-319.

143. Turrens J.F. (1997) Superoxide production by the mitochondrial respiratory chain. *Biosci. Rep.* 17, 3-8.

144. Varshney R. & Kale R. K. (1990) Effects of calmodulin antagonists on radiation-induced lipid peroxidation in microsomes. *Int. J. Rad. Biol.*, 58, 733-743.

145. Varshney R. & Kale R. K. (1996) Physico-chemical pathways in radioprotective action of calmodulin antagonists. *Rad. Phys. Chem.*, 47, 595-599.

146. Wadleigh R.G., Redman R.S., Graham M.L., Krasnow S.H., Anderson A. & Cohen M.H. (1992) Vitamin E in the treatment of chemotherapy-induced oral mucositis. *Am. J. Med.*, 92, 481-484.

147. Wang X., McGullough K.D., Franke T.F. & Holbrook N.J. (2000) Epidermal growth factor receptor dependent AKT activation by oxidative stress enhances cell survival. *J. Biol. Cem.* 275, 14624-14631.

148. Weindruch T. & Walford R.L. editors. (1988) The retardation of aging and disease by dietary restriction. *Springfield (IL): C. Thomas*, 1-29I.

149. Weisburger J.H., Rivenson A., Kingston D.G., Wilkins T.D., Van Tassell R.L. & Nagao M. (1995) Dietary modulationof the carcinogenicity of the heterocyclic amines. *Princess Takamatsu*

Symp. 23, 240-50.

150. Wong G. H. W., (1995) Protective roles of cytokines against radiation: induction of mitochondrial MnSOD. *Biochimica et Biophysica Acta,* 1271, 205-209.

151. Yie S.M., Lobb D.K. & Clark D.A. (1994) Identification of a transforming growth factor alpha-like molecule in human seminal plasma. *Fertil Seril.* 61, 129-135.

152. Yoshikawa T. (1993) Free radicals and their scavengers in Parkinson's disease. *Eur. Neurol.* (Suppl. 1) 33, 60-68.

153. Zalata A.A., Christophe A.B. & Depuydt C.E. (1998) The fatty aci composition of phospholipids of spermatozoa from intertild patients. *Mol. Hum. Reprod.* 4, 111-118.

154. Zaleska M.M., Nagy K. & Floyed R.A. (1989) Iron-induced lipid peroxidation inhibition of dopamine synthesis in stratum synaptosomes. *Neuro. Chemistry.* 14, 597-605.

155. Zhong L.T., Sarafian T., Kane D.J., Charles A.C., Mah S.P., Edwards R.H. & Bredesen D.E. (1993) *Proc. Natl. Acad. Sci.*, USA, 90, 4533-4537.

IMPAIRMENT OF AORTIC VASCULAR RESPONSES TO VASOACTIVE AGENTS IN SPONTANEOUSLY HYPERTENSIVE DIABETIC RATS

MOHAMMAD FAHIM AND SYED JAMAL MUSTAFA

Department of Pharmacology, School of Medicine East Carolina University, Greenville, NC 27858

Abstract

This study was designed to investigate the effect of streptozotocin (STZ)-induced diabetes on vascular responses to vasoactive agents in hypertensive rats. Isometric contractions were measured in isolated aortic rings. Aortic rings with or without endothelium showed significantly higher contractile response to phenylephrine (PE) in WKY than SHR. STZ treatment produced significant attenuation in the PE responses in both the groups (WKY-STZ, SHR-STZ). Endothelium removal caused attenuation of PE responses in aortic rings from all the groups except SHR-STZ. However, endothelium removal did not abolish the differences in PE response between non-diabetic and diabetic rats. N^6-monomethyl-L-arginine (30 mM) (L-NMMA), increased contractions to PE in aorta from non-diabetic rats (WKY, SHR) whereas the contractions in diabetic rats were unaltered. Indomethacin (10 mM) had no effect on the contractile responses to PE in aortic rings from WKY and WKY-STZ rats while PE contractions were significantly attenuated by indomethacin in SHR and SHR-STZ rats. Acetylcholine (ACh) produced dose-dependent relaxation in the endothelium-intact rings in all groups. Removal of endothelium abolished the ACh-mediated relaxation. Relaxant response to ACh was suppressed in SHR as compared to WKY. Diabetes caused a significant attenuation in ACh response in WKY-STZ and SHR-STZ group. Isoproterenol (ISOP) produced concentration-dependent relaxation in the aortic rings from all the groups. Rings from SHR and STZ treated rats showed attenuated response to ISOP. Endothelium removal abolished these differences. Sodium nitroprusside (SNP) produced similar dose-dependent relaxant response in endothelium-intact and -denuded rings in all groups. In conclusion, enhanced impairment of contractile and relaxant response in STZ-induced diabetes in SHR aorta demonstrates the aggravation of vascular disorder due to the added stress of diabetes in hypertensive rats.

INTRODUCTION

The major pathological features of diabetes mellitus are the morphological and functional alterations of blood vessels (Harris and MacLeod KM, 1988; MacLeod et al., 1986; Mayhan, 1992) and heart (Dai and Neill, 1992; Garvey et al., 1993). Relaxation of the aorta in response to the agonists which release endothelium-derived relaxing factor (EDRF) are impaired in diabetic animals (Durante et al., 1988; Mayhan 1992; Meraji et. al., 1987; Oyama et al., 1986; Tesfamariam et al., 1989). The mechanism of impaired responses of the aorta in diabetic animals appears to be controversial (Mayhan, 1992; Oyama et al., 1986). There are several reports showing that aerterial hypertension causes structural and functional changes in blood vessels (Azvedo and Osswald, 1992; Dai and Neill, 1992). Hypertension is known to aggravate the occurrence of cardiovascular complications associated with diabetes (Bell, 1989; Fein et al., 1989; 1980; 1990). In spontaneously hypertensive rats (SHR), experimentally induced diabetes caused a greater depression in cardiac function (Rodrigues and Neill, 1986).

The impairment of endothelium-dependent vascular smooth muscle response in hypertension is well documented (Azvedo and Osswald, 1992; Bassenge, 1992; Biaggioni, 1992; Fahim et al., 1993; Li and Bukoski, 1993; Lockett et al., 1986; Luscher et al., 1987). In diabetes, impairment of endothelium-dependent vascular smooth muscle relaxation (Mayhan, 1992; Tesfamariam et al., 1989) is described to be specific for receptor-dependent release of EDRF, since response of calcium ionophore A 23187 is reported to be unimpaired in diabetes (Pieper and Gross, 1988). Others have found attenuated response to A 23187 in diabetes (Durante et al., 1988). Since hypertension is known to be more prevalent in diabetes (Raptis, 1982), therefore, the combination of two stresses may increase the severity of circulatory disorders (Rodrigues and Neill, 1986). These studies (Bell, 1989; Fein et al., 1980; Rodrigues and Neill, 1986) suggest that in the presence of one disease (hypertension or diabetes) the occurrence of the other causes further impairment of cardiac function. However, influence of the combination of the two stresses on vascular responsiveness is not clearly understood. Therefore, the present study was conducted to examine the effects of hypertension and/or diabetes on contractile/ relaxing properties of rat aorta.

MATERIALS AND METHODS

Male WKY rats were used as normotensive animals and age matched (15-17 weeks) SHR as a hypertensive model. Rats were purchased from Taconic, NY, and housed in plastic cages at room temperature. They were kept on a twelve hour light/dark cycle and were allowed free access to standard laboratory food (Purina Rat Chow) and water *ad libitum.* Rats were divided randomly into non-diabetic normotensive (WKY), normotensive diabetic (WKY-STZ), non-diabetic hypertensive (SHR), and hypertensive diabetic (SHR-STZ) groups. Rats in WKY-STZ and SHR-STZ groups were injected with 65 mg/kg i.p. streptozotocin (STZ) to induce diabetes (Mayhan, 1992). The other two non-diabetic groups (WKY, SHR) were injected with vehicle (citrate buffer, pH = 4.5). Blood pressure, blood glucose and body weights were recorded before injections and every week thereafter till the day of experiment after 8 weeks. Blood pressure was monitored in conscious rats by using sphygmomanometer (model 20-NW), pulse amplifier (model 59) and HR-pressure meter (model 72, Inc. Woodland Hills, CA) using a polygraph (model 7D, Grass Inst. Co. Quincy, MA). Blood glucose was determined by using a blood glucose sensor (Exac.Tech, Medsense, Cambridge, MA). Rats with a blood glucose concentration of greater than 300 mg/dl were considered diabetic.

For organ bath experiments, rats were sacrificed by decapitation. Blood was collected for the measurement of total cholesterol and triglycerides using Sigma kits (St. Louis, MO). Aortae were dissected and cleaned of fat and connective tissue. Rings of approximately 4 mm in length were prepared and mounted in 10 ml organ baths filled with Krebs-Henseleit solution and oxygenated with 95% O_2 + 5% CO_2 (pH 7.4, 37°C). The composition of Krebs-Hanseleit buffer was (mM): NaCl, 118; KCl, 4.8; $MgSO_4$, 1.2; $NaHCO_3$, 25; $CaCl_2$, 2.5; and glucose, 11. Changes in isometric force were measured with force transducers (Grass FT.03) connected to Sensormedics dynographs (R 611). Rings were equilibrated for 1 hour under an initial tension of 2 g (determined separately from the length-tension relationship); the buffer being changed every 15 min. After equilibration, rings were challenged with 0.5 mM PE (ED_{75}), until constant reproducible contractions were achieved. The integrity of endothelium was assessed by the ability of Ach (10^6 M) to relax the PE-contracted vascular rings. PE was added in a cumulative fashion to obtain concentration-response curves. ACh, ISOP and SNP were added in a cumulative fashion to the bath to obtain relaxation response curves in 0.5 mM PE contracted rings. The drug additions were made only after the previous response had stabilized.

Statistical Analysis

The relaxation responses to ACh, ISOP and SNP were expressed as a percent decline in steady state contraction.

All values are expressed as mean ± SEM. Two way analysis of variance (ANOVA) was used for concentration-response curves. Tukey-Kramer multiple comparison test was used for comparison between the groups. The p values for statistical significance was set at the 0.05 level.

Drugs: Streptozotocin, phenylephrine hydrochloride, isoproterenol, acetylcholine chloride, sodium nitroprusside, indomethacin, L-arginine hydrochloride, N^6- methyl-L-arginine were purchased from Sigma Chemical Co., (St. Louis, MO). Streptozotocin was freshly dissolved in citrate buffer (pH=4.5) immediately before use at a concentration of 65 mg/ml; all other drugs were dissolved in water.

RESULTS

Diabetes mellitus in the rats was characterized by marked and sustained increase in blood glucose (> 400 mg/dl) (Fig. 1). The non-diabetic groups (WKY, SHR) did not show a significant change in blood glucose throughout the study (Fig. 1). There was a marked rise in blood glucose in STZ groups one week after injections (Fig. 1). After rapid increase in the first week following STZ injection, blood glucose continued to rise slowly until it reached a peak value at 4 weeks after STZ injections in both the groups (WKY-STZ, SHR-STZ) and remained at that level until the termination of experiment (8 weeks after STZ injection) (Fig. 1). Increase in the blood glucose levels of SHR-STZ was significantly ($P < 0.05$) higher than WKY-STZ throughout the experimental period(Fig.1).

Systolic blood pressure (SBP) of SHR was significantly ($P < 0.05$) higher than those of age matched WKY rats (Fig. 1). The STZ treatment did not alter the SBP in either group of rats. WKY had significantly higher body weight (BW) (316± 3 g) than SHR (221 ± 2 g) at the time of STZ injection and remained higher during the experimental period (Fig. 1). BW of WKY and SHR increased with time

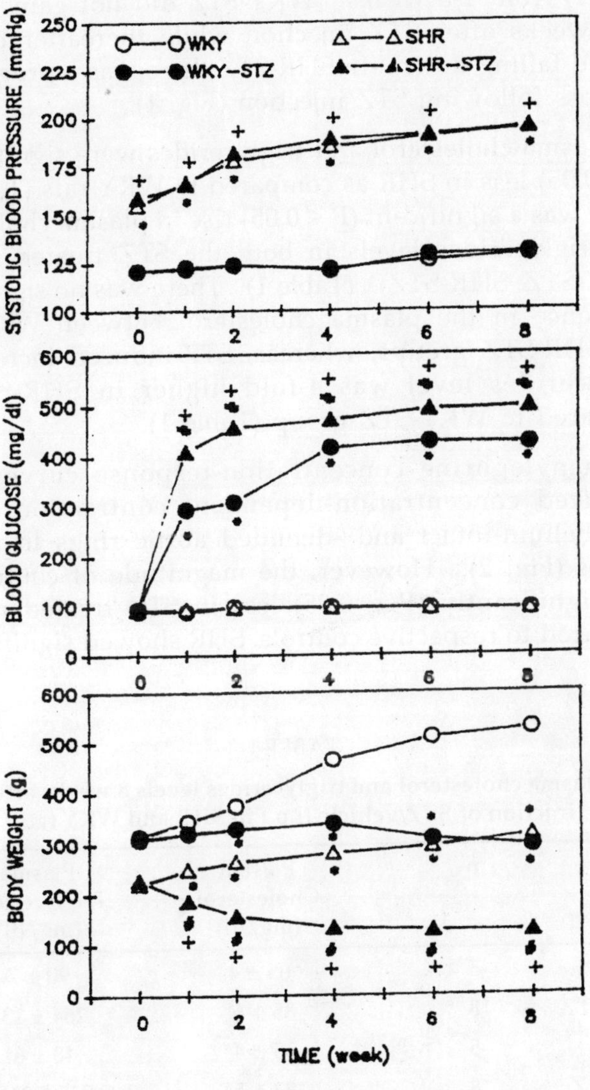

Figure 1. Time course of the effects of STZ/vehicle injection in WKY and SHR on the systolic blood pressure (top), blood glucose (middle), and body weight (bottom). Injections were given at time 0. Values are means ± SEM obtained from five WKY (o), eight WKY-STZ (•), five SHR (Δ), and eight SHR-STZ (▲) rats. * $P < 0.05$ WKY vs WKY-STZ or $P<0.05$ WKY vs SHR. # $P < 0.05$ SHR vs SHR-STZ.

(Fig. 1) from 1-8 weeks. WKY-STZ did not gain BW for four weeks after STZ injection while thereafter the BW started falling down. In SHR-STZ there was a progressive BW loss following STZ injection (Fig. 1).

Plasma cholesterol and triglycerides were significantly ($P < 0.05$) less in SHR as compared to WKY rats (Table 1). There was a significant ($P < 0.05$) rise in plasma cholesterol and triglycerides levels in both the STZ treated groups (WKY-STZ, SHR-STZ) (Table 1). There was no significant difference in the plasma cholesterol between WKY-STZ and SHR-STZ groups, whereas, STZ-induced increase in triglycerides level was 4-fold higher in SHR-STZ as compared to WKY-STZ group (Table 1).

Phenylephrine concentration-response curves: PE produced concentration-dependent contraction of the endothelium-intact and -denuded aortic rings in all the groups (Fig. 2). However, the magnitude of contraction was significantly ($P < 0.05$) less in STZ treated rats as compared to respective controls. SHR showed significantly

TABLE 1

Plasma cholesterol and triglycerides levels 8 weeks after injction of STZ/vehicle (i.p.) in SHR and WKY rats

	n	Plasma Cholesterol (mg/dl)	Plasma Triglycerides (mg/dl)
WKY	5	65 ± 4	90 ± 7
WKY-STZ	8	85 ± 6*	264 ± 13*
SHR	5	35 ± 4*	48 ± 6*
SHR-STZ	8	83 ± 5*	935 ± 21$^{\#+}$

Value are means ± SEM; n, number of animal in each group.

*P < 0.05 WKY vs. WKY-STZ or WKY vs SHR

#P < 0.05 SHR vs. SHR-STZ.

*P < 0.05 WKY-STZ vs. SHR-STZ

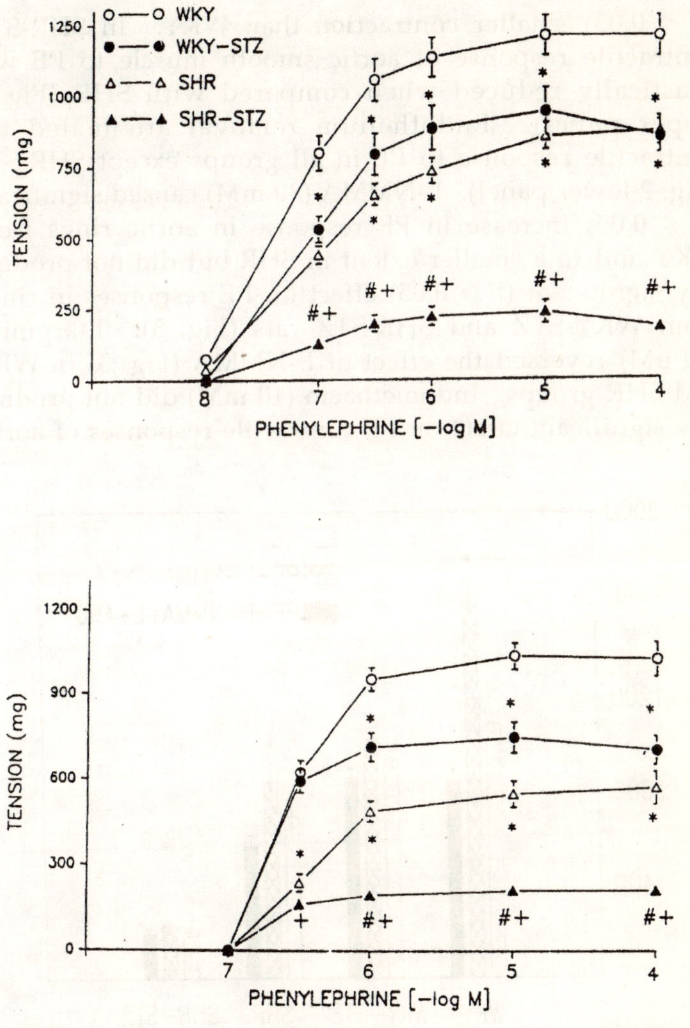

Figure 2. Cumulative concentration-response curves to phenylephrine in endothelium-intact (upper panel) and -denuded (lower panel) aortic rings from WKY (o), WKY- STZ (●), SHR (Δ), and SHR-STZ (▲). The values are mean ± SEM of four to six rings from aorta of each of five WKY, eight WKY-STZ, five SHR, and eight SHR-STZ rats. * P < 0.05 WKY vs WKY-STZ or WKY vs SHR. # P < 0.05 SHR vs SHR-STZ; + P < 0.05 WKY-STZ vs SHR-STZ.

($P < 0.05$) smaller contraction than WKY. In SHR-STZ contractile response of aortic smooth muscle to PE was drastically reduced when compared with SHR (Fig. 2 upper panel). Endothelium removal attenuated the contractile response to PE in all groups except SHR-STZ (Fig. 2 lower panel). L-NMMA (30 mM) caused significant ($P < 0.05$) increase in PE response in aortic rings from WKY and to a smaller extent in SHR but did not produce any significant ($P > 0.05$) effect on PE responses in rings from WKY-STZ and SHR-STZ rats (Fig. 3). L-arginine (50 µM) reversed the effect of L-NMMA (Fig. 3) in WKY and SHR groups. Indomethacin (10 mM) did not produce any significant effect on PE contractile responses of aortic

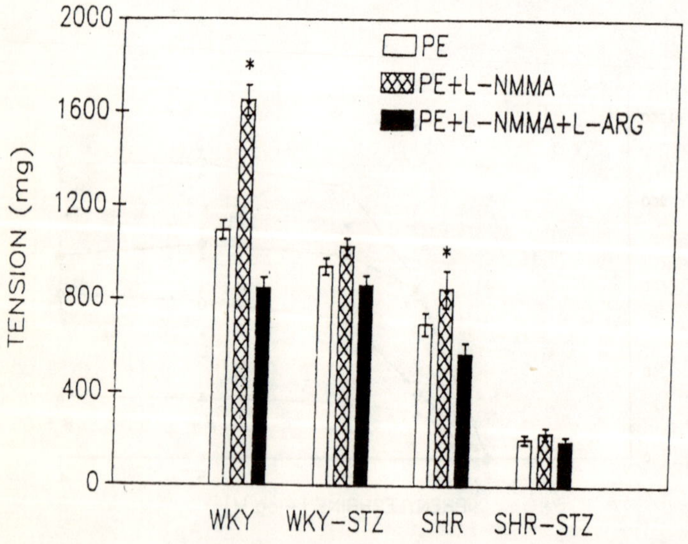

Figure 3. Changes by N^G-monometyl-L-arginine (L-NMMA, 30 mM) and L-NMMA plus L-arginine (50 mM) of phenylephrine-induced contractions in endothelium-intact aortic rings from WKY, WKY-STZ, SHR, and SHR-STZ rats. Values are means ± SEM of observations on four rings from each of five WKY, eight WKY-STZ, five SHR, and eight SHR-STZ rats. * $P < 0.05$ phenylephrine (PE) vs PE + L-NMMA in respective group.

rings with intact endothelium from WKY and WKY-STZ rats but caused significant ($P < 0.05$) attenuation of PE responses in rings from SHR and SHR-STZ rats (Fig. 4).

Acetylcholine concentration-response curves: ACh (10^{-9}- 10^{-4}M) produced concentration-dependent relaxations of the endothelium-intact aortic rings precontracted with PE. The vasorelaxant response to ACh was significantly ($P < 0.05$) smaller in SHR as compared to WKY rats (Fig. 5). Aortic rings from diabetic rats (WKY-STZ, SHR-STZ) showed significantly ($P < 0.05$) attenuated response to ACh compared to respective non-diabetic group (Figs. 5 and 6). Impairment of ACh relaxant response in the aortic rings of diabetic animals was observed in the form of

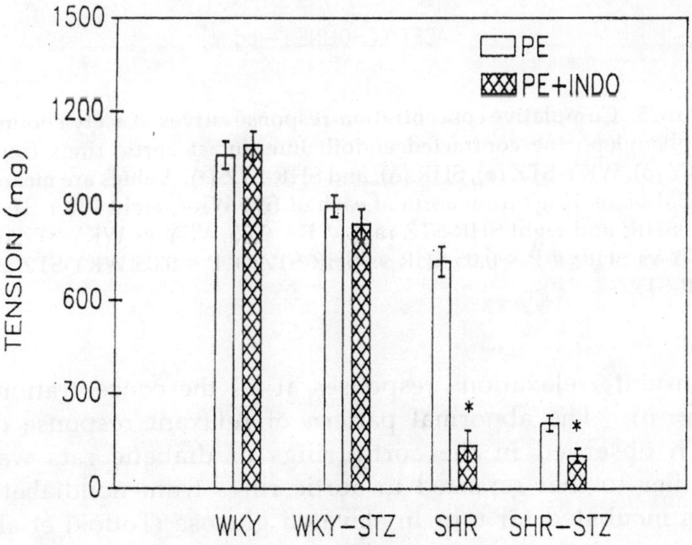

Figure 4. Responses of the endothelium-intact aortic rings to phenylephrine (PE) from WKY, WKY-STZ, SHR, and SHR-STZ in the absence and presence of 10 mM indomethacin (INDO). Values are means ± SEM of observations on three to four rings from each of five WKY, eight WKY-STZ, five SHR, and eight SHR-STZ rats. * $P < 0.05$ PE vs PE + INDO in SHR.

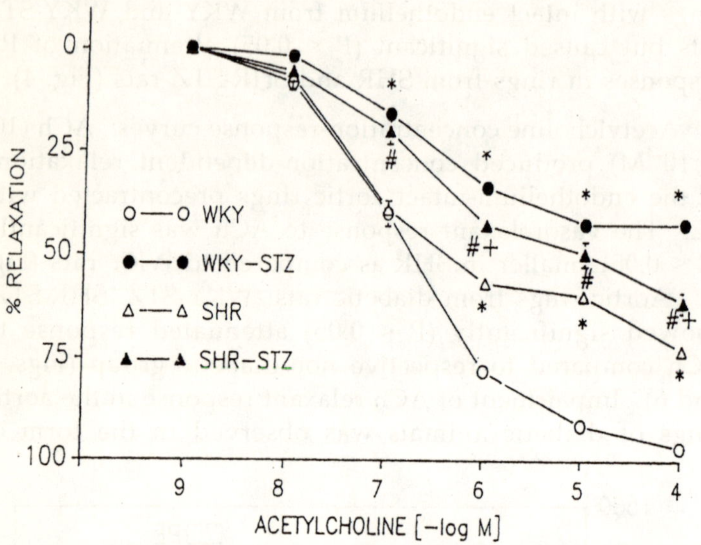

Figure 5. Cumulative concentration-response curves to acetylcholine in phenylephrine contracted endothelium-intact aortic rings from WKY (o), WKY-STZ (●), SHR (Δ), and SHR-STZ (▲). Values are means ± SEM of six rings from aorta of each of five WKY, eight WKY-STZ, five SHR, and eight SHR-STZ rats. * $P < 0.05$ WKY vs WKY-STZ or WKY vs SHR; # $P < 0.05$ SHR vs SHR-STZ; + $P < 0.05$ WKY-STZ vs SHR-STZ.

transient relaxation responses at all the concentrations (Fig. 6). The abnormal pattern of relaxant response of ACh observed in the aortic rings of diabetic rats was similar to that reported in aortic rings from nondiabetic rats incubated for 6 hr in elevated glucose (Todoki et al., 1992). Endothelium - denuded rings from rats of all the groups did not show any relaxant response to ACh (data not shown).

Isoproterenol concentration-responses curves: ISOP (10^{-9}-10^{-5}M) produced concentration-dependent relaxation of aortic rings precontracted with PE. SHR showed significantly ($P < 0.05$) smaller relaxations with ISOP as

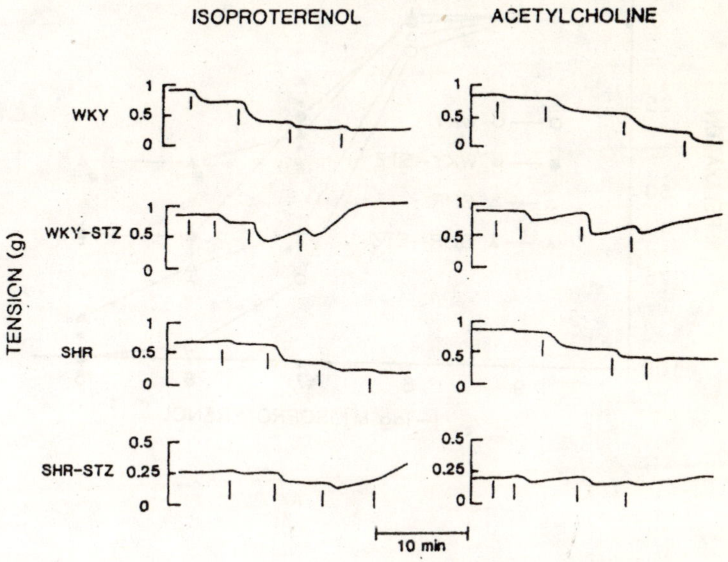

Figure 6. Tracings of isoproterenol and acetylcholine induced relaxations in phenylephrine contracted endothelium-intact aortic rings from WKY, WKY-STZ, SHR, SHR-STZ rats. Reversal of acetylcholine and isoproterenol-induced relaxant responses was observed in WKY-STZ and SHR-STZ rats. In each record, vertical lines indicate addition of cumulative concentrations (from left to right 10^{-8}, 10^{-7}, 10^{-6}, 10^{-5}M respectively) of the drug.

compared to WKY (Fig. 7 upper panel). STZ-induced diabetes caused attenuation of ISOP responses in both normotensive and hypertensive groups of rats (Figs. 6 & 7). Similar to ACh, ISOP also showed impairment of relaxation responses in the aortic rings of diabetic rats (Fig. 6). Endothelium removal abolished the differences in ISOP responses between the groups except at higher concentration (10^{-5}M) (Fig. 7 lower panel). Reversal of ISOP-induced relaxation responses were not seen in endothelium-denuded rings (data not shown).

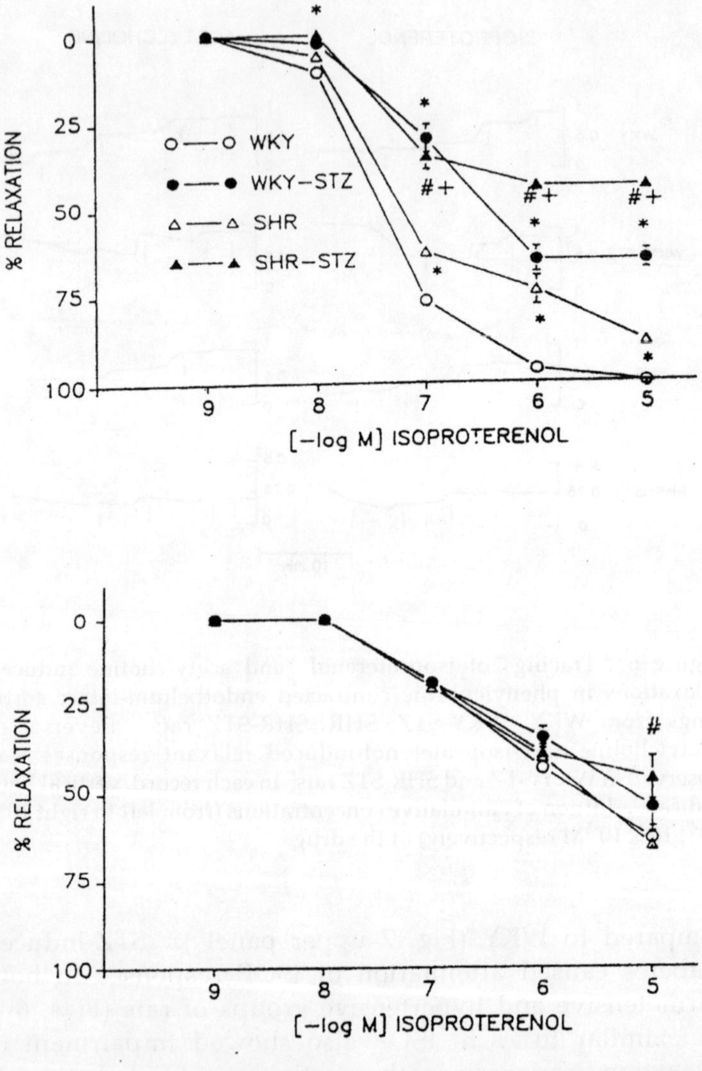

Figure 7. Cumulative concentration-response curves to isoproterenol in phenylephrine contracted endothelium-intact (upper panel) and -denuded (lower panel) aortic rings from WKY (o), WKY-STZ (•), SHR (Δ), and SHR-STZ (▴). Values are means ± SEM of six (upper panel)/four (lower panel) rings from each of five WKY, eight WKY-STZ, five SHR, and eight SHR-STZ rats. * $P < 0.05$ WKY vs WKY-STZ or WKY vs SHR; # $P < 0.05$ SHR vs SHR-STZ; + $P < 0.05$ WKY-STZ vs SHR-STZ.

Sodium nitroprusside concentration-response curves: To determine the effects of diabetes on non-receptor-mediated vasorelaxation, we examined the SNP responses on rat aortic rings precontracted with PE. SNP produced dose-dependent relaxations of the endothelium-intact and -denuded (data not shown) rings which were similar in all groups (data not shown).

DISCUSSION

This study shows that the contractions of rat aorta in response to PE were attenuated in diabetes mellitus and in hypertension. Hypertension and diabetes together added to the attenuation of PE-mediated contraction. The endothelium-dependent relaxations to ACh and ISOP were impaired in diabetes mellitus. SHR which had already attenuated responses to ACh and ISOP had further reductions in responses to ACh and ISOP following STZ induced diabetes.

Endothelial dysfunction is known to be an important factor in vascular complications in diabetes (Arbogast et al., 1984; Steiner, 1981). The scanning electron microscopic examination of rat aortae from diabetic rats revealed endothelial desquamation, attachment of platelets, leukocytes, deposition of fibrin and microthrombi (Arbogast et al., 1984). Change in the circulating levels of hormones in diabetes has also been suggested to be a contributing factor in abnormal vascular reactivity (Thorn et al., 1988). Hyperlipidemia associated with diabetes could be another factor responsible for impaired vascular response in diabetes. Hyperlipidemia has been reported to inhibit endothelium-dependent arterial relaxation through its increased lysophosphatidylcholine (Matsuda et al., 1993) and increase in platelet thromboxane generation (Andrews et al., 1987). Increased levels of cholesterol and triglycerides in our diabetic rats might have contributed to the altered vascular reactivity. Greater rise in blood glucose and plasma triglycerides following STZ-treatment in SHR might have contributed in progressive loss of BW and enhanced endothelial dysfunction and consequently altered vascular smooth muscle responsiveness in SHR-STZ.

This study demonstrates that the contractile responses to PE were attenuated after removal of vascular endothelium in rats of all the groups except SHR-STZ, but the differences between WKY/SHR and corresponding diabetic groups persisted. Therefore, the inhibition of contractile response in diabetes (WKY-STZ, SHR-STZ) does not appear to be directly related to endothelium dependent mechanism. However, the effect of diabetes on the release of EDCF and the influence of EDCF on the PE induced contraction can not be ruled out.

Markedly attenuated contractile responses of SHR-STZ aorta were not specific for a_1-adrenoceptor-stimulation (PE) as the inability of other constrictor agonists like PGF_2a and endothelin to produce stronger contractions (data not shown) suggested a reduced sensitivity of vascular smooth muscle in SHR-STZ rats. In WKY and WKY-STZ rats, indomethacin had no effect on PE contractions whereas, contractile responses to PE in aortic rings from SHR and SHR-STZ were attenuated by indomethacin. These results suggest that PE might have resulted in the production of a cyclooxygenase derived contracting factor in SHR but not in WKY vessels and the attenuation of contractile response in diabetes may not be directly related to cyclooxygenase mediated products.

In normal blood vessels, the contractile responses to agonists are enhanced by L-NMMA due to inhibition of EDRF (NO)-mediated influence on vascular tone. We observed a significant increase in PE-induced contractions by L-NMMA only in WKY and SHR. L-NMMA effect was more pronounced in WKY as compared to SHR indicating attenuated release of NO in SHR. L-NMMA did not produce any significant effect on PE-response in diabetic groups suggesting the impairment of NO release.

The attenuated vasorelaxant responses to ACh, an endothelium-dependent agonist, in diabetes/hypertension suggest malfunction of endothelium which was further enhanced in SHR-STZ. Reduced vasorelaxant response to ACh in hypertension has been attributed to malfunction of endothelium (Mayhan, 1992). The main EDRF (Furchgott, 1983) involved in this vasorelaxant response has been identified as nitric oxide (NO) which is a potent activator of the soluble guanylate cyclase and increases intracellular levels of cGMP in target tissues (Todd, 1992). Previous studies have suggested various mechanisms for alterations in the EDRF mediated responses in hypertension (Li and Bukoski, 1993; Lockett et al., 1986) and diabetes (Durante et al., 1988; Mayhan, 1992; Meraji et al., 1987; Oyama et al., 1986; Tesfamariam et al., 1989) e.g., endothelium-associated vascular pathology of hypertension (Li and Bukoski; 1993; Luscher et al., 1987); endothelial cell dysfunction caused by elevated glucose through free radicals generated by increased cyclooxygenase products in the endothelium which may interfere with the release of EDRF (NO) (Tesfamariam et al., 1989; Todoki et al., 1992). Other possible mechanisms may include impaired ability to synthesize and release of EDRF (NO) and/or the release of other endothelial substance(s) in diabetes which might be counteracting ACh and ISOP induced relaxations. Sodium nitroprusside, a direct nitrovasodilator, mediated relaxations were unaltered in hypertensive and/or diabetic groups. This suggested that the ability of smooth muscle relaxation in response to NO was not impaired. It is likely that the altered endothelial mechanism(s) may be playing a role in reduced vascular responses to ACh. ISOP-mediated relaxation also exhibited partial endothelium dependence in the aorta of non-diabetic and diabetic rats. Hypertension (SHR) or diabetes (WKY-STZ) alone caused attenuation of ISOP-induced relaxation in endothelium-intact aortic rings and diabetes in SHR (SHR-STZ) caused further attenuation of ISOP response. Removal of endothelium abolished the differences in ISOP responses between the groups. These observations further support the impairment of endothelium in vascular tissues of hypertensive and/or diabetic rats.

The attenuated vasoconstrictor response to PE observed in this study does not support either the release of vasoconstrictor agents by PE or involvement of cyclooxygenase products in diabetes. Cyclooxygenase products may be involved in altered vascular smooth muscle responses in SHR. However, the possibility of a release of a constrictor substance by cholinergic or beta-adrenergic receptor stimulation may counteract the simultaneous release of EDRF (NO) in depressed vasorelaxant response to ACh and ISOP in diabetes can not be ruled out. Inhibition of endothelium-dependent vasorelaxnt response to ACh by free-radicals induced lipid peroxidation (Tesfamariam and Cohen, 1992) or free radicals mediated increase in cyclooxygenase product catalysis occurring in the endothelium due to elevated glucose (Todoki et al., 1992) could be other possible factors in attenuated vasorelaxant response to ACh and ISOP in diabetes.

It is concluded that STZ-induced diabetes in spontaneously hypertensive rats aggravates the severity of vascular dysfunction. It is also suggested that impairment of contractile response to PE is not directly dependent on vascular endothelium whereas, impairment of vasorelaxant response to ACh and ISOP is related to endothelium-dependent mechanism(s).

ACKNOWLEDGEMENTS

The authors would like to thank Ms. Pam Wynne and Ms. Maninder for typing the manuscript.

This work was supported in part by National Heart, Lung and Blood Institute Grant HL-27339.

REFERENCES

1. Andrews, H.E., K.R. Bruckdorfer, R.C. Dunn, & M. Jacobs: Low-density lipoproteins inhibit endothelium-dependent relaxation in rabbit aorta. *Nature* 1987, 327, 237-239.

2. Arbogast, B.W., D.L Berry, & C.L. Newell: Injury of arterial endothelial cells in diabetic, sucrose-fed and aged rats. *Atherosclerosis* 1984, 51, 31-45.

3. Azvedo, I., & W. Osswald: Does adenosine malfunction play a role in hypertension? *Pharmacol Res* 1992, 25, 227-236.

4. Bassenge, E.: Clinical relevance of endothelium-derived relaxing factor (EDRF). *Br J Clinical Pharmacol* 1992, 34, 375-425.

5. Bell D, S.: Hypertension in the person with diabetes. *Am J Med Sci*, 1989, 297, 228-232.

6. Biaggioni, I.: Contrasting excitatory and inhibitory effects of adenosine in blood pressure regulation. *Hypertension* 1992, 20, 457-465.

7. Dai S. & J.H. Neill: Myocardial performance of STZ-diabetic DOCA-hypertensive rats. *Am J Physiol* 1992, 263 (Heart Circ. Physiol. 32), H1798-H1805.

8. Durante, W., A.K. Sen, & F.A. Sunahara:Impairment of endothelium-dependent relaxation in aortae from spontaneously diabetic rats. *Br J Pharmacol*, 1988, 94, 463-468.

9. Fahim, M., S.R. Makujina, & S.J. Mustafa: Vasorelaxant response to adenosine analogs in SHR and WKY rats. *FASEB J* 1993, 7(4), A547.

10. Fein, F.S., Cho, S., Zola, B.E., Miller, B. & S.M. Factor: Cardiac pathology in hypertensive diabetic rat: biventricular damage with right ventricular predominace. *Am J Pathol* 1989, 134, 1159-1166.

11. Fein, F.S., Kornstein, L.B., J.E. Storbeck, J.M. Capasso, & E.H. Sonnenblick: Altered myocardial mechanics in diabetic rats. *Circ Res* 1980, 47, 922-933.

12. Fein, F.S., E. Zola, A. Malhotra, S. Cho, S.M. Factor, J. Scheuer, & E.H.Sonnenblick :Hypertensive-diabetic cardiomyopathy in rats. *Am J Physiol* 1990, 258 (Heart Circ.Physiol. 27), H793-805.

13. Furchgott, R.F: Role of endothelium in responses of vascular smooth muscle. *Circ Res* 1983, 3, 557-573.

14. Ganz, P., P.F. Davies, J.A. Leopald, M.A. Gimbrone, & R.W. Alexander: Short- and long- term interactions of endothelium on

vascular smooth muscle in coculture: Effects on cyclic GMP production. *Proc Natl Acad Sci* USA, 1986, 83, 3552-3556.

15. Garvey, W.T., H.D.Hardin, M. Juhaszova, & J.H. Dominiguez: Effects of diabetes on myocardial glucose transport system in rats: implications for diabetic cardiomyopathy. *Am J Physiol* 1993, 264 (Heart Circ. Physiol. 33), H837-844
16. Harris, K.H., & K.M. MacLeod: Influence of the endothelium on contractile responses of arteries from diabetic rats. *Eur J Pharmacol* 1988, 153, 55-64.
17. Li, J., & R.D. Bukoski: Endothelium-dependent relaxation of hypertensive resistance arteries is not impaired under all conditions. *Cir Res* 1993, 72, 290-296.
18. Lockette, W., Y. Osaka, & O. Carretero: The loss of endothelium-dependent vascular relaxation in hypertension. *Hypertension*1986, 8 (Suppl. II), II61-66.
19. Luscher, T.F., P.M. Vanhoutte, & L. Raij: Antihypertensive treatment normalizes decreased endothelium-dependent relaxations in rats with salt-induced hypertension. *Hypertension* 1987, 9 (Suppl. III), III193-197.
20. MacLeod, K.M., K.H. Harris, & J. Diamond: Evidence that cGMP is the mediator of endothelium-dependent inhibition of contractile responses of rat arteries to α-adenoceptor stimulation. *Am Soc Pharmacol Exp Ther* 1986, 32, 59-64.
21. Matsuda, Y., K. Hirata, N. Inoue, M. Svenmatsu, S. Kawishima, H. Akita & Yokayama: High density lipoprotein reverses inhibitory effect of oxidized low density lipoprotein on endothelium-dependent arterial relaxation. *Circ Res* 1993, 72, 1103-1109.
22. Mayhan, W. G: Impairment of endothelium-dependent dilation of the basilar artery during diabetes mellitus. *Brain Res* 1992, 58, 297-302.
23. Meraji, S., L. Jayakody, M.P.J. Senartine, A.B.R. Thomson, & T. Kappagada : endothelium-dependent relaxation in aorta of BB rat. *Diabetes*, 1987, 36, 978-981.
24. Oyama, Y., H. Kawasaki, Y. Hattori, & M. Kanno: Attenuation of endothelium-dependent relaxation in aorta from diabetic rats. *Eur J Pharmacol* 1986, 131, 75-78.
25. Pieper, G.M., & V. Gross: Oxygen-derived free radicals abolish endothelium-dependent relaxation in diabetic rat aorta. *Am J Physiol* 1988, 255 (Heart Circ. Physiol .24), H825-833.

26. Raptis, S: Hypertension and diabetes mellitus. In: *Arterial Hypertension*, Ed.: by J. Rosenthal. Springer, New York,USA, 1982, pp. 93-99.

27. Rodrigues, B., & J.H. McNeill: Cardiac function in spontaneously hypertensive diabetic rats. *Am J Physiol* 1986, 251 (Heart Circ. Physiol. 20), H571-580.

28. Steiner, G: Diabetes and atherosclerosis. *Diabetes* 1981, 30 (Suppl. 2), 1-7.

29. Tesfamariam, B., J.A. Jakubowski, & R.A. Cohen: Contraction of diabetic rabbit aorta caused by endothelium-derived PGH_2-TxA_2. *Am J Physiol* 1989, 257 (Heart Circ. Physiol. 26), H1327-1333.

30. Tesfamariam, B., & R.A. Cohen: Free radicals mediate endothelial cell dysfunction caused by elevated glucose. *Am J Physiol* 1992, 263 (Heart Circ. Physiol. 32), H321-326.

31. Thorn, S., A. Hughes, & P.S. Sever: Endothelium dependent responses in human arteries. In: *Relaxing and Contracting Factors: Biological and Clinical Research*, Ed.: by P.M. Vanhoutte, Humana Press, Clifton, NJ, USA, 1988, pp. 511-528.

32. Todd, M.E: Hypertensive structural changes in blood vessels: Do endothelial cells hold the key? Can *J Physiol Pharmacol* 1992, 70, 536-551.

33. Todoki, K., E. Okabe, T. Kiyosi, T. Sekishita, & H. Ito: Oxygen free radical-mediated selective endothelial dysfunction in isolated coronary artery. *Am J Physiol* 1992, 262 (Heart Circ. Physiol. 31), H806-812.

ON THE NEUROTRANSMITTER BASIS OF MORPHINE DEPENDENCY

MOHAMMAD-REZA ZARRINDAST
Department of Pharmacology, Tehran University of Medical Sciences, Tehran, Iran

INTRODUCTION

Mechanisms by which particular drugs lead to addiction, and the genetic factors that make some individuals particularly vulnerable to addiction, have remained elucive (Nestier, 1992). Addiction is defind as the compulsive use of a drug despite adverse consequences. Three terms related to drug abuse are used commonly; tolerance, dependence, and addiction. Tolerance represents a reduced effect upon repeated exposure to a drug at a contant dose, or the need for an increased dose to maintain the same effect. Dependence is defined as the need for continued exposure to a drug so as to avoid a withdrawal syndrome (physical or psychological signs) when the drug is withdrawn.

The discovery of endogenous opiate receptors raised the possibility that opiate addiction might be mediated by changes in these receptors. A decade research has failed to identify changes in the number of opioid receptors and also changes in levels of endogenous opioid peptides (Loh & smith, 1990; Nestier, 1992). Some investigations have demonstrated that changes in the activity of Gprotein and the second messenger and protein phosphorylation pathway mediate important aspects of opioid, and possibly cocaine addiction in a number of drug responsive brain regions.

The locus coeruleus (LC) is the largest noradrenergic nucleus in brain, has served for many years as a useful model of opiate action. Several studies have indicated that modulation of LC neuronal firing rates contibutes to physical aspects of opiate addiction, namely physical dependence and withdrawal in several species (Redmond & Krystal, 1 984; Rasmussen et al. 1990).

The cAMP system in the LC can play a role in morphine dependence. Chronic administration of opiate leads to upregulation of cAMP system, which increases the intrinsic excitability of LC neurons, and thereby accounts, at least in part, for opiate tolerance, dependence, and withdrawal exhibited by these neurons (Nestler, 1 992). In the opiate-tolerant/dependent state, the combined presence of the opiate and the upregulated cAMP system would return LC firing rates toward pretreatment levels, whereas removal of the opiates would leave the upregulated cAMP system unopposed to withdrawal activation of the neurons.

In the present review, the effects of a few neurotransmitters on dependence induced by morphine in animal's experimental model are discussed. The methods used for the experiments have described elsewhere (Zarrindast & Farzin, 1996 ; Zarrindast & Mousa-Ahmadi, 1999).

MECHANISM AND EFFECT OF NICOTINE ON NALOXONE-INDUCED JUMPING IN MICE

The psychoactive component of tobacco products, nicotine is widely consumed by humans (Benowitz, 1988; Henningfield & Goldberg, 1988; Stolerman, 1988). It produces euphoria (Henningfield et al., 1 985; Pomerleau and Pomerleau, 1992), increased arousal, decreased fatigue (Perkins et al. 1993) and it particularly increases dopaminergic and cholinergic activity (Balfour, 1991; Clarke, 1990). The drug is also involved in activating opioid system(s) (Davenport et al. 1990). These findings may have some bearing on the observation that opiate addicts and cigarette smokers display parallel emotional profiles during abstinence from their habits (Gossop et al. 1990). Thus nicotine may alleviate at least some morphine abstinence signs. There is a report that nicotine suppresses naloxone-induced jumping in morphine dependent mice (Brase et al. 1974). Recently we showed that nicotine can attenuate naloxone-induced jumping in morphine-dependent mice (Zarrindast & Farzin, 1996).

We showed that, the cross-dependence between morphine and nicotine may exist. The effect of nicotine on naloxone-induced jumping is shown in table 1. Our data showed that nicotine remarkably effective in reducing the incidence of withdrawal jumping in morphne-

TABLE 1

Effects of nicotine on naloxone-induced jumping behaviour in the presence or absence of drugs

Drugs	Response	Receptor type remarks
Nicotine	↓	Nicotinic receptor agonist
Mecamylamine	N,↔N	Central nicotinic antagonist
Hexamethonium	N,NN	Peripheral Nicotininc antagonist
Atropine	N,NN	Muscarinic receptor antagonist
SCH23390	↓, ↔N	D_1 receptor antagonist
Sulpiride	N,NN	D_2 receptor antagonist
Propranolol	N,NN	β -adrenoceptor antagonist
Phenoxybenzamine	N,NN	α-adrenoceptor antagonist

↓= Decreases naloxone-induced jumping
↔N= Prevents nicotine effect
N= No effect on jumping
NN= No effect on nicotine response
Data for table I derived from Zarrindast and Farzin, 1996(5)

dependent mice. The results indicate that nicotinic receptor mechanism may be involved in the supressive action of nicotine. Nicotinic receptor stimulation activates enkephalin release and biosynthesis in discrete brain nuclei and adrenal chromaffin cells (Eiden et al. 1984; Houdi et al. 1991). Therefore nicotine may supress withdrawal jumping by such a mechanism. Mecamylamine, the central nicotinic receptor antagonist (Martin et al. 1989) but not hexamethonium, the peripheral nicotinic receptor antagonist antagonized the nicotine response. Since the muscarinic receptor antagonist atropine did not alter the effect of nicotine, both central and peripheral muscarinic receptor involvement may be excluded. It has been reported that morphine inhibits the release of substance P from the spinal cord and that substance P accumulates during the development of morphine dependence, possibly due to chronic inhibition of substance P (Bergstrom et al. 1984). There is also a report showing that the opioid receptor antagonist naloxone is able to release substance P through a presynaptic nicotinic receptor mechanism (Torrens et al. 1981), It may be that nicotine suppresses withdrawal jumping by such a mechanism.

Our data indicate that the selective dopamine D-1 receptor antagonist SCH23390 (Hyttel, 1 984), decreased the effect of nicotine on withdrawal jumping b ehaviour induced by naloxone. Therefore, nicotine may also elicit its effect upon withdrawal jumping through a dopamine D-1 receptor mechanism. Nicotine receptors are located in the striatum and the mesolimbic system at the levels of cell bodies and terminals (Glorguieff et al. 979; Clarke and Pert, 1985). Activation of nicotinic receptors has been shown to be effective in stimulating the release of dopamine from the striatum and limbic system (Goodman, 1 974; Imperato et al. 1986). One may speculate that nicotine indirectly causes the inhibition of jumping through dopamine D-1 receptor stimulation. It has also been reported that the dopamine D-2 receptor agonist bromocriptine may potentiate morphine withdrawal signs

(Gomaa et al. 1 989), and that the dopamine D- 1 and D-2 receptors exert opposite influences on morphine antinociception (Zarrindast & Moghadampour, 1989).

Administration of the dopamine D-2 receptor antagonist sulpiride (Stoof & Kebabian, 1984) did not alter the effect of nicotine. Sulpiride itself also did not affect withdrawal jumping. These data indicate that the dopamine D-2 receptor is not involved in the attenuation of withdrawal jumping. SCH23390 binds also to 5HT-2 receptors in the brain (Bischoff et al. 1986) and antagonizes 5-HT-2 receptor activation both centrally and peripherally (Bijak & Smialowski, 1 989; Hicks et al. 1 984). The administration of 5-HT-2 receptor antagonists has been shown to attenuate naloxone-precipitated withdrawal and quasi-morphine withdrawal (Kleven & Sparber, 1989; Neal & Sparber, 1986; Neal & Sparber, 1990). This may account for the reduction of withdrawal jumping by SCH23390. Since, the α and β-adrenoceptor antagonists phenoxybenzamine and propranolol did not alter the effect of nicotine. Therefore, the involvement of adrenergic mechanisms in this action of nicotine is unlikely.

ADENOSINE RECEPTOR MECHANISMS AND MORPHINE DEPENDENCE

Adenosine is a neuromodulator in the central nervous system (Bundege & Dunwiddie, 1997), which functions through different receptor sites named Al, A2, A3 and A4 receptors (Dalziel & Westfall, 1994). The Al and A2 subtypes mediate different physiological actions of adenosine, display distinct structure-activity relationships and are distributed differently in tissues, including the brain (Olah & Stiles, 1995). Adenosine receptor agonists inhibit neuronal firing (Dunwiddie, 1985), reduce neurotransmitter release (Myers & Pugsley, 1986) and influence neurotransmitter second messengers (Dalziel &

Westfall, 1994). Analgesic, anticonvulsant and hypnotic effects of adenosine receptors have been proposed (Yarbrough & McGuffin-Clineschmidt, 1981).

Our previous study also showed that adenosine receptor activation may influence the antinociception induced by GABA receptor agonists (Sabetkasai & Zarrindast, 1993) and stress-induced antinociception (Zarrindast & Sabetkasai, 1992; Zarrindast et al. 1993). Morphine has been shown to release adenosine (Sawynok et al. 1989). Adenosine-dependent mechanisms may be involved in catalepsy (Zarrindast et al., 1997), morphine antinociception (Sawynok et al. 1 989; De Lander & Keil, 1 994) and morphine tolerance (Tao et al. 1995). Opioids are known to induce behavioural reinforcing effects (Bilsky et al. 1992) and a major restricting factor in the clinical use of opioids is the fear of drug dependence (Weis et al. 1983). A change in synaptic regulation of dopamine cells in the ventral tegmentum area one week after termination of chronic treatment with morphine has been suggested. A possible long-lasting dopamine-adenosine interaction has been also implicated in dopamine-mediated craving and relapse to drug-seeking behaviours (Bonci & Williams, 1996). Adenosine receptor agonists have shown to decrease naloxone-induced jumping in rats (Dionyssopoulos et al. 1992) and in mice (Tucker et al. 1984). However, other investigators found no effect for adenosine receptor agonists in this respect in rats (Salem & Hope, 1997) or in mice (Kaplan & Sears, 1996).

We studied, effects of adenosine receptor agonists and antagonists on naloxone-induced jumping in mice. Effects of adenosine receptor agonists and antagonists on naloxone-induced jumping is shown in table 2 (Zarrindast et al. 1999). CHA (cyclohexyladenosine), and R-PIA (R(-) N^6_ (2-phenylisopropyl) adenosine, which are adenosine receptor agonists (Jacobson et al. 1992), decreased naloxone-induced jumping. Similar results have been

TABLE 2

Effects of adenosine receptor agonist on naloxone-induced jumping behaviour in mice

Drugs	Response	Receptor type remarks
CHA	↓	A_1 adenosine receptor agonist
R-PIA	↓	A_1 adenosine receptor agonist
DPCPX	↑	A_1 adenosine receptor antagonist
CPCA	↓	A_2 adenosine receptor agonist
DMPX	N	A_2 adenosine receptor antgonist

↓ = Decreases naloxone-induced jumping

↑ = Increases naloxone-induced jumping

N No effect on jumping

Data for table 2 derived from Zarrindast et al., 1999 (67)

reported by others (Tucker et al. 1984; Dionyssopoulos et al. 1992). In agreement with others (Tucker et al. 1984), we did not observe sedation with low doses (0.1 and 0. 25 mg/kg) of the adenosine agents. Thus the data may suggest that an adenosine-dependent mechanisms) is involved in morphine dependence. However, there are reports that adenosine agonists do not influence naloxone-induced jumping (Kaplan & Sears, 1996; Salem & Hope, 1997).

The adenosine A_1 receptors are widely distributed in the brain (Olah & Stiles, 1995). Since the adenosine receptor agonists, CHA and R-PIA have more affinity for adenosine A_1 receptors (Daly, 1982), and the receptor A_1 antagonist, DPCPX (8-cyclopentyl-1,3-dipropylxanthine; Jacobson et al. 1992), decreased the inhibitory response to CHA, adenosine A_1 receptors may be involved in the response. However, the adenosine A_1 receptor antagonist by itself also increased naloxone-induced jumping, which is consistence with some reports (Salem & Hope, 1997) but not with others (Kaplan & Sears, 1996).

In our study, the higher doses of the adenosine A2 receptor agonist, CPCA (5'-(N-cyclopropyl)-carboxamidoadenosine; Daly, 1982), also reduced naloxone induced jumping and the effect was not antagonized by the adenosine A_1 or A_2 receptor antagonists. This effect of CPCA may not be mediated through adenosine receptor mechanism, since the drug doses were high, no adenosine receptor antagonists reduced the response and since other authors (Dionyssopoulos et al. 1992; Kaplan & Sears, 1996; Salem & Hope, 1997) reported no effect for adenosine A_2 receptors in this respect.

Adenosine A_1 and A_2 receptors have been shown to be present in the gastrointestinal tract (Murthy et al. 1995). The adenosine A_1 receptor agonists, CHA and R-PIA, and also a higher dose of an adenosine A_2 receptor agonist, CPCA, reduced the naloxone-induced diarrhea. The response elicited by the adenosine A_1 and A_2 receptor agonists was reduced by the adenosine A_1 receptor antagonist, DPCPX (Jacobson et al. 1992), and the adenosine A_2 receptor antagonist, DMPX (3,7-dimethyl-l-propargylxanthine; Scale et al. 1988), respectively. Thus stimulation of both the adenosine A_1 and A_2 receptors may be involved in the inhibition of diarrhea by the agents. The adenosine A receptors are divided into two subtypes, A_{2A} and A_{2b} sites, and the adenosine A_{2b} receptors have been shown to be located in the gastric tissues (Olah & Stiles, 1995). Thus one may speculate that a peripheral mechanism is involved in the response induced by CPCA. However, there is a report indicating that the spinal cord may be a site of opioid effects on gastrointestinal transit in the mouse (Porreca & Burks, 1983). Presynaptic adenosine A_1 receptor blockade may release adenosine, which in turn may activate postsynaptic adenosine receptors involved in the inhibition of diarrhea induced by naloxone. This hypothesis gains support from the by fact that combination of adenosine A_2 receptor antagonist, DMPX with the adenosine A_1 receptor antagonist, DPCPX, is able to decrease this later effect induced by DPCPX. It should be mentioned that the results obtained with the adenosine receptor antagonists by some investigators (Kaplan & Sears, 1996) indicating that DPCPX has no effect on diarrhea and that DMPX increases the diarrhea induced by naloxone, are not in agreement with our findings.

GABA RECEPTOR AGENTS AND MORPHINE-DEPENDENCE

The role of several neurotransmitters including serotonin, dopamine, GABA, adenosine aspartate, and excitatory amino acid, in morphine tolerance and withdrawal has been investigated. They seem to be involved in morphine tolerance and dependence (Bhargava, 1994). A number of studies have also demonstrated that dopamine contributes to the expression of reward or morphine reinforcement (Bozarth & Wise, 1981). Interactions of GABA with dopaminergic pathways (Zarrindast & Moghadampour, 1991; Zarrindast & Farahvash, 1994), and adenosine (Sabetkasai & Zarrindast, 1993) also may indicate a greater complexity of the role of these neurotransmitters. It has been suggested that GABA-ergic and opiopeptidergic systems are interconnected through μ-opioid receptors (Desarmenien et al. 1984). GABA administration has also been shown to facilitate the development of tolerance and physical dependence (Ho et al. 1976). The present results indicate that both baclofen and muscimol, which are GABA receptor agonists (Bowery et al. 1983, 1984), inhibit naloxone-induced jumping behaviour in morphine-dependent mice in a dose- dependent manner. The data also may indicate that GABA receptor mechanisms are involved in morphine jumping behaviour.

The central inhibitory neurotransmitter, GABA (De Feudis, 1977; Hosli & Hosli, 1978; Johnston, 1978), is found in all areas of the human brain (Perry et al. 1971). It is well established that the GABA system is a target for a variety of centrally pharmacological agents including sedatives, analgesics and anticonvulsants (De Feudis, 1982; Sawynok & Labella, 1982). GABA receptors in the brain have been classified as $GABA_A$ and $GABA_B$ (Bowery et al. 1980, 1981; Hill & Bowery, 1981). Whereas $GABA_A$ receptors are directly associated with a chloride channel, the $GABA_B$ receptors seem to be G-protein coupled and linked to Ca^2 or K^+ channels (Bormann, 1988). However, a third class of $GABA_A$ binding site, the $GABA_C$ sites, resembles the $GABA_A$ receptor but is insensitive to bicuculline (Drew et al. 1984).

Since muscimol is a $GABA_A$ receptor agonist (Bowery et al. 1984) and baclofen acts on $GABA_B$ receptors (Bowery et al. 1983, 1984), it can be speculated that decreases in naloxone-induced jumping are mediated through both the $GABA_A$ and $GABA_B$ receptors. The inhibitory response induced by either intraperitoneal (IP) or intracerebroventricular (ICV) administration of the agonists, therefore, makes it likely that the responses to drugs are mediated through central GABA receptor mechanisms. Our data are consistent with data which shows that chronic administration of morphine may modify central GABA receptors (Ticku & Huffman, 1980), and the blockade of postsynaptic GABA receptors by bicuculline inhibits the development of tolerance and dependence (Ho et al. 1976), indicating that the central GABA system is involved in the expression of jumping behaviour.

The ICV but not IP administration of the competitive $GABA_A$ receptor antagonist, bicuculline, or the non-competitive $GABA_A$ receptor antagonist, picrotoxin (Ticku & Maksay, 1983), also decreased noloxone-induced jumping. Bicuculline has been shown to release GABA, which in turn may reduce jumping behaviour. The present data showed that IP injection of the higher dose of the $GABA_B$ receptor antagonist, CGP35348 (Olpe et al. 1990), increased naloxone induced jumping. This may indicate that a $GABA_B$ receptor mechanism has a dominant inhibitory influence on this behaviour. However, the ICV injection of the antagonist did not alter the naloxone-induced jumping. Therefore, a possibility may exist that the response induced by IP administration of a higher dose of the drug is mediated through a peripheral mechanism. To clarify the exact mechanisms involved will require further work.

CHOLECYSTOKININ (CCK) AND MORPHINE DEPENDENCE

The cholecystokinin octapeptide (CCK-8) is found throughout the mammalian nervous system and is present in the brain and spinal cord predominantly in the sulfated octapeptide form (CCK-8) (Vanderhaeghen et al. 1 975).

TABLE 3

Effects of GABA receptor agonist and antagonist on naloxone-induced jumping behaviour in mice

Drugs	Route	Response	Receptor type remarks
Baclofen	ICV or IP	↓	$GABA_B$ receptor agonist
Muscimol	ICV or IP	↓	$GABA_A$ receptor agonist
CGP35348	IP	↑, ↔B	$GABA_B$ receptor antagonist
CGP35348	ICV	N	$GABA_B$ receptor antagonist
Bicuculline	IP	N	$GABA_A$ receptor antagonist
Picrotoxin	IP	N	$GABA_A$ receptor antagonist

↓ = Decreases naloxone-induced jumping
↑ = Increases naloxone-induced jumping
↔B= Inhibits baclofen response
N = No effect on jumping
IP= Intraperitoneal injection
ICV = Intracerebroventricular injection
Data for table 3 derived from Zarrindast and Mousa-Ahmadi 1999(6)

High concentration of CCK have been identified in the cortical gray matter, periaqueductal gray, ventromedial thalamus and dorsal horn of the spinal cord, all of which are areas known to be involved in nociception (Vanderhaeghen et al. 1975; Dourish et al. 1990; Hughes et al. 1991).

It has been shown that the effects of CCK are mediated through at least two distinct types of binding sites. These have been referred to as type A (CCK_A) and type B (CCK_B) receptors for the predominant forms in the periphery and in the central nervous system (CNS), respectively. However, recent studies indicate that although CCK_B receptors predominate in the CNS, a smaller population of the CCK_A sites also exists (Gue & Bueno, 1991; Dourish et al. 1990; Hill et al. 1987; Hughes 1991; Moran et al. 1986; Woodruff et al. 1991). The majority of CCK, receptors are distributed throughout the brain and spinal cord (Dourish et al. 1990; Hill et al. 1987; Moran et al. 1986; Woodruff et al. 1991). There are good data suggesting that endogenous CCK may play physiologically an important role in pain transmission by modulating CNS opiate mechanisms (Zetler, 1980; Faris et al. 1983; Itoh et al. 1982; Barbaz et al. 1986; Suh et al. 1992; Stanfa et al. 1994). Our previous study showed that CCK-peptides may prevent tolerance to morphine antinociception (Rezayat et al. 1994). In this review the possible mechanisms of CCK receptor agonists on development of morphine dependence has been discussed (Rezayat Azizi & Zarrindast, 1997).

The effect of CCK receptor agonists and antagonists has been shown in tables 4 and 5. Our study showed that CCK receptor agonists caerulein, CCK-8 and unsulfated CCK-8 (CCK-8U) reduced the incidence of naloxone-induced jumping in morphine-dependent mice (Zarrindast et al., 1995). The data may indicate that CCK mechanisms may interact with morphine physical dependence. Caerulein and CCK-8 have high affinity for CCK, and

TABLE 4

Effects of CCK receptors agonists and antagonists on naloxone-induced jumping behaviour in mice

Drugs	Response	Receptor type remarks
Caerulein	↓	CCKA & B receptor agonist
CCK-8	↓	CCKA & B receptor agonist
CCK-8U	↓	CCKB receptor agonist
MK-329	↓, ↔ C, NS, NU	CCKA receptor antagonist
L-365,260	↓, ↔ C, NS, NU	CCKB receptor antagonist

↓ = Decreases naloxone-induced jumping
↔ C = Inhibits effect of caerulei on naloxone-induced jumping
N= No effect on jumping
NS, NU= No effect on response of CCK-8 or CCK-8U
Data for table 4 derived from Zarrindast et al., 1995 (109); Rezayat et al., 1997 (108)

TABLE 5

Effects of CCK dopamine, 5-HT, adrenoceptor and muscarinic receptor antagonists in the presence or absence of CCK receptor agonists, on naloxone-induced jumping behaviour in mice

Drugs	Response	Receptor type remarks
Sulpiride	↓,NC,↑S,NU	D_2 dopamine antagonist
Pimozide	↓,NC,↑S,NU	D_2 dopamine antagonist
SCH23390	↓,NC,NS,NU	D_1 dopamine antagonist
Methysergide	↓,NC	5-HT receptor antagonist
Phenoxybenzamine	N,NC	α-adrenoceptor antagonist
Propranolol	N,NC	β-adrenoceptor antagonist
Atropine	↑,NC	antimuscarinic drug

↓ = Decreases naloxone-induced jumping
↑= Increases naloxone-induced jumping
N = No effect on jumping
NC, NU= No effect on responses of caerulein or CCK-8U respectively
↑S= increase response of CCK-8
Data for table 5 derived from Rezayat et al., 1997 (108) Zarrindast et al., 1995 (109)

CCK receptors, therefore it may be possible that CCK_A and CCK_B receptor sites to be involved in the inhibition of morphine dependence elicited by these peptides. CCK-8U which have high affinity for CCK_B but not for CCK_A receptors (Woodruff & Hughes, 1991), also decrease the morphine withdrawal jumping. The response induced by CCK-8U seems to be lower than elicited by C.CK-8 or caerulein. However, it is suggested that the interaction between opioidergic and CCKergic neurotransmission at different stages of morphine treatment and withdrawal are not caused by changes of CCK receptor binding properties (Welin et al. 1994).

Although neurotransmitters i.e. norepinephrine, dopamine, serotonin and acetylcholine have been implicated in the pharmacological actions of morphine and in phenomena of opioid withdrawal (Sloan et al. 1963; Domino & Wilson, 1973), the neurochemical bases of the CCK mechanisms in the abstinence is unclear. In our study, the influences of the neurotransmitters on naloxone-induced jumping has been evaluated (Table 5). Functional relationship between CCK and dopamine in the different regions of brain has been demonstrated. There appears to be a complex interaction between dopamine and cholecystokinin systems in the nucleus accumbens (Vaccarino & Rankin 1989). CCK-8 is colocalized with dopamine in a subpopulation of A10 dopamine-containing neurons (Hokfelt et al. 1980). Moreover, the CCKpeptides may be released with dopamine. It is also possible that CCK-8 influence the release of dopamine or of CCK-8 itself by a presynaptic action. The naloxone-precipitated withdrawal jumping response in morphine-dependent animals has been suggested to be associated with an elevation of dopamine level (Iwamoto et al. 1973).

Dopamine is known to bind to separate receptor subtypes named D, and D, (Stoof & Kebabian, 1981). Present data showed that the D, dopamine receptor antagonist SCH23390 (Hyttel 1984) did not alter attenuation of naloxone-induced jumping by CCK agonists in the morphine-dependent animals, thus the involvement of D, receptor sites in CCK mechanism seems unlikely. However, SCH 23390 can decrease the naloxone-induced jumping by itself. Our results indicate that D,, dopamine receptor antagonists sulpiride (Stoof & Kebabian, 1984) and pimozide (Morley et al. 1987) potentiate CCK agonists-induced suppression of the withdrawal jumping The D2 dopamine antagonists sulpiride and pimozide also reduced naloxone-induced jumping by themselves. The data may be in agreement with those obtained by others which D2 dopamine agonists increases (Cerbo et al. 1984) withdrawal jumping and may agree with the hypothesis that dopamine is important in the rewarding effects of abused drugs, and opioid withdrawal (Harris & Astonjones, 1994). The results may be consistent with the reports that activation of D2 dopamine receptors may inhibit CCK release in brain (Hutchinson et al. 1986). However, there is some reports indicating that dopamine receptor activation cause an increase (Tseng et al. 1976) or decrease (Blasig et al. 1976 in the withdrawal jumping respectively.

The α-and, β-adrenergic receptor antagonists phenoxybenzamine and propranolol did not alter naloxone-induced jumping in the presence or absence of the caerulein. The same results have been also shown previously (Minneman & Holtzman, 1984). Thus the involvement of adrenergic system(s) in the CCK-induced attenuation of naloxone-induced jumping seems unlikely.

Our data also indicate that 5-HT receptor antagonist methysergide reduced the naloxone-induced jumping in morphinedependent mice. The 5-HT antagonist have been shown to attenuate the withdrawal jumping in morphine-dependent mice by others (Neal & Sparber, 1986). In the present study, the antagonist tends to increase caerulein's response, but not significantly. Therefore the involvement of 5-HT mechanism in the caerulein's effect should be more evaluated.

The antimuscarinic atropine used in the study increased naloxone-induced jumping, which is also in agreement with results in other laboratories (Laschka et al. 1976) that atropine increases, whereas cholinergic activation attenuates abstinence syndrome. Overall, It may conclude that CCK receptor system(s) may interact with D_2 dopamine receptor mechanism in attenuation of naloxone-induced jumping. Since CCK receptor agonists induce hypolocomotion (O'Neill et al. 1991), even this effect may interact with the naloxone-induced jumping. For exact clarification of CCK mechanism, more experiment are required.

REFERENCES

Balfour, D.J.K. (1991) The neurochemical mechanisms underlying nicotine tolerance and dependence. In the biological bases of drug tolerance and dependence. ed. by J.A. Pratt, pp. 121-151, Academic Press, New York

Barbaz, B.S., Autry, W.L., Ambrese, F.G., Hah, N.R. & Liebman, i.M. (1986) Antinociceptive profile of sulfated CCK-8. *Neuropharmacology* 25, 823-829.

Benowitz, N.L. (1988) Pharmacologic aspects of cigarette smoking and nicotine addiction. *N. Engl. J. Med.* 319, 13181330.

Bergstrom, L., Sakurada, T. & Terenius, L. (1984) Substanse P levels in various regions of rat central nervous system after acute and chronic morphine treatment. *Life Sci.* 35, 2375-2382.

Bhargava, H.N. (1994) Diversity of agents that modify Opioid tolerance, physical dependence, abstinence syndrome and self administrative behaviour. *Pharmacol. Rev.* 46, 293-324.

Bilsky, E.J., Montegut , M.J., Delong, C.L. & Reid, L.D. (1992) opioidergic modulation of cocaine conditioned place preference. *Life Sci.* 50, 85-90.

Bijak, M. & Smialowski A. (1989) Serotonin receptor blocking effect of SCH23390. *Pharmacol Biochem Behav* 32, 585-587.

Bischoff, S., Heinnch, M., Soontag, J.M. & Krauss, J. (1986) The D-1 dopamine receptor antagonist SCH23390 also interacts potently with brain serotonin (5-HT,) receptors. Eur. J. Pharmacol. 129, 367-370

Blasig, J., Gramsch, C., Laschka, E. & Herz, A. (1976) The role of dopamine in withdrawal jumping in morphine dependent rats. *Arzneimittelforschung* 26, 1104-1106.

Bonci, A. & Williams, J.T. (1996) A common mechanism mediates long-term changes in synaptic transmission after chronic cocaine and morphine. *Neuron* 16, 631-639.

Bormann, J. (1988) Electrophysiology of GABA-A and GABAB receptor subtypes. *Trends Neurosci.* 11, 112-116.

Bowery, N.G., Hill, D.R. & Hudson, A.L. (1983) Characteristics of GABA, receptors binding sites on rat whole brain synaptic membranes. *Br. J. Pharmacol.* 78, 191-206.

Bowery, N.G., Price, G.W., Hudson, A.L., Hill, D.R., Wilkin, G.P. & Turnbull, M.J. (1984) GABA receptor multipilicity: visualization of different receptor types in the mammalian CNS. *Neuropharmacology* 23, 219-231.

Bowery, N.G., Hill, D.R., Hudson, A.L., Doble, A., Middlemiss, D.N., Shaw, J. & Turnbull, M.i. (1980) (-)-Baclofen decreases neurotransmitter release in the mammalian CNS by an action at a novel receptor. Nature 283, 92-94.

Bowery, N.G., Doble, A., Hill, D.R,. Hudson, A.L., Shaw, J.S., Turnbull, M.J. & Warrington, R. (1981) Bicuculline insensitive GABA receptors on peripheral autonomic nerve terminals. *Eur. J. Pharmacol.* 71, 53-70.

Bozarth, M.A. & Wise, R.A. (1981) Heroin reward is dependent on a dopaminergic substrate. *Life Sci.* 29, 1881-1886.

Brase, D.A., Tseng, L.F., Loh, H.H. & Way, E.L. (1974) Cholinergic modification of naloxone-induced jumping in morphine dependent mice. *Eur. J. Pharmacol.* 26, 1-8.

Bundege, J.M. & Dunwiddie, T.V. (1997) Role of adenosine as a modulator of synaptic activity in the CNS. *Advances in Pharmacology* 39, 353-391.

Cerbo, R., Boni, B., De-Lena, C., Cesarino, F., Meco, G., Feliciani, M., Formisano, R. & Casacchia, M. (1984) Naloxone-induced jumping activity in morphine-dependent mice: A pharmacological study on the role of DA2 receptors. *Boll. Soc. Ital. Biol. Sper.* 60, 493-499.

Clarke, P.B.S. & Pert, A. (1985) Autoradiographic evidence for nicotine receptors on nigrostriatal and mesolimbic dopaminergic neurons. *Brain Res.*, 348, 355-358.

Clarke, P.B.S. (1990) Dopaminergic mechanisms in the locomotor stimulant effects of nicotine. Biochem. *Pharmacol.* 40, 1427- 1432 .

Daly, J.W. (1982) Adenosine receptors: targets for future drugs. *J. Med. Chem.* 25, 197-207.

Dalziel, H.H. & Westfall, D.P. (1994) Receptors for adenine nuleotides and nucleosides: subclassification, distribution and molecular characterization. *Pharmacol.* Rev. 46, 449465.

Davenport, K.E., Houdi A.A. & Van Loon, G.R. (1990) Nicotine protects against g-opioid receptor antagonism by P-funaltrexamine: evidence for nicotine-induced release of endogenous opioids in brain. *Neurosci. Lett.* 113, 40-46.

De Feudis, F.V. (1982) GABAergic analgesia-A naloxone insensitive system. *Pharmacol. Res. Commun.* 14, 383-390.

De Feudis, F. (1977) GABA-ergic in the vertebrate nervous system. *Prog. Neurobiol.* 9, 123-145.

De Lander, G.E. & Kiel, J. (1994) Antinociception induced by intrathecal coadministration of selective adenosine receptor and selective opioid receptor agonists in mice. *J. Pharmacol. Exp. Ther.* 268, 943-951.

Desarmenlen, M., Felz, P., Occhlpltl, G., Santangeto, F. & Schllcher, R. (1984) Coexistence of GABA, and GABA, receptors on AS and C primary afferents. *Br. J. Pharmacol.* 81, 327333.

Dionyssopoulos, T., Hope, W. & Coupar, I.M. (1992) Effect of adenosine analogues on the expression of opiate withdrawal in rats. *Pharmacol. Biochem. Behav.* 42, 201-206.

Domino, E.F. & Wilson, A. (1973) Effects of narcotic analgesic agonists and antgonists on rat brain acetylcholine. *J. Pharmacol. Exp. Ther.* 184, 18-32.

Dourish, C.T., O'Neill, M.F., Coughlan, J., Kitchen, S.J., Hawley, D. & Iversen, S.D. (1990) The selective CCK, receptor antagonist L-365,260 enhances morphine analgesia and prevents morphine tolerance in the rat. *Eur. J. Pharmacol.* 176, 35-44.

Drew, C.A., Johnston, G.A.R. & Weatherby, R.P. (1984) Bicuculline insensitive GABA receptors: studies on the binding of (-)-baclofen to rat cerebellar membranes. *Neurosci. Lett.* 52, 317-321.

Dunwiddie, T.V. (1985) The physiological role of adenosine in the central nervous system. *Int. Rev. Neurobiol.* 27, 63-139.

Eiden, L.E., Giraud, P., Dave, J. T., Hotchkiss, A.J. & Affolter, H. (1984) Nicotinic receptor stimulation activates enkephalin release and biosynthesis in adrenal chromaffin cell. *Nature* 312, 661-663.

Faris, P.L., Komisaruk, B.R., Watkins, L. R. & Mayer, D. J. (1983) Evidence for the neuropeptide cholecystokinin as an antagonist of opiate analgesia. *Science* 219, 310-312.

24 Giorguieff, M.F., Kemel, M.L., Wandscheer, D. & Glowinski, J. (1979) Regulation of dopamine release by presynaptic nicotinic receptors in rat striatal slices :effect of nicotine in a low concentration. *Life Sci.* 25, 1257-1262.

Goodman, F.R. (1974) Effects of nicotine on distribution and release of 14C-norepinephrine and 14C-dopamine in rat brain striatum and hypothalamus slices. *Neuropharmacology* 13, 1025-1032.

Gomaa, A., Mohamed, L.H. & Ahmed, H.N. (1989) Modification of morphine-induced analgesia, tolerance and dependence by bromocriptine. *Eur. J. Pharmacol.* 170, 129-135.

Gossop, M. , Powell, J. , Grey, S. & Hajek, P. (1990) What do opiate addicts and cigarette smokers mean by "craving"? A pilot study. *Drug Alcohol Depend.* 26, 85-87.

Gue, M. & Bueno, L. (1991) Brain CCKA receptors mediate the colonic motor response to feeding in dogs. *Peptides* 12, 523-527.

Harris, G.C. & Astonjones, G. (1994) Involvement of D2 dopamine receptors in the nucleus accumbens in the opiate withdrawal syndrome. *Nature* 371, 155-157.

Henningfield, J.E., Miyasato, K. & Jasinski, D.R. (1985) Abuse liability and pharmacodynamics of intravenous and inhaled nicotine. *J. Pharmacol. Exp. Ther.* 234, 1-12.

Henningfield, J.E. & Goldberg, S.R. (1988) Pharmacologic determinants of tobacco self-administration by humans. *Pharmacol. Biochem. Behav.* 30, 221-226.

Hicks, P.E., Schoemaker, H. & Langer, S.Z. (1984) 5-HT receptor antagonist properties of SCH23390 in vascular smooth muscle and brain. *Eur. J. Pharmacol.* 105, 339-342.

2 5 Hill, R.G., Hughes, J. & Pittaway, K.M. (1987) Antinociceptive action of cholecystokinin octapeptide (CCK-8) and related peptides in rat and mice: effect of naloxone and peptidase inhibitors. *Neuropharmacology* 26, 289-300.

Hill, D.R. & Bowery, N.G. (1981) 3 H-Baclofen and 3H-GABA bind to bicuculline-insensitive GABAB sites in rat brain. *Nature* 290, 149-152.

Ho, I.K., Loh, H.H. & Way, E.L. (1976) Pharmacological manipulation of gamma-aminobutyric acid (GABA) in morphine analgesia, tolerance and physical dependence. *Life Sci.* 18, 1111-1124.

Hokfelt, T., Rehfeld, J.F., Skirboll, L.,, Ivemark, B., Goldstein, M. & Markey, K. (1980) Evidence for coexsitence of dopamine and CCK in mesolimbic neurons. *Nature* 285: 476478

Hösli, L. & Hösli E. (1978) Action and uptake of neurotransmitters in CNS tissue culture. *Rev. Physiol. Biochem. Pharmacol.* 81, 135-188.

Houdi, A.A., Pierzchala, K., Marson, L., Palkovits, M. & Van Loon, G.R. (1991) Nicotine-induced alteration in Tyr-GlyGly and Met-enkephalin in discrete brain nuclei reflects altered enkephalin neuron activity. *Peptides* 12, 161-166.

Hughes, J., Hunter, J.C. & Woodruff, G.N. (1991) Neurochemical actions of CCK underlying the therapeutic potential of CCKB antagonists. *Neuropeptides* 19 (suppl.), 85-89.

Hutchinson, J.B., Strupish, J. & Nahorski, S.R. (1986) Release of endogenous dopamine and cholecystokinin from rat striatal slices: Effects of amphetamine and dopamine antagonists. *Brain Res.* 370, 310-314.

Hyttel, J. (1984) Functional evidence for selective dopamine D, receptor blockade by SCH 23390. *Neuropharmacology* 23, 1395-1401.

Imperato, A., Mulas, A. & Di Chiara, G. (1986) Nicotine preferentially stimulates dopamine release in the limbic system of freely moving rats. *Eur J Pharmacol* 132, 337-338.

Iwamoto, E.T., Ho, I.K. & Way, E.L. (1973) Elevation of brain dopamine during naloxone-precipitated withdrawal in morphine-dependent mice and rats. *J. Pharmacol. Exp. Ther.* 187, 558-567.

Itoh, S., Katsura, G. & Maeda, Y. (1982) Caerulein and cholecystokinin suppress B-endorphin-induced analgesia in the rat. *Eur. J. Pharmacol.* 80, 421-425.

Jacobson, K.A., van Galen, P.J.M. & Williams, M. (1992) Adenosine receptors: pharmacology, structure-activity relationships and therapeutic potential. *J. Med. Chem.* 35, 407-422.

Johnston, J.A.R. (1978) Neuropharmacology of amino acid inhibitory transmitters. *Ann. Rev. Pharmac. Toxic.* 18, 269-289.

Kaplan, G.B. & Sears, M.T. (1996) Adenosine receptor agonists attenuate and adenosine receptor antagonists exacerbate opiate withdrawal signs. *Psychopharmacology* 123, 64-70.

Kleven, M.S. & Sparber, S.B. (1989) Modification of the behavioral effects 3-isobutyl-l-methylxanthine by serotonin agonists and antagonists; evidence for a role of serotonin in the expression of opiate withdrawal. *Psychopharmacology* 98, 231-235.

Laschka, E., Herz, A. & Blasig, J. (1976) Activity of nigrostriatal dopaminergic system during precipitated morphine withdrawal investigator in rats with acute unilateral inactivation of the striatum. *Naunyn Schmiedebergs Arch. Pharmacol.* 296, 15-23.

Loh, H.H. & Smith, A.P. (1990) Molecular characterization of opioid receptors. *Pharmacol. Toxicol.* 30; 123-147.

Martin, B.R., Onaivi, E.S. & Martin, T.J. (1989) What is the nature of mecamylamine's antagonism of the central effects of nicotine. *Biochem. Pharmacol.* 38, 3391-3397.

Minneman, K.P. & Holtzman, S.G. (1984) Morphine dependence and withdrawal without alternations in cerebral P-adrenergic receptor density. *Biochem. Pharmacol.* 33, 2331-2333.

Moran, T.H., Robinson, P., Goldrich, M.S. & McHugh, P. (1986) Two brain cholecystokinin receptors: implications for behavioral actions. *Brain Res.* 362, 175-179.

Morley, M.J., Bradshow, C.M. & Szabadi, E. (1987) Attenuation by pimozide of the suppressant effect of d-amphetamine on operant behaviour. *Psychopharmacology* 91, 239-243.

Murthy, K.S., McHenry, L., Grider, J.R. & Makhlouf, G.M. (1995) Adenosine Al and A,, receptors coupled to distinct interactive signaling pathway in intestinal muscle cells. *J. Pharm. Exp. Ther.* 274, 300-306.

Myers, S. & Pugsley, T.A. (1986) Decrease in rat striatal dopamine synthesis and metabolism in vivo by metabolically stable adenosine receptor agonists. *Brain Res.* 375, 193-197.

Neal, B.S. & Sparber, S.B. (1986) Mianserin attenuates naloxone-precipitated withdrawal in rats acutely or chronically dependent upon morphine. *J Pharmacol* 38, 3391-???.

Neal, B. S. & Sparber, S.B. (1990) The serotonin2 antagonist ritanserin blocks quasi-morphine withdrawal at a time when mianserin in no longer effective. *Psychopharmacology* 100, 258-266.

Nestler, E.J. (1992) Molecular mechanisms of drug addiction. *J Neuroscience* 12; 2439-2450.

Olah, M.E. & Stiles, G.L. (1995) Adenosine receptor subtypes: characterization and therapeutic regulation. *Annu. Rev. Pharmacol. Toxicol.* 35, 581-606.

Olpe, H.R., Karlsson, G., Pozza, M.F., Brugger, F., Steinmann, N., Van Riezen, H., Fagg, G., Hall, R.G., Froestel, W. & Bittigr, H. (1990)

CGP 35348: a centrally active blocker of GABA-B receptors. *Eur. J. Pharmacol.* 187, 27-38.

O'Neil, M.F., C.T. Dourish & Iversen, S.D. (1991) Hypolocomotion induced by peripheral or central administration of CCK in the CCK-A receptor antagonist L365,260. *Eur. J. Pharmacol.* 193, 203-208.

Perkins, K.A., Grobe, J.E., Epstein, H., caggiula, A.C., Stiller, R.L. & Jacob, R.G. (1993) Chronic and acute tolerance to subjective effects of nicotine. *Pharmacol. Biochem. Behav.* 45, 375-381.

Perry, T.L.,, Berry, K., Hansen, S., Diamond, S. & Mok, C. (1971) Regional distribution of amino acids in human brain obtained at autopsy. *J. Neurochem.* 18, 513-519.

Pomerleau, C.S. & Pomerleau, O.F. (1992) Euphoriant effects of nicotine in smokers. Psychopharmacology 108, 460-465. Porreca, F. & Burks, T.F. (1983) The spinal cord as a site of opioid effects on gastrointestinal transit in the mouse. *J. Pharmacol. Exp. Ther.* 227, 22-27.

Rasmussen, K., Beitner-Johnson, D.B. & Krystal, J.H. (1990) Opiate withdrawal and the rat locus coeruleus: behavioral, electrophysiological, and biochemical correlates. *J. Neurosci.* 10, 2308-2317.

Redmond, D.E.J. & Krystal, J.H. (1984) Multiple mechanisms of withdrawal from opioid drugs. *Ann. Rev. Neurosci.* 7, 4434 4 7.

Rezayat, M., Nikfar, Sh. & Zarrindast, M.R. (1994) CCK receptor may prevent tolerance to morphine in mice. *Eur. J. Pharmacol.* 254, 21-26.

Rezayat, M., Azizi, N. & Zarrindast, M.R. (1997) On the mechanisms of cholecystokinin (CCK): receptor stimulation attenuates morphine-dependent in mice. Pharmacol. Toxicol. 81, 124-129.

Sabetkasai, M. & Zarrindast, M.R. (1993) Antinociception: Interaction between adenosine and GABA systems. *Arch. Int. Pharmacodyn.* 322, 14-22.

Salem, A. & Hope, W. (1997) Effect of adenosine receptor agonists and antagonists on the expression of opiate withdrawal in rats. Pharmacol. Biochem. Behav. 57, 671-679. Sawynok, J. & Labella, F.S. (1982) On the involvement of GABA in the analgesia produced by baclofen, muscimol and morphine. *Neuropharmacology* 21, 397-403.

Sawynok, J., Sweeney, M.I. & White, T.D. (1989) Adenosine release may mediate spinal analgesia by morphine. *Trends Pharmacol. Sci.* 10, 186-189.

Stanfa, L., A. Dickenson, X.-J. Xu & Z.W.-Hallin (1994) Cholecystokinin and morphine analgesia: variations on a them. *Trend. Pharmacol. Sci.* 15, 65-66.

Seale, T., Abla, K.A., Shamim, M.T., Carney, J.M. & Daly, J.W. (1988) 3,7 Dimethyl-1-1 propargylxanthine: a potent and selective in vivo antagonist of adenosine analogs. *Life Sci.* 43, 1671-1684.

Sloan, J.J., J.W. Brooks, A.J. Eisenman & W.R. Martin (1963) The effect of addiction to and abstinence from morphine on rat tissue catecholamine and serotonin levels. *Psychopharmacology* 4, 261-270.

Stolerman, I.P. (1988) Characterization of central nicotinic receptors by studies on the nicotine cue and conditioned taste aversion in rats, *Pharmacol. Biochem. Behav.* 30, 235-242.

Stoof, J.C. & J.W. Kebabian (1981) opposing roles for D, and D2 dopamine receptors in efflux of cyclic AMP from rat neostriatum. *Nature* 294, 366-368.

Stoof, J.C. & Kebabian, J.W. (1984) Two dopamine receptors; biochemical, phsiology and pharmacology. *Life Sci.* 35, 2281-2296.

Suh, H.H., K.A. Collins & F. Tseng (1992) Intrathecal cholecystokinin octapeptide attenuates the antinociception and release of immunoreactive Met-enkephalin induced by intraventricular B-endorphin in the rat. *Neuropeptides* 21, 131-136.

Tao, P.L., Liu, C.F., Tsai, H.C., 1995. Chronic intracerebroventricular administration of morphine down-regulate spinal adenosine Al receptors in rats. *Eur. J. Pharmacol.* 278, 233-237.

Ticku, M.K., Huffman, R.D., 1980. The effects of acute and chronic morphine administration on GABA receptor binding. *Eur. J. Pharmacol.* 68, 97-106.

Ticku, M.K., Maksay, G., 1983. Convulsant/depressant site of action at the allosteric benzodiazepine-GABA receptorionophore complex. *Life Sci.* 33, 2363-2375.

Torrens, Y., Beaujouan, J.C., Besson, M.J., Michelot, R. and Glowinski, J. (1981) Inhibitory effects of GABA, Lglutamic acid and nicotine on the potassium-evoked release of substance P in substantia slice of the rat. *Eur. J. Pharmacol.* 71, 383-392.

Tseng, L.F., D.A. Brase & H.H. Loh: Dopaminergic influence of withdrawal jumping behavior in morphine-dependent mice. *Res. Commun. Chem. Pathol. Pharmacol.* 1976, 15, 435-446.

Tucker, J.F., Plant, N.T., von-Uexkull, A., Collier, H.O., 1984. Inhibition by adenosine analogs of opiate withdrawal effects. *NIDA Res. Monogr.* 49, 85-91.

Vaccarino, F.J. & J. Rankin: Nucleus accumbens cholecystokinin (CCK) can either attenuate or potentiate amphetamineinduced locomotor activity: Evidence for rostral-caudal differences in accumbens CCK function. Behav. *Neuosci.* 1989, 103, 831-836.

Vanderhaeghen, *i.J., J.C.* Signean & W. Gepts: New peptide in the vertebrate CNS reacting with antigastrin antibodies. *Nature* 1975, 25, 604-605.

Weis, O.F., Sriwatanakul, K., Alloza, i.L., Weintraub, M., Lasagna, L., 1983. Attitudes of patients, house staff, and nurses toward postoperative analgesic care. *Anesth. Analg.* 62, 70-74.

Woodruff, G.N., D.R. Hill, Pl. Boden, R. Pinnock, L.Singh & *J.* Xu, X.J., Z. Wiesenfeld-Hallin, J.Hughes, D.C. Horwell and T. Hokfelt: CI988, a selective antagonist of cholecystokinin-B receptors prevent morphine tolerance in the rat. *Br. J. Pharmacol.* 1992, 105, 591-596

Woodruff, G.N. & J. Hughes: Cholecystokinin antagonists. Annu. Rov. Pharmacol. Toxicol. 1991, 31, 169 501.

Welin, M , J Harro, R. Yukhananov, F. Nyberg & L. Orcland: Cholecystokinin receptor binding in morphine analgesia: Tolerance, withdrawal and abstinence. *Neuropeptides* 1994, 26, 379-383.

Yarbrough, G.C., McGuffin-Clineschmidt, i.C., 1981. In vivo behavioral assessment of central nervous system purinergic receptors. *Eur. J. Pharmacol.* 76, 137-144.

Zarrindast, M.R. and Farzin, D. (1996) Nicotine attenuates naloxone-induced jumping behaviour in morphine-dependent mice. *Eur. J. Pharmacol.* 298, 1-6

Zarrindast, M.R., Elaheh Mousa-Ahmadi (1999) Effects of GABAergic system on naloxone-induced jumping in morphinedependent *Mice. Eur. J. Pharmacol.* 381; 129-133.

Zarrindast MR, Moghadampour E, 1989, opposing influences of D-1 and D-2 dopamine receptor activation on morphine-induced antinociception. *Arch Int. Pharmacodyn. Ther.* 300, 37-50.

Zarrindast, M.R., Sabetkasai, M., 1992. Stress-induced antinociception and GABAergic mechanism. *Arch. Int. Pharmacodyn.* 318, 5-12.

Zarrindast, M.R., Sabetkasai, M., Khakpour, Sh, 1993. Effects of drug active at adenosine receptors on stress-induced analgesia in mice. *Arch. Int. Pharmacodyn.* 325, 51-60.

Zarrindast, M.R., Iraie, F., Heidari, M.R., Mohagheghi-Badi, M., 1997. Effect of adenosine receptor agonists and antagonists on morphine-induced catalepsy in mice. *Eur. J. Pharmacol.* 338, 11-16.

Zarrindast, M.R., B. Naghipour, Farshad Roushan-zamir, Bijan Shafaghi (1999) Effects of adenosine receptor agents on the expression of morphine withdrawal in mice. *Eur. J. Pharmacol,* 369. 17-22.

Zarrindast, M.R., Farahvash, H., 1994. Effects of GABA-ergic drugs onpenile erection induce by apomorphine in rats. *Psychopharmacology* 115, 249-253.

Zarrindast M.R., Malekzadeh A, Rezayat M, Ghazi-Khansari M (1995) Effects of cholecystokkinin receptor agonist andantagonists on morphine dependence in mice. *Pharmacol Toxicol* 77 : 360-364.

Zetler, G. Analgesia and ptosis caused by caerulein anc chlocystokinin octapeptide (CCK-8). *Neuropharmacology* 1980, 19, 415-42.

HIGH THROUGHPUT SCREEN AND COMBINATORIAL CHEMISTRY FOR OPTIMIZED DRUG DISCOVERY

J.B. GUPTA AND ANITA CHUGH

New Drug Discovery Research, Ranbaxy Research Laboratories, 20, Sector 18, Udyog Vihar, Gurgaon–122 001

Summary

Biomolecular screening of thousands of new chemical entities in different assays to fish out a lead molecule is the foundation of drug discovery process and is followed by pharmaceutical industry world-over. Until recently, biological assays were performed manually which not only made the drug discovery costly and labour intensive, but also time-consuming. In recent years, advancement in automation and computer technology together with the judicious use of miniaturization has transformed the manual biomolecular testing into an automated, user- friendly High Throughput Screening *(HTS)*. Screening procedures are being automated with methods of selecting and optimizing ligands through several cycles. High throughput screening is an automated process by which large number of compounds present either singly or in a reaction mixture can be tested rapidly in primary activity screens against a particular target. The goal of HTS is to detect high quality 'hits' or 'leads' that are active in nanomolar concentrations and possess a new chemical structure. In order to match the rate of synthesis of compounds generated through combinatorial chemistry, the screen speed is achieved through system automation, assay miniaturization and associated bioinformatics. This permits screening of up to 50,000 - 100,000 samples a day against a given target. Complex work stations equipped with loading bay, robotic arm, autopipetting, labeling, incubation and radioactivity counting provision along with data storage and retrieval are all integral parts of the infrastructure. Several types of bioassays such as receptor binding, cell-based and those employing microorganisms have successfully been developed for HTS. Since a variety of human physiological processes can now be expressed in microbes that are easy to grow, provide selectivity and relative ease for genetic manipulation, these systems offer an attractive option for cell-based HTS.

It is a known premise for drug discovery that more you screen more are the chances of 'hit'. Advances in scientific knowledge particularly molecular biology have greatly influenced the drug discovery process today. Two main complimentary approaches have now become dominating, namely, the rational one based on computer aided structure-based design strategies and the random one based on combinatorial chemistry (Fig. 1). This nascent technology already has produced more new compounds in just a few years than the pharmaceutical industry previously did in its entire history. Almost all-major drug companies now use random screening for identification of novel leads. The limitations of employing conventional methods for screening are that these are costly, labour intensive and restrict the number of compounds that can be tested. Moreover, advancements in medicinal chemistry particularly those related to combinatorial technology have allowed investigators to generate new chemical entities with high degree of molecular diversity. Therefore, a constant challenge to biologists involved in drug discovery is to meet this demand by making a quantum leap in screening throughput that ultimately accelerates the chances of discovering a lead. This has been impacted significantly by technology advancement in the form of evolution of HTS [1–5].

High throughput screening can be defined as a tool for rapidly identifying novel pharmacologically active molecules by evaluating large number of NCEs present

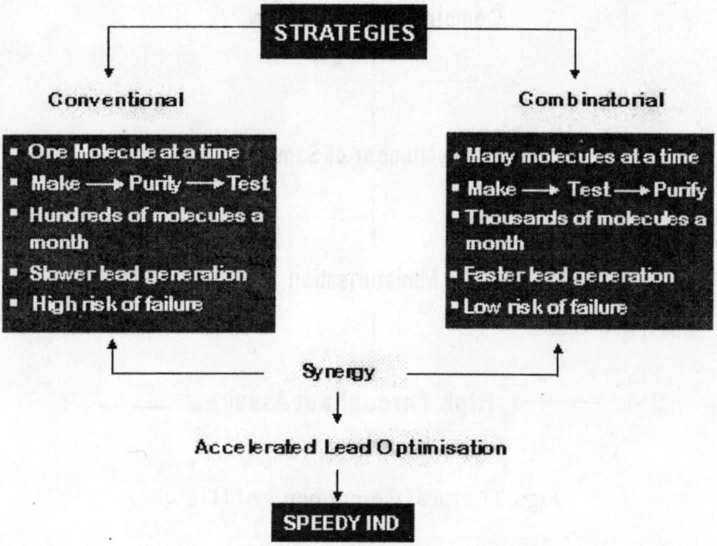

Fig 1 Druq Discovery : A Journey from Conventional to Combinatorial Technology

singly or in a mixture, employing the targeted assays. The term 'large number of compounds' is of course relative. The entire process being solely dependent on the degree of automation, assay technology developed and the ability to analyze and interpret voluminous data so generated.

CRITICAL COMPONENTS OF HTS

Speed is the buzzword for HTS where conventional manual procedures employed for the assay have been automated. The critical factors for throughput screening include accurate preparation of test samples, their evaluation in many assays, data analysis to choose quality hit and establishment of structure-activity relationship. High throughput screening demands speed and cost effectiveness in all operations. This has now been achieved by the appropriate use of robotics, miniaturization and bioinformatics (Fig. 2).

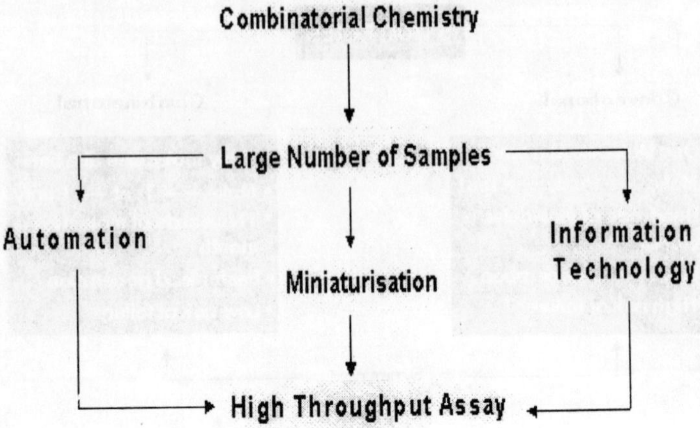

Fig. 2 Critical Components of HTS

Robotic automation of HTS provides both speed and accuracy to the assay system. A variety of steps ranging from sample weighing, dispensing, dissolving, making dilutions, addition of solvents and assay reagents, incubation and loading into quantitating devices such as scintillator counter or ELISA can be automated by using robotic arms. Automation of even a few of these steps can improve the speed substantially at a relatively low level of investment. However, a complete automation of these procedures would allow round the clock operation and increase the rate of screening many fold.

As expected, automated screening of NCEs against a variety of targets would generate large sum of data. Handling the vast amount of data so generated is also a real challenge. The requirement from data management point of view includes data bases of chemical structures, number of assays performed, results of individual screening assays and calculations, their linking with structures and getting proper SAR information. The importance of efficient information management systems cannot be ignored, as it requires solid up front planning. Miniaturization is another important component of HTS. Miniaturization not only enhances throughput but also lowers the cost of screening since it depends substantially on sample volumes. The 96-well microtitre plate has made the conventional 8 ml scintillation vials obsolete. Many advanced screening centres have already replaced 96-well microtitre plates by 384-well microtitre plates. Technologists are optimistic about further miniaturization and are actually evaluating high-density 864-well format plates[6].

SAMPLE LOGGING

Suitably arranged compound libraries and automated pipetting systems are critical aspects of sample preparation and assay automation. Synthesis of combinatorial libraries can also be accomplished in microtitre plates. Similarly, samples received from other sources such as existing libraries, fermentation broth or natural product extracts can be dispensed into microtitre plates. Each well of the microtitre plate must be marked by an appropriate

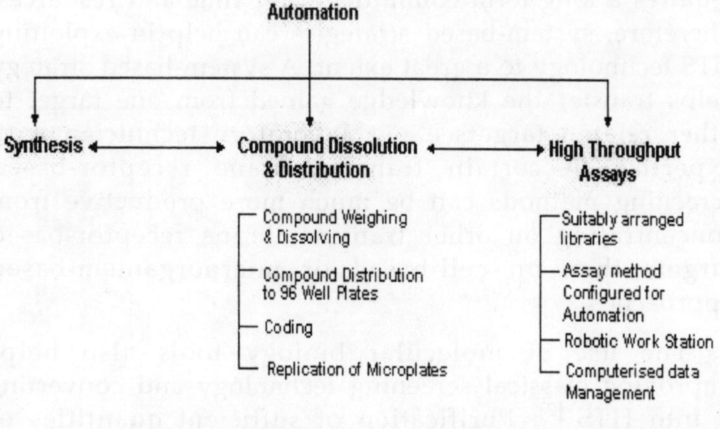

Fig 3 Redesigning Drug Discovery Through HTS

marking system to provide proper identification to each test compound. Automated sample identifiers are essential because there is considerable potential for error if manual sample logging is used (Fig. 3).

Automated pipetting system is a must for dispensing solvents to dissolve the samples and for adding reagents to perform the assay. This is an area, which traditionally has required a lot of manual involvement for repetitive liquid handling steps. The use of an automated pipetting workstation improves the quality of data and increases throughput of the assay.

DEVELOPMENT OF WELL-DESIGNED ASSAYS

While appropriate automation, miniaturization and informatics can provide accuracy and speed, the success of HTS depends on development of well-designed assays and their configuration for automation (Fig. 3). Well-designed assays are the basis of good screening and hence involve a considerable length of time to develop them. The choice of the type of assay itself is very critical. Though many types of assays (viz. *in vitro,* cell- or microorganism-based) can be converted into HTS[1,3], each requires a long term commitment for time and resources. Therefore, system-based strategies can help in exploiting HTS technology to a great extent. A system-based strategy helps transfer the knowledge gained from one target to other related targets e.g. a laboratory technician with expertise in certain transmembrane receptor-based screening methods can be much more productive from concentrating on other transmembrane receptor-based targets than on cell-based or microorganism-based approaches.

The use of molecular biology tools also helps improving classical screening technology and converting it into HTS [2]. Purification of sufficient quantities of targets like receptors or enzymes needed for massive screening is a very time-consuming task. The use of biotechnology to clone the specific gene and then overexpress the protein can circumvent this problem. In fact, many receptors and enzymes have now been cloned and used successfully for receptor ligand binding or enzyme-based HTS.

CONFIGURATION OF ASSAYS FOR HTS

Theoretically, even though most steps can be automated for HTS, the speed and accuracy cannot be assured. Moreover, procedures like centrifugation, washing or fractionation pose problems for automation. Therefore, ideally the assay most suited for HTS should be a single step and be restricted to processes such as reagent addition and incubation. Recently developed technologies like Scintillation Proximity Assay (SPA) generally require very little manipulation and are well suited for HTS. The entire assay can be performed successfully in a microtitre plate [7]. It is a versatile technology which can be applied to diverse assays like receptor binding, radioimmuno, enzyme and even for transcription factor binding assays.

In SPA, solid scintillant is coated over the plastic well of microtitre plate and the target of interest viz. receptor or enzyme is immobilized to the solid scintillant. Radiolabelled ligand when added to this well binds to the target which brings radioactivity into close proximity of the scintillant. This results in emission of a light signal which upon amplification is measured with the help of scintillation counter. However, the radioisotope which remains unbound is away from the scintillant and remains undetected. The SPA and its comparison with the conventional binding assay is depicted in Fig. 4.

DATA MANAGEMENT

Combinatorial technologies including synthesis and HTS generate vast amount of data. The data generation

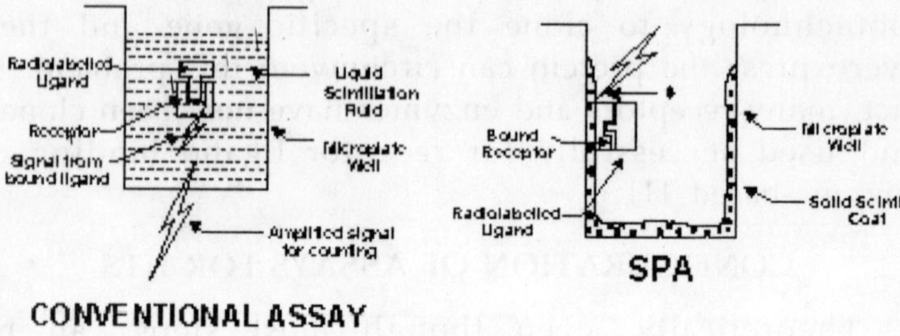

Fig. 4 - Conventional Binding Assay vs. SPA

begins from planning and synthesizing the compounds and continues to pour in from analytical and screening efforts. Additionally, there is a need to interlink data from each function so that necessary information can be extracted for a query from any perspective. The success of combinatorial technologies therefore requires a general database model and associated software tools to support the different library types, synthetic strategies and screening results.

Problems & Limitations of HTS

High throughput screening employs complicated and sophisticated systems that are problematic right from the start. Commonly seen problems are system crashes and discrepancies in results obtained with manual set up. These can occur even after months of trouble free operation. Development of assays and their configuration for automation is indeed a difficult task and building of an automation team within the HTS set up is highly desirable. False negative or false positive is inherent problems with any assay. Both create a problem for HTS as well but more so in the case of false positives since such results cause waste of time and resources.

Besides, HTS has certain other inherent limitations. It should be understood that the purpose of HTS is to identify the lead compound and provide direction for its optimization. HTS is not capable of assessing many critical aspects of drug development. viz. efficacy, safety, bioavailability etc. which have to be studied through conventional methodologies. Ideally, biologists prefer to screen individual compounds since their ratio in a given mixture may vary which would affect the assay outcome to a great extent. Moreover, the absence of a clear strategy for separating individual compounds in an active well might jeopardize the importance of the assay itself. Miniaturization, though associated with many advancements, may also compromise the sensitivity of the assay. A cloned target overexpresses the protein and facilitates HTS. In contrast to the wild receptor, cloned receptors and their expression in mammalian cells lack the second messenger system. The consequence of this in terms of assessing the affinity of a compound is not known and remains, a matter of speculation. However, the advantages offered by HTS are imminent and far outweigh these limitations.

THE COMBINATORIAL FUTURE

Combinatorial technology has provided a means of circumventing traditional limitations encountered in lead identification by permitting the synthesis and screening of immense number of NCEs. This technology is actually revolutionizing drug discovery as every large pharmaceutical company is either putting it in place in-house, buying it, partnering it, or is at least worried that it does not have it. In a nutshell, it is the ultimate high-throughput screening tool. The focus has been rapidly shifting from peptides to more of a heterocycles-small organic molecules. The potential of combinatorial chemistry was summarized as "enabling completely novel, biologically active compounds to be identified through screening without any prior structural or sequence knowledge"[8]. Future drug discovery may therefore depend less on the serendipitous findings of the past which yielded drugs such as sulphonamides and monoamine oxidase inhibitors. The future of drug discovery may lie in mass generation of locks to the keys rather keys to locks. This is in sharp contrast to Paul Ehrlich's 20th century description of drugs as chemical keys and receptors as biological locks. Indeed, one can envisage the creation of fully synthetic receptors custom designed to bind to specific ligands. With the advent of combinatorial chemistry and HTS, it is now possible to test millions of keys to a lock without precisely defining either at the outset. It may be noteworthy that the super miniaturized high-resolution robotics world of ultra-HTS is just around the corner in which hundreds of thousands of assays may be performed daily.

REFERENCES

1. Broach J.R. and Thorner J. High throughput screening for drug discovery. *Nature*, 384 (suppl), 14-16, 1996.
2. Palmer M.A.J. High throughput screening on a low budget. *Nature Biotech*, 14, 513-515, 1996.
3. Nelson N.J. Drug discovery shifts toward rapid, mass screening. *J. Natl. Canc. Inst.*, 88, 704-705, 1996.
4. Drews J. Drug discovery today - and tomorrow. *Drug Disc. Today*, 5, 2-4, 2000.
5. Lahana R. How many leads from HTS? *Drug Disc.* Today, 4, 447-448, 1999.
6. Hook D. Ultra high throughput screening - a journey into nanoland with Gulliver and Alice. *Drug Disc. Today*, 1, 267-268, 1996.
7. Cook N.D. Scintillation proximity assay: A versatile high-throughput screening technology. *Drug Disc. Today*, 1, 287-294, 1996.
8. Birmingham K. Pharmaprojects Magz., 5-7, Jan. 1996

CARDIAC REFLEXES ELICITED BY PHENYLDIGUANIDE ARE AUGMENTED BY BUTHUS TAMULUS VENOM VIA KININ RECEPTORS

SHRIPAD B. DESHPANDE*, ANITHA B. ALEX AND SOVAN BAGCHI

Department of Physiology, Institute of Medical Sciences, Banaras Hindu University, Varanasi -221 005, India

Abstract

In the present study, the role of kinin receptors in mediating the *Buthus tamulus* (BT) venom-induced reflex augmentation was evaluated. Intravenous injection of phenyl- diguanide (PDG) in adult male albino rats produced reflex hypotension, bradycardia and apnea lasting for > 60 sec. After exposure to BT venom (50 μg/kg, i.v., for 30 min), the PDG-induced reflex responses were augmented both in magnitude and time period. The reflex augmentation was associated with increase in pulmonary water content. However, at this concentration of venom, there were no great alterations in resting blood pressure, heart rate and respiratory rate.

The augmentation of cardiac reflexes and production of pulmonary oedema by venom were absent in aprotinin (kallikrein-kinin inhibitor; 6000 KIU) pretreated animals. Further, the venom-induced cardiopulmonary changes were blocked by Hoe 140, a B_2 receptor antagonist, but not by des-Arg^{10}-Hoe 140, B_1 receptor antagonist. Results of the present study indicate that BT venom exerts its action through kinins involving B_2 receptors.

INTRODUCTION

Stings due to Indian red scorpion, *Buthus tamulus* (BT), have been reported to be fatal and occur mainly in the rural parts of Andhra pradesh, Karnataka, Tamilnadu, Pondicherry and along the coastal areas of Maharashtra (Bawaskar & Bawaskar, 1994; Murthy et al., 1987; 1988). BT envenoming in human beings and experimental animals produce varying degrees of cardio-pulmonary abnormalities like cardiac dysrhythmias, acute myocarditis, hypotension followed by hypertension, increased peripheral resistance, peripheral circulatory failure, cardiac arrhythmias, abnormalities in ECG and massive pulmonary oedema, respiratory dysrhythmias, decreased ventilation, etc (Murthy & Hossein, 1986; Murthy et al., 1991; Rowan et al., 1992; Murthy & Hase, 1994). In addition, reports from this laboratory provide evidences for BT venom-induced augmentation of cardiac reflexes elicited by phenyldiguanide (Bagchi & Deshpande, 1998, 1999). Chemicals like histamine, serotonin, kinins, prostaglandins, etc are known to increase the vagal discharges evoked by PDG (Paintal, 1973; Anand & Paintal, 1988; Panzenbeck et al., 1988; Hainsworth, 1991). The venom-induced augmentation of PDG reflex was shown to be due to the sensitization of reflex components by kinins (Bagchi & Deshpande, 1998, 1999).

Since, the kinin synthesis inhibitor (aprotinin) prolonged the survival time of *Leiurus quinquestriatus* envenomed rats (Ismail et al., 1992), it was proposed that, kinins play a vital role in the pathophysiology of scorpion toxicity. Recently it has been shown that cardiac reflex changes and pulmonary oedema produced by *Buthus tamulus* venom could be reversed by aprotinin (Bagchi & Deshpande, 1998; Deshpande et al., 1999). Kinins exert its action in atleast 3 different ways, either directly on vagal C fibres, or as inflammatory mediators or indirectly through prostaglandins and other pathways. Two types of kinin receptors are identified pharmacologically, namely B_1 and B_2. Though the earlier reports demonstrate the role of kinins in scorpion envenomation, the underlying mechanisms and the receptor systems involved still remains obscure. The present study was therefore undertaken, to identify the type of kinin receptors involved in *Buthus tamulus* envenomation and the possible mechanism of action.

METHODS

Animals, anaesthesia and recording procedure

Adult male albino rats (150-250 g) of Charles Foster strain were anaesthetized with urethane (1.5 g/kg; i.p.). Tracheal cannulation was done to keep the respiratory tract patent, followed by jugular venous cannulation to deliver drugs/venom. Femoral artery cannulation was carried out for the recording of blood pressure. Animals were allowed to stabilise for atleast 30 min after the surgical procedures. Electrocardiographic (ECG) potentials were recorded with the help of needle electrodes in standard limb lead II configuration. Blood pressure was recorded from femoral artery with the help of a pressure transducer (Stathum transducer). Respiratory movements were recorded by securing skin over the xiphisternum with a thread to a force displacement transducer. All the recordings were made on Student's Physiograph.

The pulmonary water content was determined by the method described by Deshpande, et al., 1999. Briefly, lungs from saline treated (control) and venom exposed animals were taken out, weighed and then dried to a constant weight in an electric oven for more than 48 hours. The difference in wet weight and dry weight were taken and expressed as the % of wet weight.

Experimental protocol

Phenyldiguanide (PDG; 10 μg/kg; i.v) was injected and the response (initial PDG response) was obtained, followed by venom (50 μg/kg). After 30 min of venom administration, the PDG response was obtained again.

In second set of experiments, after taking the initial PDG response, aprotinin/des-Arg/Hoe 140 was injected and 15 min later the PDG response was elicited again. Subsequently, crude BT venom (CV; 50 μg/kg; i.v) was injected and 30 min after, the PDG response was obtained.

Drugs and Solutions

Lyophilized *Mesobuthus tamulus* venom was purchased from Haffkine's Research Institute, Mumbai, India. Hoe 140 and des-Arg^{10}-Hoe 140 (des-Arg) from Sigma Chemical Co., USA; Aprotinin (100,000 Kallikrein inactivating units; KIU) from Wako Pure Chemical Industries, Ltd., Japan, was gifted by Prof. H. Nishino, Nagoya City University Medical School, Japan and Phenyldiguanide, from Koch Light laboratories, Bucks, U.K, a gift from Prof. A.S. Paintal, V.P. Chest Institute, University of Delhi. Stock solutions of all the drugs were prepared in distilled water and subsequent dilutions were made in normal saline at the time of administration.

Analysis of data

All the values were presented as means ± S.E.M. The values of BP, HR and RR, before injecting PDG were taken as initial values and the values after the injection of PDG at every 5 s were normalised to the initial values and pooled to obtain mean ± S.E.M. Differences between various groups were compared by using Student's *t*-test for paired and unpaired observations. A P value < 0.05 was considered statistically significant.

RESULTS

Venom augmented the PDG-induced reflex response

Jugular venous injection of PDG (10 μg/kg) produced hypotension, bradycardia and apnea for a period of time.

The heart rate, respiratory rate or changes in mean arterial pressure were calculated for every 5 sec upto 60 sec and expressed as % of initial response. The % response values were plotted at every 5 sec and the area of the curve is calculated as shown in Fig. 1 for heart rate. Blood pressure and respiratory responses were also computed similarly.

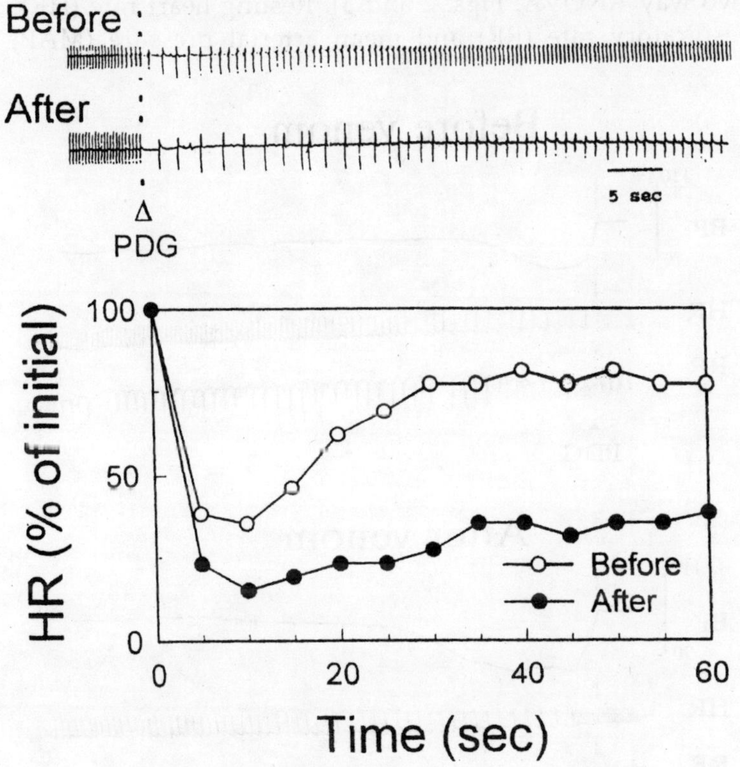

Fig. 1 Phenyldiguandide (PDG; 10 μg/kg) induced changes in heart rate (HR) before and after BT venom (50 μg/kg). Original ECG tracings before and after venom are given in the upper panels. The point of injection of PDG is indicated by Δ and dotted line. Horizontal bar denotes 5 sec. The lower panel shows the time-response plot of PDG response at every 5 sec before and after venom upto 60 sec. Area of time-response curve represents the PDG response. Note the increase in area after venom as compared to before.

Reflexes elicited by PDG were compared with those obtained after (30 min) the injection of crude BT venom (50 μg/kg).

After the administration of BT venom, the reflex hypotension, bradycardia and apnea time evoked by PDG were potentiated by about 2 times the initial ($P < 0.05$; two way ANOVA; Figs. 2 and 3). Resting heart rate (HR), respiratory rate (RR) and mean arterial pressure (MAP)

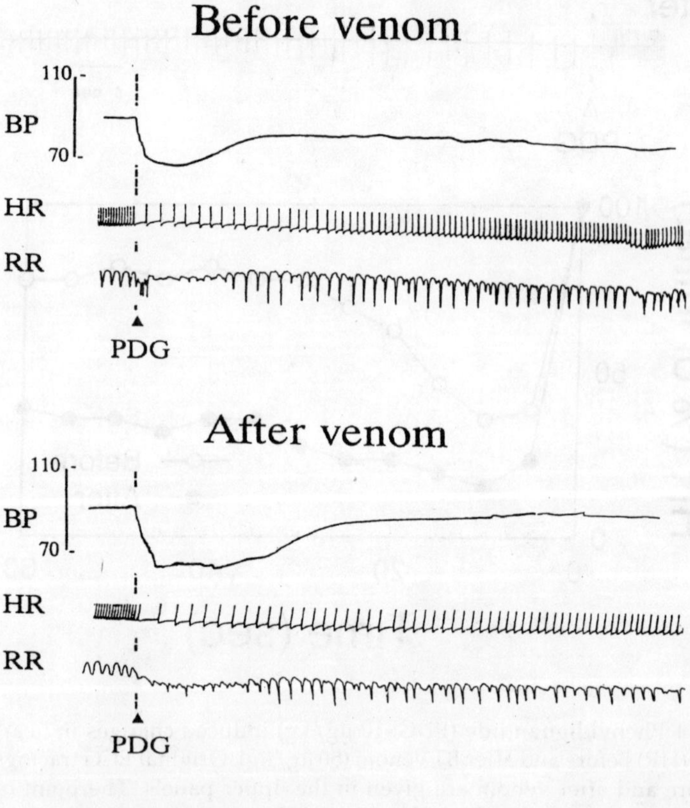

Fig. 2 Original tracings of blood pressure (BP), ECG (HR) and respiration (RR) indicating PDG-induced cardio pulmonary reflexes before and after crude venom (50 μg/kg) from the same animal. The point of administration of PDG is indicated by ▲ and the dotted line.

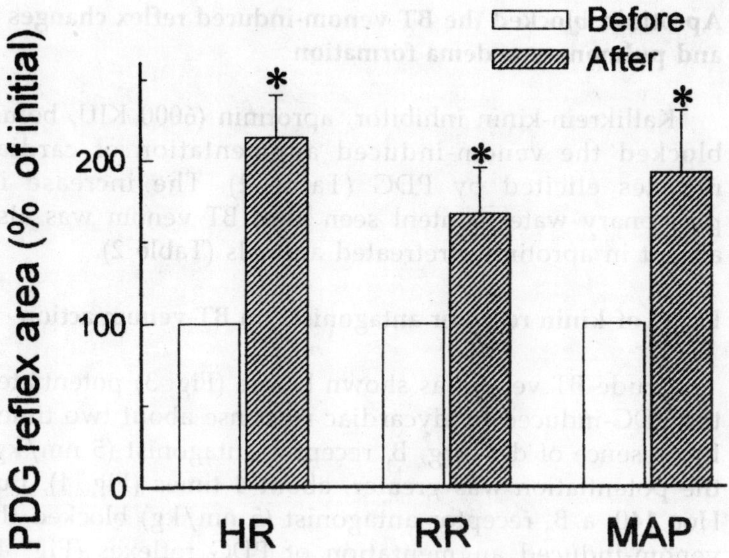

Fig. 3 Bar diagram depicting the PDG-induced reflex area of heart rate (HR), respiration rate (RR) and mean arterial pressure (MAP) before and after crude BT venom (CV). The HR, RR and MAP values after venom are expressed as percentage of initial reflex area (100 %). * $P < 0.05$ as compared to the initial reflex area (Student's t-test for paired observations).

were not altered after the exposure to venom (Table 1). The heart rate was found to be little lower than the initial, though statistically not different ($P > 0.05$, Student's t-test).

TABLE 1

Table showing the resting heart rate (HR), respiratory rate (RR) and mean arterial pressure (MAP) before and after CV (50 μg/kg). HR is indicated as beats per minute (Bpm) and RR as rate per minute (Rpm) and MAP as mm Hg.

Condition	HR (Bpm)	RR (Rpm)	MAP (mm Hg)
Before CV	270 ± 21.1	105 ± 3.0	85 ± 5.0
After CV	258 ± 24.7	108 ± 8.5	82 ± 3.5

Aprotinin blocked the BT venom-induced reflex changes and pulmonary oedema formation

Kallikrein-kinin inhibitor, aprotinin (6000 KIU, bolus) blocked the venom-induced augmentation of cardiac reflexes elicited by PDG (Table 2). The increase in pulmonary water content seen after BT venom was also absent in aprotinin pretreated animals (Table 2).

Effect of kinin receptor antagonists on BT venom action

Crude BT venom as shown before (Fig. 3) potentiated the PDG-induced bradycardiac response about two times. In presence of des-Arg, B_1 receptor antagonist (5 nm/kg) the potentiation was greater, about 4 times (Fig. 4). But, Hoe 140, a B_2 receptor antagonist (5 nm/kg) blocked the venom-induced augmentation of PDG reflexes (Fig. 4). Hoe 140 or des-Arg *per se* did not alter the PDG reflex pattern. Further, resting heart rate in the presence of antagonists before and after venom were not different from initial rate.

TABLE 2.

Crude BT venom (CV) induced reflex changes were blocked by aprotinin (6000 KIU bolus). Mean ± S.E.M values of time-response changes in reflex area in HR, RR and MAP produced by CV (50 µg/kg) in the absence (CV alone) or presence of aprotinin (Apr + CV) are presented. Pulmonary water content in saline treated animals was 79.21 ± 0.42 % of wet weight. * indicates P < 0.05 as compared to the venom alone values. @ P < 0.05, as compared to saline treated group (Student's t-test).

Condition	n	Reflex area (% of initial)			Pulmonary water (% of wet weight)
		HR	RR	MAP	
CV alone	4	203±18	185±28	218±35	82.5 ± 1.65@
Apr + CV	4	108±15*	96±17*	95±10*	79.5 ± 1.49*

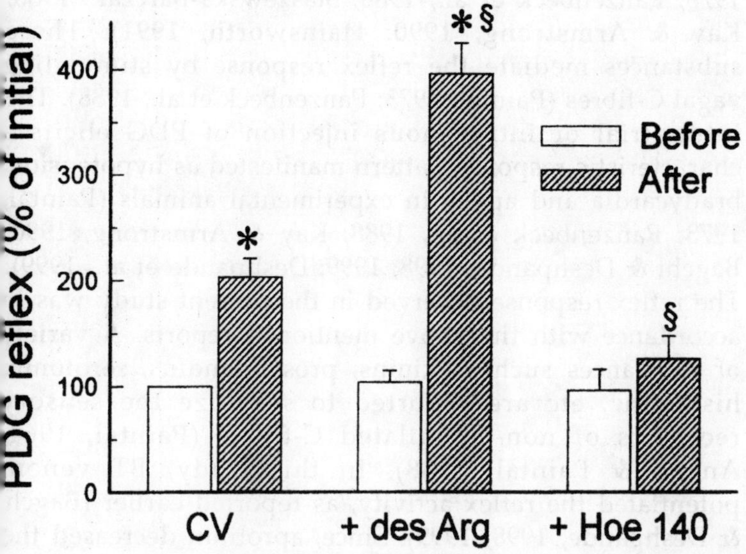

Fig. 4 Effect of kinin receptor antagonists on BT venom action. B_2 receptor antagonist blocked the crude venom (CV) -induced augmentation of PDG reflex, while B_1 receptor did not. des-Arg or Hoe 140 (5 nm/kg) per se did not produce any effect on PDG-reflex area (as indicated by open bars). * indicates $P < 0.05$, as compared to initial response (Student's t-test); § indicates $P < 0.05$ from the venom response (unpaired t-test).

DISCUSSION

The present study confirms the *Buthus tamulus* venom-induced augmentation of PDG-elicited cardiopulmonary reflexes and pulmonary oedema formation reported earlier (Bagchi & Deshpande, 1998, 1999, Deshpande et al., 1999). Further, the data demonstrate that the venom-induced augmentation is mediated through kinins via B_2 receptors.

Phenyldiguanide, phenylbiguanide, nicotine, serotonin, veratridine, etc stimulate pulmonary J receptors as well as coronary receptors (Paintal, 1973; Dey & Rao,

1978; Panzenbeck et al., 1988; Staszewska-Barczak, 1988; Kay & Armstrong, 1990; Hainsworth, 1991). These substances mediate the reflex response by stimulating vagal C-fibres (Paintal, 1973; Panzenbeck et al., 1988). The intra-atrial or intravenous injection of PDG elicits a characteristic response pattern manifested as hypotension, bradycardia and apnea in experimental animals (Paintal, 1973; Panzenbeck et al., 1988; Kay & Armstrong, 1990; Bagchi & Deshpande, 1998, 1999; Deshpande et al., 1999). The reflex response observed in the present study was in accordance with the above mentioned reports. A variety of substances such as kinins, prostaglandins, serotonin, histamine, etc are reported to sensitize the sensory receptors of non-medullated C-fibres (Paintal, 1964, Anand & Paintal, 1988). In this study, BT venom potentiated the reflex activity, as reported earlier (Bagchi & Deshpande, 1998, 1999). Since, aprotinin decreased the mortality rate of scorpion envenomed animals (Ismail et al., 1992), it is possible that kinins are also involved in venom-induced potentiation of reflex activity. Hence, the increased level of kinins may be responsible for the greater scorpion venom fatalities reported earlier (Ismail et al., 1992).

Angiotensin converting enzyme (ACE) inhibitor (captopril), besides inhibiting the formation of angiotensin II, also acts as a kininase-II inhibitor, necessary for the degradation of kinins, resulting in the accumulation of kinins (Vogel & Werle, 1970; Brown et al., 1996). Further, kinins are also shown to potentiate the metabolic and cardiovascular effects of ACE inhibitor (Linz et al. 1995; Brown et al., 1996). Hence, the endogenous kinins are implicated for the actions of ACE. Evidences for the involvement of kinins for captopril/venom-induced potentiation of cardiac reflexes are given elsewhere (Bagchi & Deshpande, 1998; 1999).

In this study as in our earlier studies, aprotinin, a kinin synthesis inhibitor blocked the BT venom-induced ugmentation of cardiac reflexes, confirming the kinin ıvolvement in BT venom action. Kinins, prostaglandins, istamine, lymphokines, leukotrienes, etc are ıflammatory mediators and can increase the vascular ermeability leading to oedema formation (Haddy et al., 970; Linz et al., 1995; Marceau et al., 1998). Recent reports ıdicates that pulmonary oedema may increase the ensitivity of vagal C fibres leading to the augmentation f cardiopulmonary reflex responses (Bagchi & eshpande, 1999; Deshpande et al., 1999). Thus, it appears ıat scorpion envenomation results in increased kinin evels, which inturn leads to increased vascular ermeability and oedema formation which inturn further ensitizes the vagal C fibre endings leading to reflex ugmentation.

Kinins exert their action atleast through 3 different ıechanisms viz., through receptors or involving second ıessenger systems or directly by altering the ermeability of tissue barriers. Bradykinin (BK) receptors ave been pharmacologically characterized and classified s B_1 and B_2 receptors (Regoli & Barabe, 1980). Under hysiological conditions majority of the tissues display B_2 eceptors, while B_1 receptors are dormant and are pregulated only after tissue injury or inflammation Marceau et al., 1983). B_1 receptors are responsible for yperalgesia and pain of inflammation, while B_2 receptors egulate capillary permeability and hence responsible for roducing oedema. The upregulation of B_1 receptors is easible in scorpion envenomation also, as it is a athological condition and induces tissue injury. loreover, B_1 receptors mediates pain and have a direct fect on vagal C fibres. However, our present results do ot favour this pathway for venom action.

The blockade of venom-induced reflex augmentation ı animals pretreated with Hoe 140, a B_2 receptor ıtagonist indicates that the venom-induced reflex ıgmentation is brought about by B_2 receptors through permeability changes. (Fig. 4). Since captopril action is mediated through B_2 receptors (Marceau, 1997; Marceau, et al., 1998), the captopril-induced augmentation of PDG reflexes reported earlier could also be mediated through B_2 receptors (Bagchi & Deshpande, 1998). This further substantiates B_2 receptor involvement in reflex augmentation seen after crude BT venom.

In conclusion, the present study indicate that cardiopulmonary reflex augmentation induced by *Buthus tamulus* venom, is mediated through kinins via B_2 receptors. The mechanism of action of venom on the vagus nerve needs to be explored further. From the present results, it appear that kinins are the primary agents for producing the cardiopulmonary manifestations of BT envenomation. Thus, kinin synthesis inhibitors or B_2 receptor antagonists may be the appropriate agents for the treatment of scorpion envenomation.

REFERENCES

Anand, A. & Paintal, A.S. (1988) Possible role of capillary permeability in excitation of sensory receptors by chemical substances. *Progress in Brain Research* 74, 337-340.

Bagchi, S. & Deshpande, S.B. (1998) Indian red scorpion (*Buthus tamulus*) venom-induced augmentation of cardiac reflexes is mediated through the mechanisms involving kinins in urethane anaesthetized rats. *Toxicon* 36, 309-320.

Bagchi, S. & Deshpande, S.B. (1999) Indian red scorpion (*Buthus tamulus*) venom-induced augmentation of cardiac reflexes is mediated through the involvement of peripheral 5-HT_3 and central 5-HT_{1A} receptor subtypes. *Toxicon* 37, 1697-1709.

Bawaskar, H.S. & Bawaskar, P.H. (1994) Vasodilators: Scorpion envenoming and the heart (an Indian experience). *Toxicon* 3[illegible] 1031-1040.

Brown, N.J., Ryder, D., Gainer, J.V., Morrow, J.D. & Nadeau, J. (199[illegible]) Differential effects of angiotensin converting enzyme inhibitors on the vasodepressor and prostacylin responses to bradykinin. *Journal of Pharmacology and Experimental Therapeutics* 27[illegible] 703-712.

Deshpande, S.B., Bagchi, S., Rai, O.P. & Aryya, N.C (1999) Pulmonary oedema produced by scorpion venom augments phenyldiguanide-induced reflex response in anaesthetized rats. *Journal of Physiology* 521, 537-544.

Dey, P.K. & Rao, K.S. (1978) Visceral reflex responses following right intra-atrial injection of phenyldiguanide in rats. *Indian Journal of Physiology and Pharamacology* 22, 347-357.

Haddy, F.J., Emerson, T.E., Scott, J.B. & Daughery, R.M. (1970) The effects of kinins on the cardio- vascular system. *Hand book of Experimental Pharmacology,* ed. E.G. Erdos, Vol. 25, pp. 362-384, Springer-Verlag, Heidelberg.

Hainsworth, R. (1991) Reflexes from the heart. *Physiological Reviews* 71, 617-658.

ISmail, M., Fatani, A.J.Y. & Davees, T.T. (1992) Experimental treatment protocol for scorpion envenomation. A review of common therapies and an effect of kallikrein-kinin inhibitors. *Toxicon* 30, 1257-1279.

Kay, I.S. & Armstrong, D.J (1990) Phenylbiguanide not phenyldiguanide is used to evoke the pulmonary chemoreflex in anaesthetized rabbits. *Experimental Physiology* 75, 383-389.

Linz, W., Wiemer, G., GOhlke, P., Unger, T. & Scholkens, B.A. (1995) Contribution of kinins to the cardiovascular actions of angiotensin converting enzyme inhibitors. *Pharmacological Reviews* 47, 25-30.

Marceau, F., Lussier, A., Regoli, D. & Giroud, J.P. (1983) Pharmacology of kinins: their relevance to tissue injury and inflammation. *General Pharmacology* 14, 173-201.

Marceau, F. (1997) Is there a role for bradykinin in the therapeutic and side effects of angiotensin-converting enzyme inhibitors? *Canadian Journal of Cardiology* 13, 187-194.

Marceau, F., Hess J.F. & Bacharov, D.R. (1998) The B_1 receptors for kinins. *Pharmacological Reviews* 50, 357-386.

Murthy, K.R.K. & Hossein, Z. (1986) Increased osmotic fragility of red cells after incubation at 37 C for 24 hr in dogs with acute myocarditis produced by scorpion (*Buthus tamulus*) venom. *Indian Journal of Experimental Biology* 24, 464-467.

Murthy, K.R.K., Subramaniam, P. & Yeolekar, M.E. (1987) Hyperglycaemia and reduction in glycogen content of atria and liver in dogs with acute myocarditis produced by scorpion *(B. tamulus)* venom. *Journal of Association of Physicians India* 35, 189-190.

Murthy, K.R.K., Hossein, Z., Medh, J.D., Kudalkar, J.A., Yeolkar, M E., Pandit, S.P., Khopkar, M., Dave, K.N., & Billimoria, F.R. (1988) Disseminated intravascular coagulation and disturbances in carbohydrate and fat metabolism in acute myocarditis produced by scorpion (*Buthus tamulus*) venom. *Indian Journal of Medical Research* 87, 318-325.

Murthy, K.R.K., Shenoi, R., Vaidyanathan, P., Kelker, K., Sharma, N., Birewar, N., Rao, S. & Mehta, M.N. (1991) Insulin reverses haemodynamic changes and pulmonary oedema in children stung by Indian red scorpion *Mesobuthus tamulus concanesis*, Pocock. *Annals of Tropical Medicine and Parasitology* 85, 651-657.

Murthy, K.R.K. & Hase, N.K. (1994) Scorpion envenoming and role of insulin. *Toxicon* 32, 1041-1044.

Panital, A.S. (1964) Effect of drugs on vertebrate mechano- receptors. *Pharmacological Reviews* 16, 341-380.

Panital, A.S. (1973) Vagal sensory receptor and their reflex effects. *Physiological Reviews* 53, 159-227.

Panzenbeck, M.J., Tan, W., Hajdu, M.A. & Zucker, H.I. (1988) Prostaglandins mediate the increased sensitivity of left ventricular reflexes after captopril treatment in conscious dogs. *Journal of Pharmacology and Experimental Therapeutics* 244, 384-390.

Regoli, D. & Barabe, J. (1980) Pharmacology of bradykinin and related kinins. *Pharmacological Reviews* 32, 1-46.

Rowan, E.G., Vatanpour, H., Furman, B.L., Harvey, A.L., Tanira, M.O.M. & Gopalakrishnakone, P. (1992) The effect of Indian red scorpion *Buthus tamulus* venom *in vivo* and *in vitro*. *Toxicon* 30, 1157-1164.

Staszewska-Barczak, J. (1988) Prostanoids and cardiac reflexes of sympathetic and vagal origin. *American Journal of Cardiology* 53, 36A-45A.

Vogel, R. & Werle, E. (1970) Kallikrein inhibitors. Bradykinin, kallidin, and kallikrein. In *Handbook of Experimental Pharmacology*, Vol. 25, ed. E.G. Erdos, pp. 213-249. Springer-Verlag, Heidelberg.

DIFFERENCES IN PHOTODYNAMIC EFFECTS OF HEMATOPORPHYRIN DERIVATIVE IN HUMAN SQUAMOUS CARCINOMA AND GLIOMA CELL LINES

*GUPTA S., #JAIN V., @MURALIDHAR K.

*Institute of Nuclear Medicine and Allied Sciences, Delhi, India, #Dr. B. R. Ambedkar Centre for Biomedical Research, University of Delhi, Delhi, India and @Department of Zoology, University of Delhi, Delhi, India.

#Current Address : Department of Emergency Medicine, Wright State University, Ohio, USA

Summary

Photodynamic therapy (PDT) of tumors utilizes photosensitizers and visible light, which in presence of oxygen, generate reactive oxygen species causing macromolecular and structural damage leading to the inactivation of cells. Optimal distribution of photosensitizers at critical intracellular targets is an important requirement, which is determined by both the nature of the photosensitizer as well as target cells. To gain further insight into the factors determining photodynamic efficiency, we have investigated the uptake, localization and photodynamic effects in two human tumor cell lines of diverse origin; a glioma (BMG-1) and a squamous cell carcinoma (4451) using hematoporphyrin derivative (PS-3), a widely used sensitizer in clinics.

Whole cell suspension spectroscopy was used to study cellular uptake, while fluorescence microscopy and image analysis were used for localization studies. Perturbations in cell cycle progression, cell death (macrocolony assay), apoptosis as well as micronuclei formation were studied as parameters of photodynamic effects.

Although, uptake of PS-3 was higher in 4451 cells, BMG-1 cells were more sensitive to the photodynamic inactivation (macrocolony assay). Most of the PS-3 was localized in the cytoplasm of both the cell lines. In both the cell lines, induction of apoptosis as well as cytogenetic damage (micronuclei) were dependent on the concentration of PS-3 and were higher in BMG-1 cells. A significant delay in the cell cycle progression (G_2 block) observed only in 4451 cells, could be related to the repair/recovery from photodynamic damage, which may be partly responsible for lower sensitivity observed. These results imply that manifestations of photodynamically induced lesions resulting in the formation of micronuclei and apoptosis are important determinants of photodynamic response besides uptake and localization.

INTRODUCTION

Photodynamic therapy (PDT) has three components: a photosensitizer, light and oxygen. The photosensitizer can be activated to a higher energy state by absorption of light of appropriate wavelength leading to the production of reactive oxygen species (ROS) in the presence of oxygen, which can damage the structure, and functions of cell constituents. Several factors influence the photodynamic efficacy including uptake and intracellular localization in addition to the quantum yield of oxidation and absorption maximum of the sensitizer.

The physico-chemical properties of the sensitizer (charge distribution, lipophilicity, aggregation state etc.) as well as the cell type and its physiological state such as pH, number of LDL receptors and lysosomes etc. (Oenbrink *et al.*, 1988; Woodburn *et al.*, 1991, 1992; Khanum and Jain, 1987; Soncin *et al.*, 1995) influence the uptake and intracellular localization of the sensitizer. Also, cells differing in their origin and radiosensitivity have been shown to respond differently to PDT (Penning *et al.*, 1994;

Gomer *et al.*, 1988).

Photodynamic treatment results in damage to membranes (Kessel *et al.*, 1995; Gaffney *et al.*, 1990; Dellinger, 1996), mitochondria (Dummin *et al.*, 1997; Munday *et al.*, 1996; Modica-Napolitano *et al.*, 1990), lysosomes (Berg and Moan, 1997; Ambroz *et al.*, 1994; Lin *et al.*, 1993) and/or other essential biomolecules including DNA (Moan *et al.*, 1980; Hong *et al.*, 1998). Even though, specific damage to cellular structures or functions has been observed at various intracellular sites, a clear causal relationship between the lesions and cell death has not emerged (Morgan *et al.*, 2000). Also, the relative contribution of the factors in the manifestation of the photodynamic response (apoptosis or necrosis) is still not very clear (Morgan *et al.*, 2000). Therefore, in the present study, we have investigated the relationship between uptake, localization and photodynamic effects (cell growth, colony forming ability, cytogenetic damage and apoptosis) of a hematoporphyrin derivative (photosan-3; PS-3) in two human tumor cell lines, a squamous cell carcinoma (4451) and a glioma (BMG-1).

MATERIAL AND METHODS

Chemicals

The hematoporphyrin derivative, Photosan-3 (PS-3) was a gift from SeeLab, Germany. Hank's Balanced Salt Solution (HBSS), Dulbecco's modified Phosphate Buffered Saline (PBS), Dulbecco's Modified Eagle's Medium (DMEM), fetal calf serum (FCS), (N-[2-Hydroxyethyl] piperazine- N'-(2-ethanesulfonic acid]) (HEPES) buffer, propidium iodide (PI), 4,6 diamidino 2-phenyl indole (DAPI), Ribonuclease-A (RNase-A), Hoechst-H33342 (bis Benzimide (2'-[4-Ethoxyphenyl]-5-[4-methyl-1-piperazinyl]-2,5'-bi-1H-benzimidazole) trihydrochloride and trypsin were obtained from Sigma Chemical Co.,

USA. All other chemicals used in the present study were of analytical grade from BDH, Glaxo laboratories (Qualigens), SRL, and E-Merck, India.

Tumor cell lines

Human cerebral glioma cell line, BMG-1 (Dwarakanath and Jain, 1989) established from a human mixed glioma and a human squamous carcinoma cell line of the oral cavity, 4451 (Zolzer *et al.*, 1995) were used in the present studies.

Monolayer BMG-1 cells were grown in DMEM with 5% fetal calf serum (FCS) and 4451 cells with DMEM containing 10% FCS, penicillin (100 units/mL), streptomycin (50 μg/mL) and nystatin (2 μg/mL). Stock cultures were passaged every third day (BMG-1) or second day (4451) after harvesting the cells with 0.05 % trypsin and seeding 8 X 10^3 cells/cm^2 in tissue culture flasks to maintain the cells in the exponential phase.

Uptake studies

Cellular uptake of PS-3 was estimated by whole cell suspension spectroscopy. Uptake was calculated using standard calibration curve of PS-3 in HBSS at 405 nm absorption and 620 nm fluorescence.

Cells were suspended in HBSS containing the sensitizer (2.5-20 μg/mL) and incubated at 37^0 C in dark for various time intervals (0.5, 1, 2, 4 h). Absorption and fluorescence spectra of cells and supernatant were obtained at 405 nm and 620 nm respectively.

To determine the cell numbers, the amount of DNA was estimated using an AT specific DNA fluorochrome, bisbenzimidazole (Hoechst-33342) (Brunk *et al.*, 1979).

Subcellular localization using fluorescence microscopy (image analysis system)

Intracellular localization of sensitizer was studied by fluorescence microscopy using image analysis system (Olympus, BX60, Japan) fitted with a monochrome CCD camera (Gründig, FA87, Germany). CCD camera contained a monochrome frame grabber of 24 Bit (Bit flow, Inc, USA) and spectrum range was 400-1000 nm with an image sensor of 596 (V) X 795 (H) total pixels.

Cells growing on coverslips were used in these studies. After incubation with PS-3, coverslips were washed in PBS, mounted on slides and examined under the fluorescence microscope using UV excitation filter (300-400 nm) and emission recorded in the red region of the spectrum (400-800 nm). Images were acquired and stored in digital pentium based computer (166 MHz) and analyzed using the software provided by Optimas Corporation, USA.

Photodynamic treatment and cell response

Treatment

Cells were incubated at 37^0 C for 4 h with varying concentrations (1.25-20 μg/mL) of PS-3 in HBSS. After the incubation, cells were washed with HBSS and exposed to red light (>610 nm; Power = 3 W/cm^2) from a high power (1000 W) Xenon arc lamp (Oriel, USA). Optical power at the cell surface was measured using radiometer. Cells were incubated for another 2 h at 37°C in HBSS before further analysis of cell response to treatment.

Macrocolony assay for survival

Nearly 150 cells were plated in GM (DMEM + 10 % FCS) after the treatment (as described above) and incubated in dark, humidified, 5 % CO_2 atmosphere at 37° C for 8-10 days to allow colony formation. Colonies having 50 or more cells were fixed with methanol and stained with 1 % crystal violet. Number of colonies were counted and plating efficiency (PE) and surviving fraction (S.F.) were calculated.

Cell cycle analysis

After photodynamic treatment, cells were grown in growth medium for varying intervals of time, harvested by trypsinization, counted (adherent+floating) and fixed in 70 % ethanol. Flow cytometric measurements of cellular DNA content were performed with the ethanol fixed cells using the intercalating DNA fluorochrome, propidium iodide (PI) (Dwarakanath *et al.*, 1999). Briefly, the cells (~ 0.5-1 million) were washed in PBS after removing ethanol and treated with Ribonuclease-A (200 μg/mL) for 30 min at 37^0C. Subsequently, cells were stained with PI (50 μg/mL) in PBS and measurements were made with a Facs calibur (Beckton and Dickenson, USA). PI fluorescence was collected on list mode and cell cycle analysis was performed using the Modfit program.

Micronuclei formation

Air-dried slides containing acetic-methanol (1:3 V/V) fixed cells were stained with 2-aminophenylindoledihydrochloride (DAPI) (10 μg/mL in citric acid (0.01 M), disodium phosphate (0.45 M) buffer containing 0.05% Tween-20 detergent) as described earlier (Dwarakanath and Jain, 1985). Slides were examined under fluorescence microscope using UV excitation filter and fluorescing nuclei were visualized using a blue emission filter.

Cells containing micronuclei were counted from >1000 cells by employing the criteria of Countrymen and Heddle (1976). The fraction of cells containing micronuclei, called the M-Fraction (%) was calculated as defined earlier (Dwarakanath and Jain, 1989) and shown below:

$$\text{M-Fraction (\%)} = N_m/N_t \times 100$$

Where N_m is the number of cells with micronuclei and N_t is the total number of cells analyzed.

Since, micronuclei formation is linked to cell proliferation, the micronuclei frequencies were normalized with respect to the cell numbers.

Detection and assay of apoptotic cells:

Apoptotic cells were detected morphologically and by flow cytometry using PI labeled cells. Presence of hypodiploid population (sub G_0/G_1) in DNA histograms obtained after PI labeling (as described for cell cycle analysis) reflected the apoptotic population. Morphologically, marked condensation and margination of chromatin, fragmentation of nuclei and cell shrinkage characterize apoptotic cells and a good correlation between these morphological changes and DNA ladder (one of the hallmarks of cells undergoing apoptosis) has been demonstrated (Yanagihara *et al.*, 1995). At least 1000 cells were counted and percent apoptotic cells determined.

RESULTS

Uptake of PS-3 in BMG-1 and 4451 cells

A linear increase in intracellular content of PS-3 was found in both BMG-1 and 4451 cells as a function of concentration (data not shown). In both the cell lines, the kinetics of PS-3 uptake studied by cell suspension spectroscopy was biphasic in nature as it accumulated rapidly up to 1 h, with a decrease in the rate of uptake subsequently (Fig. 1). These observations are similar to the earlier results reported for BHK-21 and other cell lines (Khanum and Jain, 1997; Kessel, 1981; Bohmer and Morstyn, 1985). The accumulation of PS-3 was 3-4 times higher in 4451 cells as compared to BMG-1 cells at all time points studied (Fig. 1).

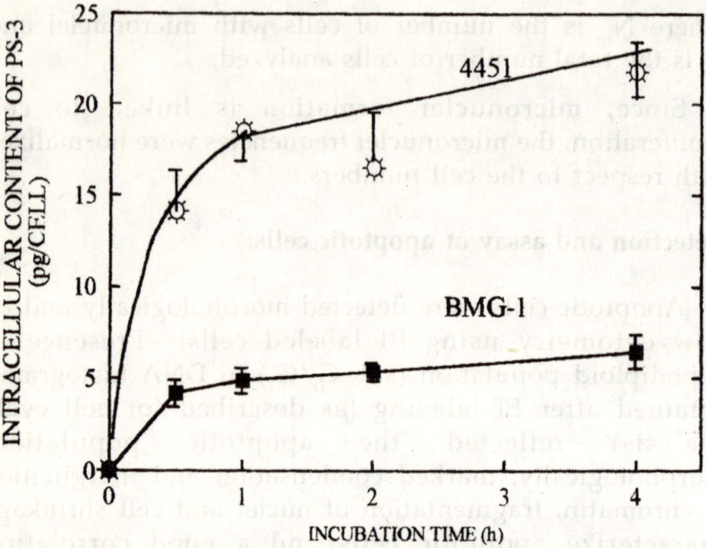

Fig. 1 Time dependent uptake of PS-3 (10 μg/mL) in exponentially growing BMG-1 and 4451 cells studied by cell suspension spectroscopy.

Subcellular localization

Subcellular localization of the sensitizer was studied by fluorescence microscopy based Image Analysis System (FMIA) using cells grown on coverslips. A time dependent distribution of PS-3 was observed in both the cell lines, with initial accumulation in the membrane followed by increase in fluorescence in the cytoplasm and in the perinuclear region by 2 h (data not shown). At 4 h, most (75-90%) of the sensitizer was localized in the cytoplasm (Fig. 2) without any significant difference in the distribution between the cell lines. Porphyrins, which accumulate mainly *via* passive diffusion in cells, are known to localize in the cytomembranous structures giving diffuse fluorescence in the cytoplasm (Hilf *et al.*, 1984).

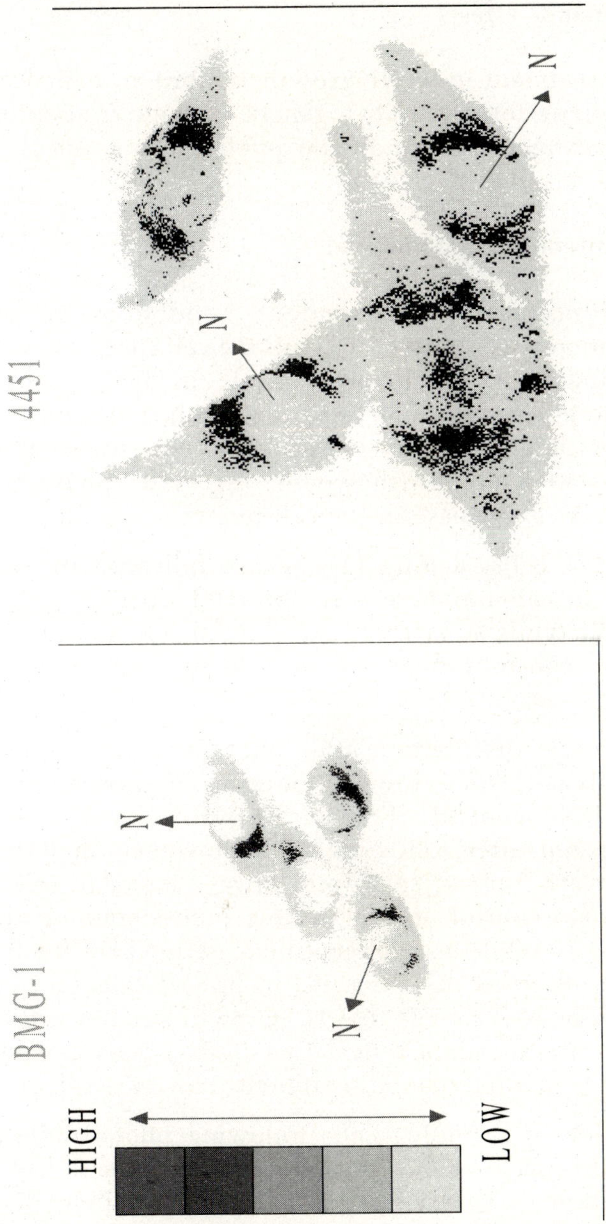

Fig. 2 Localization of PS-3 (20 μg/mL at 4 h) in BMG-1 [a] and 4451 [b] cells N-Nucleus.

Photodynamic effects

Treatment-induced growth inhibition, cell death (macrocolony formation) cytogenetic damage & apoptosis were investigated to study the photodynamic effects in both the cell lines.

Cell proliferation and survival

A concentration dependent reduction in cell proliferation was observed in both the cell lines following the photodynamic treatment (Fig. 3). In BMG-1 cells, a cytostatic effect was observed up to 40 h, followed by a recovery leading to an increase in the cell number at 2.5 μg/mL. At 5 μg/mL, however, the static phase was followed by a decrease in the cell number (Fig. 3[a]).

In 4451 cells, a long lag period followed by slow increase in cell numbers was observed up to 5 μg/mL (Fig. 3 [b]), while no increase in cell numbers was observed at higher concentrations (10 and 20 μg/mL) (data not shown).

Cell cycle distribution after photodynamic treatment was analyzed from flow cytometric measurements of cellular DNA content. Fraction of S-phase cells in 4451 cells did not alter following PDT, however, in BMG-1 cells, percent S-phase cells were always lower in treated groups than control at all the time points studied (data not shown). While a significant increase in G_2+M fraction could be observed in 4451 cells, in BMG-1 cells G_2 block could not be observed (Table 1). Growth kinetics and cell cycle distribution data reflect that BMG-1 cells are more sensitive to photodynamic treatment than 4451 cells.

Fraction of surviving cells following photoirradiation assayed by macrocolony formation are shown in Fig. 4. The fraction of surviving cells decreased exponentially with increasing content of PS-3 up to 2.2 pg/cell in BMG-1 cells and 7.4 pg/cell in 4451 cells. A further increase in

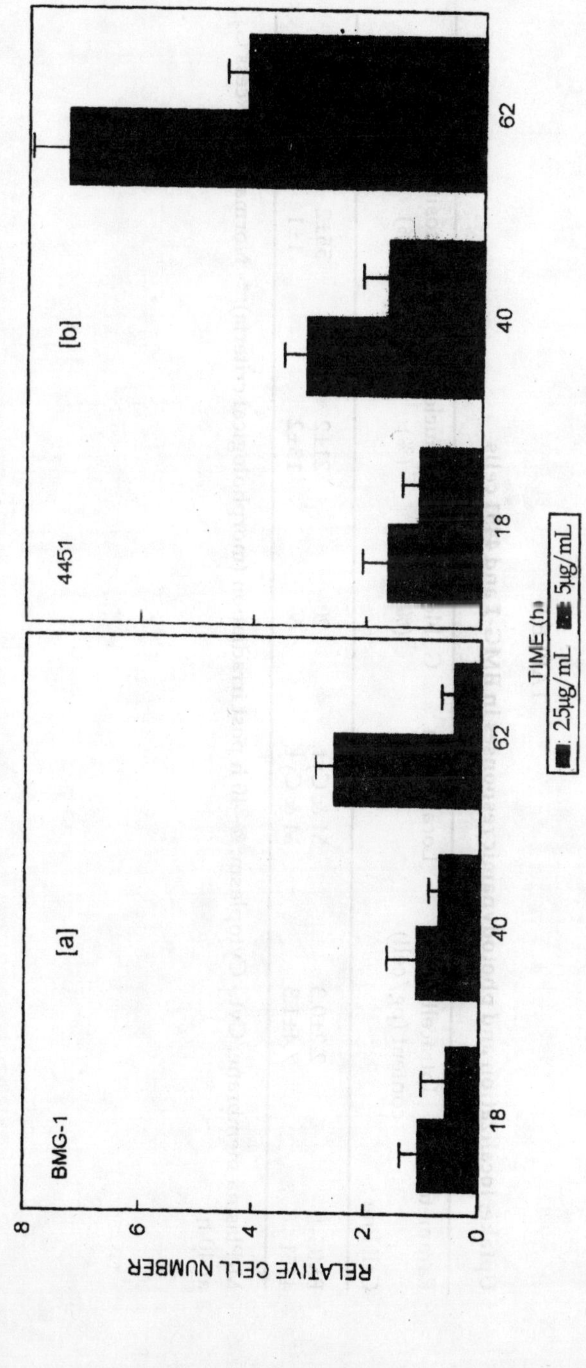

Fig. 3 Effects of photodynamic treatment on the growth of exponentially growing BMG-1 [a] and 4451 [b] cells. Cells were incubated with PS-3 (2.5 and 5 μg/mL) for 4 h in HBSS and irradiated with red light (Power = 3 W/cm^2; light dose = 4.32 KJ). Relative cell numbers observed at various post-irradiation time intervals (with reference to unirradiated control) are given.

TABLE 1

Uptake, localization and photodynamic responses in BMG-1 and 4451 cells

Parameters / Cell line	Intracellular content (pg/cell)	Localization	G_2 block* (%)	Micronuclei@ (%)	Apoptosis @ (%)	S. F (%)
BMG-1	2.2±0.3	M & Cyt.	20	21±2	55±2	0.15
4451	7.4±1.3	M & Cyt.	66	13±2	1±1	4.6

M-Plasma membrane; Cyt.- Cytoplasm; @- 40 h post irradiation (morphological criteria); *- Normalized excess G_2 at 40 h.

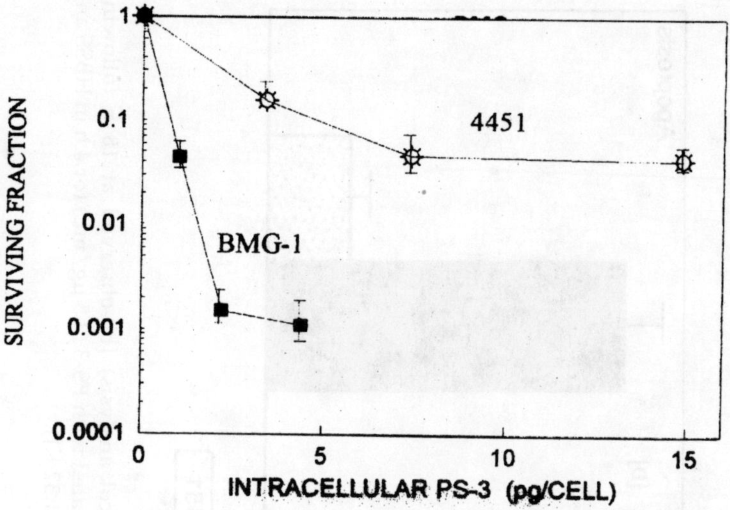

Fig. 4 Response of exponentially growing BMG-1 and 4451 cells to photodynamic treatment studied as a function of intracellular content of PS-3. Cells were incubated for 4 h in HBSS containing PS-3 and irradiated with red light (> 610 nm; Power = 3 W/cm^2; light dose = 4.32 KJ). Two hours after irradiation cells were plated for macrocolony assay (n=3).

the intracellular content of PS-3 did not result in a decrease in the cell survival in both the cell lines (Fig. 4). This may be due to relocalization of the photosensitizer to less sensitive targets (Morgan *et al.*, 2000).

Cytogenetic damage

Cytogenetic damage in the form of micronuclei was investigated in both the cell lines. Micronuclei found in the post mitotic daughter cells following treatment, arise from the chromosomal damage and cells with micronuclei are associated with loss of reproductive capacity (Midander & Revesz, 1980; Dwarakanath *et al.*, 2000). At 2.5 μg/mL, the fraction of BMG-1 cells with micronuclei

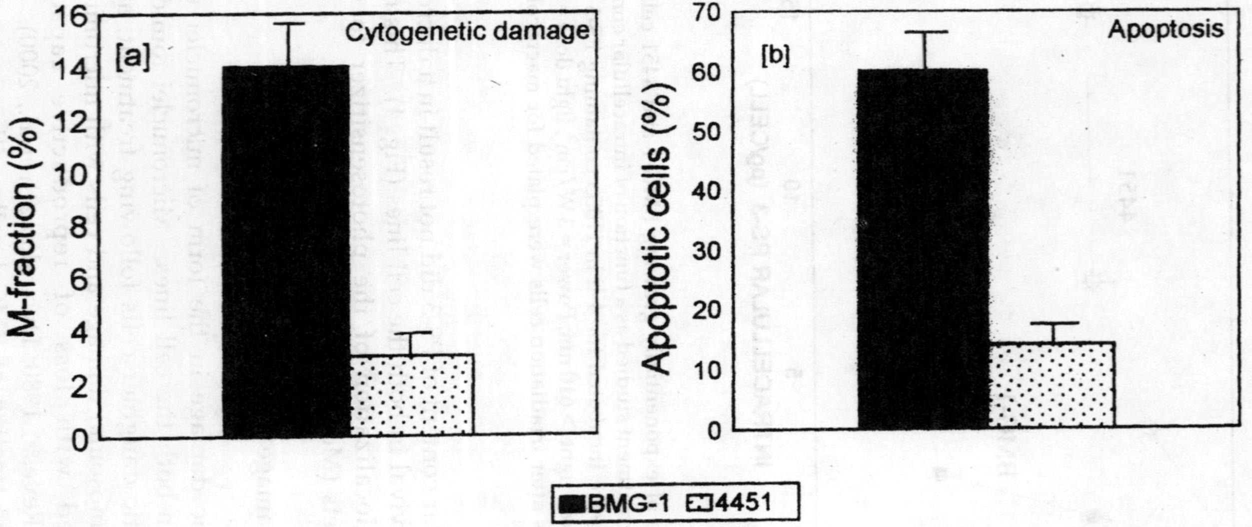

Fig. 5 Micronuclei frequency [a] and apoptosis (by morphological analysis) [b] observed at 18 h following photodynamic treatment in BMG-1 and 4451 cells. Cells were incubated with PS-3 (2.5 μg/mL) for 4 h in HBSS and irradiated with red light (> 610 nm; Power = 3 W/cm^2; light dose = 4.32 KJ).

was highest at 40 h post-treatment and decreased thereafter (data not shown). Due to extensive damage (interphase death), micronuclei expression could not be analyzed in photodynamically treated cells at higher PS-3 concentrations (10 and 20 μg/mL).

In 4451 cells also, results similar to BMG-1 cells were observed. However, fraction of 4451 cells expressing micronuclei (normalized with respect to cell proliferation) was significantly lower than BMG-1 cells at all the time points studied (Fig. 5[a] and Table 1). Comparison of the M-fraction (%) at 18 h in both the cell lines is shown in Fig. 5[a].

Apoptosis

The frequency of apoptotic cells (morphological criteria) observed at 18 h and 40 h of cell proliferation after photodynamic treatment is given in Fig. 5[b] and Table 1 respectively. While, only 0-1 % of 4451 cells were apoptotic, about 55 % of BMG-1 cells were found to be apoptotic by the morphological analysis at 40 h. Fraction of cells undergoing apoptosis increased with increase in concentration up to 5 μg/mL of PS-3. However, at 10 μg/mL number of apoptotic cells reduced (data not shown), which could be due to necrosis as shown earlier (Noodt *et al.*, 1998). The relative fraction of apoptotic cells was also reduced at 62 h when a recovery in proliferation was observed (data not shown).

These observations were complemented by flow-cytometric measurements of DNA content, which showed a hypodiploid cell population following photodynamic treatment in BMG-1 cells but not in 4451 cells (data not shown).

DISCUSSION

Cellular response to photodynamic treatment depends both on the photodynamic dose (sensitizer concentration and light dose) and the cell type. In the present study, the glioma cell line (BMG-1) was found to be more sensitive to the photodynamic treatment with PS-3 as compared to squamous carcinoma cell line (4451) that could not be accounted on the basis of uptake and localization of the sensitizer (Table 1). The amount of PS-3 was at least three times more in 4451 cells than in BMG-1 cells. Earlier studies have also reported a lack of correlation between uptake and photodynamic efficiency (Perry *et al.*, 1990).

The above results may imply that localization of the photosensitizer at critical targets could be responsible for the differences in the photodynamic response as has been observed earlier (Woodburn *et al.*, 1992). However, significant differences in the localization pattern could not be observed in these two cell lines (Fig. 2). It is also possible that PS-3 localize at different sites in the cytoplasm, which could not be resolved by the image analysis system used in the present study and may be resolved by the use of confocal microscopy (Moan *et al.*, 1994). These results suggest that not only the uptake and localization of the sensitizer, but processes that influence the manifestation of primary photodynamic lesions, leading to cell death could play an important role in determining the photodynamic efficacy.

Studies on cytogenetic damage showed that micronuclei frequency was significantly higher in BMG-1 cells (Table 1 and Fig. 5[a]). Cells with micronuclei have been found to be associated with the loss of reproductive ability (Midander and Ravesz, 1980). Centromere breaks and double minutes are the most frequent aberrations induced by HpD and light (Evensen and Moan, 1982). Since, recovery from treatment-induced DNA and chromosome damage is facilitated by delayed cell proliferation due to checkpoints at G_1-S and G_2 -M transition (Maity *et al.*, 1994), a G_2 block observed in 4451 cells (Table 1) could be partly responsible for the resistance to the treatment.

Mitotic and apoptotic death that contribute to the loss of survival following photodynamic treatment vary among tumor cells both *in vitro* as well as *in vivo* depending on the genotypic and phenotypic characteristics of cells, besides the uptake and localization of the sensitizer (Noodt *et al.*, 1999; Kessel and Luo, 1998). Therefore, cells where photodynamically-induced lesions elicit apoptotic as well as mitotic death are expected to be more sensitive to the treatment. PDT-induced apoptosis observed in several cell lines has been considered as one of the important determinants of cell sensitivity (Luo *et al.*, 1996; Carre *et al.*, 1999; Dellinger, 1996; Dahle *et al.*, 1999). Therefore, higher level of apoptotic death observed in BMG-1 as compared to 4451 cells (Table 1 and Fig. 5[b]) could be one of the reasons for higher sensitivity of BMG-1 cells to PDT. The entire process of apoptosis induced by a variety of signals is regulated by the status as well as expression of several genes and p53, bcl-2, bcl-x and bax (Oleinick *et al.*, 1993; He Xiao-Yan *et al.*, 1994; Noodt *et al.*, 1996, 1998; Agarwal *et al.*, 1996) are among the most important ones. While the wild-type p53 has been observed to facilitate the progress of apoptosis in most instances (Tong *et al.*, 2000; Denstman *et al.*, 1986; Fisher *et al.*, 1998 & 1999), bcl-2 inhibits apoptosis (He Jin *et al.*, 1996). It is pertinent to note that the BMG-1 cells have a wild-type p53 status (Dwarakanath *et al.*, 1999), while the 4451 cells carry a mutated p53 gene (Zolzer *et al.*, 1995).

Results of the present studies have important implications for improving the photodynamic therapy of cancer. Differences in the sensitivities of BMG-1 and 4451 observed here and earlier in other cell systems (He Xiao-Yan *et al.*, 1994) suggest that the responses of tumors to PDT are likely to vary among tumors and therefore, treatment regimens need to be individualized and protocols selected on the basis of their *in vitro* response to enhance the efficacy of PDT. Further, the results also emphasize that the photodynamic therapy of tumors can be more effective if nature and biological responses of individual tumors are taken into consideration, besides optimizing the photodynamic dose *i.e.* the concentration of the sensitizer and amount of the light absorbed by the tissue. Enhancing the photodynamically-induced apoptosis (an important cell death process) selectively in tumor cells, based on the information on their biological behavior, particularly the p53 and bcl-2 status could be one of the approaches to achieve this objective.

Mitotic and apoptotic death are the two major pathways of cell inactivation contributing to the tumor control. Therefore, a combination of treatments that enhance both mitotic as well as apoptotic death can significantly enhance the treatment efficacy. Earlier studies have shown that 4451 cells are more sensitive to ionizing radiation than the BMG-1 cells as evidenced by cell death and cytogenetic damage (Dwarakanath *et al.*, 1999), while the present studies indicate that the BMG-1 cells are more sensitive to PDT than 4451. Therefore, combining PDT with IRT can significantly enhance the therapeutic gain in tumors behaving like BMG-1 and possibly to a lower extent in tumors similar to 4451 as well. Earlier studies *in vitro* and *in vivo* have shown an additive or synergistic effect of combining the two treatments depending on the nature of cells (Evensen and Moan, 1982; Bellnier and Dougherty, 1986; Ben-Hur *et al.*, 1988; Kostron *et al.*, 1986; Rasch *et al.*, 1997). Further experimental and clinical studies are required to evaluate the potential of combining PDT with IRT to improve cancer therapy.

ACKNOWLEDGEMENTS

We thank Dr. N. K. Choudhury, Dr. B. S. Dwarakanath, Mr. J. S. Adhikari and Mr. Sudhir Chandna for their help in spectroscopic, flow cytometric and image analysis studies. We are grateful to Dr. T. Lazar Mathew, Director and Maj. Gen T. Ravindranath, Additional Director, INMAS, for their encouragement and support during the course of this study. S. G. was a recipient of a fellowship from UGC, Govt. of India.

REFERENCES

1. Agarwal R., Korman N. J., Mohan R. R., Feyes D. K., Jawed S., Zaim M. T. & Mukhtar H. (1996) Apoptosis is an early event during phthalocyanine photodynamic therapy-induced ablation of chemically induced squamous papillomas in mouse skin, *Photochem. Photobiol.* 63, 547-552.

2. Ambroz M., MacRobert A. J., Morgan J., Rumbles G., Foley M. S. C. & Phillips D. (1994) Time resolved fluorescence spectroscopy and intracellular imaging of disulphonated aluminum phthalocyanine, *J. Photochem. Photobiol. B: Biol.* 22, 105-117.

3. Bellnier D. A. & Dougherty T. J. (1986) Haematoporphyrin derivative photosensitization and g-radiation damage interaction in chinese hamster ovary fibroblasts, *Int. J. Rad. Biol.* 50, 659-664.

4. Ben-Hur E., Kol R., Marko R., Riklis E. & Rosenthal I. (1988) Combined action of phthalocyanine photosensitization and gamma radiation on mammalian cells, *Int. J. Rad. Biol.* 54, 21-30.

5. Berg K. & Moan J. (1997) Lysosomes and microtubules as targets for photochemotherapy of Cancer, *Photochem. Photobiol.* 63, 403-409.

6. Bohmer R. M. & Morstyn G. (1985) Uptake of hematoporphyrin derivative by normal and malignant cells: Effects of serum, pH, temperature and cell size, *Cancer Res.* 45, 5328-5334.

7. Brunk C. F., Jones K. C. & James T. W. (1979) Assay for nanogram quantities of DNA in cellular homogenates, *Anal. Biochem.* 92, 497-500.

8. Carre V., Jayat C., Granet R., Krausz P. & Guilloton M. (1999) Chronology of apoptotic events induced in the K562 cell line by photodynamic treatment with hematoporphyrin and monoglucosylporphyrin, *Photochem. Photobiol.* 69, 55-60.

9. Countryman P. I. and Heddle J. A. (1976) Production of micronuclei from chromosome aberrations in irradiated cultures of human lymphocytes, *Mutat. Res.* 41, 321-332.

10. Dahle J., Steen H. B. & Moan J. (1999) The mode of cell death induced by photodynamic treatment depends on the cell density, *Photochem. Photobiol.* 70, 363-367.

11. Dellinger M. (1996) Apoptosis or Necrosis following photofrin photosensitization: Influence of the incubation protocol, *Photochem. Photobiol*, 64, 182-187.

12. Denstman S. C., Dillehay L. E. & Williams J. R. (1986) Enhanced susceptibility to HPD sensitized phototoxicity and correlated resistance to trypsin detachment in SV40 transformed IMR-90 cells, *Photochem. Photobiol.* 43, 145-147.

13. Dummin H., Cernay T. & Zimmerman H. W. (1997) Selective photosensitization of mitochondria In HeLa cells by cationic Zn(II) phthalocyanines with lipophilic side chains, *J. Photochem. Photobiol. B: Biol.* 37, 219-229.

14. Dwarakanath B. S. & Jain V. (1985) Enhancement of the radiation-induced damage by 2-deoxy-D-glucose in organ cultures of brain tumors, *Indian J. Med. Res.* 82, 266-268.

15. Dwarakanath B. S. and Jain V. (1989) Energy linked modifications of the radiation response in a human glioma cell line, *Int. J. Radiation Oncol. Biol. Phys.* 17, 1033-1040.

16. Dwarakanath B. S., Adhikari J. S. & Jain V. (1999) Hematoporphyrin derivatives potentiate the radiosensitizing effects of 2-deoxy-D-glucose in Cancer cells, *Int. J. Radiation Oncol. Biol. Phys.* 43, 1125-1133.

17. Dwarakanath B. S., Zolzer F., Chandna S., Bauch T., Adhikari J. S., Muller W., Streffer C. & Jain V. (2000) Heterogeneity in 2-deoxy-D-glucose induced modification of radiation response in human tumor cell lines, *Int. J. Rad. Oncol. Biol. Phys.* (In press).

18. Evensen J. F. & Moan J. (1982) Photodynamic action and chromosomal damage: a comparison of hematoporphyrin derivative (HpD) and light with X-irradiation, *Br. J. Canc.* 45, 456-465.

19. Fisher A. M. R., Ferrario A., Rucker N., Zhang S. & Gomer C. J. (1999) Photodynamic therapy sensitivity is not altered in human tumor cells after abrogation of p53 function, *Cancer Res.* 59, 331-335.

20. Fisher A. M. R., Rucker N., Wong S. & Gomer C. J. (1998) Differential photosensitivity in wild-type and mutant p53 human colon carcinoma cell lines, *J. Photochem. Photobiol. B: Biol.* 42, 104-107.

21. Gaffney D. K., Schober S. L. & Sieber F. (1990) Merocyanine 540-sensitized photoinactivation of leukemia cells: role of oxygen and effects of plasma membrane integrity and mitochondrial respiration, *Exp. Hematol.* 18, 23-26.

22. Gomer D. J., Ruckter N. & Murphree A. L. (1988) Differential cell photosensitivity following porphyrin photodynamic therapy, *Cancer Res.* 48, 4539-4542.

23. He Jin, Agarwal M. L., Larkin H. E., Friedman L. R., Xue L. & Oleinick N. L. T (1996) he induction of partial resistance to photodynamic therapy by the protooncogene *Bcl-2, Photochem. Photobiol.* 64, 845-852.

24. He Xiao-Yan, Sikes R., Thomsen S., Chung L. W. K. & Jacques S. L. (1994) Photodynamic therapy with photofrin II induces programmed cell death in carcinoma cell lines, *Photochem. Photobiol.* 59, 468-473.

25. Hilf R., Small D. B. Murant R. S., Leaky P. B. & Gison S. L. (1984) Hematoporphyrin derivative sensitivity of mitochondrial succinic dehydrogenase and selected cytosolic enzymes of R3230AC mammary adenocarcinoma of rats, *Cancer Res.* 44, 1483-1488 .

26. Hong L., Shin D. S., Lee Y. E, Nguyen D. C., Trang T. C., Pan A. H., Huang S. L. J., Chong D. H. & Berns M. W. (1998) Subcellular phototoxicity of 5-aminolevulinic acid (ALA), *Lasers Surg. Med.* 22, 14-24.

27. Kessel D. and Luo Y. (1998) Mitochondrial photodamage and PDT-induced apoptosis, *J. Photochem. Photobiol. B: Biol.* 42, 89-95.

28. Kessel D., (1981) Transport and binding of HpD and relative porphyrins by murine leukemia L1210 cells, *Cancer Res.* 41, 1318-23.

29. Kessel D., Woodburn D., Gomer C. J., Jagerovic N. & Smith K. M. (1995) Photosensitization with derivatives of chlorin e_6, *J. Photochem. Photobiol. B: Biol.* 28, 13-18.

30. Khanum F. & Jain V. (1987) Studies concerning the role of energy metabolism in the photodynamic therapy, *Assoc. Med. Phys. Bull.* 12, 113-124.

31. Khanum F. & Jain V. (1997) Cellular accumulation and biological activity of hematoporphyrin derivative (L) in comparison with Photofrin II, *Ind. J. Exp. Biol.* 35, 348-355.

32. Kostron H., Swartz M., Miller D. C. & Martuza R. L. (1986) The interaction of hematoporphyrin derivative, light and ionizing radiation in a rat glioma model, *Cancer.* 57, 964-970.

33. Lin C. W., Shulock J. R., Kirley S. D., Cincotta L & Foley J. W. (1993) Photodynamic destruction of lysosomes mediated by Nile Blue photosensitizes, *Photochem. Photobiol.* 58, 81-91.

34. Luo Yu, Chang C. K. & Kessel D. (1996) Rapid initiation of apoptosis by photodynamic therapy, *Photochem. Photobiol.* 63, 528-534.

35. Maity A., McKenna W. G. & Muschel R. J. (1994) The molecular basis for cell cycle delays following ionizing radiation: review, *Radiother. Oncol.* 311-13.

36. Midander J. & Revesz L. (1980) The frequency of micronuclei as a measure of cell survival in irradiated cell populations, *Int. J. Radiat. Biol.* 38, 237-242.

37. Moan J., Berg K., Anholt H. & Madisen K. (1994) Sulfonated aluminium phthalocyanines as sensitizers for photochemotherapy. Effects of small light doses on localization, dye fluorescence and photosensitivity in V-79 cells, *Int. J. Cancer.* 58, 856-870.

38. Moan J., Waksvik H. & Christensen T. (1980) DNA single strand breaks and sister chromatid exchanges induced by treatment with hematoporphyrin and light or by X-rays in human NHIK 3025 cells, *Cancer Res.* 40, 2915-2918.

39. Modica-Napolitano J. S., Joyal J. S., Ara G., Oseroff A. R. & Aprille J. R. (1990) Mitochondrial toxicity of cationic photosensitizes for photochemotherapy, *Cancer Res.* 50, 7876-7881.

40. Morgan J., Potter W. R. & Oseroff A. R. (2000) Comparison of photodynamic targets in a carcinoma cell line and its mitochondrial DNA-deficient derivative, *Photochem. Photobiol.* 71, 747-757.

41. Munday A. D., Sriratana A., Hill J. S., Kahl S. B. & Nagley P. (1996) Mitochondria are the functional intracellular target for a photosensitizing boronated porphyrin, *Biochim. Biophys. Acta.* 1311, 1-4.

42. Noodt B. B., Berg K., Stkke T., Peng Q. & Nesland J. M. (1996) Apoptosis and necrosis induced with light and 5-aminolaevulinic acid-derived protoporphyrin IX, *Br J Cancer*, 74, 22-29.

43. Noodt B. B., Berg K., Stokke T., Peng Q. & Nesland J. M. (1999) Different apoptotic pathways are induced from various intracellular sites by tetraphenylporphyrins and light, *Br. J. Cancer.* 79, 72-81.

44. Noodt B. B., Rodal G. H., Wainwright M., Peng Q., Horobin R., Nesland J. M. & Berg K. (1998) Apoptosis induction by different pathways by methylene blue derivative and light from mitochondrial sites in V79 cells, *Int. J. Cancer.* 75, 1-8.

45. Oenbrink G., Jurgenlimke P. & Gabel D. (1988) Accumulation of porphyrin in cells: influence of hydrophobicity, aggregation and protein binding. *Photochem. Photobiol.* 48, 451-456.

46. Oleinick N. L., Antunez A. R., Clay M. E., Rihter B. D. & Kenny M. E. (1993) New phthalocyanine photosensitizers for photodynamic therapy, *Photochem. Photobiol.* 57, 242-247.

47. Penning L. C., Lagerberg., J. W. M., VanDierendonck J. H., Cornelisse C. J., Dubbleman T. M. A. R. & VanSteveninck J. (1994) The role of DNA damage and inhibition of Poly (ADP-ribosyl)-lation in loss of clonogenicity of murine L929 fibroblasts, caused by photodynamically induced oxidative stress, *Cancer Res.* 54, 5561-5567.

48. Perry R. R., Matthew W., Mitchell J. B., Russo A., Evans S. & Pass H. I. (1990) Sensitivity of different human lung cancer histologies to photodynamic therapy, *Cancer Res.* 50, 4272-4276.

49. Rasch M. H., Tijssen K., Lagerberg Johan W. M., Corver W. E., VanSteveninck J. & Dubbleman T. M. A. R. (1997) The role of protein kinase C activity in the killing of Chinese hamster ovary cells by ionizing radiation and photodynamic treatment, *Photochem. Photobiol.* 66, 209-213.

50. Soncin M., Polo L., Reddi E., Jori G., Kenney M. E., Cheng G. & Rodgers M. A. (1995) Effect of axial ligation and delivery system on the tumor-localizing and -photosensitizing properties of Ge(IV)-octabutoxy-phthalocyanines, *Br. J. Cancer.* 71, 727-732.

51. Tong Z., Singh G. & Rainbow A. J. (2000) The role of p53 tumor suppressor in the response of human cells to photofrin-mediated photodynamic therapy, *Photochem. Photobiol.* 71, 201-210.

52. Woodburn K. W., Vardaxis N. J., Hill J. S., Kaye A. H. & Philips D. R. (1991) Subcellular localization of porphyrins using confocal laser scanning microscopy, *Photochem. Photobiol.* 54, 725-732.

53. Woodburn K. W., Vardaxis N. J., Hill J. S., Kaye A. H., Reiss J. A. & Phillips D. R. (1992) Evaluation of porphyrin characteristics required for photodynamic therapy, *Photochem. Photobiol.* 55, 697-704.

54. Yanagihara K., Nii M., Numoto K., Kamiya, Tauchi H., Sawada S. & Seito S. (1995) Radiation-induced apoptotic cell death in human gastric epithelial tumor cells: Correlation between mitotic death and apoptosis, *Int. J. Radiat. Biol.* 77, 677-685.

55. Zolzer F., Hillebrandt S. & Streffer C. (1995) Radiation-induced G_1 block and p53 status in six human cell lines, *Radiother. Oncol.* 37, 20-28.

METHYLGLYOXAL : ITS ROLE IN UNDERSTANDING THE BIOCHEMICAL BASIS OF MALIGNANCY AND IN TREATMENT OF CANCER

MANJU RAY

Department of Biological Chemistry, Indian Association for the Cultivation of Science, Calcutta - 700 032, INDIA

Summary

In the 1920s, methylglyoxal, a keto-aldehyde, was widely held as one of the key intermediates of glucose breakdown. But with the elucidation of Einbden-Meyerhof pathway of glycolysis, this idea was rejected. However, in the 1970s and the 1980s the metabolic pathway for methylglyoxal in different organisms was established. Methylglyoxal has growth-inhibitory and anticancer properties and it had been generally assumed that, these properties are interrelated. But recent studies have convincingly showed that metliylglyoxal is tumoricidal. It inhibits mitochondrial respiration and glycolysis of exclusively malignant cells which critically reduces ATP level in these cells rendering them non-viable. We have obtained strong evidence that in malignant cells both mitochondrial complex I and the glycolytic enzyme glyceraldehyde-3-phosphate dehydr-ogenase, may be critically altered. Based on these results and considering the role of ATP in biological system, we have proposed a new hypothesis on cancer which suggests that excessive ATP formation in cells may lead to malignancy. Moreover, the previously reported anticancer property of methylglyoxal and recent experimental findings from our laboratory strongly suggest that methylglyoxal alone or in combination with some synthetic or natural product(s) should immediately be put to trial for the treatment of cancer patients.

HISTORICAL PERSPECTIVE

Methylglyoxal CH_3, a keto aldehyde has a chequered history in biology.

|

C=O

|

HC=O

As early 1913 it had been observed that, methylglyoxal is converted to D-lactic acid by an enzyme which is present in many animal tissues and in yeast. In the 1920s, methylglyoxal was widely held as one of the key intermediates of glucose breakdown. But with the elucidation of Embden-Meyerhof pathway of glycolysis, the idea that methylglyoxal as the key intermediate of glycolysis was abandoned. However, several investigators from time to time reported the formation of methylglyoxal in different biological systems, although no specific enzymatic reaction producing methylglyoxal could be identified at that time[1,2].

METABOLIC PATHWAY OF METHYLGLYOXAL

The present phase of interest in the biological role of methylglyoxal began with the work and hypothesis of Szent Györgyi which have suggested that methylglyoxal is growth regulatory and can serve is a carcinostatic agent[3]. During 1970s, Cooper and his co-workers isolated and purified the enzyme methylglyoxal synthese from *E. coli,* and that was the first direct demonstration of enzymatic formation of methylglyoxal in any biological system[4]. With subsequent isolation, purification and characterization of several enzymes responsible for the catabolism and anabolism of methylglyoxal, the metabolic pathways of methylglyoxal have subsequently been elucidated in mammalian system, yeast, protozoa and bacteria[2,4-6]. The main precursors of methylglyoxal are the glycolytic intermediate dihydroxyacetone phosphate and glycine and L-threonine. Methylglyoxal is degraded to D-lactic acid of lactaldehyde or to pyruvic acid (Fig. 1).

REACTION OF METHYLGLYOXAL WITH BIOLOGICAL MOLECULES

Methylglyoxal being a highly reactive compound has the potential to affect a wide variety of cellular processes. Methylglyoxal reacts with amino acids and amino groups in proteins, it induces cross-links in DNA; it inhibits protein synthesis by reacting with RNA. Evidences of reactions of methylglyoxal with other biological macromolecules have also been put forward[2,6].

Methylglyoxal has been isolated from different organisms, but it has been generally assumed that its concentration in ell pool is very small to produce many of the above mentioned biological effects[2]. However, recent experiments have suggested that its cellular concentration can be significantly increased during different metabolic conditions[7].

GROWTH INHIBITORY AND ANTICANCER PROPERTIES OF METHYLGLYOXAL

Methylglyoxal has strong growth inhibitory and anticancer properties. Significant growth inhibitory effect has been observed on germinating seeds, bacteria, tumor cells, yeast, protozoa and on other cells[2-6]. Methylglyoxal when injected into mice along with sarcoma 180 cells, no tumor developed[8]. It has also been observed that methylglyoxal significantly inhibited tumor growth and in some cases produced indefinite survivors in mice bearing several types of cancer[9]. Of all the methylglyoxal catalyzing enzymes, glyoxalase enzyme system is the most strong and ubiquitous[10]. Several inhibitors of glyoxalase were synthesized and tested for their possible cytotoxic

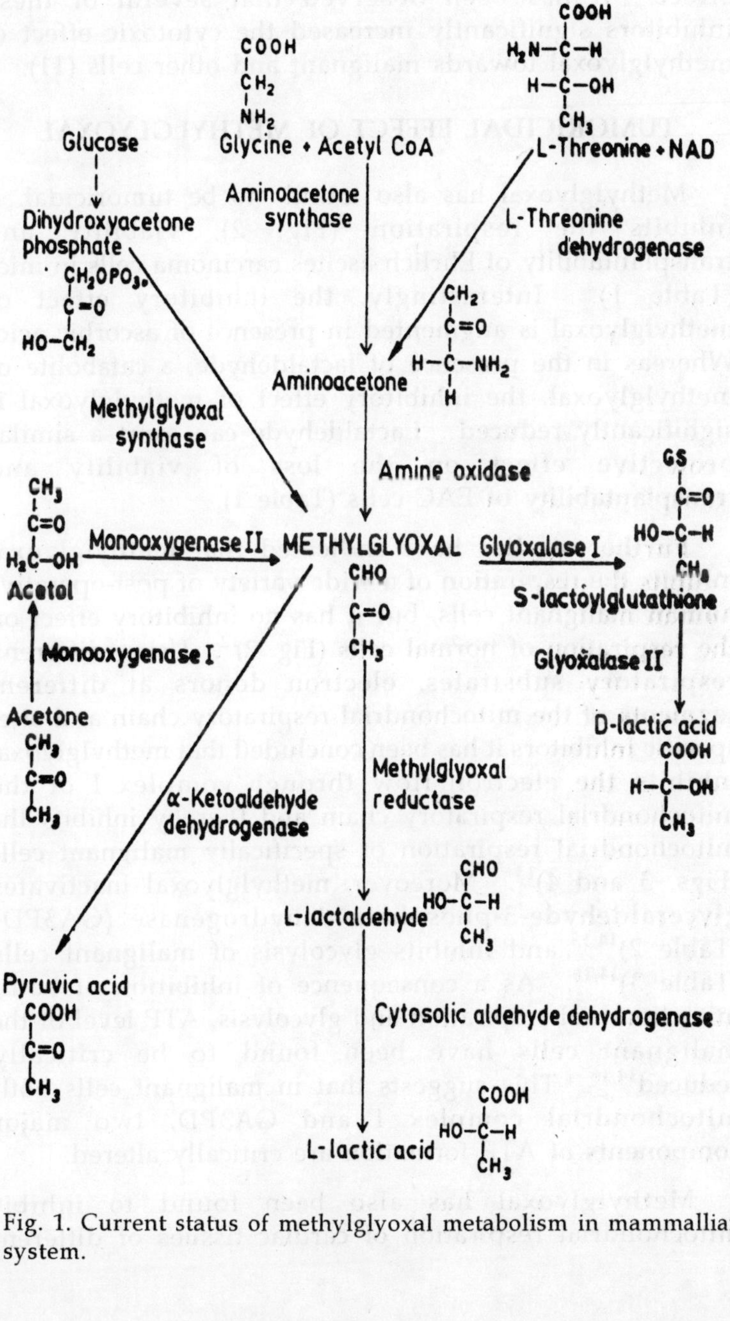

Fig. 1. Current status of methylglyoxal metabolism in mammallian system.

effect. It has been observed that several of these inhibitors significantly increased the cytotoxic effect of methylglyoxal towards malignant and other cells (11).

TUMORICIDAL EFFECT OF METHYLGLYOXAL

Methylglyoxal has also found to be tumoricidal. It inhibits the respiration (Fig. 2), viability and transplantability of Ehrlich ascites carcinoma cells in mice (Table 1). Interestingly, the inhibitory effect of methylglyoxal is augmented in presence of ascorbic acid. Whereas in the presence of lactaldehyde, a catabolite of methylglyoxal, the inhibitory effect of methylglyoxal is significantly reduced. Lactaldehyde can exert a similar protective effect on the loss of viability and transplantability of EAC cells (Table 1).

Further studies have indicated that methylglyoxal inhibits the respiration of a wide variety of post-operative human malignant cells, but it has no inhibitory effect on the respiration of normal cells (Fig. 2)[12]. Using different respiratory substrates, electron donors at different segments of the mitochondrial respiratory chain and site-specific inhibitors it has been concluded that methylglyoxal inhibits the electron flow through complex I of the mitochondrial respiratory chain and thereby inhibits the mitochondrial respiration of specifically malignant cells (Figs. 3 and 4)[13]. Moreover, methylglyoxal inactivates glyceraldehyde-3-phosphate dehydrogenase (GA3PD) (Table 2)[14,15] and inhibits glycolysis of malignant cells (Table 3)[14,16]. As a consequence of inhibition of both, mitochondrial respiration and glycolysis, ATP level of the malignant cells have been found to be critically reduced[14,16]. This suggests that in malignant cells both mitochondrial complex I and GA3PD, two major components of ATP formation are critically altered.

Methylglyoxal has also been found to inhibit mitochondrial respiration of cardiac tissues of different

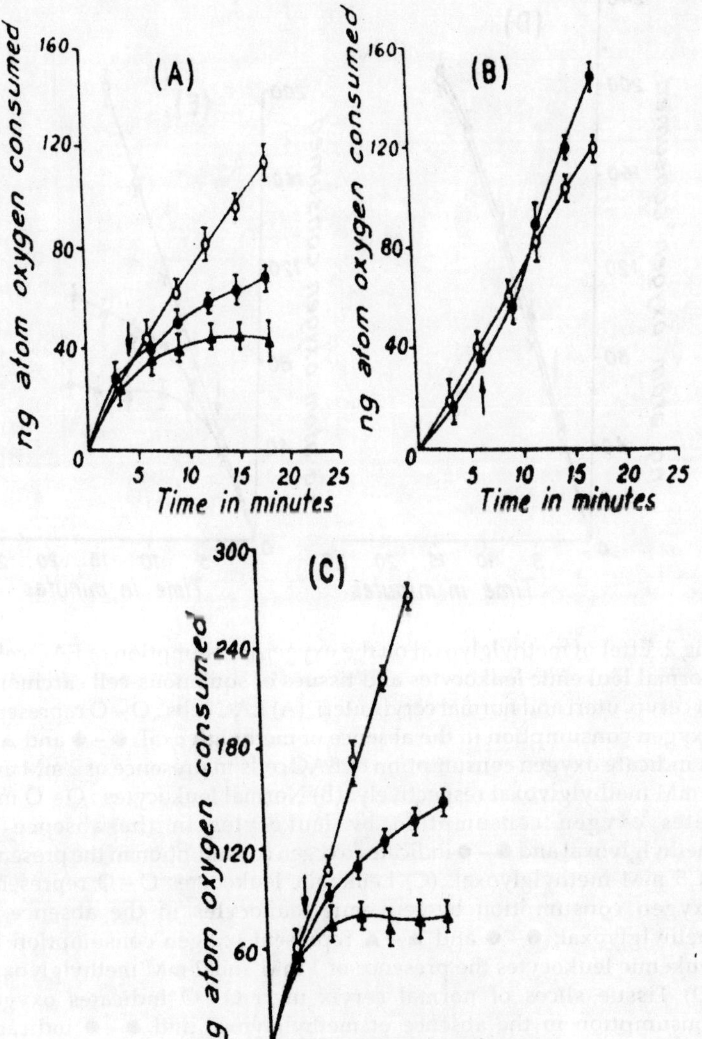

Fig 2. Contd.... on next page

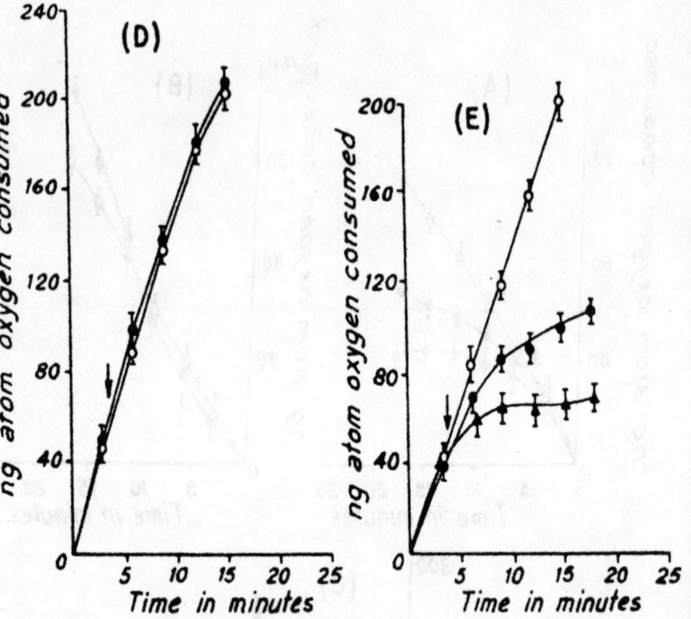

Fig 2. Effet of methylglyoxal on the oxygen consumption of EAC cells, normal leukemic leukocytes and tissues of squamous-cell carcinoma of cervix uteri and normal cervix uteri. (A) EAC cells : O – O represents oxygen consumption in the absence of methylglyoxal. ● – ● and ▲ – ▲ indicate oxygen consumption of EAC cells in presence of 2 mM and 5 mM methylglyoxal respectively. (B) Normal leukocytes : O – O indi cates oxygen consumption by leukocytes in the absence of methylglyoxal and ● – ● indicates oxygen consumption in the presence of 5 mM methylglyoxal. (C) Leukemic leukocytes O – O represents oxygen consumption by leukemic leukocytes in the absence of methylglyoxal; ● – ● and ▲ – ▲ represent oxygen consumption by leukemic leukocytes the presence of 1 mM and 2 mM methylglyoxal. (D) Tissue slices of normal cervix uteri O – O indicates oxygen consumption in the absence of methylglyoxal and ● – ● indicates oxygen consumption in the presence of 5 mM methylglyoxal. (E) Tissue slices of squamous-cell carcinoma of the cervix uteri : Oxygen consumption in the absence of methylglyoxal is represented by O – O; ● – ● and ▲ – ▲ represent oxygen consumption in the presence of 2 mM and 5 mM methylglyoxal respectively. In each figure the arrow indicates the addition of methylglyoxal. Each point represents the mean (± SD) of the experiments. Details of the incubation mixture are described in reference 12.

TABLE 1

Effect of ascorbic acid and lactaldehyde on the loss of viability transplantability of EAC cells by methylglyoxal

Addition of compounds to the control	Viable cells after incubation %	T/I
None	96.0 ± 2.5	10/1
Methylglyoxal (1 mM)	81.0 ± 6.2	10/1
Methylglyoxal (2 mM)	33.0 ± 5.3[4]	10/1
Methylglyoxal (5 mM)	8.4 ±2.7[4]	1/2
Ascorbic acid (1 mM)	92.4±2.8	10/1
Ascorbic acid (2 mM)	78.0±6.6	10/1
Methylglyoxal (1 mM) + Ascorbic acid (1 mM)	28.0±3.7[4]	8/1
Methylglyoxal (2 mM) + Ascorbic acid (2 mM)	7.3±3.1[4]	1/2
L-Lactaldehyde (1.5 mM)	97.0±1.7	10/1
L-Lactaldehyde (1.5 mM) + Methylglyoxal (5 mM)[3]	80.0±5.2	10/1
L-Lactaldehyde (1.5 mM) + Methylglyoxal (10 mM)[3]	71.0±7.2	10/1

The results represent an average (± SD) of 10 sets of experiments.

[1]Number of mice developing tumors/number inoculated.

[2]Delayed development of tumor.

[3]Cells were incubated for 2 min with L-lactaldehyde and then methylglyoxal was added.

[4]$P<0.001$.

Further details of the experimental conditions are described in reference 12.

normal animals, but has no effect on mitochondrial respiration of other organs of normal animals (17). These studies suggest an essential similarity between mitochondria of malignant cells and cardiac tissues.

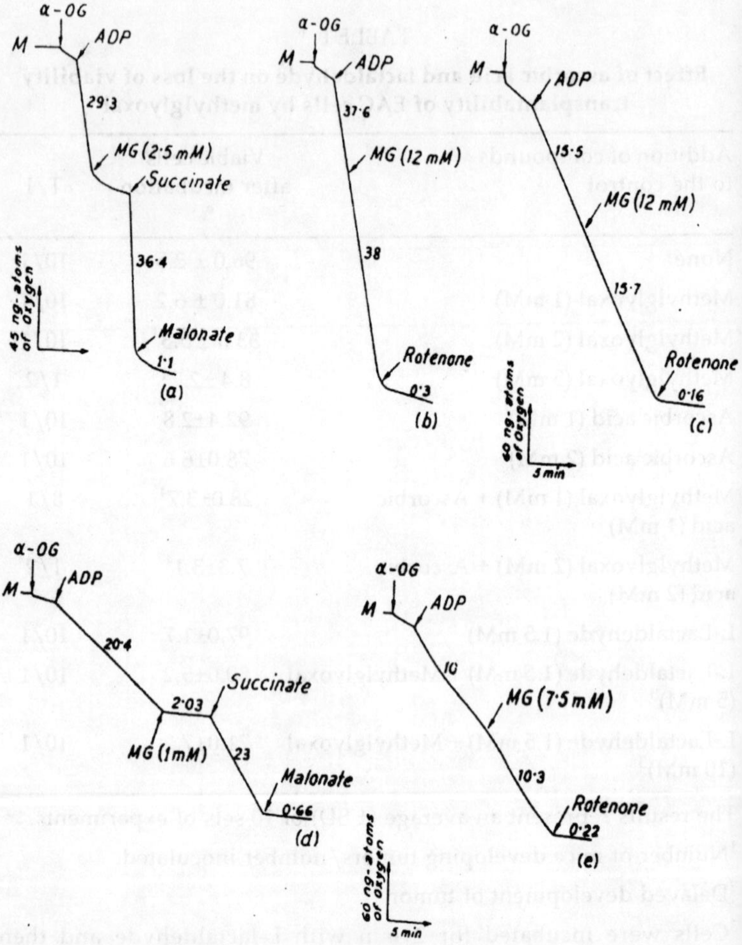

Fig. 3. Effect of methylglyoxal on mitochondrial respiration of some normal and malignant cells. The direct oxygraph tracings of some typical experiments are shown here. Traungs represent the effect of methylglyoxal on α-oxoglutarate, ADP-stimulated mitochondrial respiration of EAC cell (a), normal mouse liver (b), normal mouse kidney (c), human leukemic leukocyte (d) and normal leukocye from healthy donors(e). The numbers on the traces represent, ng-atoms oxygen consumed per minute per mg of mitochondrial protein. Abbreviations : M, mitochondria; MG, iiietliylglyoxal; α-OG, α-oxoglutaiate. Fu details of experimental procedures and result-s are available in references 12, 13 and 14.

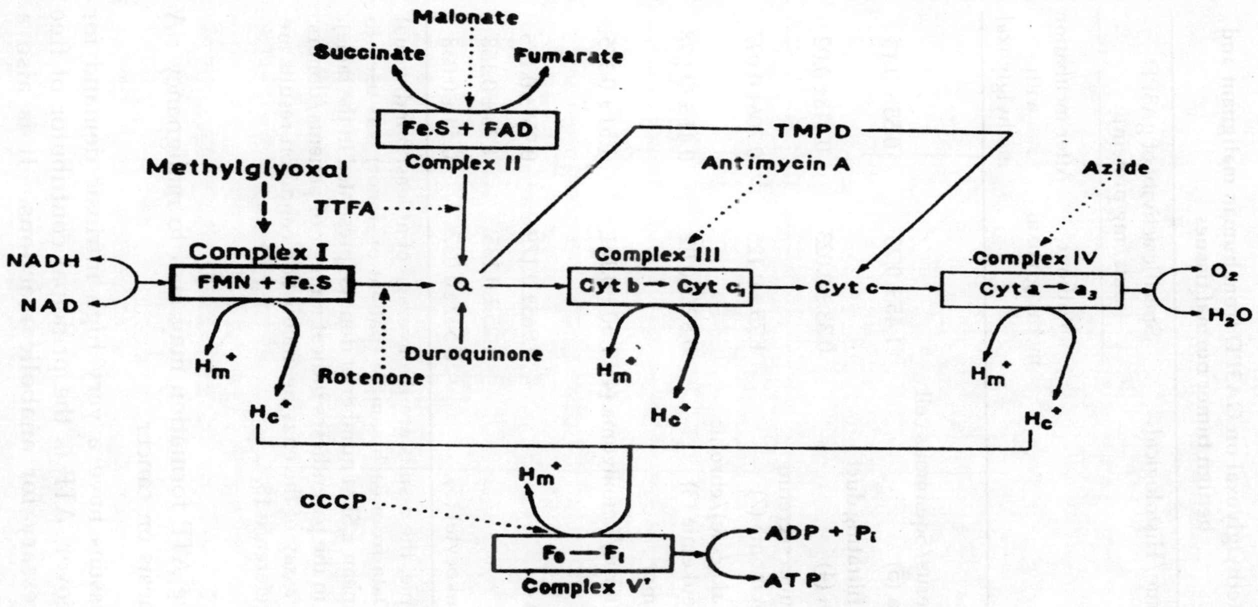

Fig. 4. Components of mitocliondrial electron transport chain and com phosphorylation and the site of inhibition by methylglyoxal. The broken arrows indicate the sites of inhibition. Abbreviations : CCP carbonylcyanide m-chlorophenylhydrazone; cyt, cytochrome; TMPD, N,N,N',N'-1 methyl-p-phenyleue-diamine; TTFA, thenoyl trifluoroacetone.

TABLE 2

Effect of methylglyoxal on GA3PD from human malignant and benign tumor normal tissues

Organ or Tissue/Histological diagnosis	Specific activity of gA3PD (units/mg protein)	
	Without methyiglyoxal	After incubation with methylglyoxal
A. Carcinoma		
Cervix uterus/Squamous cell carcinoma (5)	1.45 ± 0.25	0.55 + 0.13
Breast/Iilfiltrating duct carcinoma (4)	0.33 ± 0.023	0.118± 0.02
Colon/Mucin secreting adeno-carcinoma (7)	1.75 ± 0.125	0.706± 0.097
Blood (Leukocyte)/chronic myeloid leukemia (3)	0.896± 0.02	0.41 ± O.(;28
B. Benign tumor ,		
Fibroid, uterus/Leiomyoma (4)	1.50 ± 0.161	1.51 ± 0.175
C. Normal		
Uterus (5)	0.963± 0.179	0.951± 0.175
Colon (3)	1.25 ± 0.135	1.26 ± 0.158
Blood (Leukocyte) (5)	0.542± 0.037	0.54 ± 0.038

For each sample, the results are the average of at least 3 individual assay ± SD. Data from each sample (patient or donor) was used to calculate the mean ± SEM number of donors (presented in the table). The numbers in the parentheses indicat number of patients/donors. Details of the assay of the enzyme, incubation condition results are described in reference 15.

Excessive ATP formation may lead to malignancy : A new hypothesis on cancer

Heart tissues have a very high intrinsic demand for ATP. Moreover, ATP is the principal contributor of free energy necessary for anabolic reactions. It is also a

TABLE 3

Effect of methylglyoxal on glycolysis (L-lactic acid formation from glucos EAC cells leukemic leukocytes and leukocytes from healthy donors.

Cells	Addition to the complete system	L-Lactic acid formed in µmol/30 min
A.		
EAC cells (10, cells)	None	2.30 ± 0.12
- Do -	Metliylglyoxal (2 mM)	1.04 ± 0.07
- Do -	Methylglyoxal (5 niM)	0.15 ± 0.02
B.		
Leukemic leukocytes		
(10^6cells)	None	2.24 ± 0.076
- Do -	Metliylglyoxal (2 mM)	0.59 ± 0.042
- Do -	Methylglyoxal (5 mM)	0.23 ± 0.055
C.		
Leukocytes from healthy		
donors (100, cells)	None	0.77 ± 0.045
- Do -	Methylglyoxal (5 mM)	0.80 ± 0.03
- Do -	Methylglyoxal (10 niM)	0.77 ± 0,03

Values are mean ± SEM of five different samples from five different mice/patients/donors. Further details of the experimental procedures and results are available in references 14 and 16.

precursor of both RNA and DNA. Based on these biological functions of ATP and the results presented above, a very striking hypothesis has been proposed which suggests that excessive ATP formation in cells may lead to malignancy (17,18). Experimental evidences suggest that in malignant cells both glycolysis and mitochondrial respiration are enhanced resulting in excessive ATP formation.

The phenomenon of excessive ATP formation in malignant cells can explain several characteristics of malignancy such as metastasis and increased glucose uptake of malignant cells and generation of painful stimuli in cancer patients.

Therapy of cancer with a formulation based on methylglyoxal as the lead compound

As mentioned before, previous work have indicated that methylglyoxal can act as an agent which can prevent and inhibit tumor growth in animals[8,9]. Moreover some synthetic and natural compounds are known to augment the anticancer effect of methylglyoxal in *vitro*[11]. Based on these results we have developed a new formulation with methylglyoxal as a lead compound and have tested its efficacy in treating cancer bearing animals. This formulation when injected or orally administered into mice bearing EAC cells, a very rapidly growing malignant cells has been able to produce indefinite survivors in those animals.

All these results suggest that in order to save mankind from the dreadly disease of cancer, methyglyoxal alone or in combination with some synthetic and natural compounds should immediately be put to clinical trial for the treatment of cancer patients.

CONCLUSION

The possible alterations of GA3PD and mitochondrial complex I of malignant cells should be deciphered at the molecular level and to ascertain whether excessive ATP formation does indeed occur in malignant cells, and whether this excessive ATP formation is due to the alterations of GA3PD and complex I in these cells.

Finally, methylglyoxal alone or in combination with other synthetic and natural compounds should immediately be put to trial for the treatment of cancer.

ACKNOWLEDGMENT

The author thanks Council of Scientific & Industrial Research and Department of Science and Technology, Government of India, for their help in preparing the manuscript.

REFERENCES

1. Florkin, M. (I 975) in Comprehensive Biohemistry (eds. Florkin, M. and Stotz, E.H., Elsevier Scientific Publishing Co., Amsterdam, vol. 31, pp 39-115.
2. Thornalley, P.J. (1990) *Biochem. J.* 269, 1 -11.
3. Szent-Györgyi, A. (1979) *Ciba* Found. *Symp.* 67, 3-18.
4. Cooper, R.A. (1984) *Ann.* Rev. Microblot. 38, 49-68.
5. Misra, K., Banerjee, A.B., Ray, S. and Ray, M. (1996) *Mol. Cell. Biochem.* 156, 117-124.
6. Kalapos, M.P. (1994) *Toxicol.. Lett.* 73, 3-24.
7 Kondoh, Y., Kawase, M., Hirata, M. and Olimori, S. (1994) *J. Biochem.* 115, 590-595.
8. Egyud, L.G. and Szent-Györgyi, A. (1968) *Science* 160, 1140.
9. Apple, M.A. and Greenberg, D.M. (1968) *Cancer Chernotherp. Rep.* 52, 687-696.
10. Biswas, S., Bhattachaijee, S., Ray, M. and Ray, S. (1996) *Mol. Cell. Biochem.* 165, 9-16.
11. Vince, R. and Daluge, S. (1971) *J. Med. Chem.* 14, 35-37.
12. Ray, M., Halder, J., Dutta, S.K. and Ray, S. (1991) *Int. J. Cancer* 47, 603-609.
13. Ray, S., Dutta, S., Halder, J. and Ray, M. (1994) *Biochem. J.* 303, 69-72.
14. Halder, J., Ray, M. and Ray, S. (1993) *Int. J. Cancer* 54, 443-449.
15. Ray, M., Basu, N. and Ray, S. (1997) *Mol. Cell. Biochem.* in press.
16. Biswas, S., Ray, M., Misra, S., Dutta, D.P. and Ray, S. (1997) Biochem. *J.* 323, 343-348.
17. Ray, S., Biswas, S. and Ray, M. (1997) *Mol. Cell. Biochem.* 171, 95-103.
18. Ray, S. and Ray, M. (1997) *Med. Hypothes.* 48, 473-476.

ROLE OF TRACE ELEMENTS IN ADAPTATION TO HIGH ALTITUDE STRESS

M. V. SINGH, S.B. RAWAL , A.K. SALHAN
A.K. TYAGI AND W. SELVAMURTHY

Defence Institute of Physiology And Allied Sciences, Lucknow Road, Delhi- 110054

Summary

Research has focused mainly on the relationship of zinc, copper and vanadium contents under acute hypoxic stress at 3,500 m. It has also been reported that other forms of stresses change the concentration of these trace elements in humans. However, there are no reports on the effects of high altitudes induced hypoxic stress on the plasma levels of these metals. Since hypoxia is one of the important stresses, we considered it appropriate to observe the changes in the levels of zinc, copper and vanadium concentrations in certain zinc and copper related enzymes and hormones in the plasma of human volunteers on acute induction to high altitude. From these findings we intend to ascertain whether supplementation of these trace elements would be required for optimal health and amelioration of acute mountain sickness symptoms under such conditions.

On acute induction to hypoxic stress, the requirement of these trace elements may change in stressed organs and tissues. Hence supplementation may be beneficial under hypoxic stress for better adaptability. Volunteers were divided into four groups namely control, supplementation with zinc salt, and supplementation with copper salt, and supplementation with vanadyl sulphate. Blood samples were collected at sea level on inductions to acute hypoxia on days 3 and 10. Trace mineral contents and their related enzyme alkaline phosphatase and hormone ceruloplasmin levels were determined in plasma samples.

Plasma zinc contents were significantly reduced upon induction to high altitude in the non-supplemented group, but not in the zinc supplement group. Alkaline phosphatase activity increased significantly upon induction to the high altitude. The enzyme activity remained elevated upto day 10 of the stress. Plasma copper contents and ceruloplasmin activity did not change upon induction to high altitude. The plasma vanadium contents were significantly decreased, may be due to redistribution of vanadium from plasma into other organs/tissues: certain physiological changes take place in these organs on exposure to high altitude. Under hypoxic stress circulating levels of zinc and alkaline phosphatase in plasma changed appreciably as plasma zinc was transported into the organs and tissues. However, circulating levels of copper and ceruloplasmin in plasma did not change indicating no extra supplementation of copper is required under hypoxic stress. The difference in valence state of vanadium may be responsible for absence of diuresis in human.

INTRODUCTION

Rapid ascent to high altitude leads to symptoms of acute mountain sickness (AMS), severe enough to limit normal activity in the majority of the people. The most important stressor observed at high altitude is hypoxia, and numerous investigations of human responses to hypoxia have demonstrated many physiological changes, including endocrine reactions (Anand, 1993; Hacket, 1976; Hultgren, 1964).

During the last few years, the interest in the behavior and possible function of trace elements on biological systems has increased. Trace elements serve specific function in the metabolism, depending on their physio-chemical properties. Trace elements such as zinc, copper and vanadium are directly involved in many physiological processes that may be altered by physical exercise (Singh, 1991). Zinc is an essential trace element required for normal eating pattern, growth, protein metabolism integrity (McClain, 1985); Eating disorders and zinc deficiency may have many of the similar symptoms (Humphies, 1989; Kutti, 1984). It has been reported that strenuous exercise, whether acute or chronic, leads to decreased serum zinc concentration and also increase urinary zinc loss. Such losses are dependent on the intensity and duration of exercise (Miyamura, 1987). Little is currently known regarding the relationship between physiological function and specific levels of these trace elements in humans. It has been reported that vanadium deficiency significantly increases packed cell volume, which in turn may increase blood viscosity (Nielson, 1990). Golden (1981) has reported that administration of vanadium salt induces diuresis which may be beneficial in the process of high altitude (HA) acclimatization where ill effects of HA are mainly due to fluid retention in the body.

The effect of Zinc on Hb-O_2 affinity is quite dramatic. A large shift in the oxygen affinity of a red cell -saline suspension occurs with a low Zn/Hb molar ratio, binding experiments have indicated that Zinc can bind to more than one Hb amino acid radical, but it seems probable that the amino acid with the highest binding capacity for Zinc is also the radical involved in the oxygen affinity effect of Zinc. Only that Zinc, which is transported to the cells, whether as an enzyme cofactor or bound to a membrane or other metabolically active form, is of any significant value in the body.

Zinc plays an integral role in appetite regulation .In rats; decreased food consumption and a cyclic pattern of eating represent primary signs of Zinc deficiency (Essatara, 1984; Karaskis, 1986). Zinc deficient animals also demonstrate altered intake of a variety of solutions such as quinine sulphate and saline used to assess taste acuity (Chen, 1980). McClain (1993) has demonstrated that during the Zinc depletion period, food intake by zinc deficient group was reduced to 33% of ad-lib controls, which increased during zinc repletion three fold in comparison to depletion period. McClain (1993) also evaluated the relationship between hypothalamic neurotransmitter system and aberrant feeding behavior in zinc deficient rats. The concentration of tyrosine, DOPA, nor epinephrine, epinephrine, tryptophan, 5HT and MOA-A activity were measured in hypothalamus of rats fed zinc deficient diets and reported that NE increase 30%, MOA-A rose 20% with other transmitters unchanged compared to Zn-adequate control group. Enzyme activities are also reported to decrease significantly in zinc deficient rats.

In spite of beneficial effects of trace elements under stressful conditions, nothing has been reported on the role of trace elements on early high altitude acclimatization. Present study examines the effect of hypoxia on concentrations on these stress elements and also on the level of certain enzymes and hormones in human plasma on acute induction to high altitude.

METHODS

The study was conducted on 32 healthy male volunteers from the Indian Army ranging in age from 21-27 yr. The subjects were physically fit, low land dwellers who had never been exposed to high altitude. They were briefed about the details of the study and test procedure and their written consent was obtained. The subjects were initially tested at Delhi (altitude of 200m, subsequently referred to as sea level) and then divided into four groups of eight each. The first group of subjects served as controls and were given placebo 3 days prior to their airlift to high altitude (3500m). The second, third and fourth groups (treatment groups) were given 15 mg of zinc sulphate, 4 mg of copper chloride and 5mg of vanadyle sulphate filled in gelatin capsules), respectively, 3 days prior to their airlift to high altitude and trace elements supplementation was continued for two more days at that altitude. At high altitude these soldiers were fed on regular army diet and were physically fit. The environmental temperatures at sea level and high altitude varied between 22.6°C to 39.8°C and between 3.2°C to 18.7°C, respectively. Total time for air flight from sea level to high altitude was 50 min. The blood samples of these subjects were collected once at sea level and twice (on days 3 and 10) at high altitude by vene puncture in heparinized disposable syringes in a centrally heated hospital maintained at 19 + 1°C Plasma was separated to determine zinc and copper contents in their respective groups by atomic absorption spectrometer (Model No Varian Spectra AA-20 plus Atomic Absorption Spectrometer with GTA-96 Graphite tube Atomizer Victoria Australia).

Estimation of plasma alkaline phosphatase and ceruloplasmin was carried out using methods reported earlier (Raphel, 1976; Raphel, 1976)

Statistical analysis: The data was analyzed by employing parametric t-test between the differences of end points; i.e., differences between control and day 3 readings with control and day 10 readings.

RESULTS

Table 1 shows that in the control group at high altitude on day 3, the plasma zinc concentration significantly decreased ($p<0.01$). Plasma zinc contents on day 10 were also significantly lower, compared to sea level values ($p<0.05$). The comparison has also been made in the differences of zinc contents between SL-3d and SL-10d, which was also significant ($p<0.01$). Further difference of SL-3d of zinc level between the zinc-supplemented group and control group was also found significant.

Table II shows the values of alkaline phosphatase in the various groups. In the group not given any zinc salt supplementation, alkaline phosphatase activity rose

TABLE I

Changes in Plasma Zinc Contents (Mean±Sd) of Human Volunteers with and without Zinc Salt Supplementation on Induction to High Altitude (N=8); Height 3,500 M

	Plasma zinc contents without Zinc salt supplementation (µg/dl)	Plasma zinc contents with zinc salt supplementation (µg/dl)
Group		
Sea Level	115(±9)	121(±11)
3rd day on induction to high altitude	92(±10)**	118(±14)
10th day on induction to high altitude	105(±9)*	114(±12)
Group differences		
SL-3d	22.8(±2.59)	3.00(±4.49)
SL-10d	10.1(±7.11)**	6.9(±4.40)
3d-10d	12.9(±9.04)**	6.0(±2.19)

Values are mean and (SD) of the differences of plasma zinc at sea level(SL) and at height of 3,500 m on day 3 and day 10.
Stars indicate significantly different from sea level value
* p< 0.05
** p< 0.01

significantly on day 3 of induction to high altitude. The enzymatic value increased dramatically ($p < 0.01$). On prolonged exposure up to 10 d, this value decreased, but it still remained significantly higher than at sea level. The value of alkaline phosphatase was found appreciably changed ($p < 0.001$) in the differences of SL-3d vs. SL-10d as well as in SL-3d vs. 3d -10d ($p < 0.01$). Supplementation of zinc salt did not alter the enzyme activity caused by the high altitude exposure.

TABLE II

Changes in Alkaline Phosphatase Activities (Mean±Sd) on Induction to 3,500 M with and without Zinc Salt Supplementation (N=8)

	Alkaline phosphatase contents Without zinc salt supplementation mg P/hr/dl	Alkaline phosphatase with zinc salt supplementation mg P/hr/dl
Group		
Sea level	1.42(±0.37)	1.54(±0.26)
3rd day on induction to high altitude	4.98(±0.66)***	4.55(±0.68)***
10th day on induction to high altitude	2.22(±0.75)**	1.93(±0.48)*
Group differences		
SL-3rd day	3.55(±0.36)	3.01(±0.44)
SL-10th day	0.81(±0.52)***	0.40(±0.25)
3rd day – 10th day	2.75(±0.45)**	2.62(±0.26)

Values are mean and (SD) of the differences of alkaline phosphatase at sea level and at 3,500 m on day 3 and day 10.

Statistical significance level:

* $p<0.05$

** $p<0.01$

*** $p<0.001$

No significant changes in plasma copper contents and ceruloplasmin levels were observed between the sea level values and the group inducted to high altitude with and without copper salt supplementation (Tables III & IV). A similar picture was revealed by the difference between the two responses.

TABLE III

Changes in Plasma Copper Contents (Mean±Sd) of Human Volunteers with and without Copper Salt Supplementation on Acute Induction to High Altitude (N=8); Height 3,500 M

	Plasma copper contents without supplementation (µg/dl)	Plasma copper contents copper salt with copper salt supplementation (µg/dl)
Group		
Sea level	85(±8)	91(±11)
3rd day on induction to high altitude	78(±10)	86(±10)
10th day on induction to high altitude	80(±11)	81(±11)
Group differences		
SL-3rd day	6.9(±3.50)	5.0(±2.88)
SL-10th day	5.1(±5.70)	9.8(±5.57)
3rd day-10th day	2.1(±1.98)	5.1(±1.68)

Values are mean and (SD) of the differences of plasma copper at sea level and at height of 3,500 m on day 3 and day 10.

Fig. 1 depicts the changes in plasma vanadium contents of human volunteers at sea level with and without supplementation of vanadium salt. And also after induction to high altitude in both groups on days 3 and 10. At sea level the contents of vanadium in plasma were 27.33 + 2.13 ng/ml, which likely increased after oral administration of vanadium salts to 31.9 + 3.1 ng/ml. On the 3rd and 10th day of induction to high altitude a significant decrease ($p<0.001$) in plasma vanadium contents

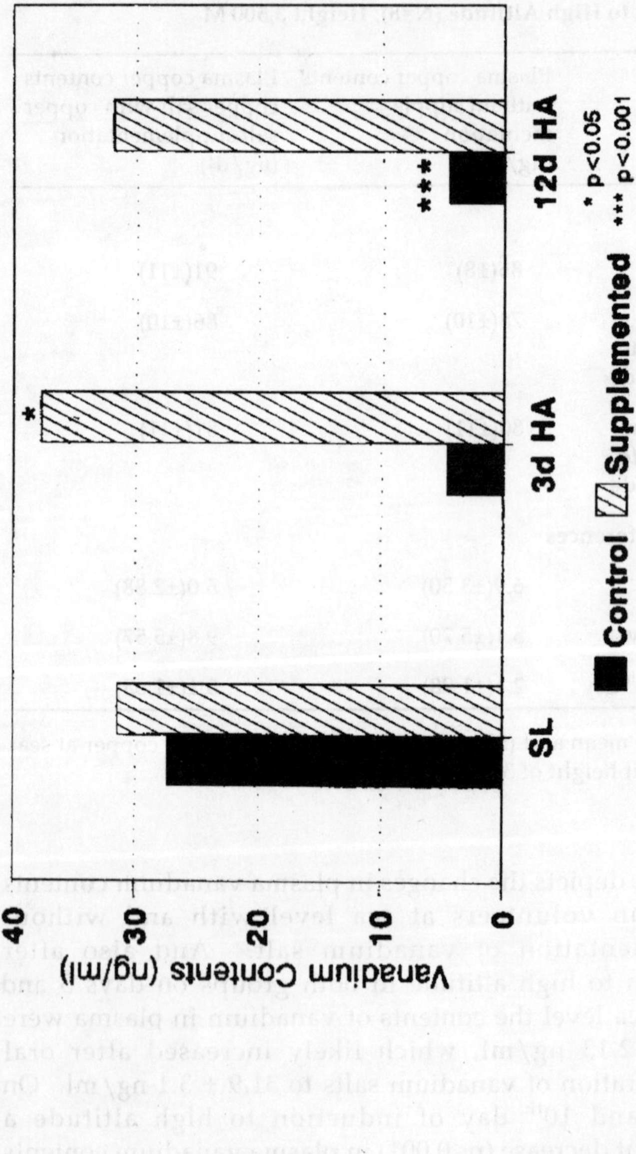

Fig 1. Relationship between vanadium contents in plasma of control and supplemented groups at sea-level and on various days of high altitude exposure. ■ Control; ▨ Supplemented. * $P < 0.05$; *** $P < 0.001$

TABLE IV

CHANGES IN CERULOPLASMIN CONTENTS (MEAN±SD) IN PLASMA ON ACUTE INDUCTION TO HIGH ALTITUDE WITH AND WITHOUT SUPPLEMENTATION OF COPPER SALT (n=8); HEIGHT 3,500 M

	Plasma ceruloplasmin contents without copper salt supplementation (mg/100 ml)	Plasma ceruloplasmin contents with copper salt supplementation (mg/100 ml)
Group		
Sea level	42.5(±3.5)	43.7(±3.8)
3rd day on induction to high altitude	36.3(±2.6)	39.9(±4.1)
10th day on induction to high altitude	39.3(±1.8)	40.7(±2.6)
Group differences		
SL-3rd day	6.1(±1.26)	3.7(±1.46)
SL-10th day	3.3(±2.06)	3.1(±2.11)
3rd day-10th day	3.1(±1.13)	0.9(±1.34)

Values are mean and (standard deviation) of the differences of plasma copper at sea level and at height of 3,500 m on day 3 and day 10

was observed in the control group. On both days the vanadium contents of less than 5 ng/ml were significantly reduced in comparison with the value at sea level. In the experimental group, which was fed orally for 6 days with vanadium salt, the vanadium contents rose dramatically to a level of 37.7 + 4.3 ng/ml on the 3rd day of high altitude exposure. Even after the cessation of oral vanadium feeding, the vanadium contents remain elevated and reach a value of 31.7 + 2.9 ng/ml.

Table 5 shows the liquid intake and urine output for the first 24 hr of the stay at high altitude in control and experimental group. The experimental group consumed more liquid than the control group, compared with the increased urinary output of the control group.

DISCUSSION

The significance of the biochemical and nutritional roles of zinc, copper and vanadium trace elements is widely recognized because they are found to be in-vivo constituents of many metalloenzymes and metalloproteins (McClain, 1993). Use of plasma has been preferred instead of serum for zinc estimation. This is because serum may have relatively high levels of zinc due to the hemolysis of red blood cells and disintegration of platelets during the serum separation process. Furthermore, these levels may fluctuate depending on the degree of hemolysis and platelet disintegration.

Zinc is an essential cofactor for, and in some instances leads structural stability to, key metabolic enzymes that may be important during stress (Richardson, 1979). It has been shown by Van Rij (1986) that plasma zinc concentration decreases immediately following prolonged running and decreases even further at 6 h after running. In the present study, it was observed that upon acute hypoxic exposure, plasma zinc content significantly decreased. The mechanism for regulating the plasma zinc deficiency in this case is by redistribution of this metal ion

TABLE V

Liquid Intake and Urine Output in Control and Vanadyle Sulphate Treated Group(mean±Sem) after Exposure to High Altitude (N=8)

	CONTROL GROUP	EXPERIMENTAL GROUP
Fluid Intake (ml)	2291±554	2458±657
Urine Output (ml)	1795±631	1339±403

to other tissues that were enduring hypoxic stress. It has been reported that stressors stimulate the uptake of trace minerals by the liver and synthesis of metallothionine, accompanied by a reduction in plasma mineral concentration (Ohno, 1985). However, in the zinc-supplemented group, plasma zinc contents upon acute high altitude exposure remained unchanged, comparable to sea level. The reason may be that under stressful conditions various organs and tissues require more zinc and this need is fulfilled from the plasma

In the zinc-supplemented group, extra zinc was available in plasma for redistribution to stressed organs and tissues, while maintaining the normal plasma zinc levels.

It is clear from the above discussion that zinc deficiency usually occurs when biological systems undergo stress. Dressendorfer (1980) reported that under strenuous exercise, whether acute or chronic, serum zinc content decreased. Physical trauma is yet another stress, which leads to changes in zinc parameters. Cousins, (1985) and Rofe, (1992) have also reported that under acute response to stress, trauma, inflammation and infection, a prominent decrease occurred in the serum zinc concentration and an internal distribution of total body zinc stores, with increased levels of zinc in the liver. Although internal redistribution of zinc during the acute phase of response might explain hypozincemia in humans, other mechanisms have also been reported to play an important role. These include increased urinary zinc excretion, decreased serum albumin concentration, and changes in serum albumin zinc binding (Rofe, 1992). Kikukawa, (1996) have reported that after the +Gz acceleration exposure {another stressful situation) the serum zinc concentration significantly decreases. The mode of activity (aerobic or anaerobic) and the duration of exposure may account for different results. From the above observations, one can conclude that under stressful situations, whether exercise stress, +Gz acceleration stress, or hypoxic stress, more zinc is required to combat that stressful situation. It has also been reported that during zinc depletion, food intake was reduced by 33% in animals, and after zinc depletion, food intake increased approximately threefold (McClain, 1993). The most widely postulated mechanism for zinc-induced anorexia is an alteration in the brain neurotransmitter metabolism (Young, 1996). Alkaline phosphatase is a very important zinc-dependent enzyme. It has been reported that activity of alkaline phosphatase significantly decreases in the plasma for zinc deficient rats. The alkaline phosphatase in plasma responds rapidly to zinc depletion through a significant reduction in its activity.

Zinc deficient diet, the enzyme lost 27% and 48% of its activity on 2 and 4 d, respectively (McClain, 1993), under normal conditions without any external stressors. In the present study, the activity of plasma alkaline phosphatase increased significantly in both the groups, not given zinc and zinc treated group on acute induction to high altitude. In the untreated group this increase in alkaline phosphatase activity may be at the cost of plasma zinc contents, which decreased on high altitude induction.

The additional zinc supplementation did not bring about any further increase in alkaline phosphatase activity. Cousins, (1985) and Rofe, (1992) have also reported that zinc levels in liver increase under various stressful situations due to internal distribution of total body zinc stores. The mechanism of alkaline phosphatase increase is due to increased production of enzyme in the liver. This results in the liver secreting more of the alkaline phosphatase into the blood (Hultgren, 1964). Under a similar mechanism, significant increase of alkaline phosphatase in plasma was observed in this study.

On day 10 of exposure, the increase in alkaline phosphatase activity was found to be significantly lower than on day 3 in both the groups. It can be concluded from this finding that zinc plasma contents in the subjects under study were sufficient, and additional zinc supplementation would not increase alkaline phosphatase activity when the zinc supply was optimal.

Copper is another trace element that has attracted the attention of exercise physiologists because it is a part of the cytochrome oxidase complex, the final step in the electron transport system. An increase in serum copper level has been reported during both graded bicycle exercise to exhaustion and prolonged cycling (Olha, 1982). In the present study, copper contents in plasma of both the groups (copper salt supplemented and non-supplemented groups) did not change from their sea level value. It indicates that the tissues and organs under stressful conditions do not require extra copper, and hence no variation in plasma coppers contents. The subjects of this study were not found copper deficient because none of our subjects were anemic and values for median corpuscular volume (MCV), median corpuscular hemoglobin concentration (MCHC), and median corpuscular hemoglobin (MCH) were normal in our study (data not reported here) as these values are significantly reduced in copper deficiency (Hacket, 1976). It has been reported by Ohno, (1985) that plasma copper concentration increased immediately after brief intensive aerobic exercise but returned to normal after 30 min of rest.

Ceruloplasmin is an essential copper transporting protein in plasma, and copper deficiency reduces the value of ceruloplasmin. About 94% of the circulating copper can be accounted for in ceruloplasmin. Plasma levels of this protein can be used to confirm copper deficiency or excess accumulation. Because of the short half-life of ceruloplasmin; its activity responds very rapidly to inadequate copper intake. In the present study, the ceruloplasmin contents of both the control and copper-supplemented groups did not show any change from their sea level values, indicating again that neither of these groups was copper deficient nor is copper supplementation required under hypoxic stress.

Another important parameter, which is very useful for high altitude acclimatization, is diuresis: intravenous vanadate has been reported to be a potent diuretic. Rats with a control urine output of 26 ml/h produced 36.2 ml/h after intravenous injection of sodium vanadate at a dose of 250 µg/kg body wt. (Balfour, 1978). In the presence of vanadate, extracellular potassium (at physiological concentrations) inhibits the sodium pump whereas, in the absence of vanadate, potassium is stimulatory. Our results on human volunteers, upon administration of vanadyl sulphate do not support the above findings. A possible explanation for this discrepancy is that in our study vanadyl sulphate was administered orally while vanadate was injected intravenously in the rat. The difference in valency state of vanadium may be responsible for these varied responses. Moreover, in our studies the experimental group (treated with vanadyl sulphate) drank more water with a lower amount of urine output than the control group. This indicates that vanadium in the tetravalent state may not act as a diuretic as reported in the case of pentavalent valency (i.e. sodium vanadate). The body is retaining the extra water. Macara, (1980) also reported that in vivo vanadium might function as a physiological regulator of sodium pump activity. Vanadate inhibits Na.K ATPase by binding to the ATP hydrolysis site but reduction of vanadate to vanadyl reverses that inhibition.

It has been confirmed from the use of radioactive vanadium (^{48}V) that vanadium was mainly present in plasma and disappeared from blood stream quickly. Hence plasma was estimated for vanadium contents and its probable retention on HA exposure. In our study the plasma vanadium contents were significantly decreased on day 3 and 10 of HA exposure. The decreased contents on hypoxic exposure may be due to redistribution of vanadium from plasma into the other organs/tissues: certain physiological changes take place in these organs on exposure to HA and hence uptake of radioactive vanadium may vary in these organs under stressful conditions. In the vanadium supplemented group. The plasma level of vanadium returned to normal. It has been reported that radioactive vanadium is taken up selectively by the various organs and for up to 96 h remains in the blood. Therefore, it is presumed that supplemented vanadium salt was responsible for the increased plasma vanadium contents, which were significantly reduced after hypoxic exposure.

From these findings, it can be concluded that under hypoxic stress zinc plasma content decreased due to redistribution of plasma zinc to other organs where the requirement may increase, due to the stressful situation. The internal redistribution of zinc may have important functional consequences causing certain tissue stores to be deprived of zinc.

In spite of decreases in plasma zinc, alkaline phosphatase concentration in plasma significantly increased due to increased induction of this enzyme in the liver. This causes the liver to secrete more alkaline phosphatase into the blood. However circulating levels of copper and ceruloplasmin in plasma did not change, again indicating no extra supplementation of copper is required under hypoxic stress.

ACKNOWLEDGMENT

The authors are thankful to volunteers from Indian Army for their whole-hearted cooperation and Mrs. Saroj Bala Chopra for secretarial assistance.

REFERENCES

1, Anand IS, Chandrashekhar Y, Rao SK. et al. Body fluid compartments, renal blood flow and hormones at 6000 m in normal subjects. *J Appl Physiol* (1993), 74:1234-9.

2. Balfour WE, Grantham JJ, Glynn IM. Stimulated Natriuresis. *Nature* (London) (1978); 275-768.
3. Chen SY. Morphologic alterations in oral mucosa in zinc deficient rabbits. *Arch Oral Biol*, (1980); 25:377-83.
4. Cousins RJ. Absorption, transport, and hepatic metabolism of copper and zinc: special reference to metallothionein and ceruloplasmin. *Physiol Rev* (1985); 65:238-309.
5. Dressendorfer RH, Sockolov R. Hypozincemia in runners. *Phys Sports Med* (1980); 8:97-100.
6. Essatara MB, Levine AS, Morley JE, McClain CJ. Zinc deficiency and anorexia in rats : Normal feeding patterns and stress induced feeding. *Physiology and Behaviour* (1984); 32:469-74 .
7. Golden MHN, Golden BE. Potential importance in human nutrition with particular reference to zinc and vanadium *Br.Med. Bull* (1981);37: 31-36.
8. Hacket PH, Rennie D, Levine HD. The incidence importance and prophylaxis of acute mountain sickness. *Lancet* (1976); 2:1149- 54.
9. Hultgren HN, Lopez CE, Lundberg E, Miller H. Physiologic studies of pulmonary edema at high altitude. *Circulation* (1964); 9:393-408.
10. Humphies L, Vivian B, Stuart M, McClain CJ. Zinc deficiency and eating disorders. *J Clin Psych* (1989); 50:456-9.
11. Karaskis EJ, Sparks DL, Slevin JT: Changes in hypothalamic noradrenergic systems during the anorexia of zinc deficiency. *Bio Trace El. Res.* (1986); 9:25-35.
12. Kikukawa A, Miyamoto Y, Akamatsu T. +Gz Acceleration affects to trace minerals zinc, copper and chromium in serum and urine of humans. *Aviat Space Envrion Med* (1996); 67:1166-9.
13. Kutti SS, Kuti J. Zinc and anorexia nervosa. *Ann Intern Med* (1984); 100:317-8.
14. Macara IG, Kustin K, Cantly LC. Glutathione reduces cytoplasmic vanadate. Mechanism in physiological implications. *Biochem Biophys Acta* (1980); 629:95-106.
15. McClain CJ, Kasarskis EJ, Alien JJ. Functional consequences of zinc deficiency. *Frog Food Nutr Sci* (1985); 9:185-226.
16. McClain CJ,Stuart M, Kasarskis EJ, Hamphries L. Zinc appetite regulation and eating disorders. Essential and toxic trace elements in human health and disease. An update New York: *Wileey-Liss, Inc.* (1993); 47-64 .

17. Miyamura JB, McNutt SW, Lichton IJ, Wenkam NS. Altered zinc status of soldiers under field conditions *J Am Diet Assoc* (1987); 87:595-7.

18. Nielson FH. New essential trace elements for the life sciences. *Biol Trace Elem Res.* (1990); 26-27 : 599-611.

19. Ohno H, Yamashita K, Doi R, et al. Exercise induced changes in blood zinc and related proteins in humans. *J Appl Phsyiol* (1985); 58:1453-8.

20. Olha AE, Klissouras V, Sullivan JD, Skoryna SC. Effect of exercise on concentration of elements in the serum. *J Sports Med Phys Fitness* (1982); 22:414-25.

21. Raphel SS, ed. Lynch's Medical Laboratory Technology, 3rd ed (Asian ed) Tokyo: WE Saunder's Company Ligaku Shoin Ltd. (1976); 2: 74-75.

22. Raphel SS ed Lynch's Medical Laboratory Technology. 3rd ed (Asian ed) Tokyo: WE Saunder's Company, Ligaku Shoin Ltd. (1976); 345-46.

23. Richardson JH, Drak PD. The effects of zinc on fatigue of striated muscle. *J Sports Med Phys Fitness* (1979); 19:133-4.

24. Rofe AM, Philcox JC, Haynes DR, Whitehouse MW, Coyle P. Changes in plasma zinc, copper, iron and hepatic metallothionein in adjauvant-induced arthritis treated with cyclosporin. *Biol Trace Elem Res.* (1992); 34:237-48.

25 Singh A, Smoak BL, Patterson Ky et al. Biochemical indices of selected trace elements in men : effect of stress. *Am J Clin Nutr* (1991);53: 126-31

26. Van Rij AM, Hall MT, Dohn GL, et at. Changes in zinc metabolism following exercise in human subjects. *Biol Trace Elem Res.* (1986); 10:99-105.

25. Young B, Ott L, Kasayskis E, et al. Zinc supplementation improves neurological recovery rate in patients with severe closed head injury. *J Neurotrauma* (1996); 13:25-34.

26. Brewer GI, Yuzbasiyan-Gurkan V, Dohyeel L. Molecular genetics and zinc-copper interaction human Wilson's disease and canine copper toxicosis. In Essentia1 and .toxic trace elements in human healath and disease: An update wiley-Liss, Inc,1993;129-45.

27. Ashkenazi A, Levin.C, Djaldeni M. The syndrome of neonatal copper deficiency 1973; 52:525-33.

ENDOCRINE FUNCTION AT HIGH ALTITUDE IN MAN

R.C. SAWHNEY, A.S. MALHOTRA, M. BASU, K. PAL & R. PRASAD

Defence Institute of Physiology and Allied Sciences, Lucknow Road, Timarpur, Delhi - 110 054

Summary

The neuroendocrine system, particularly the hypothalamic-pituitary-adrenal system is put up to maximum test during exposure to the altitude stress. Though cortisol levels are increased on immediate arrival at high altitude (HA), plasma cortisol returns to sea level (SL) values within 3-4 weeks of stay. When subjects acclimatized to a lower altitude are taken to a higher altitude, the cortisol secretion is not further augmented indicating that once acclimatisation is achieved to a lower altitude, increased secretion of cortisol may not be necessary for acclimatization to subsequent higher altitudes. In acclimatised low landers, the cortisol rhythmicity is well maintained suggesting a perfect acclimatization to the changed environment. Those who are unable to acclimatize show a decline in cortisol on immediate arrival at HA and showed marked symptoms of acute mountain sickness (AMS). Administration of glucocorticoids in physiological doses is able to curtail severity of AMS to a great extent. The thyroidal secretion of hormones is also increased at HA. This increase in thyroid hormones is essential not only for mobilization of fuels, but also important in stimulation of 2, 3-DPG synthesis and activation of Na^+-K^+-ATPase activity for utilizing the available oxygen more efficiently. The rise in thyroid hormones appears to be independent of the cold stress since the levels are increased following exposure to simulated altitude under thermoneutral conditions, and do not show any increase during prolonged stay in an Antarctic environment where the minimum temperature decreases up to –45°C. The GH secretion is increased at HA, mainly to compensate for hypoxia induced protein catabolism and to stimulate erythropoiesis and 2, 3-DPG synthesis for enhancing cellular availability of oxygen. This increase in GH appears to be independent of the cold exposure since the levels are not altered during prolonged stay at Antarctica. The glucoinsulinar axis appears to be operating at a higher level at HA. The gonadal secretion of testosterone is decreased on immediate arrival at HA and is due to hypoxia induced hyperprolactinemia rather than its effects on the gonadotrops. After the acclimatization is achieved the pituitary-gonadal function reverts to the normal sea level status.

INTRODUCTION

On arrival at high altitude (HA), man faces a variety of physical factors like decreased partial pressure of oxygen (PO_2), cold, low humidity and increased amounts of solar and ultraviolet radiations which can affect various physiological processes of the body. The amount of O_2 in the atmosphere remains constant (20.93%) even at an altitude of 110,000m. only the barometric pressure decreases with increase in altitude resulting in a decline in partial pressure of O_2, thereby limiting its availability to the tissues. Despite decreased O_2 availability man is able to acclimatize to the hypoxic environment and has been able to reach even Mount Everest (8854m) without supplementary oxygen. This acclimatization to high altitude is achieved through adjustments of various body functions by stimulating circulatory, haemopoietic and cardiorespiratory systems for maximal oxygen delivery to the vital organs like heart, lungs, brain and other tissues (Ramirez et al, 1999). These regulatory and adaptive changes to hypoxia are brought about through the fine modulatory interplay of hormones in the blood by endocrine glands, especially those related to maintenance of blood circulation, blood pressure and mobilization of nutrients for energy requirements.

PITUITARY-ADRENAL FUNCTION

The neuroendocrine system, particularly the hypothalamic-pituitary-adrenal system is put up to maximum test to combat the stressful environment. Both adrenomedullary and adrenocortical systems are activated by the hypoxic stress. The urinary excretion of catecholamines is increased during initial days of arrival at high altitude, peaks by day seven and returns to sea level values within three to four weeks of stay at HA (Hoon et al, 1977). The main catecholamines of the central nervous system is norepinephrine whereas epinephrine is predominantly secreted by the adrenal medulla. Acute exposure to hypoxia does not stimulate norepinephrine secretion and may cause a decline in resting values, whereas prolonged exposure results in an increase in blood norepinephrine (Brooks et al, 1991). The epinephrine levels are increased on immediate arrival at HA, decreases thereafter but are maintained at higher levels during three to four weeks of stay at high altitude (Brooks et al, 1991). Stimulation of the pituitary-adrenal function, monitored as rise in ACTH can be detected within 8h of arrival at high altitude. During the initial ten days of stay at high altitude, the ACTH rhythmicity is disturbed (Figure 1), whereas that of cortisol is well-maintained (Sawhney, Malhotra & Singh, 1991; Sawhney et al, 1996). Like catecholamines, the highest cortisol levels are seen on day 7 of the stay at HA, start declining thereafter and return to initial SL values within three to four weeks of stay (Figure 2a). When the subjects acclimatised to a lower altitude (3450m) for three to four weeks were taken to further higher altitude (5080m), plasma cortisol did not show any appreciable change indicating that once acclimatization to a lower altitude is achieved increased secretion of cortisol may not be necessary for acclimatization to higher altitudes. The cortisol levels in acclimatised low landers at high altitude are slightly but not significantly higher than the SL values.

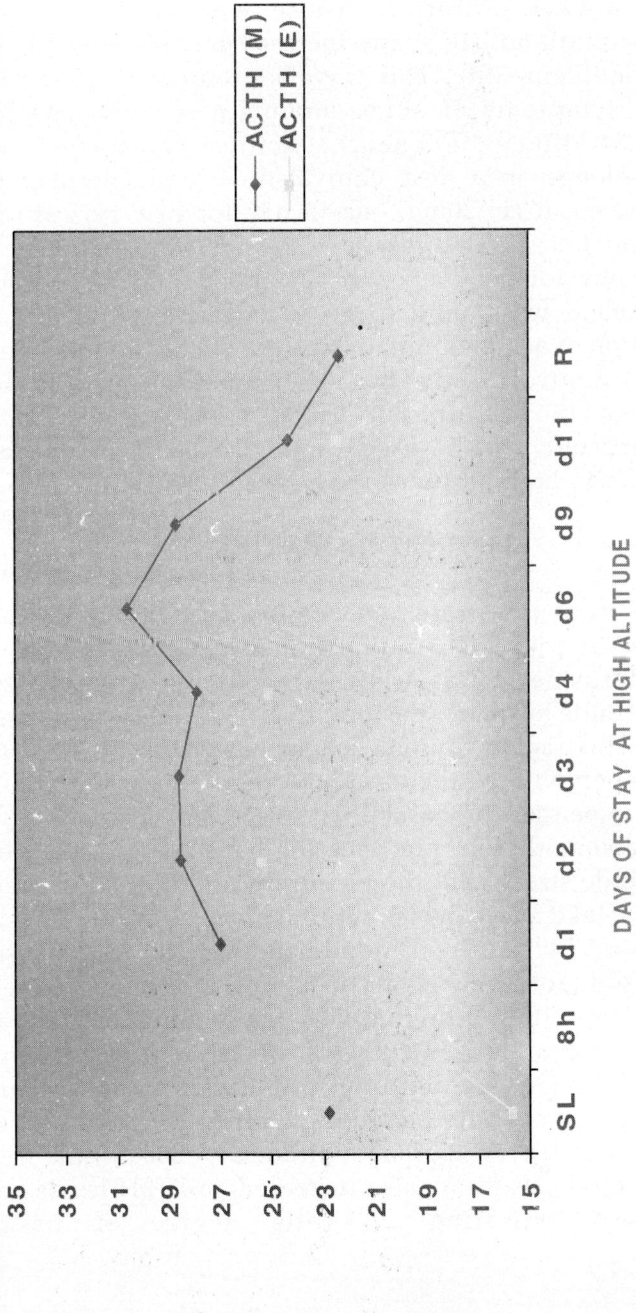

Fig 1. Morning and Evening ACTH Level on Different Days of Stay at High Altitude

Nevertheless, the cortisol response to the hypoxic stress is not always uniform. Those who are unable to acclimatize do not show any increase in cortisol but show a decline (Figure 2b). This was the group, which showed typical symptoms of acute mountain sickness (AMS). Administration of short acting glucocorticoid prednisolonge, in a dose equivalent to daily production rate of cortisol i.e. 20mg, once a day for two days at sea level and for initial three days at high altitude to meet higher physiological need of the body under stressful environment was found to be an effective modality for prevention of acute mountain sickness. In the double blind placebo control study the AMS symptoms could be curtailed by about 80 to 90% suggesting that glucocorticoids can be used prophylactically for quicker induction to high altitudes (Basu et al, 1995).

THYROID HORMONES

The hypoxic stress also causes activation of the pituitary-thyroid axis resulting in increased secretion of both thyroxine (T_4) as well as triiodothyronine (T_3) at high altitude in man (Rastogi et al, 1977; Mordes et al, 1983). This rise in thyroid hormones at HA appeared to be independent of increased secretion of thyrotropin (TSH), as neither the basal TSH levels nor its response to hypothalamic thyrotropin releasing hormone is altered by the altitude stress and the rise in thyroid hormone levels can also take place when pituitary secretion of TSH is suppressed by exogenous administration of T_4. This rise in thyroid hormone levels is also not due to altered binding capacities of thyroid hormone binding proteins as binding capacities and levels of thyroxine binding globulin, thyroxine binding pre-albumin and serum albumin are not altered at high altitude (Sawhney & Malhotra, 1991). At extreme altitudes, (> 5080m) the free T_4 and free T_3 levels are also increased and TSH levels are decreased indicating a subtle degree of tissue

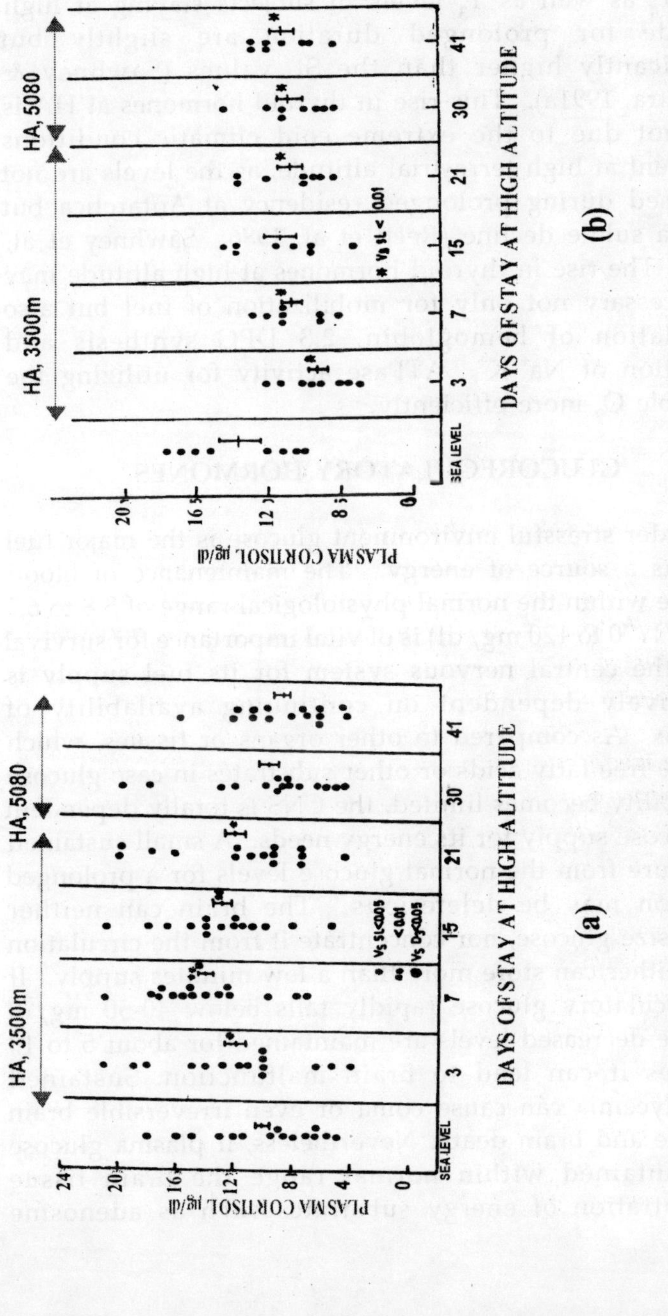

Fig 2. a & b Alterations in Cortisol Levels in Sea Level Residents at Sea Level and on Different Days of Stay at High Altitude

hyperthyroidism at high altitude in man (Basu et al, 1995). Both T_4 as well as T_3 levels in subjects staying at high altitude for prolonged duration are slightly but significantly higher than the SL values (Sawhney & Malhotra, 1991a). This rise in thyroid hormones at HA is also not due to the extreme cold climatic conditions prevalent at high terrestrial altitude, as the levels are not increased during prolonged residency at Antarctica but show a subtle decline (Reed et al, 1986; Sawhney et al, 1995). The rise in thyroid hormones at high altitude may be necessary not only for mobilization of fuel but also stimulation of hemoglobin, 2,3 DPG synthesis and activation of Na^+-K^+ ATPase activity for utilizing the available O_2 more efficiently.

GLUCOREGULATORY HORMONES

Under stressful environment glucose is the major fuel used as a source of energy. The maintenance of blood glucose within the normal physiological range of 3.8 to 6.7 mmol/l (70 to 120 mg/dl) is of vital importance for survival since the central nervous system for its fuel supply is exclusively dependent on continuing availability of glucose. As compared to other organs or tissues, which can use free fatty acids or other substrates in case glucose availability becomes limited, the CNS is totally dependent on glucose supply for its energy needs. A small sustained departure from the normal glucose levels for a prolonged duration may be deleterious. The brain can neither synthesize glucose, nor concentrate it from the circulation and neither can store more than a few minutes supply. If the circulatory glucose rapidly falls below 40-50 mg/dl and the decreased levels are maintained for about 5 to 10 minutes it can lead to brain malfunction. Sustained hypoglycemia can cause coma or even irreversible brain damage and brain death. Nevertheless, if plasma glucose is maintained within normal range the brain tissue concentration of energy substrates such as adenosine triphosphate, adenosine diphosphate and adenosine monophosphate remain close to normal even during severe hypoxia. Unlike hypoglycemia, abnormal elevation of blood glucose is not totally disabling, yet prolonged hyperglycemia is also life threatening. Prolonged hyperglycemia for a few days can lead to dehydration, decrease in blood volume, hypertension, shock and coma. Besides energy, glucose is also required for synthesis of ribose and deoxyribose for RNA and DNA synthesis, glycolipids as components of membranes and complex carbohydrates are components of connective tissue mattress.

Despite wide variations in glucose influx such as following meals and efflux due to its utilization as predominant energy fuel, the blood glucose under hypoxic conditions is well maintained within the normal physiological range by an efficient mechanism of hormonal, neural and substrate glucoregulatory factors. The islets of Langerhans of pancreas secrete four hormones viz. insulin, glucagon, somatostatin and pancreatic polypeptide. Insulin and glucagon have important functions in regulation of intermediary metabolism of carbohydrates, fats and proteins. Somatostatin may play a role in the regulation of insulin and glucagon secretion from the pancreas, whereas the physiological function of pancreatic polypeptide remains unsettled. Nevertheless, insulin is the most potent and critical regulator and is the key hormone controlling rate of glucose removal from the blood.

An increased glucose dependency (Brooks et al, 1991) evident as enhanced glucose utilization and increased glucose release by the liver with a concomitant decline in blood glucose has been suggested as a strategy in maintaining tissue energy in acclimatized low landers at high altitude. However, on acute exposure to hypoxia following arrival at high altitude or under simulated altitude conditions, the fasting blood glucose rises to about 5.51 mmol/l (100 mg/dl) followed by a decline to even less than the initial sea level values within the next 5 to 7 days (Brooks et al, 1991; Sawhney, Malhotra & Singh, 1991). Thereafter, the glucose levels tend to increase but are maintained within the normal or, low normal range during the first three to four weeks of the acclimatization period. When the low landers acclimatized to lower altitudes for about four to five weeks are taken to further heights a secondary rise in blood glucose takes place to meet the additional energy requirements of the hypoxic stress. In low landers who stay at high altitude for an extended duration of 3 months to 2 years, the fasting glucose values are found to be slightly higher than the sea level values, though a decline after ten months of stay at high altitude has been also recorded (Srivastva et al, 1975).

The mechanism that alters blood glucose at high altitude appears to be different in animals from humans. In animals depressed insulin secretion is primarily responsible (Baum, Griapp & Porle, 1979), while in humans the insulin secretion is not impaired, instead shows a moderate increase at lower altitudes and also following prolonged exposure to extreme altitudes (Brook set et al, 1991; Sawhney, Malhotra & Singh, 1991; Young et al, 1992). Like blood glucose, the fasting insulin levels are also increased by about two fold on acute exposure to hypoxia and tries to come down to sea level values within the next two weeks of stay. When sea level residents acclimatized to lower altitudes are taken to further heights blood insulin trends to increase again (Sawhney, Malhotra & Singh, 1991). This rise in insulin is also evident at different times of the day and after oral glucose administration (Sawhney et al, 1986). One of the most important functional role of insulin is to control whether carbohydrate or fat is to be utilized as a fuel for energy. The rise in insulin at HA may be important to counteract the hyperglycemic effects of stress hormones cortisol, catecholamines and GH. Hypoxia induced rise in insulin does not appear to be due to the cold stress as prolonged residency at Antarctica does not cause any increase in insulin levels but rather causes a decline (Malhotra et al, 1998). The triglyceride levels are increased under hypoxic conditions. At high altitude as there is an increased dependency on glucose as a source of energy, increased secretion of insulin appears to be necessary not only for enhancing glucose utilization but also for maintaining the glucose stores in the form of glycogen in liver and muscles. There appears to be no impairment in insulin sensitivity under hypoxic environment.

The glucose raising or counter-regulatory hormones are glucagon, epinephrine, cortisol, growth hormone and thyroid hormones. Glucagon secreted by the alpha cells of the pancreatic islets mobilizes energy stores and is a hormone of energy release. It is the most important physiological regulator of glycogen degradation and release of glucose from the liver. Nevertheless, the glucagon secretion is not stimulated either by acute or chronic altitude stress and the blood levels remain unchanged even at extreme altitude (Young et al, 1992). The insulin-to-glucagon molar ratio is also not altered indicating lack of catabolic metabolic state under hypoxic environment. Moreover, glucagon induced rise in blood glucose is always transient and cannot account for observed changes in blood glucose following acute or chronic exposure to altitude stress.

The increased blood glucose concentration on immediate arrival at high altitude may also be the result of enhanced hepatic glycogenolysis and glucose release due to activation of the sympatho-adrenomedullary and adrenocortical system or to the direct effect of hypoxia on glucose metabolism. Epinephrine directly stimulates glycogen breakdown in the liver thus releasing glucose into the circulation. It also limits glucose utilization. The major glycogenolytic action of epinephrine is due to its alpha-adrenergic effects by inhibiting insulin release thus reducing the action of its major antagonist on glycogen metabolism. However, the altitude stress does not inhibit the insulin secretion but causes a moderate increase. The rise in epinephrine at high altitude in man is always mild to moderate and never exceeds more than 800 pg/ml. Although high circulatory levels of norepinephrine have been shown to have an inhibitory effect on insulin secretion, a mild to moderate elevation even upto 1800 pg/ml as seen during severe stress, heavy exercise, complicated myocardial infarction and severe surgical trauma seems to cause hyperglycemia by stimulating basal hepatic glucose output without changing basal glucose utilization or insulin and glucagon secretion (Sacca et al, 1980).

The hypoxic stress also causes activation of the hypothalamic-pituitary-adrenal system resulting in an enhanced secretion of cortisol, the major glucocorticoid hormone in man. Cortisol increases blood glucose by inhibiting peripheral glucose utilization, over production of glucose by the liver, increased gluconeogenesis and causing hyperinsulinism. It also stimulates protein degradation and flow of substrate amino acids to the liver for glucose synthesis. Cortisol interacts in a permissive manner with other hormones including insulin, glucagon, catecholamines and growth hormone to achieve full homeostasis. The glucocorticoids oppose cellular action of insulin and thereby decrease glucose entry into the cells.

GROWTH HORMONE

Pituitary secretion of growth hormone (GH) is not changed during the first five to six weeks of arrival at high altitude but the levels are found to be higher in acclimatized low landers and high altitude natives (Sawhney, Malhotra & Singh, 1991; Anand et al, 1993). Growth hormone has a biphasic effect on blood glucose.

Acute elevation of GH in the blood has an insulin like effect, increasing glucose uptake, but this effect is transient lasting only an hour or so. Long-term elevation of GH increases blood glucose by limiting glucose uptake by muscles and adipose tissues. It also decreases peripheral actions of insulin. Growth hormone dose not stimulate insulin secretion directly but the hyperglycemia produced secondarily stimulates pancreatic secretion of insulin. Pituitary secretion of GH undergoes cyclic variations over the 24 hour period and maximum GH secretion is observed after about one to two hours of onset of sleep. In acclimatized low landers and high altitude natives the pattern of GH secretion is identical to that of sea level natives, but the GH levels at different times of the day are higher than the sea level residents (Sawhney & Malhotra, 1991b). This rise in GH at high altitude is under normal physiological control mechanism as it is further stimulated by exercise stress and inhibited following glucose administration (Sutton & Garmendia, 1982).

PITUITARY-GONADAL FUNCTION

The gonadal secretion of testosterone is decreased during initial days of arrival at high or extreme altitude (Sawhney et al 1985,; Basu et al, 1997). This decline in testosterone appeared to be related to increased secretion of prolactin by the altitude stress. The FSH levels are not altered by the altitude stress. In acclimatised low landers and high altitude natives, levels of LH, FSH, prolactin, testosterone and dihydrotestostosterone are not significantly different than the SL native values. Prolonged residency at high to extreme altitude does not cause any marked alterations in gonadotropin, prolactin, testosterone, dihydro-testosterone and estradiol levels. At extreme altitude, the progesterone levels are increased following extended stay. The exact mechanism and significance of increase in progesterone at high altitude remains unknown but may be important in increasing the sensitivity of the hypoxic ventilatory response and activation of hemoglobin synthesis (Basu et al, 1997).

ATRIAL NATRIURETIC (ANP), ADH AND ERYTHROPOIETIN

Plasma antidiuretic hormones (ADH) shows a transient decline on day 3 of arrival at high altitude but returns to SL values thereafter. The cardiac hormone atrial natriuretic peptide (ANP) is also increased on arrival at HA and remained high during initial ten days of observations. The ADH and ANP levels in acclimatised low landers and high altitude natives are not significantly different than the SL values (Sawhney et al, 1996). In patients of acute mountain sickness and high altitude pulmonary edema (HAPE), the ADH levels are not significantly different than the sojourner's values suggesting that the pituitary secretion of ADH may not be participating in the genesis of altitude induced maladies. As compared to sojourners, in HAPE patients, the increase in ANP did not take place either on the day of admission, during treatment or following recovery indicating a blunting of ANP response to hypoxia in HAPE. It appears that ANP may not be the major contributing factor towards genesis of HAPE but lack of adequate ANP may accentuate the pressure effects of hypoxia and or sympatho-adreno-medullary and adreno cortical hormones.

The erythropoietin (EPO) levels are also increased on arrival at HA but return to initial SL values within two to three days of stay. The rise in EPO in AMS is not significantly different than that of sojourners. Patients of HAPE show an exaggerated rise in EPO and the levels remain higher, even when these patients were discharged from the hospital (Figure 3). Estimation of EPO in the plasma can be confidently used as a marker for the differential diagnosis of AMS and HAPE. There is a need

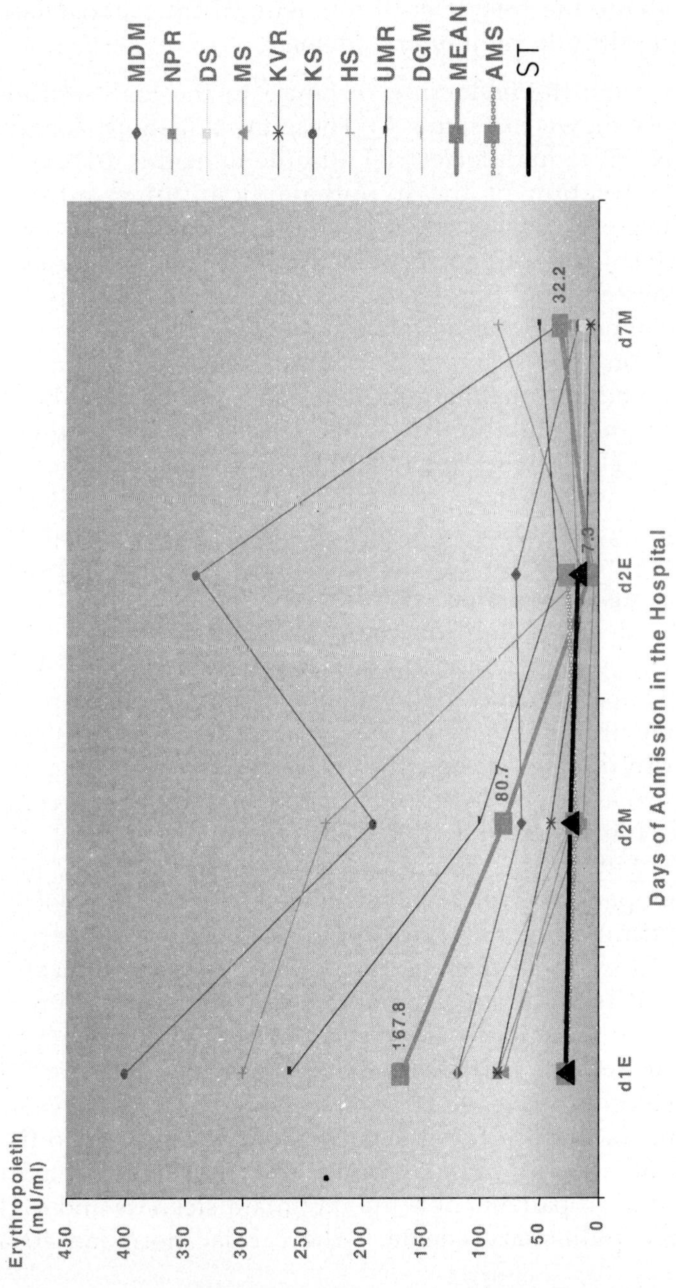

Fig 3. Erythropoietin Levels in Patients of High Altitude Pulmonary EDEMA

to evaluate the role of erythropoietin in the pathogenesis of high altitude pulmonary edema.

In brief, the endocrine response to the high altitude stress is shown in Figure 4. These investigations suggest that ascent to high terrestrial altitude in man is associated with activation of the hypothalamic-pituitary-adrenal system resulting in an increase in sympatho-adreno-medullary and adreno-cortical activity. This activation of HPA system resulting in increased secretion of cortisol is essential not only for mobilization of fuels but also provide protection against hypoxia induced transvascular protein leakage besides maintaining integrating of the endothelial barrier and inhibition of ADH release by the pituitary gland. Those who are not able to acclimatize show a decline in plasma cortisol. Prophylactic use of physiological doses of glucocorticoids can be used for prevention of acute mountain sickness. Hypoxic stress in man is also associated with increase in circulatory levels of T_4 and T_3 which in turn may be essential for 2, 3 DPG and hemoglobin synthesis and activation of Na^+ - K^+ ATP activity for utilizing the available O_2 more efficiently. At extreme altitude, there is present a subtle degree of tissue hyperthyroidism. The altitude stress is also associated with existence of hyper-insulinism and hyperglycemia. The GH levels are not altered during initial period of stay at HA but are increased following prolonged residency for compensation of hypoxia induced protein catabolism and stimulation of erythropoesis. Plasma testosterone shows a transient decline during initial days of arrival at high altitude due to hypoxia induced stimulation of prolactin secretion. However, prolonged residency at high or extreme altitude does not cause any alterations in testosterone levels. The ADH levels show a transient decline and return to sea levels values within four to five days of stay at high altitude and the levels remain unaltered in patients of acute mountain sickness and high altitude pulmonary edema. The cardiac hormone atrial

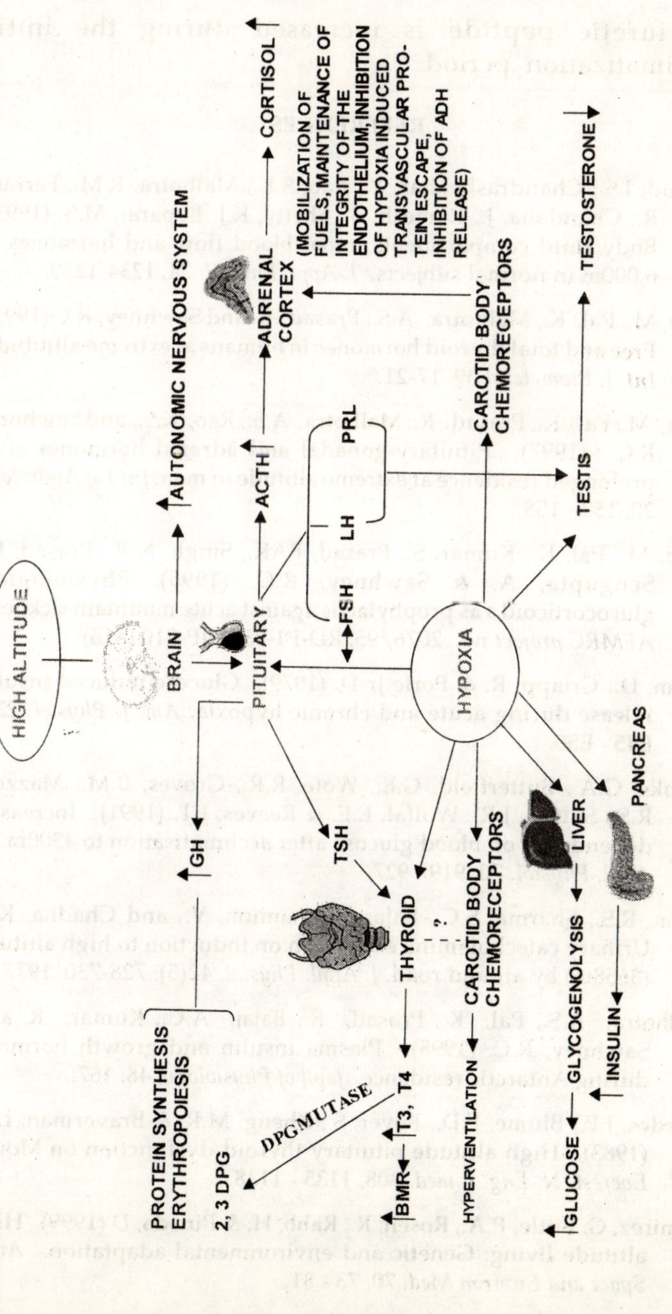

Fig 4. Endocrine Function at High Altitude

natriuretic peptide is increased during the initial acclimatization period.

REFERENCES

Anand, I.S., Chandrashekhar, Y., Rao, S.K., Malhotra, R.M., Ferrari, R., Chandana, J., Ramesh, B., Shetty, K.J. Boparai, M.S. (1993). Body fluid compartments, renal blood flow and hormones at 6,000m in normal subjects. *J. Appl. Physiol.* 74, 1234-1239.

Basu, M., Pal, K., Malhotra, A.S., Prasad, R. and Sawhney, R.C (1995). Free and total thyroid hormones in humans at extreme altititude. *Int. J. Biometerol* 39, 17-21.

Basu, M., Pal, K., Prasad, R., Malhotra, A.S., Rao, K.S., and Sawhney, R.C. (1997). Pituitary-gonadal and adrenal hormones after prolonged residence at extreme altitude in man. *Int J of Andrology* 20, 153 - 158.

Basu, M., Pal, K., Kumar, S., Prasad, BAK., Singh, N.P., Prasad, R., Sengupta, A. & Sawhney, R.C. (1995). Physiological glucocorticoid s as prophylactic against acute mountain sickness. *AFMRC project* no: 2076/95, RD-P1-95/DIP-210 (MB).

Baum, D., Griapp. R. & Porle Jr D. (1979). Glucose induced insulin release during acute and chronic hypoxia. *Am. J. Physiol.* 237, E45 - E50.

Brooks, G.A., Butterfield, G.E., Wofe, R.R., Groves, B.M., Mazzeo, R.S., Sutton, J.R., Wolfal, E.E. & Reeves, J.T. (1991). Increased dependence on blood glucose after acclimatisation to 4300m. *J. Appl. Physiol.* 70; 919 - 927.

Hoon, R.S., Sharma, S.C., Balasubramanium, V., and Chadha, K.S. Urinary catecholamine execretion on induction to high altitude (3658m) by air and road. *J. Appl. Physiol.* 42(5): 728-730, 1977

Malhotra, A.S., Pal, K., Prasad, R., Bajaj, A.C., Kumar, R. and Sawhney, R.C. (1998). Plasma insulin and growth hormone during Antarctic residence. *Jap J of Physiology*, 48: 167.

Mordes, J.P., Blume, F.D., Boyer, S., Zheng, M.R. & Braverman, L.E. (1983). High altitude pituitary thyroid dysfunction on Mount *Everest. N. Eng. J. med.* 308, 1135 - 1138.

Ramirez, G, Bittle, P.A., Rosen, R., Rabb, H. & Pineda, D (1999). High altitude living: Genetic and environmental adaptation. *Avia. Space and Environ Med.* 70, 73 - 81.

Rastogi, G.K., Malhotra, M.S., Srivastava, M.C., Sawhney, R.C., Dua, G.L., Sridharan, K., Hoon, R.S. & Inder, Singh (1977). Study of the pituitary-thyroid function at high altitude in man. *J. Clin. Endocrinol. Metab.* 44: 447 - 452.

Reed, H.L., Burman, K.D., Shakir, K.M.M., & O'Brain, J.T. (1986). Alterations in the hypothalamic-pituitary-thyroid axis after prolonged residence in Antarctica. *Clin. Endocrinol.* 25, 55 - 65.

Sacca, L., Morrone, G., Cicala, M., Corco, G. & Ungaro, B. (1980). Influence of epinephrine, norepinephrine and isoproterenal on glucose homeostasis in man. *J. Clin. Endocrinal & Metab.* 50, 680 - 684.

Sawhney, R.C., Chhabra, P.C., Malhotra, A.S., Singh, T., Riar S.S. & Rai R.M (1985). Hormone profiles at high altitude in man. *Andrologia,* 17, 178 - 184.

Sawhney, R.C. & Malhotra, A.S (1991a). Thyroid function in sojourners and acclimatised low landers at high altitude in man. *Horm. Met. Res.* 23, 81 - 84.

Sawhney, R.C. & Malhotra, A.S (1991b). Circadian rhythmicity to growth hormone at high altitude in man. *Ind J Physiol and Pharmacol* 35, 55 - 57.

Sawhney, R.C., Malhotra, A.S., Singh, T., Rai, R.M. and Sinha, K.C. (1986). Insulin secretion at high altitude in man *Int. J. Biometerol.* 30, 231.

Sawhney, R.C., Malhotra, A.S., Bajaj, A.C., Rajan, K.C., Pal, K. & Nair, C.S (1995). Thyroid function during prolonged stay in Antarctica. *Eur. J. Appl. Physiol.* 72: 127-133.

Sawhney, R.C., Malhotra, A.S., Pal, K., Prasad, R., Kumar, R., Basu, M. and Prasad, B.A.K (1996). Role of atrial natriuretic peptide and hypothalamic-pituitary-adrenal hormones in the genesis of high altitude maladies. *Project Report DIP-207,* DIPAS/27/96

Sawhney, R.C. Malhotra, A.S. and Singh, T (1991). Glucoregulatory hormones at high altitude in man. *Eur. J. Appl. Physiol,* 62, 286 - 291.

Srivastva, K.K., Kumaria, M.M.L., Grover, S.K., Sridharan, K. & Malhotra, M.S. (1975). Glucose tolerance of low landers during prolonged stay at high altitude and among high altitude natives. *Aviat Space, Environ. Med.* 46, 144 - 146.

Sutton, J.R. & Garmendia, F (1982). Hormonal response to exercise at altitude is sea level and mountain man. In: High Altitude Physiology and Medicine, Brendel, W. & Zink, R.A. (eds). Springer - Verlog, New York pp 165 - 171.

Young, P.M., Sutton, J.R., Green, H.J., Reeves, J.T., Houston, C.S. and Cymerman, A. (1992). Operation Everest II: metabolic and hormonal responses to incremental exercise to exhaution. *J. Appl. Physiol.* 73, 2574 - 2579.

ROLE OF SLEEP AND WAKE AREAS OF THE BRAIN STEM IN THE REGULATION TO REM SLEEP

BIRENDRA N. MALLICK AND STEPHEN THANKACHAN

School of Life Sciences, Jawaharlal Nehru University, New Delhi 110 067

Abstract

1. Wakefulness and rapid eye movement (REM) sleep are two distinct behavioural states. However, certain associated electrolophysiological parameters viz., desynchronization and eye movements are apparently, similar, while some others are opposite to that associated to wakefulness.

2. There are sleep active, wake active, REM-ON and REM-OFF neurons in the brain stem, however, the precise mechanism of REM sleep generation is not known.

3. We proposed that the REM-ON and REM-OFF neurons (neurons related to REM sleep) are likely to receive inputs from wake and sleep inducing areas. Therefore, brain stem neurons were first classified on the basis of their firing rate associated to sleep-wake behaviour and then their responses to stimulation of wake inducing area, midbrain reticular formation (MRF) and sleep inducing area, caudal brain stem (CBS) were studied in freely moving normally behaving cats.

4. Out of the 36 neurons studied, two-third increased firing during wakefulness (including five REM-OFF neurons) and the rest increased firing during REM sleep (including 5 REM-ON neurons). A majority of the wake active neurons were excited while most of the REM-ON neurons were inhibited by MRF stimulation. The CBS influence was broadly opposite to that of the influence of MRF. These observations help in understanding the mechanism for triggering of REM sleep generation.

INTRODUCTION

Sleep-wakefulness are behavioural phenomena. The sleep state has been electrophysiologically classified into rapid eye movement (REM) and non-REM sleep stages. Normally REM sleep appears at certain depth of sleep, however, some of the electrophysiological attributes of REM sleep viz., EEG desynchronization and eye movements are apparently similar to that observed during wakefulness while EMG tone and PGO waves are grossly opposite to that during wakefulness. Thus, although some of the electrophysiological signs during wakefulness and REM sleep are apparently similar, they are separated by a distinctly different state viz. non-REM sleep. Recently, we have shown that separate group of neurons are possibly responsible for desynchronization of the EEG during wakefulness and REM sleep (Mallick et al., 1998). It is known that some of the neurons in the brain stem either increase or decrease their respective firing rates selectively during wakefulness (wake active) or REM sleep (Hobson et al., 1975; Vertes, 1984; Mallick et al., 1989; Steriade and McCarley, 1990). Those neurons which increase firing during wakefulness and decrease during REM sleep are REM-OFF neurons (Aston-Jones and Bloom, 1981; Jacobs, 1986- El Mansari et at., 1989) while those which decrease firing during, wakefulness and increase firing during REM sleep are REM-ON neurons (Sakai, 1988, El Mansari et at., 1989; Steriade and McCariev, 1990- Kayama et al., 1992). Hence, we hypothesized that the REM-ON and REM-OFF neurons in the brain stem may be differentially influenced by the wake inducing, midbrain reticular formation (MRF) and the sleep inducing, caudal brain stem (CBS) areas.

Therefore, in this study, the behaviour of the brain stem neurons during spontaneous wakefulness and REM sleep were studied and then their responses to stimulation of wake area, MRF, and sleep area, and CBS were observed in freely moving normally behaving cats. Preliminary data was presented earlier (Mallick, 1999).

MATERIAL AND METHODS

Experiments were performed on 7 adult cats (5 male and 2 female), weighting between 2.5 and 3.4 Kg. Under surgical anaesthesia (sodium pentobarbitone) cats were prepared for chronic sleep-wakefulness (S-W) recording (Mallick et. al., 1989, 1998). One stainless steel tripolar epoxy coated stimulating electrode (200 μm diameter, 1.0-1.5 mm tip separation) was implanted in the MRF at stereotaxic co-ordinates of A2.0, L3.0 and H- 1.0 (Berman, 1968) while another one in the CBS at P9.5, L1.5, H-7.5 (Mallick et al., 1984,1986). Two bundles of microwires were lowered into each side of the brain stem through the guide cannulae mounted on a mechanical microdrive fixed to the skull at an angle of 45'. This arrangement allowed to record single neuronal activity from P0-3, L1.5 to 3.5. H-1 to -4. The other ends of the recording and the stimulating electrodes were soldered to two separate 15-pin female plugs and fixed to the skull with dental acrylic. The details of surgical procedures and implantation of electrodes have been reported earlier (Mallick et al., 1989, 1998). During recovery period of about two weeks the cat was acclimatized to the recording chamber.

After recovery, wake and sleep inducing regions in brain stem were confirmed by delivering high frequency stimulation (100Hz, 200-300μA, 300μsec) to MRF or low frequency stimulation (6Hz, 250-350μA, 300μsec) to CBS, which resulted in induction of desynchronization or synchronization, respectively, of the EEG. Thereafter, once a well isolated (S:N 3:1) signal from single neuron was encountered it was simultaneously recorded along with EEG, EOG, EMG and PGO in separate channels of the polygraph. At least three sleep-wake-REM sleep cycles along with single neuronal activity were recorded on the polygraph. The effects of stimulation of MRF and CBS on the neuronal activity were recorded by overlapping 10-12 stimulus bound responses on the oscilloscope. The MRF and the CBS were stimulated by 1Hz rectangular pulses of 500-600μA, 300μsec. The stimulation was done at the background of quiet wakefulness except for the REM-ON neurons where the stimulation had to be given during sleep period. This stimulation did not induce any change in EEF or in behavioural response. At least three sets of 10-12 overlaps were studied and the responses noted.

At the end of the recording sessions the cats were deeply anaesthetized (sodium pentobarbitone, 45mg/Kg) and the stimulation as well as recording sites were marked by electrolytic lesion by passing amodat Current (D.C. Lesion maker, Grass, USA) through stimulating and recording electrodes. The cat was then euthanasized by intracardial perfusion and then the lesioned sites were identified in 40μm coronal sections stained with cresyl violet or hematoxylin and eosin. The sites of the recorded neurons were reconstructed.

Standard criteria were followed to classify the sleep-wake states into active wakefulness (AW), quiet wakefulness (QW), sleep (S) and REM sleep (Ursin and Sterman, 1981; Mallick et al., 1989, 1998). The neuronal activities during different states were statistically compared by applying ANOVA and classified into wake active, REM-ON and REM-OFF types based on their firing rates during those states. The latency and the duration of' the neuronal responses to stimulation of MRF and CBS were calculated from the overlapped responses.

RESULTS

Thirty six well isolated single neuronal activity was recorded from chronically prepared freely moving normally behaving cats. Based on their spontaneous discharge (spikes per second) rate profile during S-W-REM sleep states compared to QW, the neurons were classified into 5 groups. Thereafter, the effects of I Hz stimulation of MRF and CBS were observed (TABLE 1 & 2).

Responses of the same brain stem neurons to influence from both CBS and MRF.

Wake active and REM sleep active neurons: Out of 36 neurons recorded, 17 increased firing during spontaneous wakefulness and REM steep (TABLE 1& 2; Fig. 1). Out of

TABLE 1

Effect of 1Hz MRF Stimulation on the Spontaneous Behaviour of Brain Stem Neurons

Responses	Spontaneous Response of Brain Stem Neurons				
	↑ AW ↑ REM	↑ AW → REM	↑ AW ↓ REM	→ AW ↑ REM	↓ AW ↑ REM
Excitation	8	2	5	-	-
No Change	9	-	-	4	-
Inhibition	-	-	-	3	5

TABLE 2

Effect of 1Hz CBS Stimulation on the Spontaneous behavoiour of Brain Stem Neurons

Responses	Spontaneous Response of Brain Stem Neurons				
	↑ AW ↑ REM	↑ AW → REM	↑ AW ↓ REM	→ AW ↑ REM	↓ AW ↑ REM
Excitation	5	-	-	2	5
No Change	11	2	5	5	-
Inhibition	1	-	-	-	-

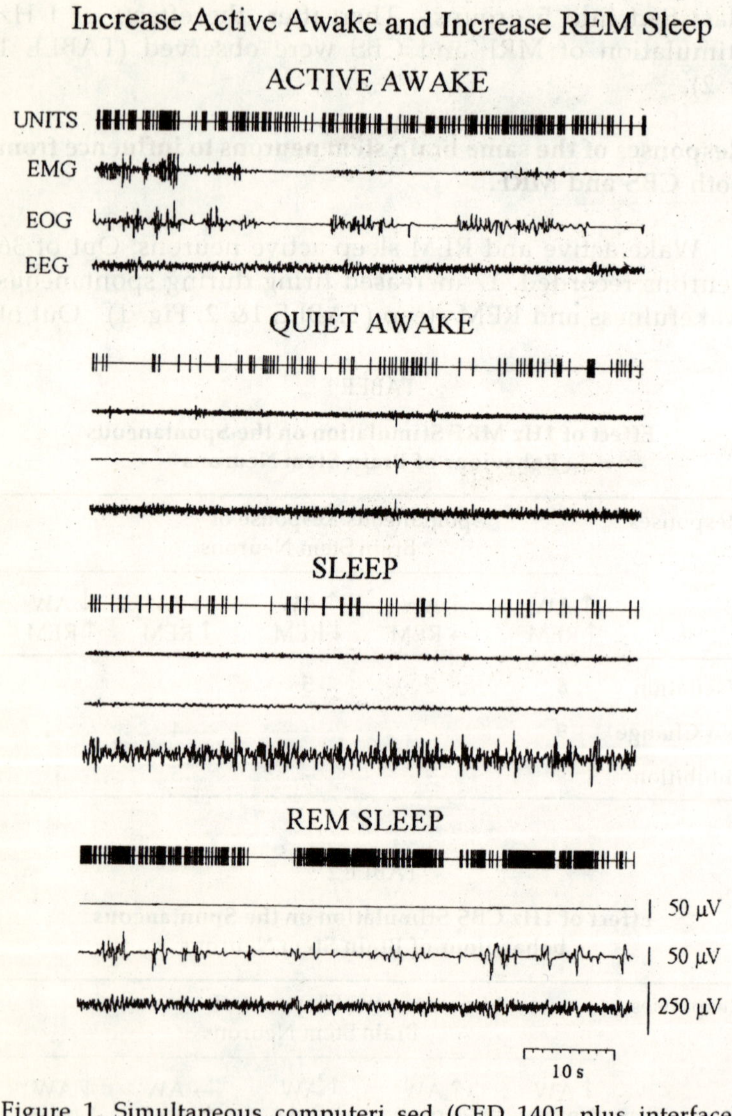

Figure 1. Simultaneous computeri sed (CED 1401 plus interface) recording of EEG, EOG, EMG and spontaneous activity of a neuron during active awake, quiet awake, sleep and REM sleep are shown in this figure. The window discriminator processed output of the neuronal activity (spike/sec) is shown in the upper trace. This neuron showed increased firing during wakefulness and REM sleep.

the 17 neurons, MRF stimulation excited 8 neurons (Fig. 2A) while 9 remained unaffected however, on CBS stimulation, 11 neurons remained unaffected (Fig. 2B), 5 neurons showed excitation and one showed inhibition. There were 2 wake active neurons that showed increased firing during spontaneous wakefulness but showed no change in firing during spontaneous REM sleep. I Hz stimulation of MRF excited while on CBS stimulation both the neurons remained unaffected. The mean latency and duration of excitation of the wake active neurons to MRF stimulation were 6.26±0.41 and 8.0±0.20msec, respectively.

REM-OFF neurons: Five REM-OFF neurons were recorded which showed increased firing during spontaneous wakefulness and decreased or ceased their firing during spontaneous REM sleep (TABLE 1 & 2; Fig. 3). All of them were excited by I Hz MRF stimulation (Fig. 4A) but remained unaffected by I Hz CBS stimulation (Fig. 4B). The mean latency and duration of excitation of REM-OFF neurons were 6.15±0.20 and 8.9±0.25msec, respectively.

REM active neurons: There were seven REM active neurons which showed increased firing during spontaneous REM sleep while during spontaneous wakefulness there was no change in their firing rate. Out of these seven, there were 2 neurons which were excited by CBS stimulation but were inhibited by MRF stimulation while the test remained unaffected by stimulation of both the areas.

REM-ON neurons: Five REM-ON neurons were recorded that showed increased firing during spontaneous REM sleep while decreased/ceased during spontaneous wakefulness (Fig. *5).* 1 Hz stimulation of MRF inhibited (Fig. 6A,) white CBS stimulation excited all of these neurons (Fig. 6B). The mean latency and duration of the excitation by CBS stimulation were 5.92 7±0.35 and 7.10± 0.25msec respectively, and inhibition by MRF were - 8.2 6.3 and 12.0 + 2.20 msec.

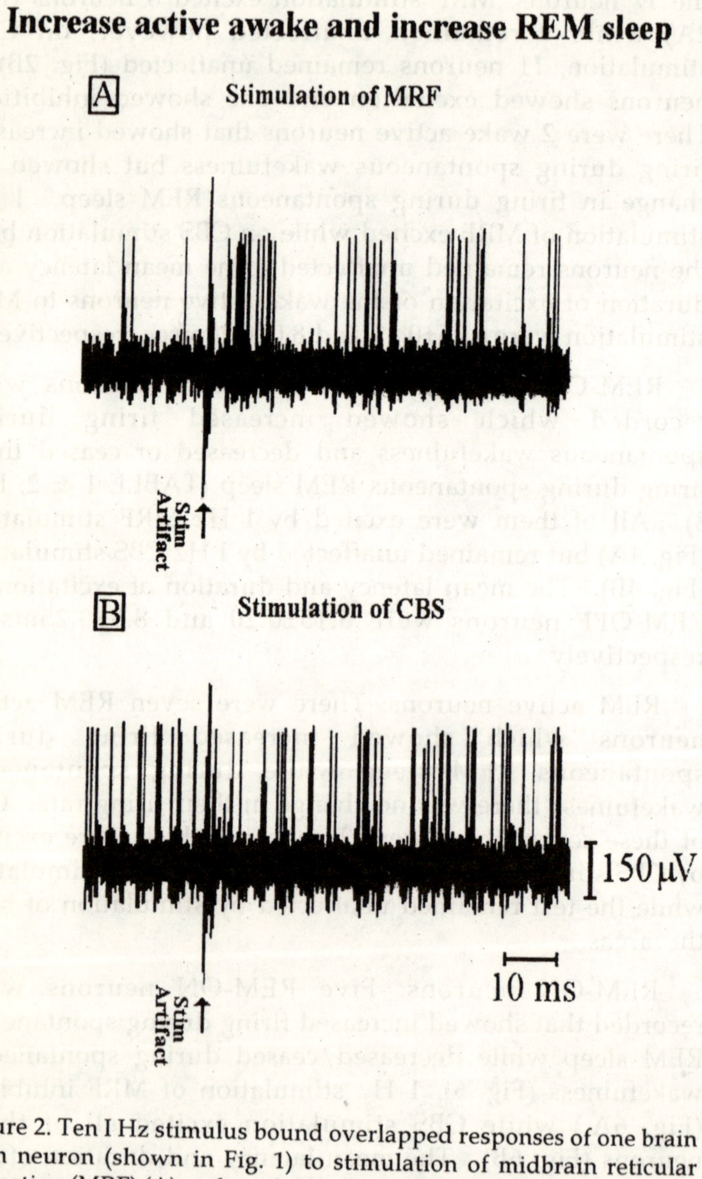

Figure 2. Ten I Hz stimulus bound overlapped responses of one brain stem neuron (shown in Fig. 1) to stimulation of midbrain reticular formation (MRF) (A) and caudal brain stem (CBS) (B) are shown here. The neuron was excited by MRF (A) but remained unaffected by CBS (B).

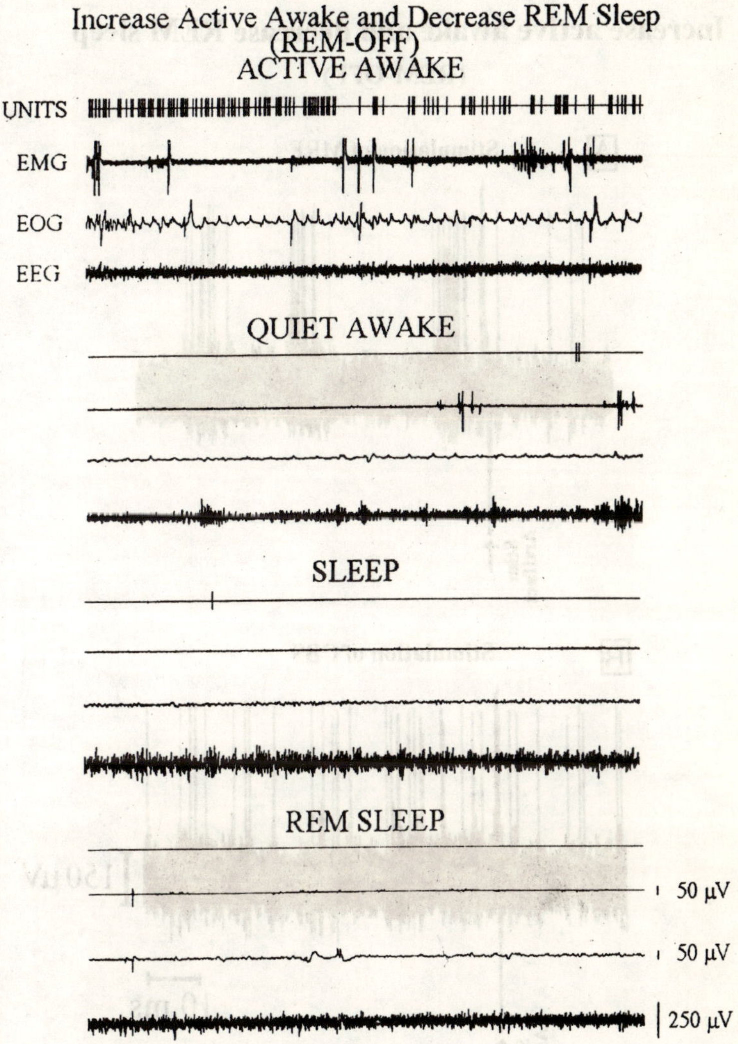

Figure 3. Recording of (computerised- CED 1401 plus interface output) EEG, EOG, EMG and spontaneous activity of a REM-OFF neuron during active awake, quiet awake, sleep and REM sleep are shown in this figure. The neuron showed increased activity during active awake and ceased firing during REM sleep.

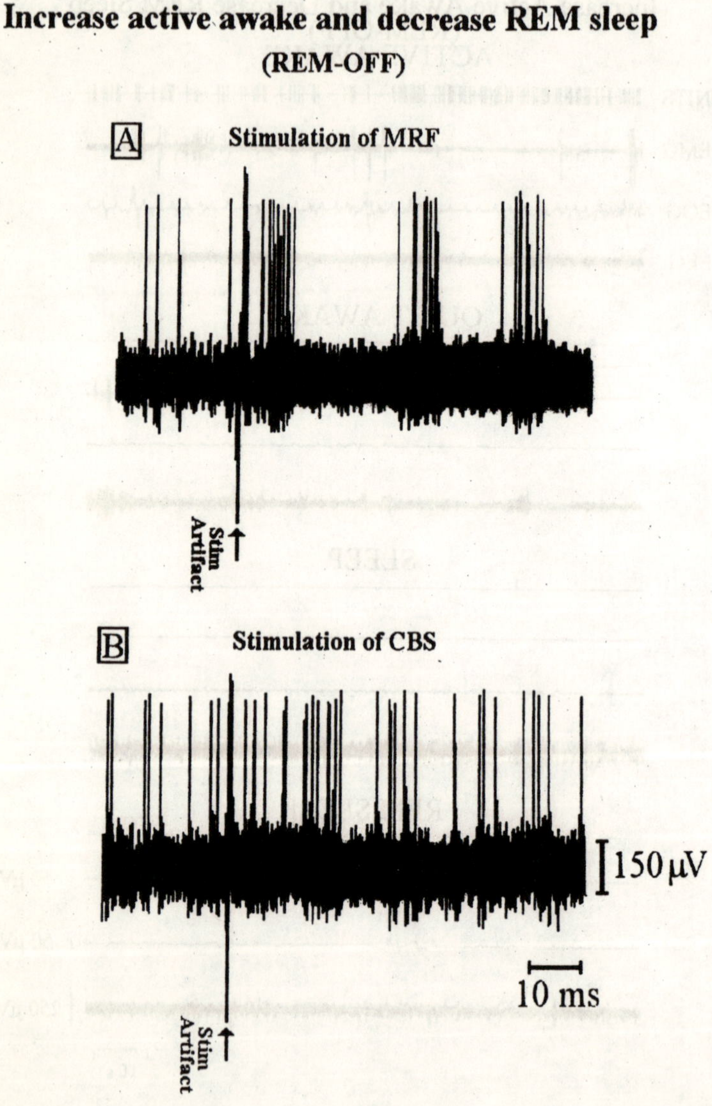

Figure 4. Ten 1Hz stimulus bound overlapped responses of one REM-OFF neuron (shown in Fig. 3) to stimulation of MRF and CBS are shown here. The neuron was excited by MRF (A) while remained unaffected by CBS (B) stimulation.

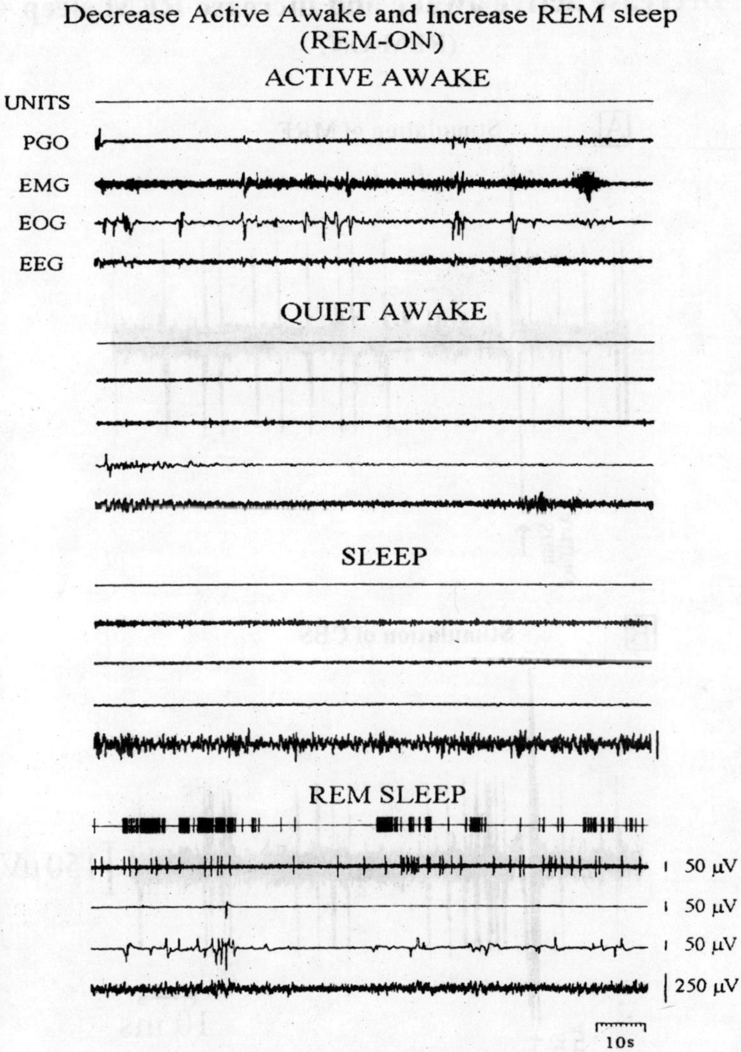

Figure 5. Simultaneous recording of EEG, EOG, EMG, PGO waves and spontaneous activity from a REM-ON neuron during active awake, quiet awake, sleep and REM sleep are shown in the figure. The window discriminator processed output of the neuronal firing during each of the states is shown in the upper trace. The neuron showed activity only during REM sleep while remained silent or ceased during other states.

Decrease active awake and increase REM sleep
(REM-ON)

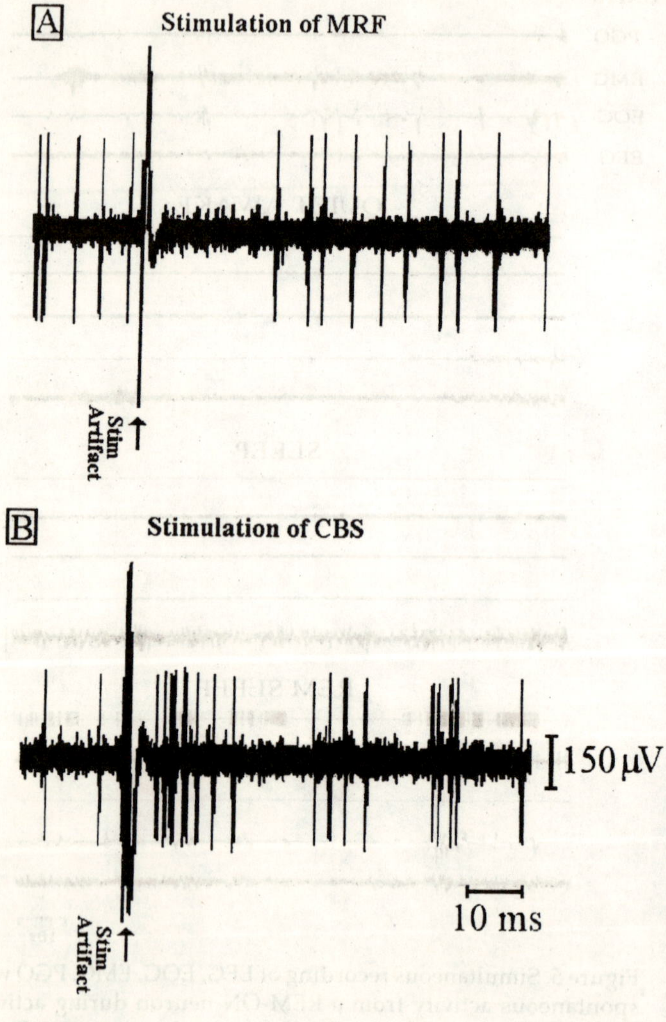

Figure 6. Ten 1Hz stimulus bound overlapped responses of one REM-ON neuron (shownin Fig. 5) to stimulation of MRF and CBS are shown here. The neuronal activity was inhibited by MRF while CBS excited this neuron (B).

DISCUSSION

Extracellular recordings of brain stem reticular neurons through S-W REM sleep cycle were done in the the unanesthetized freely moving cats. The firing rates of these neurons during wakefulness and REM sleep states were compared to that of respective quiet awake state. Since neurons responsible for these two states are distributed in the brain stem it was necessary to identify them based on specific behaviour first and then study their responses to inputs from other areas (wake and sleep) in the brain. Thereafter, the wake (MRF) as well as sleep areas (CBS) were stimulated and responses of the same neurons, were studied in freely moving normally behaving cats.

The REM-OFF and the REM-ON neurons remained inhibited during spontaneous REM sleep and waking states, respectively, although the EEG remained apparently desynchronized during both the states. The mechanism of action of activation and inhibition of those neurons and their relation with sleep-waking areas were unknown. Some of the electrophysiological signals during REM sleep have been shown to be apparently similar to that during wakefulness, while some others are similar to that seen during sleep (Aserinsky and Kleitman, 193; Demerit, 1958, Jouvet, 1999). Also REM sleep normally comes spontaneously only at certain depth of sleep period and not after wakefulness. Therefore, it was proposed that theneurons related to REM sleep (REM-ON and REM-OFF) are likely to receive inputs from wake (MRF) and sleep (CBS) inducing areas. This may be supported by our recent report that there are likely to be separate groups of neurons in the brain stem responsible for EEG desynchronization during these two distinct behavioural states (Mallick et al.., 1 998).

The results of this study showed that 1Hz stimulation of MRF affected 23 neurons (64%), 15 were excited and 8 were inhibited (Table 1). On the other hand, 1 Hz stimulation of CBS affected 13 neurons. out of which a majority 92% (N=12) of the neurons showed excitation while one neuron showed inhibition (Table 2). Interestingly, the neurons excited by MRF stimulation were those which increased firing during wakefulness irrespective of their behaviour during REM sleep. A majority (66%) of these neurons remained unaffected by CBS stimulation. Among these were the neurons which showed increased firing during wakefulness and decreased firing during REM sleep (REM-OFF) or no change during REM sleep (wake active). All of the REMOFF (N=5) and wake active neurons (N=2) were excited by I Hz MRF stimulation, but, remained unaffected by 1 Hz stimulation of CBS. Thus, MRF excited only those neurons which increased firing during wakefulness and not to those which increased firing during REM sleep although EEG remained desynchronized during both the behavioural states. Also that the MRF inhibited those neurons which increased firing during REM sleep only therefore, it may be said that the neurons which showed increased firing during wakefulness are likely to receive excitatory input from MRF and the neurons may possibly be responsible for EEG desynchronization during wakefulness only.

There were 17 neurons which showed increased firing during wakefulness and REM sleep. Out of these seventeen neurons, MRF stimulation excited 8 neurons and 9 remained unaffectd. On the other hand, on CBS stimulation 11 neurons remained unaffected, 5 showed exciation and one neuron was inhibited. Thus the results suggest that there may be a few neurons that may be common to be involved in a certain other characteristics features of wakefulness and REM sleep in addition to EEG desynchronization.

The neurons (N = 8) which were inhibited by MRF stimulation were those which howed no change or decreased firing during spontaneous wakefulness while increased firing during REM sleep. However, except for one neuron, CBS stimulation excited all the neurons which were inhibited by MRF stimulation. All the REM-ON neurons were excited by 1Hz stimulation of CBS while they were inhibited by 1Hz stimulation of the MRF. Thus, CBS stimulation excited neurons which increased firing during REM sleep only, while same neurons showed opposite effect ie., inhibition, by MRF stimulation.

FUNCTIONAL SIGNIFICANCE

REM sleep repeats a number of times during sleep, however, its frequency of occurrence and duration per bout increases with the progress of sleep (Kleitman, 1939). Although there arc varying degree and depth of occurrence of these states, normally REM sleep does not follow wakefulness. Normally, wakefulness and REM sleep stages are separated by sleep when the EEG is synchronized. None of the so far proposed models viz., the reciprocal (Hobson et al.. 1975) or mutual interaction (Sakai, 1988) models have succeeded in explaining transition from non-REM to REM sleep and possible interaction between the two states. The explanations for these appear to be incomplete in view of the pacemaker role of pontine neurons, which by themselves initiate the REM sleep process (Vertes, 1984, Sakai, 1988, Siegel. 1989. Steriade and McCarley, 1990). The non-REM sleep process, therefore, may act as a switch because the REM sleep is normally initiated after a period of sleep episode and the "clock" appear to stop during waking episodes. We propose and our data suggests that for triggering or for proper regulation of REM sleep both sleep and wakefulness regulating areas of the brain stem are likely to maintain a dialogue with those of the REM sleep related (REM-OFF and REM-ON) neurons.

Based on our results we hypothesize and propose that during wakefulness when the wake related neurons in the MRF are active, they excite the REM-OFF neurons which are likely to be norepinephrinergic located in the locus coeruleus. Activation of these neurons is likely to increase the level of norephinephrine in the brain during cortical activation (Tanaka, 1976; Vanderwolf and Baker, 1996). Such neurons (REM-OFF) may contribute to the type of EEG desynchronization associated to wakefulness and not to that REM sleep, since the REM-OFF neurons were excited while the REM-ON neurons were inhibited by the wake inducing area, MRF. At the onset of the sleep the MRF activity is reduced which withdraw the inhibitory influence from the REM-ON neurons. Thereafter, activation of the CBS (sleep inducing areas) neurons bias the system for gradual induction of the sleep. Subsequently, at certain depth of sleep (when some yet to be determined conditions are fulfilled), CBS neurons actively excite the REM-active (including the REM-ON) neurons and then REM sleep is initiated. Therefore atleast some of the sleep active neurons in the CBS possibly act as a switch to trigger REM sleep by stimulating the REM-ON neurons.

REFERENCES

Aserinsky, E., & Kicitman, N. (1955). Regularly occuring periods of eye motility, and concomitant phenomena during sleep. *Science* 118, 273-274.

Aston-Jones, G. & Bloom, F.F. (1981). Activity of norepinephrine-containing locus coeruleus neurons in behaving rats anticipates fluctuations in the sleep-waking cycle. *J. Neuroscl.* 1, 876-886.

Berman, A.I. (1968). The brain stem of the cat. A cytoarchitectonic atlas with stereotaxic co-ordinates. University of Wisconsin Press, Madison.

Dement, W.C. (1958). The occurrence of low voltage, fast, electroencephalographic patterns during behavioral sleep in the cat. *EEG Clin. Neurophysiol.* 10, 291-295.

El Mansarl, M., Sakai, K. & Jouvet, M. (1989). Unitary characteristics o presumptive cholinergic tegmental neurons during the sleep waking cycle in freely moving cats. *Exp. Brain Res.* 76, 519-529

Hobson, J.A., McCarlev, R.W. & Wyzinski, (1975). Steep cycle oscillation: reciprocal discharge by two brainstem neuronal groups, *Science* 189,

Jacobs, B.L. (1986). Single unit activity of locus coeruleus neurons in behaving animals. Prog. *Neurobiol.* 27, 183-194.

Jouvet, M. (1999). Around the discovery of REM sleep in cats. In *Rapid eye movement sleep eds.* Mallick, B.N. & Inoue, S., pp. v-ix. Marcel and Dekker. Inc., New York,

Kayama, Y., Ohta, M. & Jodo, E. (1992). Firing of 'possibly' cholinergic neurons in the rat laterodorsal tegmental nucleus during sleep and wakefulness. Brain Res. 560. 210-220.

Kleitman, N. (1939). Sleep and wakefulness. University of Chicago press, Chicago.

Mallick, B.N., Kumar, V.M., Chhlna, G.S. & Singh, B., (1984). Response of preoptic neurons to stimulation of caudal and rostral brain stem reticular structures. *Brain Res. Bull.* 13 : 354-356.

Mallick, B.N., Kumar, V.M., Chhina, G.S. & Sinah, B., (1986). Comparison of rostral-caudal brain stem influence on preoptic neurons and cortical EEG. *Brain Res. Bull.* 16:121-125.

Mallick, B.N., Siegel, J.M. & Fahringer, H., (1989). Changes in pontine unit activity of REM sleep deprivation. *Brain Res.* 515, 94-98.

Mallick, B.N., Thankachan, S. & Islam, F. (1998). Differential responses of brain stem neurons during spontaneous and stimulation-induced desynchronization of the cortical EEG in freely moving cats. *Sleep Res. Online* 1, l32-146.

Mallick, B.N., (1999). Presented in the Focus Group, 3 (FG3) titled "Where does REM sleep begin?", *Third International Congress of World Federation of Sleep Research Societies.* Oct. 5-9, Dresden, Germany.

Sakai, K. (1988). Executive mechanisms of the paradoxical sleep. *Arch. Ital. Biol.* 126, 239-257.

Siegel, J. (1989). Brainstem mechanism of generating REM sleep. In *Principles and practice of sleep medicine ed Kryger,* M.H., Roth, T. &, Dement, W.C. pp. 104-120. W.B. Saunders, Co., Philadclphia.

Steriade, M. & McCarley, R.W. (1990). Brain stem control of wakefulness and sleep. Plenum press, New York.

Tanaka,. D.J. (1976). Labelled NA release front rat cerebral cortex following electrical stimulation of LC. *Brain Res.* 106: 384-389.

Vanderwolf, C.H. & Baker, G.B. (1996). The role of brain noradrenaline in cortical activation and behavior: A study of lesions of locus coeruleus, medial thalamus and hippocampusneocortex and of muscarinic blockade in the rat. *Beliav. Brain Res.* 78, 225-234.

Ursin, R. & Sterman, M.B. (I 98 1). A manual for standardized scoring of sleep and walking states in the adult cat. Brain Infomiation Service/Brain Research Institute, University of Califomia, Los Angeles.

Vertes, R.P. (1984). Brainstem control of the events of REM sleep. *Prog. Neurobiol.* 22. 241-288.

SENSORY BRAIN DYSFUNCTION IN PROTEIN ENERGY MALNUTRITION

O.P. TANDON

Department of Physiology, University College of Medical Sciences & GTB Hospital, Delhi-110095

Summary

Brain, during its critical period of growth is uniquely vulnerable to nutritional insults. Animal studies have shown that protein-energy malnutrition results in microcephaly, delay in cerebral circulation and defective neurotransmitter synthesis. Human studies have shown that such malnutrition reduces neuronal number, synapes, glial proliferation and myelination. Our studies in newborns, infants and children having different grades of ptotein-energy malnutrition provide an electrophysiological evidence of delayed conduction in brainstem auditory pathways. At least 33% of such subjects had abnonnal inter peak latencies, and of these, 25% had abnormal morphology of brainstem auditory evoked potentials (BAEPs) characterized by absence of waveform pattern. These abnomalities were more common in younger children in whom malnutrition predominantly affected developmental processes in the rostral (ponto-mesencephalic) component of the brainstem auditory pathways.

These findings suggest that protein-energy malnutrition perinatally and in early life does affect conduction in the auditory sensory pathways. It could be due to deficits in various normal processes like myelination, synaptogenesis, glial proliferation and neurotransmitter synthesis seen in such malnourished states.

INTRODUCTION

Most of the brain regions are vulnerable to protein energy malnutrition (PEM) during its growth and development. The critical period of rapid brain growth extends from midgestational through infancy and the early pre-school years. During this rapid period of growth the brain is uniquely vulnerable to nutritional deprivation (Dobbing and Sands 1973, Levitsky and Strupp 1995). The effect of PEM on brain growth and development depends on its duration and severity of malnutrition. PEM is known to cause microcephaly, reduction in neuronal arborisation and glial proliferation (Dhopeshwarker 1983). The latter adversely affects the process of myelination essential for axonal conduction (Dobbing 1984). Thus the areas of brain where myelination is most rapid are most vulnerable to the effects of early malnutrition. Hence the early involvement of sensory motor systems, cerebellum and limbic areas, might explain the alterations in motor behaviour, reflex activity, sleep wakeful cycle, sensory and cognitive function induced by PEM during intrauterine and early life. Electrophysiological studies in rats have shown that prenatal PEM alters the response of hippocampal A-1 pyramids to electrical stimulation and that this alteration results in marked changes in both the electrographic and behavioural correlates of kindling (Bronzino et al 1986). Dietary protein rehabilitation in these malnourished rats was incapable of reversing or significantly ameliorating the effects of gestational PEM on susceptibility to seizure activity and acquisition of kindled state. Bronzino et al 1990, have thus shown that electrographic and behavioral correlates of kindling induced by neuronal changes in hippocampus due to PEM are long lasting. Similarly cerebellar purkinje cell circuitary shows changes in firing frequency and firing patterns in PEM which are resistant to rehabilitation (Sharma et al 1987, Warren and Bedi 1990, Yuckel et al 1994). Since sensory system in CNS particularly the auditory pathways seem to be rapidly myelinating regions of the brain, we conducted studies in newborns, infants and children having different grades of PEM and evaluated the functional integrity of brainstem auditory pathways in them.

MATERIAL AND METHODS

Subjects of this study were having different grades of PEM and they belonged to three groups:

Group I: Twenty five malnourished neonates of PEM mothers born 38-41 wks of gestation and equal number of healthy neonate controls.

Group II: Infants below 2 yrs. of age having PEM and age and sex matched healthy controls.

Group III: Children between 2-5 yrs of age having PEM and age and sex matched healthy controls.

Weight, height, mid arm circumference, head circumference and skin fold thickness were accurately recorded in all these subjects. A detailed physical and neurological examination was done to rule out pre-existing neurological deficit. Conductive deafness was excluded by impedance audiometry. The degree of malnutrition was graded using the Gomez classification with NCHS standards; those subjects having more than 90% of expected weight for age were considered as normal; 76%-90% as grade I, 61%-75% as grade II and 60% or less as grade III of malnutrition.

The malnourished neonates were those having birth weight less than tenth percentile for the gestational age. Most of these were small for date babies born of mothers having PEM during pregnancy

METHODS

BAEPs were recorded using MEB 5200 Neuropack II Plus (Nihon Kohden, Japan) Evoked Potential Recorder. Crying neonates and apprehensive children were sedated with oral promethazine (0.5 mg / kg) administered 30 min before the procedure. The international 10 - 20 electrode placement system was used. Ag / AgCl scalp electrodes were affixed with collodion. First the threshold of the click intensity stimulus producing wave V of BAEP was determined in each case, then alternating sound clicks of 0. I ms duration were delivered at 70 dB above hearing threshold mono-aurally through shielded headphones with - 40 dB pure white noise for contralateral ear masking. 2,048 Averages were recorded and replicated from CZ-Al and CZ-A2 with filter band pass of 150 - 3,000 Hz and automatic artifact rejection. The absolute peak latencies and interpeak latencies (IPLSs) and amplitude of waves I and V were analyzed in three grades of malnutrition and compared with healthy groups. Subjects whose IPLs were more than 3 standard deviations (SDs) of control or where the wave forms were missing were labelled as abnormal. Statistical significance was determined by analysis of variance, and pair-wise comparison in similar grades of malnutrition in groups 11 and III was done by the Tukey-HSD procedure at the 0.05 level. The technical details of the methods followed are given in our previous report (Tandon 1990).

RESULTS

The mean±SD of absolute peak latencies in milliseconds of waves I-V in control and malnourished subjects showing normal morphology of BAEPs are shown in table 1. There was no significant difference between the absolute peak latencies of wave I-V in the three grades of malnutrition and their age matched controls. In the malnourished neonates, there was slight increase in absolute peak latencies of all waves but significant difference was not seen when compared with controls.

There was also no significant difference between the amplitude of waves I and V in the three grades of malnutrition and their age-matched controls (table 2).

Overall, there was no significant difference between the IPLs of the various grades of malnutrition and their

TABLE 1

Absolute peak latencies of wave I - V in control and malnourished subjects

Age and grades of malnutrition	Absolute peak latency (ms)				
	I	II	III	IV	V
Neonates (Group I)					
Controls (n=25)	1.82±0.29	2.89± 0.83	4.05± 0.5	5,05± 0.83	6.09± 0.76
Malnourished (n=25)	1.89±0.46	3.02± 0.55	4022± 0.8	5.09± 0.77	6.31± 0.81
Less than 2 years (Group II)					
Control (n=13)	1.72 ±0.20	2.77± 0.24	4.10± 0.29	5.22± 0.23	6.05± 0.25
Grade I (n=8)	1.76 ±0.23	2.74± 0.37	4.12±0.38	5.19 ±0.09	6.13 ±0.25
Grade II (n= 15)	1.75 ±0.25	2.66± 0.22	4.17± 0.33	5.43± 0.36	6.23± 0.34
Grade III (n=18)	1.91 ±0.36	2.95 ±0.39	4.26 ±0.41	5.39 ±0.43	6.27 ±0.52
Age 2 - 3 years (Group III)					
Control (n=31)	1.61 ±0.17	2.64± 0.19	3.82 ±0.18	4.93± 0.22	5.77± 0.29
Grade I (n=12)	1.69 ±0.36	2.73 ±0.35	4.14 ±0.73	5.12 ±0.43	5.76 ±0.31
Grade R (n=15)	1.60 ±0.17	2.71 ±0.19	3.90± 0.18	4.96 ± 0.19	5.77±0.23
Grade III (n=19)	1.72±0.18	2.67±0.15	3.84±0.17	5.00±0.21	5.91±0.29

Malnourished subjects with absent wave forms were excluded.
The values are mean ± SD

TABLE 2.

I-III, I-V and III - V IPLs and amplitude of waves I and V in control and malnourished subjects (results expressed as mean ± standard deviation)

Age and grades of malnutrition	IPL, (ms) I-III	I-V	III-V	Amplitude (μV) I	V
Neonates					
Group I					
Controls (n=25)	2.27±0.40	4.30 ± 0.46	2.01±0.38	0.18 ± 0.01	0.12 ± 0.01
Malnourished (n=25)	2.34±0.58	4.52 ± 0.61	2.17±0. 52	0.15 ± 0.09	0.10 ± 0.07
Less than 2 years					
(Group II)					
Control (n= 13)	2.41 ± 0.15	4.33 ± 0.18	1.97 ± 0.07	0.31 ± 0.13	0.40 ± 0.18
Grade I (n=8)	2.44 ± 0.17	4.37 ± 0.15	1.97 ± 0.22	0.29 ± 0.18	0.30 ± 0.17
Grade II (n=15)	2.42 ± 0.28	4.47 ± 0.30	2.08 ± 0.26	0.29 ± 0.18	0.30 ± 0.17
Grade III (n=18)	2.33 ± 0.16	4.38 ± 0.33	2.04 ± 0.21	0.32 ± 0.14	0.27 ± 0.12
Age 2 - 3 years					
Group III					
Control (n=31)	2.21 ± 0.11	4.13 ± 0.22	1.94 ± 0.17	0.34 ± 0.20	0.30 ± 0.11
Grade I (n=12)	2.24 ± 0.15	4.12 ± 0.17	1.87 ± 0.15	0.37 ± 0.21	0.38 ± 0.15
Grade H (n=15)	2.28 ± 0.23	4.11 ± 0.21	1.83±0.21	0.46 ± 0.17	0.36 ± 0.10
Grade III (n=19)	2.16 ± 0.27	4.20 ± 0.34	2.07±0.33	0.34 ± 0.13	0.29±0.08

Malnourished children with absent wave forms were excluded. The values are mean ±SD age-matched controls (table 2).

The criterion of abnormality of BAEPs was taken as prolonged IPL beyond 99% tolerance (mean + 3 SDs of control). Thus, values of 3.47, 6.88 and 3.25 ms in malnourished neonates, 2.86, 4.87 and 2.18 ms in malnourished children < 2 yrs. were taken as upper tolerance limits for IPLs of I-III, I-V and III-V, respectively, and of 2.54, 4.79 and 2.15 ms as upper tolerance limits for I-III, I-V and III-V, respectively, in malnourished children between 2 and 5 years.

Five out of 25 malnourished neonates had abnormal values for BAEPs giving an incidence of 20%. Of the 96 malnourished children studied 32 had abnormal BAEPs, giving an incidence of 33.3%. Of these, 24 had one or more prolonged IPLs (based on the criterion given above) and 8 had absent wave forms.

The incidence of abnormal BAEPs in malnourished neonates (group 1) was 20% whereas it was more common in younger malnourished subjects (group II). thus 14 subjects out of 46 (30.3%) in group II had prolonged IPLs as compared to 10 out of 50 in group III. Similarly, 5 out of 46 (10.8%) in group II had absent wave forms compared to 3 out of 50 (6%) in group III. The difference is most obvious in grade III (most severe) malnutrition where 8 out of 21 children (38%) in group II had abnormal BAEPs compared to 5 out of 20 (25%) in group III. Fig. I shows the representative recordings of normal and abnormal BAEPs in malnourished subjects.

Another irfteresting observation in our study was that 4 out of 5 (80%) in group I, 13 out of 14 malnourished children (92.8%) with abnormal BAEPs in group II showed significant prolongation of III - V IPL compared to 3 out of 10 (30%) in group III. On the other hand, 7 out of 10 (70%) malnourished subjects with abnormal BAEPs in group III had significant prolongation of I - III IPL compared to I out of 5 in group I and 3 out of 13 (23%) in

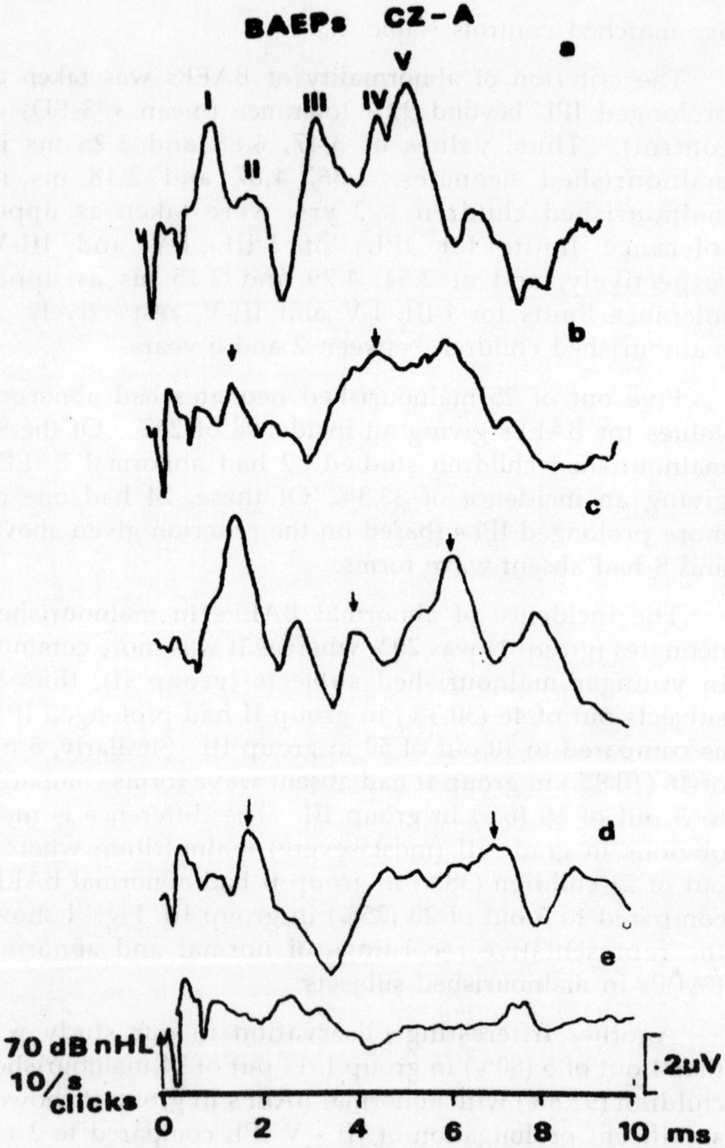

Fig. 1 Showing normal and abnormal records of BAEPs in malnourished subjects. Normal BAEPs showing waves I - V a, BAEPs showing prolonged IPL, I - III b, III - V c, I - V d, Whereas e shows absence of wave form.

group II (table 3). Thus, a delay in the conduction of the pontomesencephalic pathways (III-V) was a more common abnormality in the young; malnourished neonates and younger children while the delay in older children was predominantly in the medullopontine pathways (I-III).

DISCUSSION

Various electrophysiological studies have shown abnormalities of brain functions in PEM. Robinson et al 1995 have shown abnormalities in malnourished subjects which persisted even after somatic rehabilitation. Increased percentage of slow wave activity and / or slow background theta and delta waves have also been reported by Levav et al 1995. These EEG changes could

TABLE 3

Abnormal IPLs in different grades of malnutrition in three groups of subjects

Age and grades of malnutrition	Prolonged I - III latency	Prolonged I -V latency	Prolonged III - V latency
Neonates (Group I)			
Malnourished (n=25)	1	0	4
Less than 2 years (Group II)			
Grade I (n=9)	0	0	3
Grade II (n=16)	3	2	5
Grade III (n=21)	0	1	5
Total (n=46)	3	3	5
Age 2-3 years (Group III)			
Grade I (n=14)	2	0	1
Grade II (n=16)	3	0	0
Grade III (n=20)	2	2	2
Total (n=50)	7	2	3

result in disorganisation of both REM and NREM sleep and shortening of sleep cycle (Bhatia et al 1980).

In our study most of the PEM subjects have comparable values of BAEP's with their healthy controls (table I and II). It is only in the malnourished neonate subjects all the interpeak latencies are on higher side as compared to controls but not statistically significant. This means that maternal PEM does affect speed of sensory conduction in the auditory pathways in the brainstem. Regression analysis shows negative correlation of maternal haemoglobin with BAEP latencies. Equation being:

$$\text{IPL I - V} = \text{Maternal Hb} \times (-0.0835) + 5.1056$$

(where $r = 0.29$, $r^2 = 0.08$, $SE = 146$ and significance of $F = 0.048$)

This delay in conduction could be due to many factors, the common denominator being improper myelination of sensory tracts, as PEM does adversely affect myelination (Wiggins et al 1984).

In three groups of PEM subjects, incidence of abnormality of BAEPs was different (Table III). Five out of 25 neonates had abnormal BAEPs (20%) whereas in infant group (group II) 19 out of 46 (41.2%) cases showed abnormal BAEP either as prolonged IPLs or absent wave forms, compared to 13 out of 50 children of group III (26%). Hence the incidence of abnormality increased from neonates to infancy and childhood, maximum being during infancy (group II, below 2 yrs. of age). These observations confirm that PEM in critical perinatal periods of brain growth affects progression of neurodevelopment in central transmission of complex brainstem auditory pathways.

The subjects of present study (group II and III in particular) were gmded into three categories of malnutrition using Gomez classification to study the impact of degree of malnutrition on extent of abnormality in BAEPs. However, the abnomudity of IPLs did not show any correlation with extent of malnutrition. This may be due to the fact that exact time of onset of malnutrition in these under-privileged subjects residing in urban slums were not known. Thus, neither the birth weight of these home born children was recorded nor was the growth chart of these subjects available. The time of onset of malnutrition, apart from its degree, may be an important factor predicting extent of BAEP abnormality. Since I-V of BAEP provides an index of centnd transmission. the various IPLs reflect, developmental changes in the myelin composition along the auditory pathway (Salamy et al 1978). Prolonged IPLs thus reflect slow axonal conduction. Since axonal conduction is dependent on myelination, it is inferred that malnutrition had affected myelination in auditory pathways in these PEM subjects showing prolonged IPLs. Although excellent data on prenatal brainstem myelration and development are available, the quantitative neurorhistological information necessary to evaluable the contribution of postnatal myelination to the observed IPL changes do not exist (Magoon and Robb 1981).

Complete absence of wave form pattern indicates severe sensorineural hearing loss. This pattern was seen in 5 out of 46 children (10.8%) in group 11 and 3 out of 50 children in group III. Three out of 5 children in group 11 belong to grade III (most severe) form of malnutrition whereas, absent wave form was seen in one malnourished child each in all grades of malnutrition in group III (table III).

Since predominantly IPLs III-V is delayed in malnourished group I, II and I-III in group III as compared to age matched controls, it is inferred that conduction is more delayed in pontomesencephalic pathways during intrauterine life and in younger children and medullopontine pathway in older children, Differential effect of malnutrition on growth and develolmnent of brain has been reported by other workers, who observed that, the effect of malnutrition was more pronounced in cerebellum and medulla as compared to cerebrum (Sarma and Rao 1974). Our study suggests that effect of PEM on malnutrition of auditory brainstem pathways is time based. During gestation and up to (2 years) effect is more pronounced centrally and in early childhood, caudal pathways are affected. Since centrifugal patterns of myelination has been reported in the visual pathways (Magoon and Robb 1981) it follows that similar pattem might exist in auditory pathways too. Thus it is inferred that the progress of neuro-developmental process in auditory pathways is differentiaby affected in PEM during perinatal and early years of life, more rostral auditory pathways (Ponto-mesencephalic) are involved in contrast to caudal auditory pathways (medullopontine) in children between 2 and 5 years.

Animal experiments on malnutrition clearly demonstrate that myelination might be insufficient in neural tracts / fibres to cause reduction in diameter and depressed conduction. These have been amply confirmed by electrophysiological methods like nerve conduction studies. In general, malnutrition has been shown to cause prolongation in conduction time, delay in impulse transmission and complex information processing, increased latency time and abnormalities in response pattern (frequency, amplitude and wave form) (Rorke and Riggs 1969). Our study has substantially confirmed that even in human beings, malnutrition during critical brain growth period, affects these conduction processes in auditory pathways in the brainstem, resulting in abnormal pattern of electrophysiological responses i.e. BAEPs. However, BAEPs has limitation of its interpretation as its abnormality cannot separate inadequacy of axonal, dendritic or synaptic events. The only other report involving small group of marasmic infitnts showed abnormality in auditory evoked potential in form of evoked potential index (EPI) being more in marasmic infants as compared to control (Barnett et al 1978). This index was based on absolute peak latencies and amplitudes. It is now generally accepted that prolongation of IPLs beyond three standard deviation is the only criterion for BAEP abnormality and abnormal IPL prolongation usually reflects a pathological disturbance of central auditory conduction (Stockard et al 1986). The evoked potential index based on absolute peak latencies and amplitude is therefore less predictable and is of no clinical application.

The present study therefore, has shown that protein calorie malnutrition in neonates, infants and young children affects neuronal conduction processes in brainstem auditory pathways. The incidence of abnormal BAEP as reflected by abnormally prolonged IPLs or absent BAEP wave forms is 25% in neonates of malnourished mothers and 33.3% in malnourished children. It remains to be seen whether these changes are reversible with subsequent supplemental nutrition. Whether other sensory afferents (visual, somatosensory) are also involved in PEM, remains to be seen.

REFERENCES

1. Barnett AB, Weiss IP, Sottillo MV et al (1978). Abnormal auditory evoked potentials in early infancy malnutrition. *Science* 201, 450-452.
2. Bhatia VP, Katiyar GP, Agrawal KN, Das TK and Dey PK (1980). Sleep cycle studies in babies of undernourished mothers. *Archives Diseases of Child* 55, 134-138.
3. Bronzino JD, Austin LA, France RJ, Siok CJ and Morgane PJ (1986). Effect of protein malnutrition on hippocampal kindling: electrographic and behavioural measures. *Brain Research* 384, 348-354.
4. Bronzino JD, Austin LA, France RJ and Morgone PJ (1990). Effect of prenatal protein malnutrition on performance path kindling in the rat. *Brain Research* 515, 45-50.

5. Dhopeshwarker GA, (1983). Nutrition and brain development Plenum Press London.

6. Dobbing J., Sands J. (1973). Quantitative growth and development of human brain. *Archives Diseases of Child* 48, 757-767.

7. Dobbing J. (1984). Infant nutrition and later achievement. *Nutrition Review* 42, 1-7.

8. Levav M, Cruz ME, Nfirsky AF (1995). EEG abnormalities malnutrition, parasitism and goiter: a study of school children in Equador. *ACTA Paediatrics* 84, 197-202.

9. Levitsky DA, Strupp BJ (1995). Malnutrition and the brain: changing concertos, changing concerns. *Journal of Nutrition* 125, 2212-2220.

10. Magoon EH, Robb RM (1981). *Development of myelin in human optic nerve and Archives ophthalmology* 99, 655-659.

11. National Center for Health Statistics Growth Charts in WHO (ed): Measuring changes in nutritional status, guidelines for assessing the impact of supplementary feeding proformas for vulnerable groups. WHO Geneva.

12. Robinson S, Young RE, Golden (1995). Electrophysiological assessment of brain function in severe malnutrition. *ACTA Paediatrics* 84: 1245-1251.

13. Rorke L, Riggs H (1969). Myelination of brain in the new bom, Lippencott, Philadelphia.

14. Salamy A, McKean CM, Pettet G et al (1978). Auditory brainstem recovery process from birth to adulthood. *Psychophysiology* 15, 214-220.

15. Sarma JMK, Rao KS (1974). Biochemical composition of different regions in brain of small for date infants. *Journal of Neurochemistry* 22, 671-677.

16. Sharma SK, Nayar U, Maheshwari MC and Singh B (1987). Effect of undernutrition on developing rat cerebellum - some electro physiogical and neurological correlates. *Journal of Neurological Sciences* 78, 261-272.

17. Stockard JJ, Stockard JE, Sharbrough FW (1986). Brainstem auditory evoked potentials, methodology, interpretation and clinical application; in Aminoff MS (Ed): Electrodiagnosis in clinical neurology, New York, Churchill Livingston 467-503.

18. Tandon OP (1990). Auditory brainstem evoked responses in healthy North Indian. Indian Journal of Medical Research 92, 252-266.

'19. Warren MA, Bedi KS (1990). Synapse to neuron ratios in rat cerebellar cortex following lengthy periods of undernutrition. *Journal of Anatomy* 170, 173-182.

20. Wiggins RC, Fuller GN, Brizzee L, Bissel AC and Samorajski T (1984). Myelination of rat optic nerves during postnatal undernourishment and recovery. *Brain Research* 368, 277-286.

21. Yuckel F, Warren MA and Gumusburm E (1994). The effect of undernutrition on connectivity in cerebellar cortex of adult rats. *Journal of Anatomy* 184, 59-64.

LIPOPOLYSACCHARIDE EFFECT ON PROTEIN DEGRADATION AND LIPID PEROXIDATION OF ERYTHROCYTE

JHARNA BHATTACHARYYA, TAPASI DAS CHOWDHURI AND ASOKE G. DATTA

Indian Institute of Chemical Biology, Department of Life Sciences and Biotechnology, Jadavpur University, Calcutta-700032

Summary

1. In vivo (20 μg LPS/100 g) studies in rats showed increased tyrosine production from erythrocyte
2. In vitro studies using 25μg to 250μg LPS per ml blood also showed- similar response of LPS in protein degradation
3. Washed erythrocytes free from plasma and leukocytes did not show increased- effect after LPS treatment.
4. In vitro, lipid peroxidation was also increased after LPS treatment.
5. Increased degradative damages of erythrocytes may be related to increase Ca^{2+} flux, overproduction of cytokines or other mediators which are ultimate regulators of septic shock

INTRODUCTION

During sepsis, endotoxin (Lipapolysaccharide, LPS) from gram-negative bacteria is released which causes metabolic disturbances and hematological changes also. Microcirculatory failure is one of the ultimate results of septic shock. Among other reason, this failure of microcirculation is supposed due to reduced deformability of circulating erythrocytes. Mechanistic defect of erythrocytes may in turn results in reduced tissue perfusion, which ultimately leads to multiple organ failure or shock.

Bellary et al (1995) and Butterfield et al (1994) studied the effect of LPS on physical conformation of cytoskeletal proteins and lipid motion of erythrocytes and have shown alteration of the two parameters. Protein degradation and lipid peroxidation are two extremes- of. a-spectrum of damage in erythrocytes exposed to infection. Recently Bhattacharyya et al(1999) have shown the effet of LPS on protein degradation and lipid peroxidation of erythrocytes. Alteration in the two degradative parameters will probably help to understand the mechanism of septic shock.

METHODS

For in vivo studies with LPS (E. coli LPS, 026:B6 Sigma) we used male Sprague-Dawley rats of 150 g wt and for in vitro studies goat blood was mainly used. Blood was collected in anticoagulant solution and erythrocytes separated from plasma and leukocytes by centrifugation. For protein degradation we followed the principles of Waalkes and Udenfriend (1957) and for lipid peroxidation malondialdehyde (MDA) from erythrocyte was estimated according to Buege and Aust (1987). Protein was estimated following Bradford's method (1976).

All the values were expressed as tSD. The statistical significance was determined by student's t-test.

RESULTS AND DISCUSSION

In vivo administration of LPS (20 ug/100g) for 24h, causes a significant (2.31±0.26 vs 0.92±0.10 ug tyr/ng) 2.5

fold increase in tyrosine production of erythrocytes, when compared to control receiving saline - only. Similarly when goat blood was incubated with inreasing doses of - LPS (25 ug to 250 ug/ml blood) at 37°C, 90 min, a dose dependent linear increase- of tyrosine production was observed. With increasing incubation time the values of tyrosine produced, was elevated but non-linearly. When washed erythrocytes free from plasma and leukocytes were trated with LPS, tyrosine production was not prominent with even higher doses.

Lipid peroxidation of erythrocyte was also elevated after treatment of blood with LPS *in vitro* (Table 1). Like protein degradation in washed erythrocytes MDA production was negligible when treated with 250 ug LPS/ ml, this value is comparable to control values. In contrast, *in. vivo* lipid peroxidation does not show much changes after injection of LPS into animals (1.09±0.63 with LPS vs 0.903±0.52 without LPS)

Protein degradation as well as lipid peroxidation are generalised terms often caused by septic or bacteremic injury. The implication of these phenomena in erythrocytes is a subject of research. Short lived or abnormal proteins may get hydrolysed during endotoxin treatment. our hypothesis is that possibly cytoskeletal/membrane proteins of the erythrocyte, responsile for maintaining

TABLE 1

Effect of *in vitro* LPS on lioid peroxidation of erythrocytes.

System	n moles LMDA Produced/protein*
Control Blood	4.11 ± 0.41
Control Blood + 125 ug LPS/ml	5.90 t 0.43
Control Blood + 250 ug LPS/ml	8.22 t 0.44
Washed erythrocyte + 250 ug LPS/ml	4.29 t 0.62

*Results are mean ± SD

integrity of the cells are disrupted during infection, thus making erythrocytes incapable to deliver oxygen to the tissues properly. The role of Ca 2+ in our experimental findings cannot be overruled, as Ca 2+ has got an important role during septic injury (Bhattacharyya et al 1993, Bhattacharyya et al 1994, Bhattacharyya 1995).

Besides Ca^{2+}, oxygen free radicals are secondary mediators in septic shock. Oxygen radicals have been shown to stimulate intracellular proteolysis in and lipid peroxidation of erythrocytes through independent mechanism (Davies and Goldberg 1987). It is evident that protein degradative and lipid peroxidative changes of erythrocytes do not occur without non-specific interactions of plasma and leukocytes (Morrison 1985) mediated via cytokines etc. Further studies are in progress to elucidate the mechanism of interaction of mediators involved in LPS-induced alterations of erythrocytes.

REFERENCES

Bellary SS, Anderson KW, Arden WA, Bulterfield DA (1995) Effect of lipopolysaccharide on the physical conformation of the erythrocyte cytoskeletal proteins. *Life Sciences* 56, 91-98.

Bhattacharyya J, Thompson KD, Sayeed MM.(1993) Skeletal muscle calcium flux and catabolic response during sepsis. *Am. J. Physiol.* 265 R487- R493.

Bhattacharyya J, Ahmad S, Sayeed MM (1994) Role of Ca^{2+} in skeletal muscle metabolic and functional disturbances in pathophysiological states. In "Environment and Physiologyll (eds: Mallick 3N 6 Singh R) *Narosa* pp.122-130.

Bhattacharyya J.(1995) Protein catabolic response and proteases during pathophysiological injury of skeletal muscle. *Ind. J. Physiol and Allied Sci.* 49, 59-67.

Bhattacharyya J, Das Chowdhury T. Datta AG (1999) Effect of endotoxin on protein degradation and lipid peroxidation of erythrocytes. *J. Physiol.. Pharmacol.* 50(2): 321-326.

Bradford MM (1976) A rapid and sensitive method for the quantification of microgram quantities of protein utilizing the principal of protein dye binding. *Anal. Biochem.* 72, 248-254.

Buege JA, Aust- SD (1987) Microsomal lipid peroxidation. *Methods in Enzymol*, 52, 302-310.

Butterfield DA, Sun B, Bellary S, Arden WA, Anderson KW (1994) Effect of endotoxin on lipid order and motion in erythrocyte membranes. *Biochim. Biophys. Acta* 1225, 231-234.

Davies KJA, Goldberg AL (1997) Oxygen radicals stimulate intracellular proteolysis and lipid peroxidation by independent mechanisms in erythrocytes. *J. Biol. Chem.* 262, 8220-8226.

Morrison DC (1985) non-specific interaction of bacterial lipopolysaccharides with membranes and membrane component. In Handbook of endotoxin : Cellular biology of endotoxin, ed. *Berry LJ*, pp25-53, Elsevier.

Waalkes TP, Udenfriend S (1957) A fluorometric method for the estimation of tyrosine in plasma and tissues. *J.Lab.Clin.Med.* 50, 733-736.

PULMONARY FUNCTION PATTERN IN AGE MATCHED (10 TO 17 YEARS) SCHOOL GOING BOYS AND GIRLS

RAJESH CHINTALA*, PRATIBHA GUPTA, NEELAM VANEY

Department of Physiology, University College of Medical Sciences, GTB Hospital, Shahdara Delhi 110095.

Summary

Spirometric tests using a computerized lung function monitor (SPIRO 232, P. K. Morgan) were performed in 200 healthy boys and girls in the age group of 10 to 17 years, selected from urban population of Delhi. The results were analyzed by separating the pulmonary functions by age and sex. All pulmonary functions showed an increase with age. Females achieved a maximal peak in the lung functions at the age of 16 years thereafter it decreased. In males no peak was seen and the lung functions continued to increase throughout. FEF_{25}%, FEF_{50}%, FEF_{75}% were lower in boys up to 13 years of age. FVC, FRC, TLC, FEV_1 and PEFR were similar in both sexes till the age of 13 years, after which the boys out-performed the girls in all the lung functions. Prediction equations were calculated using independent variables (Age, Height, Weight, Arm-span, chest circumference and pubertal status). Step-wise regression analysis (Forward selection) was carried out on the independent variables to choose the best equation for each of the dependent variable. Maximum variance in the pulmonary functions was explained with age in males and weight in females. Regression equations obtained in males were more consistent as compared with that of females.

INTRODUCTION

Normograms for pulmonary functions in different age groups have been worked out by a number of researchers. These values are however incumbent upon various anthropometric and patho-physiological factors. There is also evidence that over a period of time the demographic trends have a tendency to effect the measured normal values. Certain age groups are especially vulnerable to these secular trends (Taranger 1983). The age of onset of puberty in females, has been consistently decreasing over the years. (Sidhu et al 1982, Singh et al 1998, Trananger 1983, Wyshak 1983). Such change is also observed in boys (Sidhu et al 1982). This causes an increase in height, weight, body mass index etc much before the expected age and which in due course, causes a change in the lung functions. It is thus imperative that laboratories periodically establish a normative data so that observed lung functions can be compared.

It is now well documented in literature that the wide range of geographical, ethnic and climatic conditions, are associated with regional differences in lung functions (Mahajan, 1997 and Katherine, 1979). At the onset of puberty there is a sudden growth spurt which results in change in the body morphology, especially increase in the height, weight, fat distribution and other associated pubertal changes. These alterations further effect the thoracic dimensions, causing a change in the lung functions. Various laboratories have established their normative data, recording the lung functions in a given population. However very few have concentrated on the pubertal age group, which is subject to wide fluctuation in measured values. It is thus crucial that the lung functions are assessed to establish a normative data for a particular population.

The present study is aimed at reporting lung functions of healthy children in the age group of 10 to 17 years, in order to perform a comprehensive study to evaluate the dependency of the lung functions on various anthropometric parameters.

METHODS

Equipment: The basic instrument used in the study consisted of a roll-seal type spirometer equipped with a linear electrical output for volume and flow measurement. These measurements were further analyzed by a computer (486 DX) using the software provided by P K Morgan Spiro 232. A portable two-liter precision calibration pump was used for periodic checking of the spirometer. These have been in accordance to the recommendation by the GAP conference committee on standardization of pulmonary function testing. (Tausing et al 1980, American Thoracic Society 1991).

Study Group: The subjects were drawn from a near by school. A questionnaire was prepared for screening purpose, which included a brief personal and family history, to exclude any obvious cardio-respiratory abnormalities. A group was then selected and a prior parental consent was obtained from them. In a separate questionnaire, with the help of a nurse, proper detailed history was elicited, which included the following exclusion criteria (Tausing et al 1980 and Sharma et al, 1997):

1. No history of chronic respiratory or cardiac illness.
2. No history of any major thoracic surgery in the past.
3. No history of any acute respiratory tract infection preceding three weeks of the test.
4. No history of systemic disease influencing the respiratory tract.
5. Non-smoker.

In addition the pubertal development was assessed by including the following factors: (Pamecha et al 1984, Kaul et al 1983, Marshal et al 1970)

1. **Males:** deepening of voice, appearance of facial hair and pubic hair (any two of the factors present)
2. **Females:** onset of menarche.

Detailed clinical examination, including the anthropometric measurements were carried out.

* **Height:** standing height was measured without shoes along a tape suspended from a wall. (centimeters)
* **Weight:** recorded using standard weighing machine (Kilograms). Care was taken to use the same weighing scale for all the subjects.
* **Chest:** measured (centimeters) using an inch tape at the level of nipples in the mid-inspiratory period.
* **Arm-span:** the subject was asked to stand erect with outstretched arms, and measurement was obtained as the farthest distance between the tips of the middle finger of the two outstretched arms.

Procedure for measuring lung functions: once the group was selected the lung functions were carried out at the University College of Medical Sciences, GTB Hospital, in our Environmental Physiology Laboratory. At a time the lung functions were assessed in groups of 4 to 5 students, this was important as it was seen that the student performed better in the maneuvers involving forced expiratory effort, this could be attributed to a sense of competition that the students felt in their own peer group.

Before the start of the procedure, each student was briefed about the maneuvers involved in the whole procedure. A demonstration also followed the briefing and adequate care was taken such that the students understood the procedural details involved. All procedures were carried out in the sitting position during the morning hours between 10 am to 12 noon in a quite laboratory setup in order to alleviate the emotional and psychological stress. During the tests the subject was adequately encouraged to perform at their optimum level. Tests were repeated at least 3 times and the best matching results were considered for analysis. All recordings were done at the BTPS.

The following measured and derived values were obtained:

(i)	FVC	Forced vital capacity. (liters)
(ii)	FIVC	Forced inspiratory vital capacity (liters)
(iii)	RV	Residual Volume. (liters)
(iv)	TLC	Total Lung Capacity. (liters)
(v)	RV/TLC	Residual Volume / Total lung capacity
(vi)	FRC	Functional residual capacity. (liters)
(vii)	FEV_1	Forced expiratory volume in 1st second. (liters)
(viii)	FEV_1%	FEV_1 as a percentage of FVC
(ix)	FEF_{25}%	Forced expiratory flow at 25% of expired vital capacity. (Liters/ Second)
(x)	FEF_{50}%	Forced expiratory flow at 50% of expired vital capacity. (Liters/ Second)
(xi)	FEF_{75}%	Forced expiratory flow at 75% of expired vital capacity. (Liters/ Second)
(xii)	PEFR	Peak expiratory flow rate. (Liters/ Second)
(xiii)	PIFR	Peak inspiratory flow rate. (Liters/ Second)

Statistical analysis: The data was analyzed using a computer software programs by SPSS 7.5.2 and STATISTICA 5.0. Standard statistical test including t-test and analysis of variance was used for comparison of various parameters. Lung functions and anthropometric measurements were correlated by Pearson's correlation test. The observed lung functions for males and females, were further analyzed as a function of age, height, weight, arm-span, and pubertal status using the forward selection (step-wise) regression analysis. First the dependent variable (observed pulmonary function) was correlated with all the independent variables. The independent variable having the highest absolute correlation (positive or negative) was then selected and entered into the equation. If the probability associated with the F-test was less that 0.05, it was included in the equation. If the first variable did not meet this criterion, then it was reported as no variable entered the equation. If the first variable satisfied the criterion then forward selection continued and the next variable showing the maximum correlation entered the equation. This continued until all variables were exhausted or when a particular variable entered did not show any significance at probability level. The predicted values as obtained by the equations generated through forward selection method were calculated. The residuals were identified and a normal probability plot was constructed for the residuals between observed and predicted values. The outliners were located and removed from the analysis (Munro BH 1997, Saunders DB 1990).

RESULTS

Altogether 200 children were included in the study. All those not meeting the standards as suggested in the exclusion criteria were not considered for testing. After selection only those children were included in the analysis who satisfied the 'adequate respiratory effort'. A total of 30 subjects were rejected in this process, the measurement of the lung function is purely an effort dependent process hence the subject cooperation is a prerequisite.

The children were broadly classified as males and females, according to their ages. Table-1 gives the anthropometric data of males and females. Table- 2 depicts the mean values of pulmonary functions classified according to the age and sex. All the lung functions increased with age (ANOVA: one way interaction for age $p \leq 0.05$), except $FEV_1\%$. In general, the boys and girls had almost comparable lung functions up to the age of 13 years, there-after the boys outperformed the girls ($p \leq 0.05$) in almost all the lung functions at 17 years, baring RV.

To assess the correlations between anthropometric and spirometric data, product moment correlations (Pearson's r) was computed for males and females separately. (Table 3 and 4) A significant correlation was found with age, height, weight, arm-span, chest circumference, pubertal status for most of the lung functions, barring RV/ TLC and $FEV_1\%$. In general the correlation coefficient for males was greater than females. $FEV_1\%$ was negatively correlated to all the anthropometric parameters in males.

Table 5 and 6 gives the regression equation for the dependent variables of males and females respectively. The equation did not violate the assumptions of the regression model adopted and all the residuals were found to be normally distributed. The outliners for each variable were removed before the equation went in to the regression sequence.

In another classification, to include the pubertal status, the subjects were further classified as pre-pubertal and post-pubertal (Table 7). Total of 81 subjects were in the pre-pubertal age and 119 subjects were in the post-pubertal age. Independent sample T test showed a significant change in all the lung functions except RV/ TLC.

The mean values of lung functions were plotted in the pre-pubertal and the post-pubertal group for males and

TABLE 1

The distribution by age and sex of the height, weight, arm-span and chest diameter in the subjects studied. The means and standard deviation are given.

Age (years)	SEX	N (200)	Height (cm)	Weight (Kg)	Arm-span (cm)	Chest (cm)
10	Male	10	132.50 ± 4.48	28.60 ± 3.92	132.50 ± 5.36 *	61.50 ± 3.06 *
	Female	10	134.50 ± 4.09	32.60 ± 5.46	141.80 ± 7.00	70.10 ± 4.58
11	Male	11	135.91 ± 6.28 *	30.45 ± 2.62	138.00 ± 6.93 *	65.09 ± 3.14 *
	Female	14	140.50 ± 5.46	39.64 ± 6.27	148.21 ± 8.28	81.21 ± 7.13
12	Male	14	145.0 ± 10.25	35.57 ± 9.48 *	144.29 ± 11.47 *	69.21 ± 6.81*
	Female	15	147.13 ± 5.37	46.13 ± 6.00	157.73 ± 5.85	82.53 ± 6.01
13	Male	14	148.07 ± 11.20	38.50 ± 7.72	149.79 ± 15.13	64.71±11.40 *
	Female	12	146.50 ± 5.89	40.50 ± 7.56	152.75 ± 7.19	78.50 ± 6.29
14	Male	12	162.25 ± 11.35 *	48.25 ± 10.38	165.08 ± 13.37	80.17 ± 10.02
	Female	14	148.93 ± 3.63	46.36 ± 7.08	159.07 ± 7.90	77.57 ± 12.53
15	Male	8	160.13 ± 7.95 *	49.75 ± 12.09	165.00 ± 8.05 *	72.50 ± 6.72
	Female	13	151.00 ± 4.40	42.62 ± 3.91	155.23 ± 4.92	76.85 ± 3.80
16	Male	13	168.85 ± 11.35 *	55.85 ± 11.02	172.69 ± 6.06 *	83.15 ± 12.49
	Female	10	150.80 ± 2.82	49.70 ± 9.04	157.10 ± 6.79	83.90 ± 6.06
17	Male	18	167.56 ± 5.03 *	58.89 ± 5.97 *	165.94 ± 5.34 *	71.39 ± 8.34 *
	Female	12	149.75 ± 4.11	46.42 ± 5.45	158.83 ± 5.15	82.75 ± 6.17

* $p \leq 0.05$.

TABLE 2

Means and standard deviation of the lung volumes and capacities in different ages and sex categories.

Age (yr)	SEX	N	FVC (L)	FIVC (L)	RV (L)	TLC (L)	RV/TLC	FRC (L)	FEV_1 (L/s)	FEV_1%	FEF_{25} (L/s)	FEF_{50} (L/s)	FEF_{75} (L/s)	PEFR (L/s)	PIFR (L/s)
10	Male	10	1.52± 0.16	1.30± 0.18	0.38± 0.04	1.80± 0.30	19.77± 2.14*	0.94± 0.38	1.47± 0.17	96.80± 6.39	3.10± 0.46*	2.57± 0.31	1.56± 0.32	3.29± 0.38*	3.43± 0.61*
	Female	10	1.38± 0.26	1.40± 0.25	0.59± 0.38	1.93± 0.24	23.99± 2.27	0.95± 0.13	1.32± 0.30	93.64± 6.01	2.40± 0.52	2.30± 0.56	1.62± 0.53	2.47± 0.62	1.93± 0.62
11	Male	11	1.97± 0.32	1.54± 0.27 *	0.55± 0.19	2.60± 0.50	21.03± 4.18 *	1.10± 0.32	1.78± 0.27	91.79± 6.70	3.38± 0.75	2.60± 0.58 *	1.28± 0.21*	3.74± 0.81	3.19± 1.20
	Female	14	1.83± 0.41	1.91± 0.47	0.70± 0.20	2.57± 0.76	26.77± 4.59	1.36± 0.36	1.79± 0.39	94.46± 5.67	3.73± 1.03	3.23± 0.82	2.07± 0.59	3.86± 0.94	2.75± 0.51
12	Male	14	2.10± 0.44	1.74± 0.55	0.67± 0.25	2.83± 0.65	23.07± 5.32 *	1.44± 0.44	1.96± 0.42	93.99± 7.59	3.36± 0.91	2.70± 0.98	1.64± 0.55*	3.56± 0.88	3.07± 0.87
	Female	15	1.85± 0.39	1.87± 0.38	0.79± 0.15	2.69± 0.44	29.94± 5.32	1.45± 0.24	1.86± 0.40	98.10± 3.37	3.64± 0.94	3.21± 0.70	2.08± 0.52	3.93± 0.96	2.96± 0.59
13	Male	14	1.89± 0.30	1.69± 0.39	0.67± 0.30	2.56± 0.49	25.02± 7.91	1.39± 0.45	1.81± 0.33	95.50± 6.05	3.72± 1.16	2.85± 0.53	1.62± 0.49*	3.95± 1.26	2.69± 1.04
	Female	12	1.74± 0.52	1.76± 0.51	0.73± 0.20	2.50± 0.66	29.68± 5.05	1.34± 0.36	1.72± 0.51	97.86± 3.82	3.59± 1.11	3.02± 0.81	2.01± 0.42	3.63± 1.13	2.58± 0.92

TABLE 2 (Contd..)

Age (yr)	SEX	N	FVC (L)	FIVC (L)	RV (L)	TLC (L)	RV/TLC	FRC (L)	FEV_1 (L/s)	FEV_1%	FEF_{25} (L/s)	FEF_{50} (L/s)	FEF_{75} (L/s)	PEFR (L/s)	PIFR (L/s)
14	Male	12	2.80± 0.53*	2.68± 0.85	1.03± 0.15*	4.03± 0.61*	24.16± 8.22	2.14± 0.29*	2.58± 0.52*	92.38± 5.46	5.34± 1.23*	4.23± 1.45	2.01± 0.63	5.47± 1.22	3.51± 0.66
	Female	14	2.19± 0.33	2.19± 0.41	0.67± 0.21	2.88± 0.48	23.81± 6.64	1.32± 0.48	2.06± 0.35	95.01± 4.27	3.73± 0.75	3.25± 0.54	1.93± 0.45	4.12± 0.82 *	3.05± 0.67
15	Male	8	2.86± 0.48 *	2.08± 0.71	0.77± 0.19	3.72± 0.41*	20.64± 4.51*	1.86± 0.53*	2.71± 0.38 *	96.28± 6.27	4.55± 0.61*	4.36± 1.11*	2.31± 0.48	4.60± 1.28	2.85± 1.36
	Female	13	2.04± 0.37	2.05± 0.38	0.68± 0.15	2.71± 0.33	26.42± 7.49	1.37± 0.22	1.90± 0.29	94.53± 5.34	3.53± 0.54	3.05± 0.39	1.90± 0.33	3.89± 0.59	3.14± 0.94
16	Male	13	3.36± 0.83 *	3.21± 0.54 *	1.13± 0.44 *	4.71± 1.01 *	23.79± 4.71	2.33± 0.56 *	3.09± 0.65 *	93.25± 8.76	5.69± 1.14 *	4.73± 1.40	2.68± 0.77	6.34± 1.18*	4.15± 0.78*
	Female	10	2.22± 0.33	2.26± 0.35	0.83± 0.13	3.30± 0.46	25.54± 5.94	1.63± 0.29	2.24± 0.38	97.64± 3.71	4.48± 1.24	3.88± 0.97	2.60± 0.62	4.65± 1.18	3.08± 0.56
17	Male	18	3.97± 0.63*	5.57± 11.74 *	0.95± 0.39	4.19± 0.96*	18.77± 4.24*	2.15± 0.99*	3.65± 0.49 *	92.32± 5.94 *	7.65± 1.13 *	5.76± 1.06 *	2.88± 0.84 *	8.05± 1.03 *	4.84± 0.98*
	Female	12	2.02± 0.30	2.12± 0.30	0.81± 0.10	2.96± 0.29	28.26± 3.93	1.60± 0.14	2.00± 0.29	97.81± 3.58	3.32± 1.01	3.29± 0.96	2.32± 0.64	3.46± 1.14	2.98± 0.80
Anova (P) value: one-way with age.			0.00	0.00	0.00	0.00	0.036	0.00	0.00	0.50	0.00	0.00	0.00	0.00	0.00

* **Males compared with females in each category (p £ 0.05)**

TABLE 3

Correlation coefficient 'r' between Lung Function Tests and Anthropometric measurements of males.

Lung Functions	Anthropometric Measurements					
	Age	Height	Weight	Arm-Span	Chest	Pubertal Status
FVC	0.821**	0.703**	0.679**	0.636**	0.367**	0.735**
FIVC	0.252*	0.220*	0.219*	0.089	0.157	0.210*
RV	0.552**	0.604**	0.540**	0.684**	0.486**	0.477**
TLC	0.810**	0.745**	0.697**	0.739**	0482**	0.712**
RV/ TLC	-0.065	0.137	0.069	0.247*	0.149	-0.122
FRC	0.606**	0.631**	0.534**	0.638**	0.434**	0.528**
FEV_1	0.839**	0.734**	0.700**	0.679**	0.369**	0.766**
FEV_1%	-0.100	-0.017	-0.108	-0.049	-0.099	-0.012
FEF_{25}	0.788**	0.683**	0.680**	0.626**	0.327**	0.667**
FEF_{50}	0.742**	0.724**	0.653**	0.635**	0.356**	0.663**
FEF_{75}	0.666**	0.653**	0.634**	0.599**	0.421**	0.663**
PEFR	0.794**	0.694**	0.694**	0.640**	0.355**	0.676**
PIFR	0.448**	0.363**	0.349**	0.311**	0.079	0.412**

**Correlation is significant at the 0.01 level (2-tailed).

* Correlation is significant at the 0.05 level (2-tailed).

females. (Figure 1 and 2). All lung functions were significantly increased in males and females in the post-pubertal phase, however in females FEV_{75}% was not significantly increased. When the lung functions were plotted against height and age, (Figure 3 and 4) a linear relationship with height is seen up to the age of 14 years in males and 12 years in females. Thereafter the linear relationship of lung functions is lost. In males a general increasing trend of all lung functions is observed after 13

TABLE 4

Correlation coefficient 'r' between Lung Function Tests and Anthropometric measurements of females

Lung Functions	Anthropometric Measurements					
	Age	Height	Weight	Arm-Span	Chest	Pubertal Status
FVC	0.424**	0.451**	0.490**	0.318**	0.299**	0.400**
FIVC	0.425**	0.423**	0.433**	0.328**	0.314**	0.351**
RV	0.199*	0.141	0.284**	0.166	0.410**	0.181
TLC	0.469**	0.452**	0.531**	0.326**	0.435**	0.383**
RV/ TLC	0.011	0.027	0.062	0.134	0.258**	0.075
FRC	0.389**	0.370**	0.383**	0.319**	0.458**	0.299**
FEV_1	0.421**	0.463**	0.496**	0.321**	0.357**	0.408**
FEV_1%	0.154	0.148	0.182	0.135	0.199*	0.276**
FEF_{25}	0.205*	0.335**	0.447**	0.307**	0.335**	0.256*
FEF_{50}	0.281**	0.385**	0.527**	0.325**	0.340**	0.240*
FEF_{75}	0.286**	0.299**	0.451**	0.254*	0.397**	0.190
PEFR	0.230*	0.393**	0.461**	0.341**	0.282**	0.294**
PIFR	0.311**	0.322**	0.334**	0.198*	0.229*	0.329**

**Correlation is significant at the 0.01 level (2-tailed).

* Correlation is significant at the 0.05 level (2-tailed).

years or 148 cms of height. In females the flow rates (FEF_{25}% - FEF_{75}%) increase more rapidly than the lung volumes (FVC and TLC) in same age group.

DISCUSSION

The main use of lung function assessment in the clinical practice is for the comparison of a normal measurement

TABLE 5

Regression equation for predicting lung functions of healthy Delhi Boys. (10-17 years).

Variable Y	Constant C	(a) Age	(b) Height	(c) Weight	(d) Pub-Status	(e) Chest	(f) Arm-span	R^{2*}	β
FVC	-2.034	0.341	-	-	-	-	-	0.675	0.821
FIVC	-4.845	0.549	-	-	-	-	-	0.063	0.252
RV	-1.371	-	-0.0123	-	-	-	0.0261	0.494	-0.531
TLC	-4.282	0.321	-	-	-	-	0.0218	0.689	0.284
RV/TLC	-1.331	-	-0.290	-	-6.945	-	0.505	0.320	-0.785
FRC	-2.425	0.089	-	-	-	-	0.0188	0.439	0.281
FEV_1	-1.402	0.240	-	-	0.381		-	0.719	0.222
FEV_1%			*No Variable entered the equation*						
FEF_{25}	-3.929	0.635	-	-	-	-	-	0.621	0.788
FEF_{50}	-5.741	0.300	0.0929		-	-	-0.0569	0.629	-0.606
FEF_{75}	-1.750	0.075	0.0136		0.460	-	-	0.505	0.263
PEFR	-4.102	0.669	-	-	-	-	-	0.630	0.794
PIFR	0.476	0.225	-	-	-	-	-	0.201	0.448

The equation is to read as Y = c + a (Age) + b (Height) + c (Weight) + d (Pub-status) + e (Chest) + f (Arm-span)

All regression coefficients were statistically significant at $p \leq 0.01$

TABLE 6

Regression equation for predicting lung functions of healthy Delhi Girls. (10-17 years).

Variable	Constant Y	(a) C	(b) Age	(c) Height	(d) Weight	(e) Pub-Status	(f) Chest	R^{2*} Arm-span	β
FVC	0.335	0.0504	-	0.0209	-	-	-	0.294	0.258
FIVC	0.396	0.0590	-	0.0177	-	-	-	0.255	0.290
RV	-0.112	-	-	-	-	0.01.6	-	0.168	0.410
TLC	-0.481	0.0795	-	0.0209	-	0.0152	-	0.378	0.207
RV/TLC	12.227	-	-	-	-	0.185	-	0.067	0.258
FRC	-0.590	0.0469	-	-	-	0.0169	-	0.297	0.303
FEV_1	-1.530	-	0.0176	0.0191	-	-	-	0.303	0.280
FEV_1%	91.176	-	-	-	2.885	-	-	0.076	0.276
FEF_{25}	1.061	-	-	0.0581	-	-	-	0.199	0.447
FEF_{50}	0.831	-	-	0.0530	-	-	-	0.278	0.527
FEF_{75}	0.665	-	-	0.0326	-	-	-	0.203	0.451
PEFR	-3.008	-	0.323	0.0476	-	-	-	0.245	0.209
PIFR	1.232	-	-	0.0224	0.369	-	-	0.146	0.216

The equation is to be read as Y = c + a(Age) + b(Height) + c(Weight) + d(Pub-status) + e(Chest) + f(Arm-span)

All regression coefficients were statistically significant at $p \leq 0.01$

TABLE 7

Lung function tests in pre-pubertal and post-pubertal children of the study population. (* Independent Sample T test between Pre and post pubertal children)

Variable	Mean Pre-Pubertal (N= 81)	Mean Post-Pubertal (N = 119)	P*
FVC (L)	1.86 ± 0.48	2.57 ± 0.90	0.000
FIVC (L)	1.69 ± 0.55	2.33 ± 0.62	0.000
RV (L)	0.64 ± 0.28	0.84 ± 0.28	0.000
TLC (L)	2.54 ± 0.77	3.48 ± 1.08	0.000
RV/TLC	23.92 ± 5.52	24.85 ± 6.70	0.225
FRC (L)	1.30 ± 0.48	1.71 ± 0.62	0.000
FEV_1(L)	1.75 ± 0.43	2.44 ± 0.77	0.000
FEV_1%	93.96 ± 6.36	95.68 ± 5.48	0.049
FEF_{25}(L/s)	3.45 ± 1.11	4.68 ± 1.75	0.000
FEF_{50}(L/s)	2.86 ± 0.93	3.93 ± 1.31	0.000
FEF_{75}(L/s)	1.66 ± 0.51	2.32 ± 0.68	0.000
PEFR (L/s)	3.64 ± 1.12	4.97 ± 1.84	0.000
PIFR (L/s)	2.87 ± 0.92	3.42 ± 1.09	0.000

with that of a pathological state. As a practical precept normal values are predicted through regression equations derived from population studies of healthy individuals. In the present study, a cross-section of apparently healthy school children were examined for determining the prediction equations. The model was prepared taking into consideration the effects of increasing anthropometric measurements (Height, Weight, Arm-span and thoracic diameter) on the lung functions in the pubertal age group. Further we also attempted to observe the apparent change in the pre-pubertal and the post-pubertal lung functions in males and females respectively.

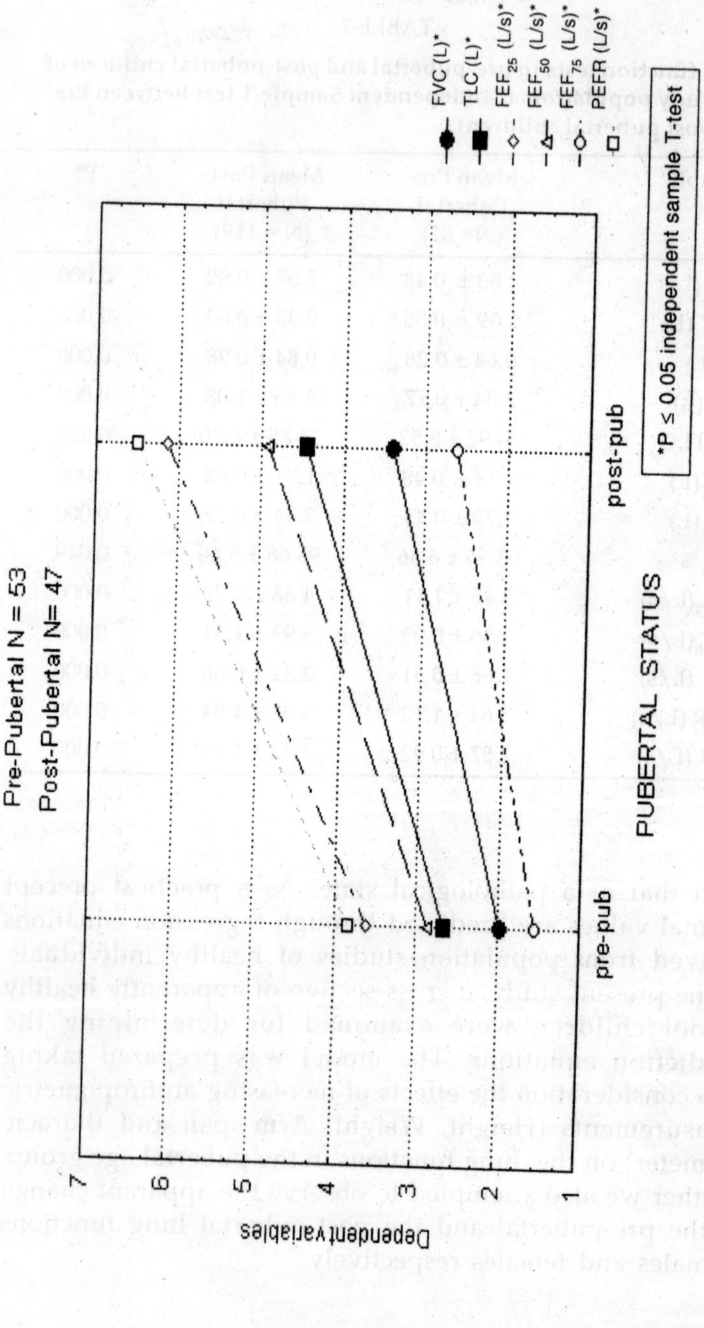

Fig. 1 Plot of mean lung funtions in pre-pubertal and post-pubertal males

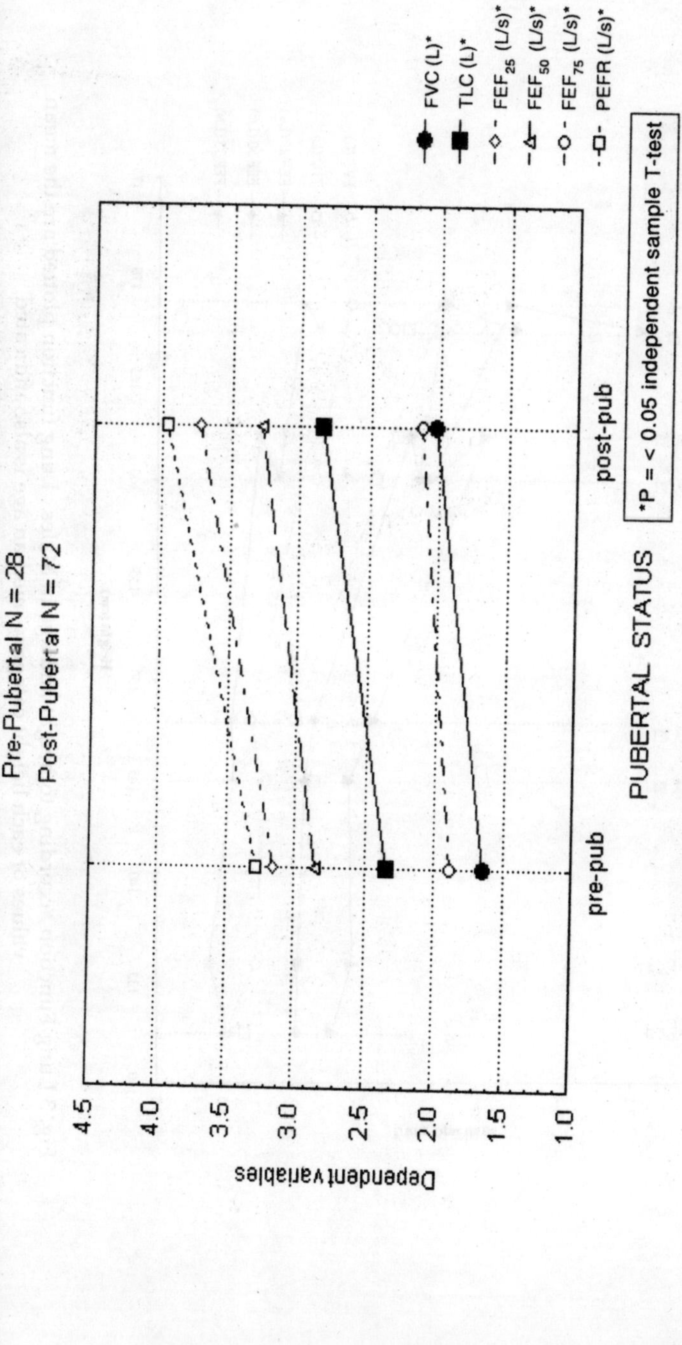

Fig. 2 Plot of mean lung function in pre-pubertal females

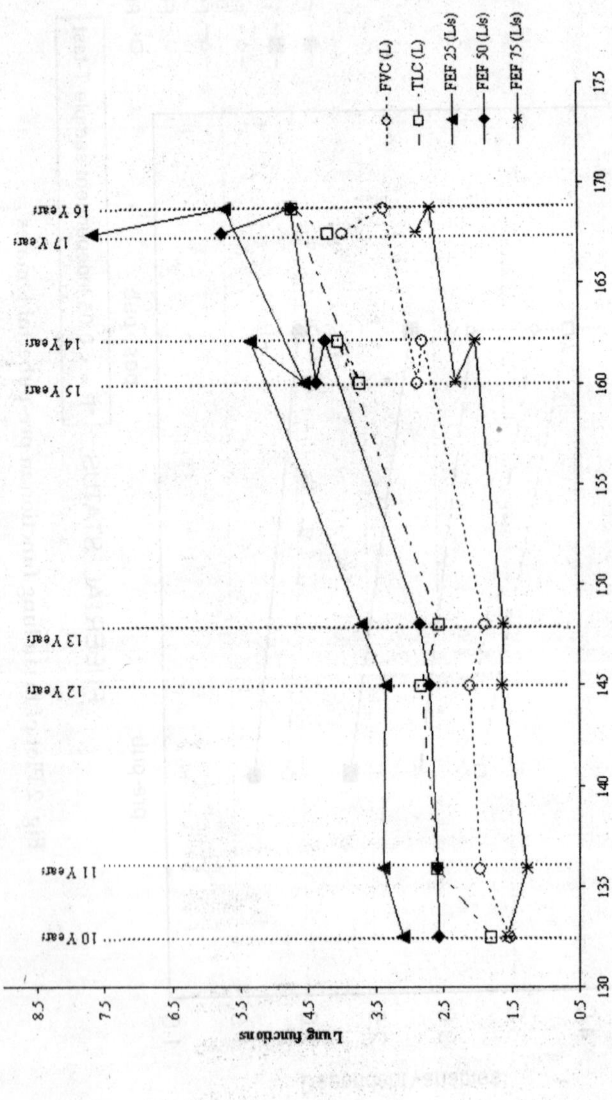

Fig. 3 Lung Function according to height and age in Males : Lung function plotted are the mean values of each height category, median age is also indicated

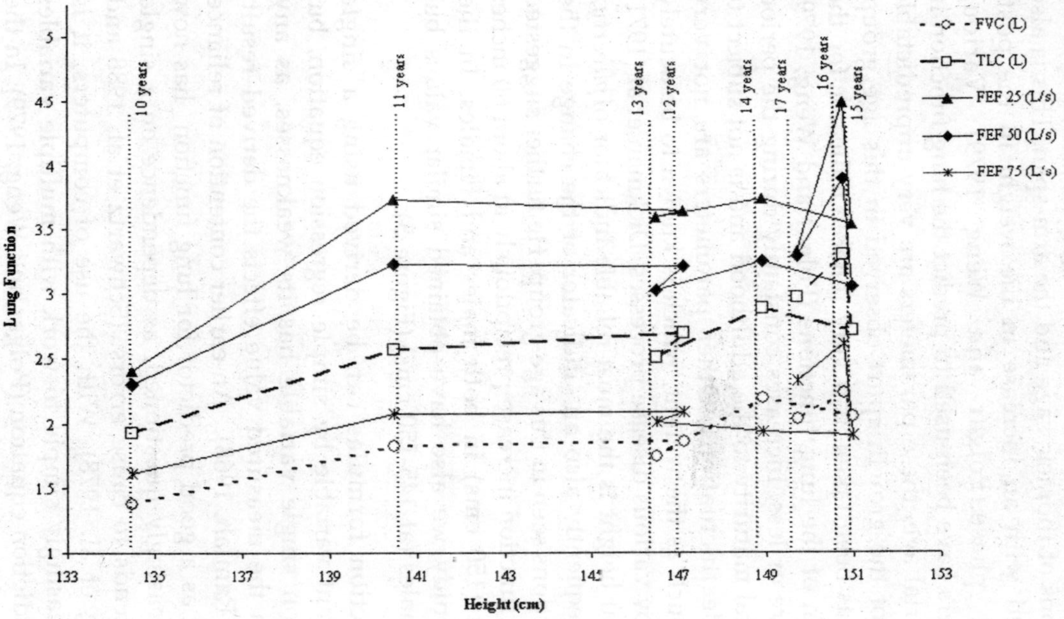

Fig. 4 Lung Function according to height and age in Males : Lung function are the mean value of each height category, median age is also indicated

The pubertal age is characterized by a sudden increase in height (growth spurt), accompanied by changes in the general skeletal architecture, causing an alteration in the dimensions of thoracic cage and the arm-span. This is also associated with an increase in the weight in the post-pubertal phase.(Polgar and Weng 1979). Various parameters have been used to predict the lung function in the pubertal age, these parameters are very unpredictable because of the growth spurt observed in this age group. Height has been taken as a very reliable indicator for the prediction of the lung functions (Polgar and Weng, 1979) as it, more or less, increases constantly during the period of pubertal maturity to the adulthood and is not subject to very wide fluctuations. Other parameters are not very reliable such as the weight, which is known to be acutely effected by various disease processes. Dickman et al (1971) stated that height is the most reliable indicator of*puberty*, and consequently also an indicator of the change in the lung functions seen in this age group. He further suggested that lung function increase precipitously at about 60 inches of height (150 cms) in both males and females. In the present study we also have obtained similar values but only in males (at 145-150 cms).(Figure 3).

Prediction formulas can be derived using a single independent variable by simple regression equation, but reliance on single variable has its weaknesses, as any change in the measured value effects the derived result. (Jain and Ramiah, 1968). An earlier contention of reliance on height as a good predictor for lung function has now been increasingly questioned, as dependence on a single variable tends to cause errors. (Schwartz et al, 1988 and Scoenberg et al, 1978). With the use of computers, it is now increasingly simple to work with multiple variables in the prediction equation (Polgar and Weng, 1979). In the present study we have attempted to include the commonly measured indices as independent variables, to predict the lung functions. A linear model for representation was used in this study. We have also used the forward selection regression analysis (stepwise regression), discarding those variable which precluded the accuracy of the resultant prediction formula. The residuals from the equation were normally distributed and did not show hetroscedasticity, hence a logarithimic transformation into power model was not performed. Care was also taken to include the commonly measurable indices as it facilitates its use in population studies.

We have used age, height, weight, arm-span, chest diameter and pubertal status as independent variables. These are the commonly measured variables and can be recorded in the out-patient clinic very conveniently with minimal equipment and expertise. Earlier studies have used combinations such as the sitting and standing height (Roizin et al, 1993 and Pierson et al, 1976) as a predictor and have concluded that the standing height is the best predictor of lung functions. In our study we have used the standing height, it is seen to be correlated with majority of the lung functions except RV/ TLC and FEV_1% in males and RV/ TLC, FEV_1% and RV in the females. The strength of correlation coefficient for height was however consistently more in the boys (0.724 to 0.220) than in girls (0.463 to 0.299). The regression equation also reflects a similar pattern. The R^2 for FVC is 0.675 (33% unexplained) for males with age, height did not fit the equation. In females the R^2 for FVC was 0.294 (71% unexplained) with age and weight (correlated best with age). Although the values are significant in females but the reliability is questionable, in fact the highest R^2 obtained in females is for TLC $R^2 = 0.378$. The reason for such a low level of R^2 in females could be attributed to:

1. **Hormonal fluctuation:** In the pubertal age group the females show a great fluctuation in the hormonal secretions (from very high levels to a low level) (Penfold et al 1980, Marshall et al 1969). The cycles are annovulatory at the beginning of the menarche and it

takes on an average of two years for the regular cycles to get established. These hormonal fluctuations may influence the various lung functions (Rajesh et al 2000).

2. **Population distribution:** the females were unequally distributed (28 Pre-pubertal ; 72 Post-pubertal females and 53 pre-pubertal ; 47 post-pubertal males) in the present study. As the group mainly consisted of girls in the age group of 10 to 18 years age, most of them had already attained their puberty. The subjects belonging to the lower age group may have confounded the results of the whole group.

3. **Performance level:** another factor which may have contributed could be the performance levels of the respiratory maneuvers in the females. (Dickman et al 1971) It was observed that the females in general performed the maneuvers with lesser efficacy as compared with the males and required more retrials. This may have led to recording of lower values.

Age became an important factor, in determining the regression equation in boys, except for RV and RV/TLC where height and arm-span were more important. Earlier studies (Sharma et al 1997, Cotes et al 1993,Chowgule et al 1995) have found height accounted for most of the lung functions and is independent of age. In females weight accounted for most of the lung functions except FIVC, RV/TLC and FEV_1%. Other studies have found that age (Sharma et al 1997) explained most of the equations. The R^2 obtained in males (range 0.201 - 0.719) were higher than those obtained in the females (range 0.146 - 0.378), hence the males have a more consistent findings in their lung functions than females when compared with independent factors. Sharma et al (1997) have also observed a similar trend. The major limitation of our study is in its being a cross-sectional study, its accuracy is effected when used to observe a longitudinal change in the individuals.

The onset of puberty is associated with an increase in height (Dickman et al 1971), it has been suggested that height is a reliable indicator of puberty in children. It is difficult to associate the onset of puberty in children based on a single identifying variable, we have included some of the criteria as suggested by earlier studies (Pamecha et al 1984, Kaul et al 1983, Marshal et al 1970). Though not very accurate they do give a rough idea about the onset of puberty in both sexes. All lung functions were seen to be increased in the post-pubertal age group in males. (Figure 1) On the other hand, in females only FEF_{75}% was not in the significant levels. (Figure 2). Pagtakhan et al (1985) suggested that there is a differential growth of the lung parenchyma and the airways in children. They have reported that the rapid growth of lung airways, out grow the parenchymal development during the pubertal growth spurt. Hence the values of flow rates increase to a more extent as compared with the lung volumes in the pubertal age group. (Kauffmann, 1989) When lung functions are compared with height and age we obtained a linear relationship with height up to 12 years of age in both sexes (Figure 3 and 4). In males the lung functions increased rapidly thereafter. In females a very erratic response was seen. The flow rates in females remain static until 15 years of age (height 151 cms), then reach a maximum at 16 years age (height 150cms) and then show a decrease in the flow rates at 17 years (height149 cm). Here although the variation in the height is not very significant but the lung functions (Figure 4) show wide fluctuations reaching a maximal at 16 years of age. Kauffman et al (1989) in a similar evaluation on a lower age group (6 to 10 years) obtained comparable results, they have attributed this to the dysanaptic growth of the lungs during the growth spurts. We observed similar changes in boys also, but as the boys attain sexual maturity after the girls these changes were not completely recorded as they were outside the scope of the study.

The values of the observed lung functions in the present study were compared with the western data. (Schoenberg 1978, Polgar 1979, Dickman 1971, Binder 1976) Our values were consistently lower than their age matched western counterparts. American Blacks were found to have lower lung volumes than whites. In our study we obtained lower values as compared with the American Blacks. Similar trend was seen when compared with other authors of European and Australian origin.

Our values were comparable with the studies done in Bombay (Chowgule et al 1995) and Delhi (Sharma et al 1997) school children. However the Bombay school children had higher PEFR. The low PEFR in our study could be due to the high levels of environmental pollution in Delhi. (Sharma et al 1997). Our values were higher when compared with that of Chetty et al (1975) and Nair et al (1997) in the same age and sex matched subjects. The study population of Chetty et al (1975) was from Delhi (North India) and Nair et al (1997) were from Kerala (South India). This indicates that even with in the same region there is a variation in the observed lung functions. This might be attributed to various factors such as method of study, type of instrument used for study [Chetty et al (1975) used a conventional spirometer and Nair et al (1997) used a portable spirometer] and more importantly the study population (North Indian and South Indian population). Sharma et al (1997) studied the lung functions in a similar population of Delhi and obtained a higher values. Similar results are echoed in studies of Rajkapoor et al (1997) and Mahajan et al (1997) in a population of Rohtak (North India).

In conclusion the results in the present study indicate that comparison of the lung functions in the pubertal age group is dependent on the growth patterns and is different for males and females. The wide fluctuations in the hormonal levels during pubertal age group might alter the respiratory mechanics. An important but very perplexing variable, which was not included in this study was the environmental pollution, which should also be taken into account before commenting on lung functions. We found that the school children in the pubertal age group represent a good stock population, where a mixture of children form different population sub-classes gather in a single area. Hence the lung functions in this segment of population could serve as a good indicator for the prediction formulas. Multiple regression formulas should be used to predict the lung functions as dependence on single variable is avoided.

REFERENCES

1. American Thoracic Society (1991). Lung Function testing: selection of reference values and interpretative strategies. *Am Rev Respir Dis* 144, 1202-1218.
2. Chetty, A., Ghai, O.P., Guleria. (1975). Pulmonary Functions studies in normal children. *Indian Pediatr* 12 (8), 647-651.
3. Chowgule, R.V., Shetye, V.M., Parmar, J.R. (1995). Lung function tests in normal Indian children. *Indian Pediatr* 32, 185-191.
4. Cotes, J.E. (1993). Lung functions throughout life: Determinants and reference values. Lung function: Assessment and Application in Medicine, 5th edn, Ed Cotes JE. London, Blackwell Scientific Publications, 445-513.
5. Dickman, M.L., Schmidt, C.D., Gardener, R.M. (1971). Spirometric standards for normal children and adolescents. *Am Rev Respir Dis* 104, 680-687.
6. Jain, S.K. and Ramiah,T.J. (1968). Lung volumes and mechanics of breathing in healthy boys 7-14 years old. *Indian J of Chest Dis* 10, 63-68.
7. Jain, S.K. and Ramiah, T.J. (1968). Prediction of ventilatory 'norms' in healthy boys 7-14 years age. *Indian J of Chest Dis* 10, 69-78.
8. Katharine, H.K., Daniel, E.J., Bartholomew, P.H., Thompson, V., Hsieh, B.S. (1979). Ventilatory functions of normal children and young adults-Mexican-American, White and black. I. Spirometry. *J of Pediatr* 95 (1), 14-23.

9. Kauffmann, F., Trager, I.B., Munoz, A., Speizer, F.E. (1989). Familial factors related to lung function in children aged 6-10 years. *Am J Epedemol* 129 (6), 1289-1299.

10. Kaul, K.K., Mukherji, B., Sundaram, K.R., Goel, R.K.(1983). Growth at adolescence II. A study of the development of secondary sex characters in urban boys.. *Indian Pediatr* 20, 249.

11. Mahajan, K.K., Mahajan, A., Misra, N. (1997). Pulmonary Functions in healthy females of haryana. *Indian J Chest Dis Allied Sci* 39, 163-171.

12. Marshall, W.A., Tanner, J.M. (1970). Variations in the pattern of Pubertal changes in boys. *Arch. Dis Child* 45, 13.

13. Miller, G.J., Aschcroft, M.T.,Swan, A.V.,Beadnell, H.M.S.G. (1971). Ethnic variation in forced expiratory volume and forced vital capacity of African and Indian adults in Guyana. *Am Rev Respir Dis* 104, 128- 131.

14. Munro, B.H. (1997). Regression. In Statistical Methods for Health Care Research, 3rd edn, Ed Munro BH. Lippincott., 246-309.

15. Nair, H.R., Kesavachandran, C., Sanil, R., Sreekumar, R. (1997). Prediction equation for lung functions in South Indian children. *Indian J Physiol Pharmacol* 41, 390-396.

16. Pagtakhan, R.D., Bjelland, J.C., Landau, L.I. (1985). Sex differences in growth patterns of the airways and lung parenchyma in children. *J Appl Physiol* 56, 1204-10.

17. Pamecha, R.K. (1984). Sequential changes at puberty in boys. *Indian J Pediatr* 51, 533-536.

18. Penfold, J.L., Boulton, T.J.C., Thomsett, M.J., Harvey, G., Crompton, S.E., Vimpani, A. (1980). Hormonal profile of puberty in south Australian children II. *Austr Paediatr* 16, 17-28.

19. Pierson, D.J., Nathern, P.D., Thomas, P.L.(1976). A comparison of spirometric values with subjects in standing and sitting positions. *Chest* 70, 17-20.

20. Polgar, G., Weng, T.R. (1979). The functional development of the respiratory system from the period of gestation to adulthood. *Am Rev Respir Dis* 120, 675-695.

21. Rajesh, C..S., Gupta, P., Vaney, N. (2000). Status of pulmonary function tests in adolescent females of Delhi. *Indian J Physiol Pharmacol* 44(4), 442-448.

22. Rajkapoor, K., Mahajan, K., Mahajan, A. (1997). Ventilatory Lung function tests in school children of 6-13 years. *Indian J Chest Dis Allied Sci* 39, 97-105.

23. Roizin, H., Sceinberg, A., Tabachunk, E., Morico, M. (1993). Ethnic differences in lung function in Israeli children. *Thorax* 48, 906-910.

24. Saunders, D.B., Trapp, R.G. (1990). Comparing three or more means (Chapter 8), Statistical methods for multiple variables (Chapter 12). In Basic and Clinical Biostatistics, Appelton & Lange, 124-282.

25. Schoenberg, J.B., Beck, B.J., Bouhuys, A. (978). Growth and decay of pulmonary functions in healthy blacks and whites. *Resp Physiol* 33, 367 - 393.

26. Schwartz, J.D., Katz,A.S., Fegley, R.W., Tockman, M.S. (1988). Analysis of spirometric data from a national sample of healthy 6 to 24 year olds (NHANES II). *Am Rev Respir Dis* 138, 1405-1414.

7. Sharma, P.P., Gupta, P., Deshpande, R., Gupta, P. (1997). Lung Function values in healthy children (10-15 years). *Indian J Pediatr* 64, 85-91.

8. Sidhu, L.S., Bhatnagar, D.P. and Dubey, A.P. (1982). Secular trends in heights and weights of Punjabi boys. *Anthrop. Anz* 40, 187-192.

9. Singh, S.P., Singh, P.P. and Bala, S. (1998). Menarcheal status and physical structure of Punjabi Girls. *J. Hum. Ecol* 9, 47-52.

). Taranger, J.(1983). Secular changes in sexual maturation. *Acta Med. Auxol* 15, 137-150.

. Taussing, L.M., Chernick, V., Wood, R. (1980). Standardization of lung function testing in children: Proceeding and recommendations of the GAP conference committee. *J Pediatr* 97, 668-676.

. Wyshak, G. (1983). Secular changes in age at menarche in a sample of U.S. women . *Ann. Hum. Biol* 10, 75-77.

AIRWAY RAPIDLY ADAPTING RECEPTORS, INFLAMMATORY MEDIATORS AND ASTHMA

K. RAV

Department of Physiology, V. P. Chest Institut
University of Delhi, Delhi - 11000

SUMMARY

1. Experiments performed in the rabbit, cat, dog and the monkey demonstrate that an increase in the pulmonary extra-vascular volume produced by mild elevations of left atrial pressure stimulates the airway rapidly adapting receptors (RARs). A reduction in the plasma oncotic pressure and an obstruction to pulmonary lymph flow also stimulate them. These findings suggest that the natural stimulus for the RARs is a fluid flux in the pulmonary extra-vascular space. This conclusion is supported by the following findings:

A. Lung autocoids such as histamine, bradykinin and prostaglandins stimulate the RARs. Since these chemicals increase bronchovenular permeability, their excitatory effect upon the RARs is partly due to fluid flux in the pulmonary extra-vascular space.

B. Inhalation of irritant gases such as smoke from cigarettes and injection of tachykinins such as substance P stimulate the RARs. Since pulmonary congestion sensitises the RARs and produces an exaggerated stimulation during smoke inhalation and substance P injection, it is proposed that the underlying mechanism behind the stimulation is again in part due to a fluid flux in the pulmonary extra-vascular space.

2. Evidence is presented to show that following the activation of the RARs, there is a reflex increase in tracheal tone, bronchial secretion and cough. A mechanism has been proposed for the cough response wherein it has been

proposed that the C-fiber receptors cause cough indirectly by liberating chemicals which increase permeability of bronchial blood vessels which in turn stimulates the RARs.

3. Asthma is an inflammatory disease and airway inflammation is caused by a number of chemicals. These chemicals stimulate the RARs, the activation of which results in bronchoconstriction, airway secretion and cough. Thus, the RARs constitute an important afferent mechanism for the respiratory symptoms of asthma.

INTRODUCTION

Asthma is a disease characterized by airway inflammation with infiltration of lymphocytes, mast cells, eosinophils etc.,. There is epithelial desquamation and thickening of the tissues of the airways. During an acute attack of asthma, there is dyspnea and wheezing with cough. Atopy is a predisposing factor for asthma and most of these subjects have hyper-reactive airways. An attack of bronchial asthma may be precipitated by several triggering factors such as pollens from grasses, weeds and trees, house dust mite, fungi, animal dander, certain food items and environmental factors such as cigarette smoke, diesel fumes etc., On exposure to these triggering factors, there is the liberation of mediators such as histamine, bradykinin, leucotrines, neuropeptides, prostaglandins, thromboxanes, and platelet activating factor which promote inflammation by increasing the permeability of bronchial blood vessels. Additionally, these chemicals may act directly upon the hyper-reactive airways and produce a bronchospasm. Alternatively, they may stimulate the underlying sensory receptors and produce reflex mechanisms which account for some of the respiratory symptoms of asthma. The present review will deal with this 'neural component' of asthma only. Recent studies indicate that among the airway sensory receptors, the rapidly adapting receptors (RARs) are particularly sensitive to fluid fluxes in the airways (Ravi & Kappagoda, 1990). Thus, the main focus would be the responses of

RARs to stimuli which promote fluid fluxes in the extra-vascular space of the airways, their stimulation by histamine, bradykinin, prostaglandins, 5-HT, substance P and cigarette smoke, and their role in increasing airway tone, mucus secretion and cough. For information on the behaviour of the remaining vagal sensory receptors to these stimuli, the reader should consult some excellent reviews which have been written on this subject (Coleridge & Coleridge, 1984,1986).

CLASSIFICATION OF AIRWAY SENSORY RECEPTORS

There are four major types of vagal sensory receptors in the airways. These include: the slowly adapting pulmonary stretch receptors (SARs), the rapidly adapting "irritant" receptors (RARs), the bronchial C-fiber receptors and the pulmonary C-fiber (type J) receptors. Among these, the SARs and RARs are connected to myelinated vagal afferents. The SARs are identified by their characteristic respiratory rhythm and slow adaptation to a maintained inflation (Fig. 1). The RARs have an irregular resting discharge and they are identified by their rapid adaptation to a maintained inflation (Fig. 1). The bronchial C-fiber receptors, as the name implies, are preferentially accessible to chemicals such as bradykinin injected into the bronchial circulation and the pulmonary C-fiber receptors, to capsaicin and phenyl diguanide injected into the pulmonary circulation (Coleridge & Coleridge, 1984). Both these groups of receptors have negligible spontaneous activity.

PULMONARY EXTRA-VASCULAR FLUID AND RARS

Experimentally, an increase in the pulmonary extra-vascular fluid volume can be achieved by raising the intra-vascular hydrostatic pressure, lowering the plasma oncotic pressure and by interfering with the mechanisms which promote the clearance of fluid from this region.

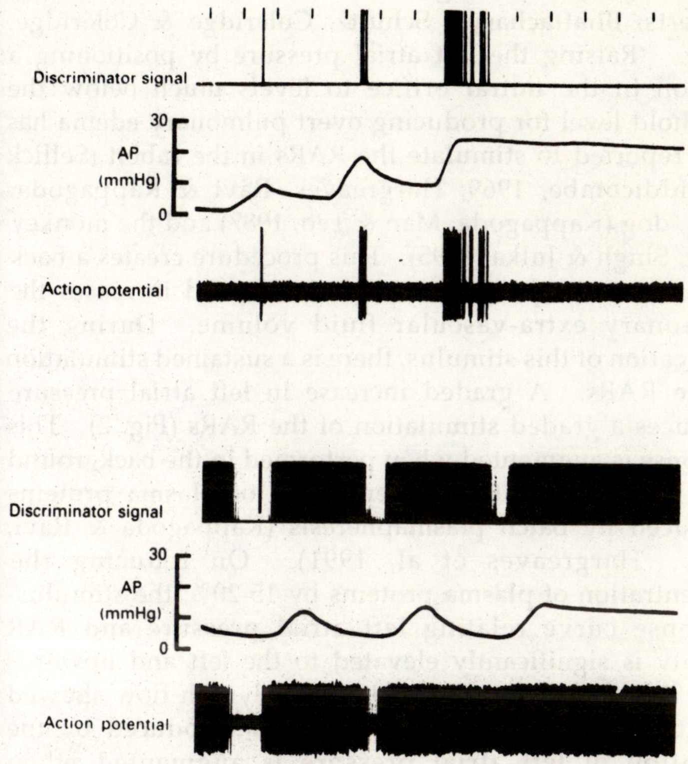

Figure 1 : Examples of RAR (top) and SAR showing response to a maintained inflation. Note that during the maintained inflation, the RAR alone shows rapid adaptation. The lungs were inflated for three successive breaths by occluding the expiratory port of the ventilator and at the peak of the third breath, the inspiratory port was also occluded. From above downwards, the tracings are: time marker (s), the processed signal from discriminator, airway pressure (AP) and action potentials (Reproduced from J. Physiol. 432: 81-97, 1991).

The hydrostatic pressure inside the vasculature can be increased by volume overload and by raising the pressure in the heart. It has been demonstrated that in the dog during intravenous infusion of isotonic Krebs-Henseleit solution (20% of body weight), along with the C-fiber receptors, there is a significant stimulation of the RARs (Roberts, Bhattacharya, Schultz, Coleridge & Coleridge, 1986). Raising the left atrial pressure by positioning a balloon in the mitral orifice to levels much below the threshold level for producing overt pulmonary edema has been reported to stimulate the RARs in the rabbit (Sellick & Widdicombe, 1969; Hargreaves, Ravi & Kappagoda, 1991), dog (Kappagoda, Man & Teo, 1987) and the monkey (Ravi, Singh & Julka, 1995). This procedure creates a back pressure in the pulmonary vasculature and increases the pulmonary extra-vascular fluid volume. During the application of this stimulus, there is a sustained stimulation of the RARs. A graded increase in left atrial pressure produces a graded stimulation of the RARs (Fig. 2). This response is augmented when performed in the background of a reduction in the concentration of plasma proteins produced by batch plasmapheresis (Kappagoda & Ravi, 1989; Hargreaves et al. 1991). On reducing the concentration of plasma proteins by 15-20%, the stimulus-response curve relating left atrial pressure and RAR activity is significantly elevated to the left and upwards (Fig. 3). Measurement of pulmonary lymph flow showed that the increase in basal lymph flow produced by the elevation of left atrial pressure is augmented when performed in the background of batch plasmapheresis (Kappagoda & Ravi, 1989). There is an intense stimulation of the RARs when the left atrial pressure is raised to levels sufficient enough to cause overt pulmonary edema (LAP > 20 mmHg) (Ravi & Kappagoda, 1992).

Since an increase in extra-vascular fluid volume stimulates the RARs, it is conceivable that a mechanical obstruction to the clearance of fluid from this region should stimulate these receptors. It is known that the lymph from the lungs is drained mainly by the right lymphatic ducts and these ducts open into the right external jugular vein at the lower part of the neck (Warren & Drinker, 1942; Uhley, Leeds, Sampson & Friedman, 1961). A vascularly isolated pouch was created in this

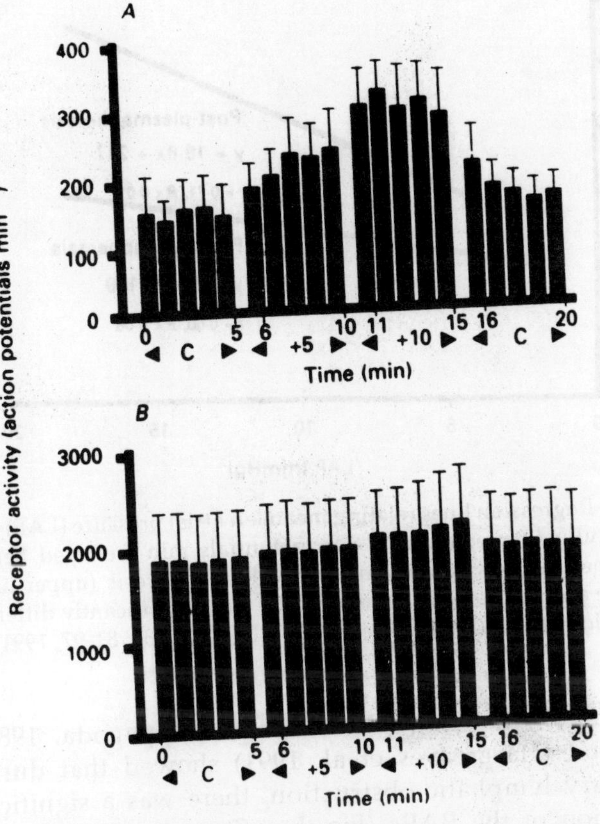

Figure 2 : Receptor activity (mean + SEM) expressed as action potentials min^{-1} during: initial control period (C), elevation of mean left atrial pressure by 5 (+5) and 10 (+10) mmHg and final control period (C). A - RAR activity (n=12); the values during +5 and +10 were significantly different from each other and from the control values ($P < 0.05$). The control values were similar to each other ($P > 0.05$). B - SAR activity (n=12); the values during +10 were significantly different from the other values ($P < 0.05$) (Reproduced from J. Physiol. 432: 81-97, 1991).

region by tying off the venous tributories and a cannula connected to a saline reservoir was placed in it (Fig. 4). By raising the level of the reservoir, it was possible to obstruct the outflow of lymph from the lung. Experiments

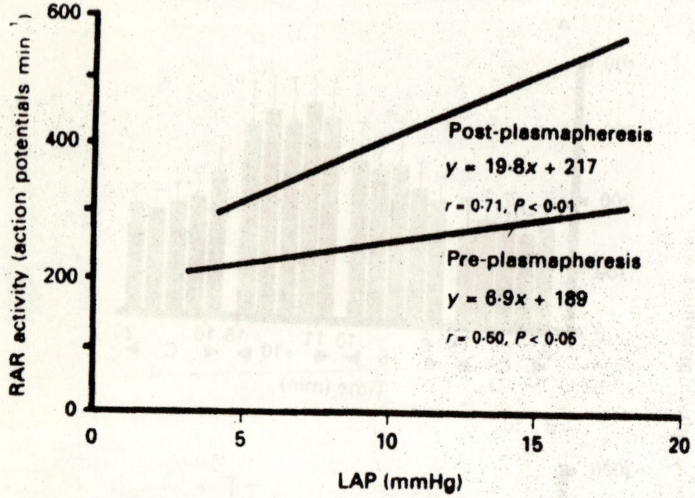

Figure 3 : Regression lines relating mean left atrial pressure (LAP) and RAR activity (expressed as action potentials min^{-1}) elicited before plasmapheresis (lower line) and after plasmapheresis (upper line). The slope and intercept of the upper line were significantly different from the lower line (Reproduced from J. Physiol. 432: 81-97, 1991).

performed in the dog (Ravi, Teo & Kappagoda, 1988a) and rabbit (Hargreaves et al. 1991) showed that during pulmonary lymphatic obstruction, there was a significant stimulation of the RARs (Fig. 5). Since the basal lymph flow in the dog is about 1.6 ml/hr (Uhley et al. 1961) and that in the rabbit is 0.35 ml/hr (Hughes, May & Widdicombe, 1956), it is proposed that the RARs are exquisitely sensitive to fluid fluxes in the pulmonary extra-vascular space. Thus, the natural stimulus for the RARs is a fluid flux in the extra-vascular space of the airways.

RARS AND LUNG AUTOCOIDS

The role of vagal afferents in the respiratory symptoms of asthma has been primarily due to the effect of lung autocoids on different sensory receptors of the airways. Even though the effects of lung autocoids have been

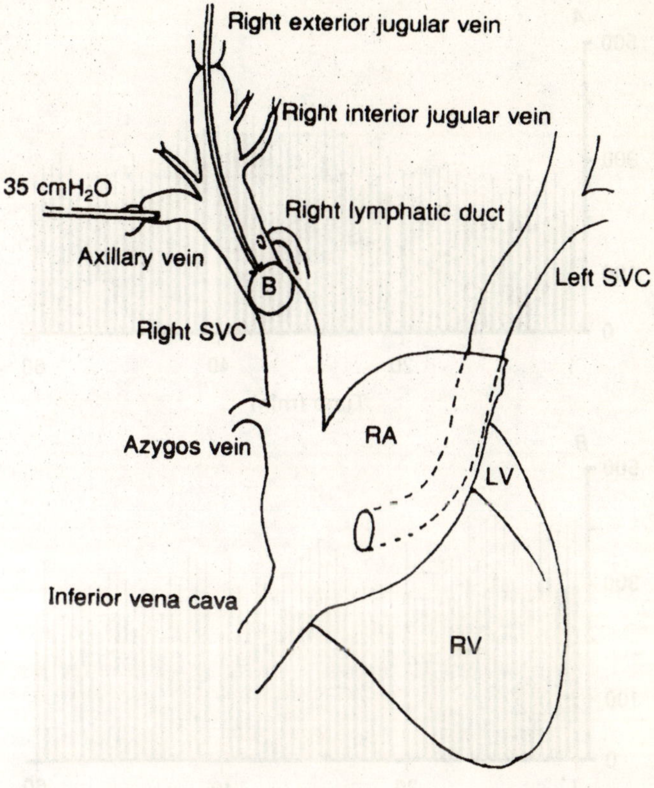

Figure 4 : Mechanical obstruction of pulmonary lymph flow. Pulmonary lymphatic obstruction was produced by creating a pouch in the right external jugular vein after inflating the balloon (B) and by connecting the cannula in the axillary vein to a saline reservoir which was kept at a height of 35 cm above the right atrium. Pulmonary lymphatic obstruction was relieved by deflating the balloon and lowering the level of the reservoir to that of the right atrium. The rest of the venous tributories were ligated. RA, right atrium; RV, right ventricle; SVC, superior vena cava (Reproduced from J. Physiol. 503: 833-840, 1997).

evaluated mostly upon the RARs and the C-fibers, the present review will be centered around the studies pertaining to RARs only.

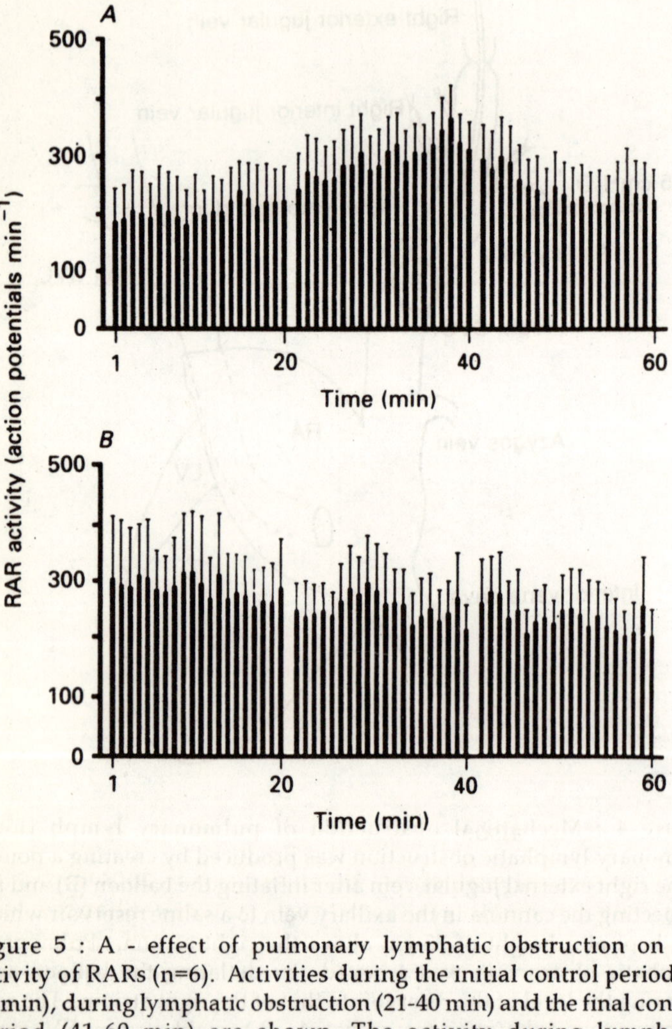

Figure 5 : A - effect of pulmonary lymphatic obstruction on the activity of RARs (n=6). Activities during the initial control period (1-20 min), during lymphatic obstruction (21-40 min) and the final control period (41-60 min) are shown. The activity during lymphatic obstruction was significantly different from those during the control periods ($P < 0.05$). B - spontaneous variation in the activity of RARs (n=5) with time. Activities were recorded continuously for 60 min. Note that the increase in RAR activity observed during lymphatic obstruction in A is different from the changes attributable to spontaneous variation. Bars represent +SEM (Reproduced from J. Physiol. 432: 81-97, 1991).

HISTAMINE

Administration of histamine as an injection or as an aerosol activates the RARs in a number of species - guinea-pigs (Bergren & Sampson, 1982), rabbits (Mills, Sellick & Widdicombe, 1969), cats (Armstrong & Luck, 1974), dog (Sampson & Vidruk, 1975) and the monkey (Ravi et al. 1995). The mechanism of action of histamine may either be direct or indirect. Since the RARs are located adjacent to airway smooth muscle (Das, Jeffery & Widdicombe, 1979), it has been postulated that the effect of histamine on RARs could be secondary to the bronchoconstriction produced by histamine. Evidence in support of this proposition was provided in the studies in rabbits, in which it was shown that the stimulatory effect of histamine on RARs was reduced after the administration of isoproterenol (Mills et al. 1969). Unlike the rabbit, in the dog, isoproterenol failed to inhibit the histamine-induced RAR excitation. Moreover, compared to histamine, acetylcholine produced only a weaker stimulation of RARs even though it produced an equal degree of bronchoconstriction (Vidruk, Hahn, Nadel & Sampson, 1977; Dixon, Jackson & Richards, 1979). These findings suggest that histamine may have a direct excitatory effect upon the RARs also.

In the peripheral circulation, histamine increases the permeability of the systemic venules and enhances the lymph flow (Haddy, Scott & Grega, 1972). In the bronchial circulation also, histamine causes bronchial edema by increasing bronchovenular permeability (Pietra & Fishman, 1978). Since an increase in the extra-vascular fluid volume stimulates the RARs, it is likely that histamine induced excitation of RARs may be due to this fluid flux. Experiments performed in the dog showed that during pulmonary lymphatic obstruction, even sub-threshold doses of bolus injections of histamine stimulated the RARs. This response occurred in spite of no significant change in airway pressure (Ravi, Teo & Kappagoda, 1988b). In the background of pulmonary lymphatic obstruction, the stimulus-response curve relating histamine and RAR activity was shifted to the left when compared with that elicited in the control state (Fig. 6). An infusion of histamine not only produced a sustained stimulation of RARs, but also increased the pulmonary lymph flow

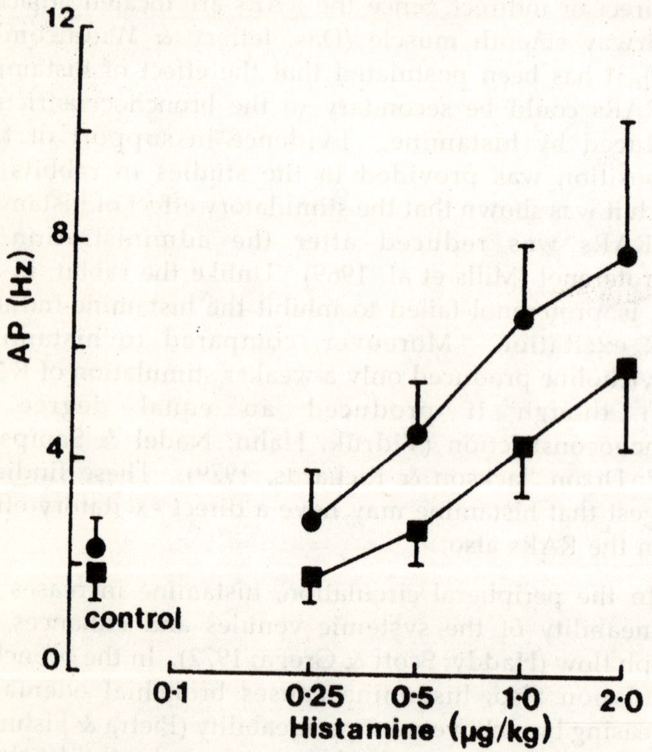

Figure 6 : Dose-response curve relating histamine and RAR activity (n=7) before (•) and after (▪) pulmonary lymphatic obstruction. "Control" denotes the activities during the control periods before injecting histamine. The shift to the left observed after lymphatic obstruction was significant ($P < 0.05$). Abscissa - histamine doses (mg/kg - log scale. Ordinate - RAR activity (Hz). AP - action potentials (Reproduced from Can. J, Physiol. & Pharmacol. 67: 1499-1505, 1989.

(Kappagoda, Ravi & Teo, 1988). All these findings suggest that fluid flux is one way by which histamine stimulates RARs.

BRADYKININ

Bradykinin has a variable effect upon the RARs. In the dog, it stimulates a few of them only (Kaufman, Coleridge, Coleridge & Baker, 1980). Even when there was a stimulation, it appeared to be secondary to changes in lung compliance. In contrast, in the rabbit, bradykinin produced a significant activation of the RARs (Hargreaves, Ravi, & Kappagoda, 1993) (Fig. 7). At the threshold dose, the excitation occurred without a significant change in airway pressure. Since bradykinin also increases bronchovenular permeability (Pietra & Fishman, 1978), it is postulated that its mechanism of action upon RARs may be similar to histamine.

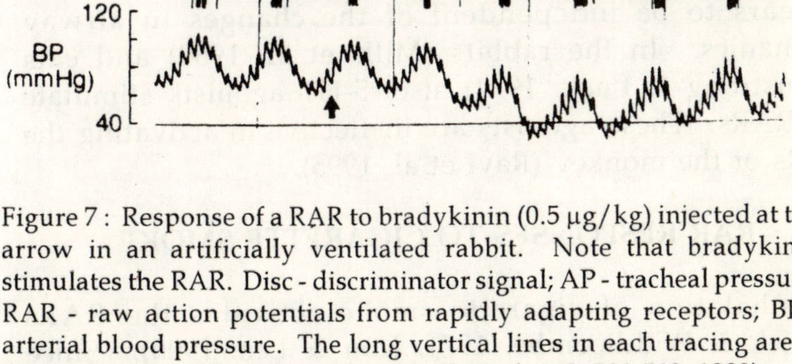

Figure 7 : Response of a RAR to bradykinin (0.5 μg/kg) injected at the arrow in an artificially ventilated rabbit. Note that bradykinin stimulates the RAR. Disc - discriminator signal; AP - tracheal pressure; RAR - raw action potentials from rapidly adapting receptors; BP - arterial blood pressure. The long vertical lines in each tracing are at intervals of 5 s (Reproduced from J. Physiol. 468: 501-513, 1993).

PROSTAGLANDINS

Several prostaglandins stimulate the RARs. In the dog, when prostaglandin $F_2\alpha$ was injected into the right atrium, it stimulated the RARs (Coleridge, Coleridge, Ginzel, Baker Banzett & Morrison, 1976). This effect was attenuated in presence of isoproterenol. Injection of prostaglandin E_2 into the right atrium produced only a mild stimulation of RARs (Roberts et al. 1985). In the cat also, the thromboxane A_2 mimetic, U46619 produced only a moderate stimulation of RARs (Karla, Shams, Orr & Scheid, 1992). Another study in the cat showed that administration of increasing doses of prostaglandin E_2 as an aerosol caused a dose-dependent increase in RAR activity and bronchoconstriction (Mohammed, Higenbottam & Adcock, 1993). Even though bronchoconstriction by itself can activate the RARs, the prostaglandin induced stimulation may be due to an increase in the fluid flux also as during bronchoconstriction, there would be passive compression of the veins draining the bronchial mucosa.

5-HYDROXYTRYPTAMINE

5-hydroxytryptamine agonists also have a variable effect upon RARs. In the dog, i.v. injection of 5-HT activates the RARs (Dixon et al. 1979). This activation appears to be independent of the changes in airway mechanics. In the rabbits (Mills et al. 1969) and cats (Armstrong & Luck, 1974) also, 5-HT agonists stimulate the RARs. These agonists are ineffective in activating the RARs of the monkey (Ravi et al. 1995).

RAR RESPONSES TO CIGARETTE SMOKE

Inhalation of cigarette smoke activates the RARs (Sellick & Widdicombe, 1971; Kou & Lee, 1990). Since nicotine injection also stimulates the RARs, it appears that nicotine in the cigarette smoke contributes to this response

(Zhang & Bonham, 1995). Nicotine may produce a direct excitation of RARs. It may stimulate the RARs by promoting a fluid flux also. For instance, in the background of mild degrees of pulmonary congestion just below the threshold level required to stimulate the RARs (mean left atrial pressure increased by 2-4 mm Hg only), inhalation of smoke from low-nicotine cigarettes produces a response which is markedly exaggerated compared to the one elicited by smoke alone (Ravi, Kappagoda & Bonham, 1994) (Fig. 8).

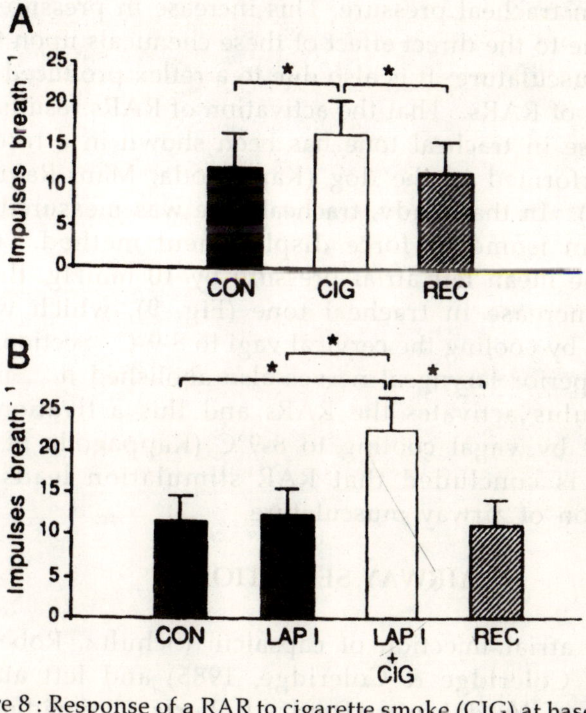

gure 8 : Response of a RAR to cigarette smoke (CIG) at baseline (A), sub-threshold increases in left atrial pressure (LAP1) alone and mbination of LAP1+CIG (B). Note that CIG alone stimulates the AR and this stimulation is exaggerated in presence of mild degress pulmonary congestion. RAR activity expressed as impulses/breath. ON - control period; REC - recovery period. *Significantly different, < 0.05 (Reproduced from J. Appl. Physiol. 77(6): 2633-2640).

REFLEX RESPONSES

During an asthma attack, there are three prominent respiratory symptoms. These are: bronchoconstriction, airway secretion and cough. Inflammation of the airways enhances the excitability of the RARs and activation of RARs produces all these responses.

BRONCHOCONSTRICTION

As reviewed above, during the exogenous administration of inflammatory mediators, there is an increase in tracheal pressure. This increase in pressure is in part due to the direct effect of these chemicals upon the airway musculature It is also due to a reflex produced by activation of RARs. That the activation of RARs results in an increase in tracheal tone has been shown in a recent study performed in the dog (Kappagoda, Man, Ravi & Teo, 1988). In that study, tracheal tone was measured *in vivo* by an isometric force displacement method. On raising the mean left atrial pressure by 10 mmHg, there was an increase in tracheal tone (Fig. 9), which was abolished by cooling the cervical vagi to 8-9°C. Sectioning of the superior laryngeal nerves also abolished it. Since this stimulus activates the RARs and this activation is abolished by vagal cooling to 8-9°C (Kappagoda et al. 1988), it is concluded that RAR stimulation leads to constriction of airway musculature.

AIRWAY SECRETION

Right atrial injection of capsaicin (Schultz, Roberts, Bratcher, Coleridge & Coleridge, 1985) and left atrial injection of bradykinin (Davis, Roberts, Coleridge & Coleridge, 1982) increase tracheal sub-mucosal gland secretion in dogs. Inhalation of cigarette smoke also increases airway secretion. These responses are due to the stimulation of RARs (Ravi et al. 1994) and the C-fiber

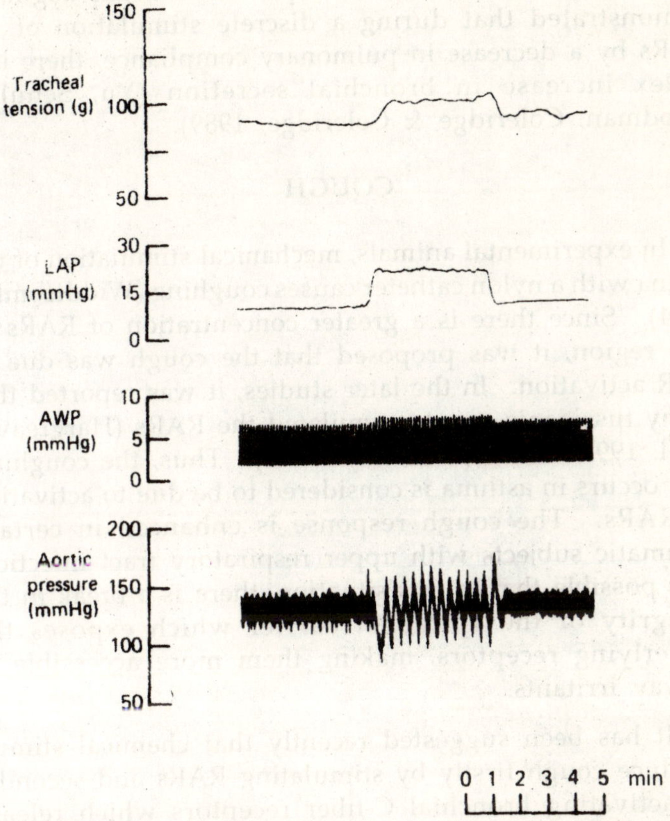

Figure 9 : Effect of pulmonary venous congestion on tracheal tension. Pulmonary venous congestion was produced by raising mean left atrial pressure by 10 mmHg. Note the increase in tracheal tension and the increase in peak airway pressure following elevation of left atrial pressure. During this procedure, there were "swings" in the aortic blood pressure; but, the mean blood pressure was prevented from falling by inflating a balloon positioned in the lower descending aorta. LAP - left atrial pressure; AWP - airway pressure (Reproduced from J. Physiol. 402: 335-346, 1988).

receptors (Lee, 1988). Recent experiments in the dog have demonstrated that during a discrete stimulation of the RARs by a decrease in pulmonary compliance, there is a reflex increase in bronchial secretion (Yu, Schultz, Goodman, Coleridge & Coleridge, 1989).

COUGH

In experimental animals, mechanical stimulation of the carina with a nylon catheter causes coughing (Widdicombe, 1974). Since there is a greater concentration of RARs in this region, it was proposed that the cough was due to RAR activation. In the later studies, it was reported that many tussigenic agents stimulated the RARs (Hargreaves et al. 1992; Mohammed et al. 1993). Thus, the coughing that occurs in asthma is considered to be due to activation of RARs. The cough response is enhanced in certain asthmatic subjects with upper respiratory tract infection. It is possible that in this situation, there is a break in the integrity of the epithelial barrier which exposes the underlying receptors, making them more accessible to airway irritants.

It has been suggested recently that chemical stimuli produce cough firstly by stimulating RARs and secondly by activating bronchial C-fiber receptors which release tachykinins (Widdicombe, 1995). The tachykinin liberated from C-fibers increases the bronchovenular permeability which in turn activates the RARs (Bonham, Kott, Ravi, Kappagoda & Joad, 1996). That such a mechanism is possible has been shown recently in the rabbit (Bonham et al. 1996) (Figs. 10 and 11). In that study, it was reported that substance P produced a dose-dependent excitation of the RARs. Additionally, even sub-threshold doses of substance P stimulated the RARs when injected in the background of mild degrees of pulmonary congestion just below the threshold level required for the excitation of RARs (mean left atrial pressure increased by 2 mmHg, Fig. 10). It has been proposed that selective stimulants for

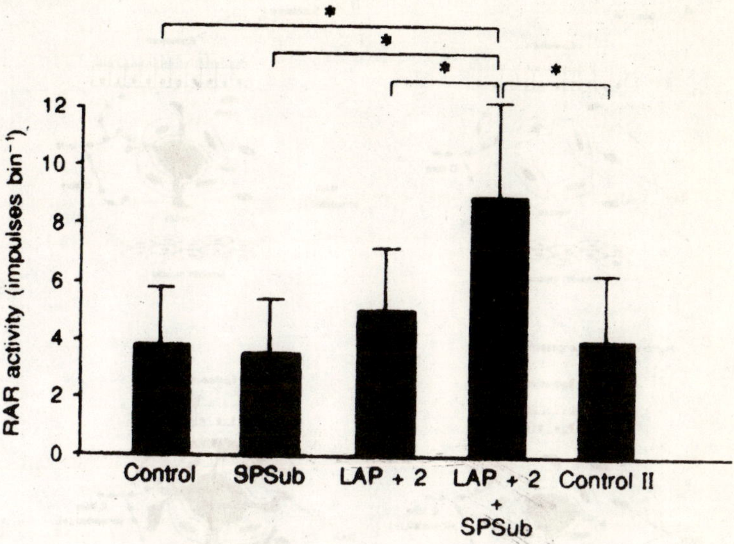

Figure 10 : Responses of a RAR to sub-threshold doses of substance P (SPSub), near-threshold increases in left atrial pressure (LAP + 2 mmHg) and the combination of the two (LAP + 2 + SPSub). Neither SPSub nor LAP + 2 changed RAR activity from control; but, their combination increased RAR activity significantly (n=7, * $P < 0.05$) (Reproduced from J. Physiol. 493(1): 229-238, 1996).

C-fiber receptors liberate tachykinins from these endings. These neurokinins would promote bronchovenular permeability and produce a subtle increase in extra-vascular fluid volume. When this stimulus is paired with near threshold levels of pulmonary congestion, the combination stimulates the RARs (Fig. 11).

In summary, the materials reviewed thus far suggest that airway inflammation is a potent stimulus for the RARs and their activation accounts for some of the respiratory symptoms of asthma..

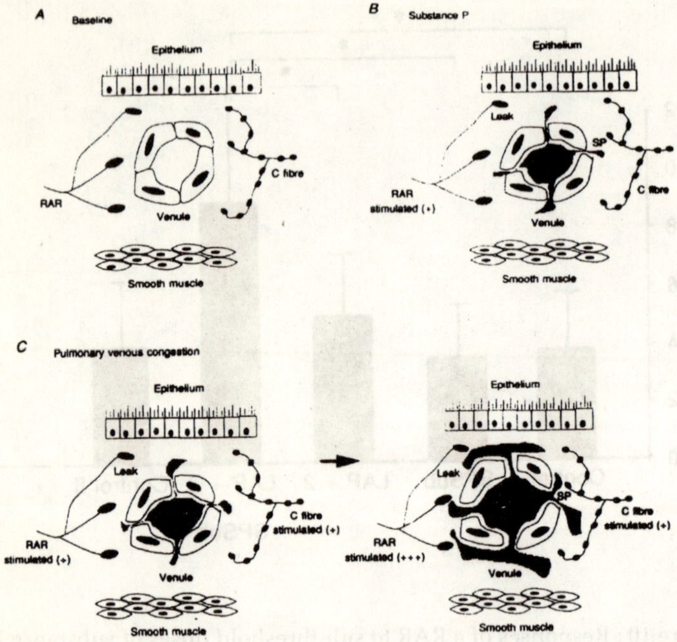

Figure 11 : Model for the interaction between RAR and C-fiber receptors. A: nerve endings of RAR and C-fiber receptors in close proximity to bronchial venule. B: Release of substance P from C-fiber receptors which increases endothelial permeability. The resulting fluid flux stimulates the RAR. C: Mild levels of pulmonary venous congestion produce moderate increases in hydrostatic pressure (↑Pv) within the venule which causes a mechanically induced microvascular leak that stimulates the RAR and C-fiber receptor. C-fiber stimulation releases substance P and the substance P induced microvascular leak augments the fluid flux. Thus, there is further stimulation of the RAR (Reproduced from J. Physiol. 493(1): 229-238, 1996). Such an interaction may account for the cough caused by some selective stimulants of C-fiber receptors such as capsaicin.

ACKNOWLEDGEMENTS

The author is grateful to Indian Council of Medical Research, New Delhi, for partial financial assistance.

REFERENCES

ARMSTRONG, D.J. & LUCK, J.G. (1974). A comparative study on irritant and type J receptors in the cat. *Respiration Physiology* 21, 47-60.

BERGREN, D.R. & SAMPSON, S.R. (1982). Characterization of intrapulmonary rapidly adapting receptors in guinea-pigs. *Respiration Physiology* 47, 83-95.

BONHAM, A.C., KOTT, K.S., RAVI, K., KAPPAGODA, C.T. & JOAD, J.P. (1996). Substance P contributes to rapidly adapting receptor responses to pulmonary venous congestion in rabbits. *Journal of Physiology* 493 (1), 229-238.

COLERIDGE, H.M. & COLERIDGE, J.C.G. (1986). Reflexes evoked from the tracheobronchial tree and lungs. In: *Handbook of Physiology, Section 3, The Respiratory System*, Vol. II, ed. CHERNIACK, N.S. & WIDDICOMBE, J.G., pp. 395-429. American Physiological Society.

COLERIDGE, H.M., COLERIDGE, J.C.G., GINZEL, K.H., BAKER, D.G., BANZETT, R.B. & MORRISON, M.A. (1976). Stimulation of irritant receptors and afferent C-fibers in the lungs by prostaglandins. *Nature* 264, 451-453.

COLERIDGE, J.C.G. & COLERIDGE, H.M. (1984). Afferent vagal C-fiber innervation of the lungs and airways and its functional significance. *Review of Physiological and Biochemical Pharmacology* 99, 1-110.

DAS, R.M., JEFFREY, P.K. & WIDDICOMBE, J.G. (1979). Experimental degeneration of intra-epithelial nerve fibers in the cat airways. *Journal of Anatomy* 128, 259-267.

DAVIS, B., ROBERTS, A.M., COLERIDGE, H.M. & COLERIDGE, J.C.G. (1982). Reflex tracheal gland secretion evoked by stimulation of bronchial C-fibers in dogs. *Journal of Applied Physiology* 53, 985-991.

DIXON, M., JACKSON, D.M. & RICHARDS, I.M. (1979). The effects of histamine, acetylcholine and 5-hydroxytryptamine on lung mechanics and irritant receptors in the dog. *Journal of Physiology* 287, 393-403.

HADDY, F., SCOTT, J. & GREGA, G.J. (1972). Effects of histamine on lymph protein concentration and flow in the dog forelimbs. *American Journal of Physiology* 223, 1172-1177.

HARGREAVES, M., RAVI, K. & KAPPAGODA, C.T. (1991). Responses of slowly and rapidly adapting receptors in airways of rabbits to changes in the Starling forces. *Journal of Physiology* 432, 81-97.

HARGREAVES, M., RAVI, K & KAPPAGODA, C.T. (1993). Effect of bradykinin on respiratory rate in anesthetized rabbits; role of rapidly adapting receptors. *Journal of Physiology* 468, 501-513.

HUGHES, R., MAY, A.J. & WIDDICOMBE, J.G. (1956). The output of lymphocytes from the lymphatic system of the rabbit. *Journal of Physiology* 132, 384-390.

KAPPAGODA, C.T., MAN, G.C.W., RAVI, K. & TEO, K.K. (1988). Reflex tracheal contraction during pulmonary venous congestion in the dog. *Journal of Physiology* 402, 335-346.

KAPPAGODA, C.T., MAN, G.C.W. & TEO, K.K. (1987). Behaviour of canine vagal afferent receptors during sustained acute pulmonary venous pressure elevation. *Journal of Physiology* 394, 249-265.

KAPPAGODA, C.T. & RAVI, K. (1989). Plasmapheresis affects responses of slowly and rapidly adapting airway receptors to pulmonary venous congestion in dogs. *Journal of Physiology* 416, 79-91.

KAPPAGODA, C.T., RAVI, K. & TEO, K.K. (1988). Effects of histamine (H) infusion on rapidly adapting receptor (RAR) activity and pulmonary lymph flow (PLF). *Physiologist* 31(4), A172.

KARLA, W., SHAMS, H., ORR, J.A. & SCHEID, P. (1992). Effects of the thromboxane A2 mimetic U46619, on pulmonary vagal afferents in the cat. *Respiration Physiology* 87, 383-396.

KOU, Y.R. & LEE, L.Y. (1990). Stimulation of rapidly adapting receptors in canine lung by a single breath of cigarette smoke. *Journal of Applied Physiology* 68(3), 1203-1210.

KAUFMAN, M.P., COLERIDGE, H.M., COLERIDGE, J.C.G. & BAKER, D.G. (1980). Bradykinin stimulates afferent vagal C-fibers in intrapulmonary airways of dogs. *Journal of Applied Physiology* 48(3), 511-517.

LEE, L.Y. (1988). Acute effects of cigarette smoke on the upper airways. In: *Respiration: Functions of the Upper Airways* Vol. 35, ed. MATHEW, O.P. & SANT'AMBROGIO, G. pp. 561-597. Marcel Dekker Inc., New York.

MILLS, J.E., SELLICK, H. & WIDDICOMBE, J.G. (1969). Activity of lung irritant receptors in pulmonary microembolism, anaphylaxis and drug induced bronchoconstriction. *Journal of Physiology* 203, 337-357.

MOHAMMED, S.P., HIGENBOTTAM, T.W. & ADCOCK, J.J. (1993). Effects of aerosol-applied capsaicin, histamine and prostaglandin E2 on airway sensory receptors of anesthetized cats. *Journal of Physiology* 469, 51-66.

PIETRA, G.G. & FISHMAN, A.P. (1978). Bronchial edema. In: *Lung Biology in Health & Disease,* Vol. 7, Lung Water & Solute Exchange, ed. STAUB, N.C. pp. 407-422. Marcel Dekker Inc., New York.

RAVI, K. & KAPPAGODA, C.T. (1990). Reflex effects of pulmonary venous congestion: Role of vagal afferents. *News in Physiological Sciences* 5, 95-99.

RAVI, K. & KAPPAGODA, C.T. (1992). Responses of pulmonary C-fiber and rapidly adapting receptor afferents to pulmonary congestion and edema in dogs. *Canadian Journal of Physiology and Pharmacology* 70, 68-76.

RAVI, K., KAPPAGODA, C.T. & BONHAM, A.C. (1994). Pulmonary venous congestion enhances the responses of lung rapidly adapting receptors to cigarette smoke inhalation in the rabbit. *Journal of Applied Physiology* 77, 2633-2640.

RAVI, K., SINGH, M. & JULKA, D.B. (1995). Properties of rapidly adapting receptors of the airways in monkeys (Macaca mulatta). *Respiration Physiology* 99, 51-62.

RAVI, K., TEO, K.K. & KAPPAGODA, C.T. (1988a). Stimulation of rapidly adapting pulmonary stretch receptors by pulmonary lymphatic obstruction in dogs. *Canadian Journal of Physiology & Pharmacology* 66, 630-636.

RAVI, K., TEO, K.K. & KAPPAGODA, C.T. (1988b). Action of histamine on the rapidly adapting receptors in the dog. *Canadian Journal of Physiology & Pharmacology* 67, 1499-1505.

ROBERTS, A.M., BHATTACHARYA, J., SCHULTZ., H.D., COLERIDGE, H.M. & COLERIDGE, J.C.G. (1986). Stimulation of pulmonary vagal afferent C-fibers by lung edema in dogs. *Circulation Research* 58, 512-522.

ROBERTS, A.M., SCHULTZ, H.D., GREEN, J.F., ARMSTRONG, D.J., KAUFMAN, M.P. et al. (1985). Reflex tracheal contraction evoked in dogs by bronchodilator prostaglandins E2 and I2. *Journal of Applied Physiology* 58, 1823-1831.

SAMPSON, S.R. & VIDRUK, E.H. (1975). Properties of lung irritant receptors in canine lung. *Respiration Physiology* 25, 9-22.

SCHULTZ, H.D., ROBERTS, A.M., BRATCHER, C., COLERIDGE, H.M. & COLERIDGE, J.C.G. (1985). Pulmonary C-fibers reflexly increase secretion by tracheal sub-mucosal glands. *Journal of Applied Physiology* 58, 907-910.

SELLICK, H. & WIDDICOMBE, J.G. (!969). The activity of lung irritant receptors during pneumothorax, hyperpnea and pulmonary vascular congestion. *Journal of Physiology* 203, 359-381.

SELLICK, H. & WIDDICOMBE, J.G. (!971). Stimulation of lung irritant receptors by cigarette smoke, carbon dust, and histamine aerosol. *Journal of Applied Physiology* 31(1), 15-19.

UHLEY, H.N., LEEDS, S.E., SAMPSON, J.J. & FRIEDMAN, M. (1961). Some observations on the role of the lymphatics in experimental acute pulmonary edema. *Circulation Research* 9, 688-693.

VIDRUK, E.H., HAHN, H.L., NADEL, J.A. & SAMPSON, S.R. (1977). Mechanisms by which histamine stimulates rapidly adapting receptors in dog lungs. *Journal of Applied Physiology* 43, 397-402.

WIDDICOMBE, J.G. (1974). Reflexes from the lungs in the control of breathing. In: *Recent Advances in Physiology Series* 9, ed. LINDEN, R.J., pp. 239-278. Churchill Livingstone, London.

WIDDICOMBE, J.G. (1995). Neurophysiology of the cough reflex. *European Respiratory Journal* 8, 1193-1202.

YU, J., SCHULTZ, H.D., GOODMAN, J., COLERIDGE, J.C.G., COLERIDGE, H.M. & DAVIS, B. (1989). Pulmonary rapidly adapting receptors reflexly increase airway secretion in dogs. *Journal of Applied Physiology* 67, 682-687.

ZHANG, Z.& BONHAM, A.C. (1995). Lung congestion augments the responses of cells in the rapidly adapting pathway to cigarette smoke in rabbit. *Journal of Physiology* 484(1), 189-200.

SCAVENGING FREE RADICALS: A NOVEL APPROACH FOR POST TRAUMATIC EPILEPSY

Y.K. GUPTA AND A.K. SRIVASTAVA

Neuropharmacology lab, Department of Pharmacology
All India Institute of medical sciences, New Delhi -29

INTRODUCTION

Epilepsy is one of the most common neurological disorder affecting nearly 0.5% of the world population (Sander and shrovan 1996). Of all the epilepsies post traumatic epilepsy (PTE) has a high clinical relevance. Posttraumatic epilepsy as a consequence of head trauma is known since Hippocrates times. In the 19th century John Huglings Jacknosn established the association between location of wound and seizure pattern. Duretus (1527-1586) attributed epilepsy in 18-year-old man to a skull fracture that had occurred 6 year earlier. Bryan Jenett studied the prevalence, nature and course of posttraumatic epilepsy and suggests a distinction between immediate, early and late seizures (Jenet 1975, Jenet1975). Modern concepts of head injury and epilepsy come from studies of British and American veterans of four major twentieth century wars. Traumatic brain injury, which is a major cause of morbidity and mortality world wide, has been reported to be one of the major risk factor for epileptic seizures. Post-traumatic epilepsy occurs following severe head injury and is characterized by recurrent epileptic seizures due to brain damage (Yokoi 1995). It complicates the management of the head injuries patients by increasing the intracranial pressure and altering the level of unconsciousness. Among the long term complications of traumatic brain injury, post traumatic epilepsy remains one of the most troubling and in the long term, PTE can have a negative effect on patients functioning. The more severe the injury the more likely that post traumatic seizure will occur.

EPIDEMIOLOGY OF PTE

The reported incidence of post-traumatic epilepsy vary from under 5% for head injury in general to 25 to 30% for severe closed head injury with hematoma and up to 51% in survivors of military penetrating head injury (Caveness 1962). In the United States, the annual incidence of head injury is about 200/100,000 population, and men are more often affected than women. All studies show a peak incidence of brain injury in young adults 15 to 24 years of age (Langendorf and Pedley 1997). Next most affected are young children and the elderly. About 10 % of the head injuries are fatal. Early seizures occur in 2-5% of all patients with head injuries and they are more common in children than adults (Annegers et al 1980, Desai et al 1983). The frequency of early seizures after severe head injuries is even higher 10 –15% for adults and 30 –35% for children. Early seizures are followed by late seizures in 25-35% of adults (De santis et al 1992, Jennet 1960). The appearance of seizures late after head injury is a major residual complication and an event that is difficult to predict. Late PTE complicates head trauma in about 7% of the civilians and 34% of combat injured patients, increasing up to 50 % in patients with severe neurotrauma (Annegers et al 1980, Credener 1993). Annegers calculated the relative risk of late post traumatic epilepsy and found it to be 12.7% in the first year, 4.4% during the next four years, 4.4% during the next four years and 1.4% thereafter in the follow up (Annegers 1980).

NATURE AND COURSE OF PTE

A principal form of brain dysfunction after trauma is epilepsy both in acute setting and in the form of chronic epilepsy. Depending on the time interval following head trauma the epilepsy can be classified in to three major types, i.e. (i) impact seizures, (ii) early seizures and (iii) late seizures.

Impact seizures are sometimes considered as subgroup of early seizure and occur immediately after the trauma or within 24 hours after injury.

Early seizures are acute symptomatic seizures that occur as a reaction of the brain to the physical effects of trauma and appear within one week after injury.

Late seizures might have a chronic course and occur after the recovery from the acute effects of the injury. Late seizures may be single or multiple. Only recurrent late seizures are referred as post-traumatic epilepsy proper (Kollevold 1976).

Although trauma accounts for only about 5% of all epilepsy cases, this is still a problem of considerable magnitude. More importantly because it is potentially preventable cause of epilepsy.

RISK FACTORS FOR POST-TRAUMATIC EPILEPSY

Several risk factors complicate the post traumatic epilepsy. Traumatic brain injury is one of the prominent one. Other factors that enhances the risk of PTE are neural location, agent of injury, severity, missile injuries, loss of consciousness, intracerebral hemorrhage, diffuse cerebral contusions, presence of focal neurological deficits and prolonged (>3days) post traumatic amnesia (Ludice and Murri 2000). The presence of an intracerebral hematoma may reflect the intensity of injury; factor such as fiber tract disruption or focal cellular change could be causal in initiation of epileptogenesis.

GENETIC FACTORS AFFECT SUSCEPTIBILITY TO POST TRAUMATIC EPILEPSY

Genetic susceptibility may also increase the risk for epilepsy in the setting of head trauma, especially in individuals with moderate injuries. Genetic influences have long been suspected as a factor in the development of post traumatic seizures. Although some investigators have reported that a family history of epilepsy is more common in subjects in whom epilepsy develops following head injury than those in whom it does not (Caveness 1963,Schaumann et al 1994). The , most careful study to date was unable to demonstrate any increase in the frequency of seizures among relatives of probands with head injury. Specific brain genetic factors that cause a liability to develop post traumatic epilepsy remains unknown; however a possible genetic predisposition has been observed with detection of decreased levels of serum haptoglobin in familial epilepsy (Panter et al 1885)

Haptoglobins are acute phase glycoprotiens in the alpha 1-globulin fraction of serum that forms stable complexes with hemoglobin. Sequestration of free hemoglobin with haptoglobin is one of the mechanisms against oxidative stress. Impairment in the synthesis of these glycoproteins may identify an inherent susceptibility to development of epilepsy after head trauma.

MECHANISM OF POST -TRAUMATIC EPILEPSY

The precise mechanism of epileptogenesis in post - traumatic epilepsy is still poorly understood. However many structural, physiologic and biochemical changes takes place in the brain following head trauma which may accounts for epileptogenesis. Early post traumatic seizures are thought to be due to mechanical damage to the neurons, caused by extravasated blood. Head trauma initiates a sequence of responses that includes altered blood flow and vasoregulation, disruption of blood brain barrier, increase in intracrainal pressure , focal or diffuse ischemia, hemorrhage, inflammation, necrosis and disruption of fiber tract and blood vessels (Gannarelli et al 1982). Histopathologic assessment of traumatized neural tissue reveals formation of axonal retraction balls, reactive gliosis, wallerian degeneration and microglial scar formation with in cystic white matter(Langfitt et al 1966, Tornheim et al 1983). Reports have suggested that iron (hemorrhage) induced neuronal lipid peroxidation and excitotoxicity could be the probable mechanism, involved in the post traumatic epilepsy.

EXCITOTOXICITY AS A MECHANISM

Both clinical and experimental studies have demonstrated immediate and marked increased in the extracellular level of excitatory amino acid following brain injury(Bullock et al 1998;Katayama et al 1990). In rats seizure occurring immediately or shortly after traumatic injury are accompanied by increased glutamate and aspartate levels(Nilson et al 1994). This may be responsible for epileptogenesis. Release of excitatory amino acid may also be responsible for the large calcium - dependent increase in extra cellular potassium seen after experimental brain injury (Katayama et al 1990). Increased extra cellular potassium further increases neuronal excitability and may contribute to epileptogenesis.

OXIDATIVE STRESS MECHANISM

It has been proposed that reactive oxygen species (ROS), especially OH, are involved in the mechanism responsible for post-traumatic epilepsy. In 1978 Willmore et al reported an animal model of post traumatic epilepsy. They showed that epileptic seizure discharge in electrocorticogram (ECOG) was induced 15 minutes after a single injection of $FeCl_2$ solution into the rat cerebral cortex (Willmore 1978). In 1979, Rosen and Prumin also suggest that convulsive seizures were induced by intracortical hemoglobin (Hb) injection with a few days latency (Rosen and Prumin 1979). Willmore and Rubin suggested that after intracranial hemorrhage red blood cells break down and release iron ions from hemoglobin and then ROS are generated in brain tissue by iron or Hb mediated reaction. These free radicals react with methylene group adjacent to double bond of (PUFA) and lipids with cellular membranes causing hydrogen abstractions and subsequent propagation of peroxidation reaction.

This non enzymatic initiation and propagation of lipid peroxidation causes disruption of membranes and subcellular organelles, degrades deoxyrylose and amino acids and yields diene conjugates and florescent chromo fore. Injury to membranes impairs Na^+-K^+ ATPase activity. As Na^+K^+ ATPase in neuronal membranes maintains ionic gradients of neuron, a decrease in its activity decreases the convulsive threshold. Injury to the membrane also leads to neurotransmitter disorders.

The release of aspartic acid, which is a well known excitatory neurotransmitter increases and the release of GABA, which is an inhibitor neurotransmitter decreases (Zhang et al 1989). Apart from this OH accelerates the production of methylguonidine a known endogenous convulsant from creatinine (Matsumoto et al 1976) . These may result in early seizures, which is a major risk factor of post traumatic epilepsy. These studies suggest that oxidation by ROS specially hydroxyl radicals is involved in the mechanism responsible for post traumatic epilepsy.

CONVENTIONAL TREATMENT AND PROPHYLAXIS FOR POST TRAUMATIC EPILEPSY: STILL NOT SATISFACTORY

Evidence demonstrate that following head injury early seizure activity may increase the associated risk of PTE

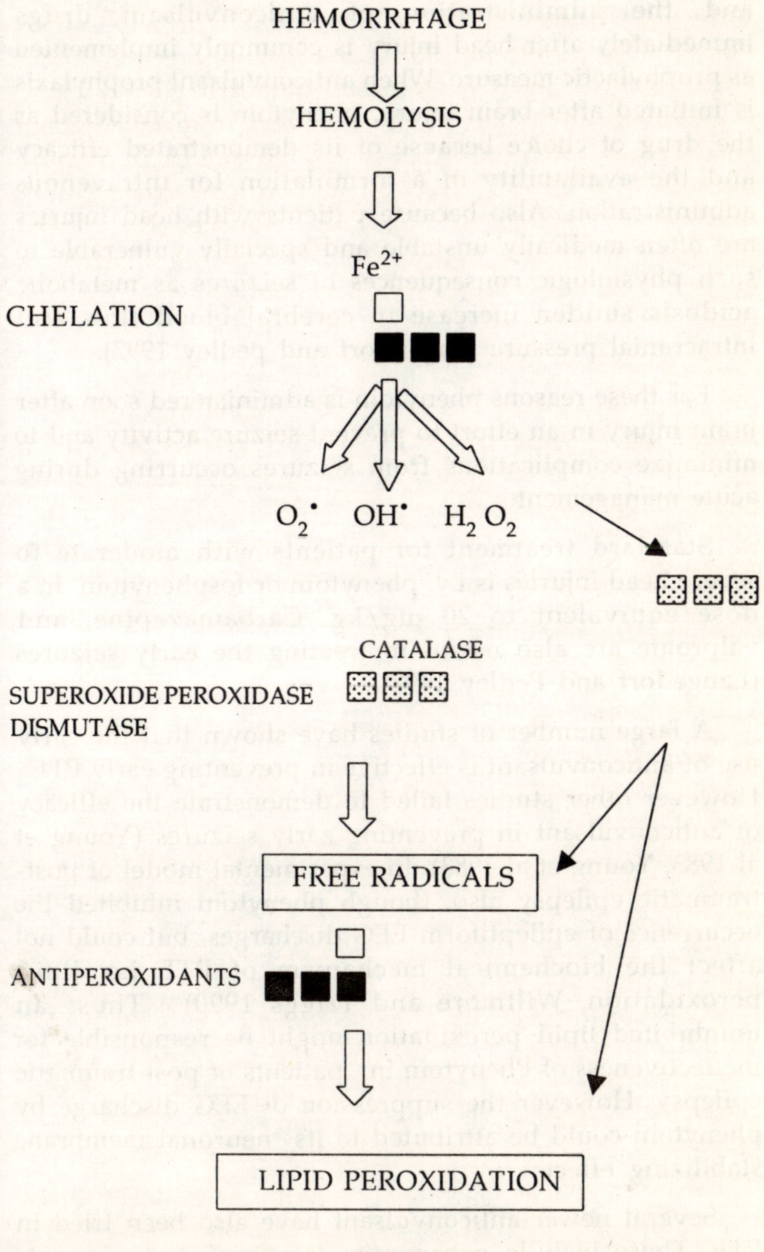
HEMORRHAGE
HEMOLYSIS
Fe^{2+}
CHELATION
$O_2^{\bullet}$ $OH^{\bullet}$ H_2O_2
CATALASE
SUPEROXIDE PEROXIDASE
DISMUTASE
FREE RADICALS
ANTIPEROXIDANTS
LIPID PEROXIDATION

Fig 1

and the administration of anticonvulsant drugs immediately after head injury is commonly implemented as prophylactic measure. When anticonvulsant prophylaxis is initiated after brain injury, phenytoin is considered as the drug of choice because of its demonstrated efficacy and the availability of a formulation for intravenous administration. Also because patients with head injuries are often medically unstable and specially vulnerable to such physiologic consequences of seizures as metabolic acidosis sudden increase in cerebral blood flow and intracranial pressure (Lagendorf and pedley 1997).

For these reasons phenytoin is administered soon after brain injury in an effort to prevent seizure activity and to minimize complications from seizures occurring during acute management.

Standard treatment for patients with moderate to severe head injuries is i.v. phenytoin or fosphenytoin in a dose equivalent to 20 mg/kg. Carbamazepine, and valproate are also useful in treating the early seizures (Langedorf and Pedley 1997).

A large number of studies have shown that the early use of anticonvulsant is effective in preventing early PTE . However other studies failed to demonstrate the efficacy of anticonvulsant in preventing early seizures (Young et al 1983, Young et al 1983). In experimental model of post-traumatic epilepsy also, though phenytoin inhibited the occurrence of epileptiform EEG discharges, but could not affect the biochemical mechanism of PTE i.e. lipid peroxidation. Willmore and Triggs 1990) . Thus an uninhibited lipid peroxidation might be responsible for ineffectiveness of Phenytoin in patients of post traumatic epilepsy. However the suppression of EEG discharge by phenytoin could be attributed to its neuronal membrane stabilizing effect.

Several newer anticonvulsant have also been tried in PTE. These include gabapentin, lamotrigine, topiramate and vigabatrin. Among these only vigabatrin has been shown to induced some protective effect in an experimental model of PTE (Shin et al 1986)

NEED FOR EFFECTIVE AND ALTERNATIVE PHARMACOLOGICAL AGENT

The limited success with which anticonvulsant drugs prevent PTE points to the need for an alternative treatment strategy. This is particularly important because the currently used anticonvulsant possess a high potential for side effect, which can be complicated further by the presence of brain injury. Preventive measures, however appears to be ineffective at preventing the development of PTE and may therefore unnecessarily expose brain injured patient to anticonvulsant drugs, moreover the anticonvulsant agents administered are not effective against cognitive impairment after post traumatic epilepsy and may themselves cause deleterious effect on cognition.

Since post traumatic epilepsy involves ROS in its pathogenesis, treatment designed to prevent peroxidation may be more effective in epilepsy prophylaxis, than the administration of anticonvulsant drugs that makes convulsive seizures, while bio-chemical brain injury continues.

Anti-epileptic with antiperoxidant properties may be one of the promising agents as it has the potential to alter the basic pathology of the disease. Many antioxidants have been examined in experimental model of PTE.

Levy et al 1990 have reported that a tocopherol (Vit. E) significantly released the onset of EEG seizures induced by intracerebral $Fecl_2$ (Levy et al 1990). Tocopherol prevented both peroxidation and epilepsy caused by iron injection into hippocampus in rats as did Phenobarbital (Willmore et al 1986, Demopoulos et al 1997). The early use of the antioxidant methylprednisolone showed limited ability to present both epilepsy and peroxidation (illmore and Triggs 1984). Free radicals scavenge, such as

TABLE II

New compounds currently assessed in experimental models of post-traumatic epilepsy and their mode of action (Ludice and Murri 2000)

Compound	Mechanism of Action
Selfotel	Glutamate antagonist
Aptiganel	Glutamate antagonist
Eliprodil	Glutamate antagonist
Lubeluzole	Glutamate antagonist
Licostinel (ACEA-1021)	Glutamate antagonist
Gavestinel (GV-150526)	Glutamate antagonist
Sipatrigine (619C89)	Glutamate antagonist
Nalmefene	κ-opiate antagonist
Tirilazad	Lipid peroxidation inhibitor
Montirelin (CG 3703)	Protirelin (thyrotrophin-releasing hormone; TRH) analogue
S-Nitrosoglutathione	Antioxidant
MDL-74180	Tocopherol (vitamin E) analogue
OPC-14117	Superoxide radical scavenger
Perporgotein (PEG-SOD)	Superoxide radical scavenger
TJ-960	Superoxide radical scavenger
Dizocilpine (MK-801)	Superoxide radical scavenger
Melatonin	Superoxide radical scavenger
EUK-8	Superoxide radical scavenger
EUK-134	Superoxide radical scavenger
NG-Mono-methyl-arginine (NMMA)	Nitric oxide synthesis inhibitor

polyethylene glycol (PEG) monomer with SOD or PEG-catalase have also demonstrated beneficial activity in animal model (Muizellar 1993). It has also been reported that (-) epigallocatechin and (-) epigallocatechin-3-0 gallate isolated from green tea leaves (Rheirhizoma), scavenged hydroxyl and superoxide radicals and prevented or slowed the occurrence of epileptic discharges induced by $FeCl_3$ (Kabuto et al 1990). An antiepileptic effect of combination of Vit C and E, L-ascorbic acid, 2 – [3-4, dihydro 2, 578 – tetramethyl) – 2 (4,8,12-trimethyltridecyl)-2H-1-benzopyrcen-6-yl hydrogenophonphate) potassium salt has also been observed (Yokoi et al 1990, Mori et al 1992). TJ 960, a Japanese herbal medicine has been found to have scavenging activity for free radicals generated within an iron induced epiteptogenic region of rat brain (Komatsu 1996).

ADENOSINE IN POST TRAUMATIC EPILEPSY

Adenosine which is an endogenous neuromodulator, has been found to be an effective antiepileptic agent in different animals modal (Malhotra and Gupta 1997). Adenosine has also been shown to have free radical scavenging activity and neuroprotective action. Yokoi et observed scavenging effects of adenosine and 2-chloroadenosine on hydroxyl radicals and also their effect on ferric chloride induced cortical EEG discharge in an experimental model of post traumatic seizures(Yokoi et al 1995)

MELATONIN IN POST TRAUMATIC EPILEPSY :

The hormone melatonin (5-methoxy-N-acetyltryptamine) was first successfully isolated and identified from bovine pineal. Melatonin is released in the blood stream with a circadian rhythm that peaks during the night. Pinealectomy has been shown to produce convulsions (Philo and Reiter, 1978). On the basis of this, it was hypothesized that *melatonin or some other substance released from the pineal gland may have anticonvulsant properties*. Melatonin has shown both antiepileptic (Alberson et al 1981,Srivastava et al 2001, Srivastava et al

1997) and free radical scavenging activity . Numerous in vitro, in vivo and clinical studies have shown potent antioxidant actions with melatonin (Pierrefiche et. al. 1993; Poeggeler et. al.1995). As a direct scavenger, melatonin inactivates free radicals by electron donation (Poeggeler et. al. 1994) but its ability to resist oxidative damage seems not exclusively attributable to this process (Chan and Tang 1996; Marshall et. al. 1996). Pharmacological levels of melatonin have been reported to stimulate the activity of glutathione peroxidase (GSH-Px) in the brain, a major antioxidant defensive mechanism in the central nervous system. Melatonin, crosses the blood brain barrier with ease and enters both neurons and glia. It has been seen that after peripheral administration of melatonin, its brain concentration rises quickly (Reiter et. al. 1997).

A second feature that has directed interest to melatonin is its a possible neuroprotective action. Melatonin has been shown to alter the neuronal and behavioral changes inflicted by KA in both in vitro and in vivo studies (Reiter et al. 1997). The antiexcitotoxic action of melatonin has been related to its capability to scavenge free radicals (Giusti et al. 1997).

Melatonin has been found to be effective in reducing the in vitro lipid peroxidation and epileptic EEG discharged induced by intracortical FeCl3 in rats (Kabuto Yokoi and Ogawa 1998). Recently Melatonin has shown in vivo inhibition of lipid peroxidation in intracortical ferric chloride model of post traumatic epilepsy (Srivastava and Gupta 2000).

TRANS RESVERATROL IN POST TRAUMATIC EPILEPSY

After the realization of reduced cardiac risk in the consumers of red wine popularly referred as French paradox, much interest has emerged in resveratrol, which is the active constituent of red wine. Resveratrol (3,4,5 tri hydroxy stilbene) is a naturally occurring phytoalexin present in high concentration in skin of grapes and wine (Fremont 1999). It has been shown to have a potent free radical scavenging activity proven in various invitro and in vivo studies (Cadenas 1999,Virgili and Contestabile 2000). Recently transresveratrol has shown its effectiveness in neurological disorders including stroke and epilepsy. Sinha et. al 2001 reported that transresveratrol is protective against middle cerebral artery occlusion model of stroke. Protective effect of transresveratrol against kainic acid induced seizures and oxidative stress has also been reported (Gupta et. al 2001). Resveratrol has also showed the protective effect of Resevratrol against ferric chloride model of post traumatic epilepsy in rats. Resveratrol reduced the lipid peroxidation and epileptiform EEG discharge in intracortical ferric chloride treated rats. (Gupta et al 2001).

CALCIUM CHANNEL BLOCKERS

Experimental studies have shown that the total brain tissue calcium level is increased in injury areas, a sustained increase in intracellular calcium levels initiates a series of damaging events (Fineman 1993). The calcium antagonist nimodipine, a strongly lipophilic agent has been tried but with limited benefit (Robinson and Teasdale 1990).

EXCITATORY AMINO ACID ANTAGONIST

Excitatory amino acids have been shown to play a major role in neuronal damage after experimental brain trauma (Benveniste 1991). Both clinical and experimental studies demonstrated immediate and marked increase in the extra cellular level of excitatory amino acids following injury (faden 1989). Various glutamate antagonists, acting at different sites have been developed, of which 4 were carrier forward into phase III trials. These are eliprodil, selfotel, D-3 (2-carboxy-piperazine-4-yl) propenyl -1 phosphonic acid (D-) and aptigonel (Bullock 1998, Toulmond et al 1993))

All these non-anticonvulsant components may represent future pharmacological interventions, aimed at limiting damage caused by reactions under lying epileptogenesis. However partial effectiveness of anticonvulsant drugs, refractoriness of epilepsies and adverse effects associated with the use of conventional antiepileptic drugs, advocate the necessity of newer antiepileptic drugs with antioxidant and neuroprotective activity, as oxidative stress has been implicated in epilepsy recently.

REFERENCES

Albertson TE, Peterson SL, Stark LG, Lakin ML and Winters WD. The anticonvulsant properties of melatonin on kindled seizures in rats. Neuropharmacology 1981; 20:61-66.

Alfonso Ludice and Luigi Murri . Pharmacological Prophylaxis of post traumatic epilepsy 2000. Drugs; 59(5) 1091-1099.

Annegers JF, Grabow JD, Groover RV, Laws ER, Eleveback LR, Kurland LT. Seizure after head trauma a population study. Neurology 1980; 30 : 683-689.

Annegers JF, Grabow JD, Groover RV, Laws ER, Eleveback LR, Kurland LT. Seizure after head trauma a population study. Neurology 1980; 30 : 683-689.

Barraco RA, Swanson TH, Phillis, JW, and Berman RF. Anticonvulsant effects of adenosine on amygdaloid kindled seizures in rats. Neurosci Lett.46:317-322 1984.

Benveniste H. The excitotoxic hypothesis in relation cerebral ischemia. Cerebrovascular Brain Metabolism Review 1991;3: 213-45.

Benveniste H. The excitotoxic hypothesis in relation cerebral ischemia. Cerebrovascular Brain Metabolism Review 1991; 3: 213-45.

Bullock R, Zauner A, Woodword JJ et al. Factor affecting excitatory aminoacid release following severe human head injury. J Neurosurg 1998; 89:507-518.

Cadenas, S., Barja, G. Resveratrol, melatonin, vitamin E and PBN protect against renal oxidative DNA damage induced by the kidney carcinogen Kbro$_3$. Free Radical Biol. Med. 1999, 26: 1531-1537

Caveness W F. Onset and cessation of fits following craniocerebral trauma. J neurosurg 1963;10:570-582.

Caveness WF, walker AE, Ascroft PB. Incidence of post traumatic epilepsy in Korean veterans as compared with those from World war 1 and world war 11. J neurosurg. 1962; 19: 122-129.

Chan TY and Tang RL. Characterization of the antioxidant effects of melatonin and related indoleamines in vitro. J Pineal Res.1996; 20: 187-191.

Constant, J. *Alcohol, ischemic heart disease and French paradox*. Coron. Artery Dis. 1997, 8: 645-649

Credner L, Klinische and Sociale Auswirkungen Von Hirnschadigungen Zgesmate . Neurol Psychiat 1993; 126:721-57.

De Santis A, Sganzerela E, Spagnoli D, Bello L, Tiberio F. Risk factors for late post traumatic epilepsy Acta Neurochir 1992; 55(Suppl): 64-67.

Demopoulos HB, Flamm ES, Seligman, ML,et al. Antioxidant effects of barbiturates in model membranes undergoing free radical damage, Acta Neurol Scand 1997;7:12-13.

Desai BT, Whitman S, Coonley- Hoganson R, Coleman TE, Gabriel G, Dell J. Seizures and civilians head injuries. Epilpesia1983; 24: 289-296.

Faden AI, Demediuk P, Panter SS et al. The role of excitatory amino acid on NMDA receptors in traumatic brain injury. Science 1989; 244: 798-800

Faden AI, Demediuk P,Panter SS et al. The role of excitatory amino acid on NMDA receptors in traumatic brain injury. Science 1989; 244: 798-800

Fermont, L. *Biological effects of resveratrol.* Life Sci. 1999, 66: 663-673

Fineman I . Hovda DA, Smith M et al. Concussive brain injury is associated with prolonged accumulation of calcium : a 45 Ca autoradiographic study. Brain Res 1993; 624: 94-102.

Fineman I . Hovda DA, Smith M et al. Concussive brain injury is associated with prolonged accumulation of calcium: a ^{45}Ca autoradiographic study. Brain Res.1993; 624: 94-102.

Frederick Langendorf and Timothy A. Pedley Post traumatic seizures in Eiplepsy : A comprenhensive text book edited by J Engel, Jr and TA Pedley 1997; 2469-2474.

Gannarelli TA, Thiabault LE, Adams JH,et al . Diffuse axonal injury and traumatic coma in the primate. Ann Neurol. 1982; 12: 564-574.

Giusti P, Lipartiti M, Gusella M, Floreani M, Manev H. In vitro and in vivo protective effects of melatonin against glutamate oxidative stress and neurotoxicity. Ann NY Acad Sci 1997; 825: 79-84.

Isao Yokoi, Junji Toma, Jiankang Liu, Hideaki Kabuto, and Akitane Mori. Adenosine scavenged hydroxyl radicals and prevented post traumatic epilepsy. Free radical Biology and Medicine 1995; 19(4): 473-479.

Jennet B. Epilepsy after non missile head injury. 2nd ed. London William Heinemann medical Books,1975.

Jennet B. Epilpesy and post trauamtic intracortical hematoma. J Neurol Neurosurg.Psych. 1975; 38:378-81.

Jennett WB, Lewin W. Traumatic epilepsy after closed head injuries. J Neurol. Neurosurg. Psyichator 1960;23: 295-301

Kabuto H, Yokoi I, Okamura Y, Yamamoto, M, Suyama K, Mori A. Effeects odf ferric iron and (-) epigallocatechin 3-o-gallate on monoamine metabolite levels in rat striatum by brain dialysis. Neurosciences 16: 377-382;1990.

Kabuto H, Yokoi I, Ogawa N. Melatonin inhibits iron induced epileptic discharges in rats by suppressing peroxidation. Epilpesia 1998; 39: 237-243.

Kabuto H, Yokoi I, Ogawa N. Melatonin inhibits iron induced epileptic discharges in rats by suppressing peroxidation. Epilepsia 1998; 39: 237-243.

Katayama Y, Becker DP, Tamura T et al. Massive increase in extracellular potassium and indiscriminate release of glumate following concussive brain injury. J Neurosurg 1990; 73: 889-900.

Katayama Y, Becker DP, Tamura T et al. Massive increase in extracellular potassium and indiscriminate release of glutamate following concussive brain injury. J Neurosurg 1990; 73: 889-900.

Kollevold, T. Immediate and early seizures after head injuries. Part1 J oslocity Hospital 26: 99-114 1976.

Komatsu M, Hiramatsu M, Yokoyama H, et al . Effect of TJ- 960 (a Japanese herbal medicine) on free radical changes within an iron induced focal epileptogenic region in rat brain measured by in vivo L band electron spin resonance. Neurosci Lett 1996, 205: 189-92.

Langfitt TW, Weinstein JD, Kassell NF. In Caveness WE , Walker Ae (eds): Head Injury. Philadelphia, JB Lippincott 1966,172-194.

Levy S.L, Burnham M, Hwang PA. An evaluation of the anticonvulsnat effects of vitamin E. Epilepsy Res.1990 6:12-17.

Malhotra J and Gupta YK,Effect of adenosine receptor modulation on pentylenetetrazole induced seizures in rats. Br J Pharmacol 1997 120: 282-288.

Marshal KA, Reiter RJ, Poeggeler B, Aruoma OI and Halliwell B. Evaluation of the antioxidant activity of melatonin in vitro. Free Radical Biol Med 1996; 21: 307-315.

Matsumoto M, Koabyoshi K, Kishikawa H, Mori A. A convulsive activity of methylguanidine in cats and rabbits. IRCS Med Sci 1976 4: 65.

Mori A, Yokoi I, Kabuto H. Effects of vitamin E and its derivative on post traumatic epilepsy and seizures. In packer L, Funch J,eds. Vitamin E in health and disease. Newyork: Marcel Dekker Inc 1992,851-858

Muizellar JP, Marmarou A, Young HF, Et al. Improving the out come of severe head injury with the oxygen radical scavenger polyethylene glycol- conjugated superoxide dismutase. A phase 2 trial. J Neurosurg 1993; 78: 375_82.

Nilson P, Ronne- Engstrom E, Flink R, Ungerstedt U, Carlson H, Hillered L. Epileptic seizure activity in the acute phase following cortical impact trauma in rat. Brain Res 1994. 637: 227-232.

Panter S S, Sadrzadesh SM, Hallaway PE et al . Hypohaptoglobinemia associated with familial epilepsy. J Exp Med. 1985. 161: 748-754.

Philo R and Reiter RJ. Characterization of pinealectomy-induced convulsions in the Mongolian gerbil (Merioner-unguicalabes). Epilepsia 1978; 19: 485-492.

Pierreficta G, Topall G, Canboin G, Henreit I, Laborit H. Antioxidant activity of melatonin in mice. Res Common Chem Pathol Pharmacol. 1993; 80: 211-223.

Poeggeler B, Reiter RJ, Tan DX, Chen LD, Manchester LC. Melatonin hydroxyl radical mediated oxidative damage and aging. J Pine Res 1993; 14: 151-168.

Poeggeler BS, Saarela, Reiter RJ Tan DX , Chen LD Monchester LC and Barlow-Walten LR . Melatonin a highly potent endrogenoon radical scavenger and electron donor. New aspects of the oxidation chemistry of this indole assessed in vitro. Ann NY Acad Sci 1994; 738: 419-420.

Reiter RJ, Guerrero JM, Escames G, Pappolla MA, Acuna-castroviejo D, prophylactic action of melatonin in oxidative neurotoxicity. Ann NY Acad Sci 1997; 825: 70-78.

Reiter RJ, Tang L, Garcia JJ, Munoz-hoyos A. Pharmacological actions of melatonin in oxygen radical pathophysiology. Life Sci. 1997; 60 (25): 2255-2271.

Robinson MJ, Teasdale GM. Calcium antagonists in the management of subarrachnoid haemorrhage. Cerebrovascular Brain Metabolism Review. 1990.;2: 205-26.

Robinson MJ, Teasdale GM. Calcium antagonists in the management of subarrachnoid hemorrhage. Cerebrovascular Brain Metabolism Review. 1990; 2: 205-26.

Rosen AD, Frumin NV. Focal epileptogenesis after intracortical haemoglobin injection. Exp Neurol 66: 277-284.1979.

Sander JWAS Shrovan SD: Epidemiology of the epilepsies. J neurol Neurosurgerery Psychiatry 1996; 61: 433-443.

Schaumann BA, Annegers JF, Johnson SB, Moore KJ, Lubozynski MF, Salinsky MC. Family history of seizures in post traumatic and alcohal associated seizure disorders. Epilepsia 1994. 35: 48-52.

Shin C, Rigsbee LC, Mc Namara JO. Antiseizure and Antiepileptogenic effect of gamma- vinyl gamma- aminobutyric acid in amygdaloid kindling. Brain res. !986; 398: 370- 374

Sinha K, Chaudhary G and Gupta YK Protective effect of resveratrol against oxidative stress middle cerebral artery occlusion model of stroke in rats. Life Sci.2001 (In press).

Smith DH, Gennarelli T A, Macintosh TK. The potential of 21 amino steroids (Lazorids) on neuroprotective therapies in a CNS Injuries. CNS Drugs 1995; 3: 159-63.

Srivastava A.K, and Gupta Y.K. (2000): Role of melatonin in experimental model of posttraumatic epilepsy in rats. Indian J Pharmacol; 32(1):76.

Srivastava A.K, Chaudhary G, and Gupta Y.K (1997): Protective effect of melatonin in lithium pilocarpine model of status epilepticus in rats. Indian J Physiol Pharmacol ;41(5):484A .

Srivastava A.K, Malhotra J and Gupta Y.K. Adenosine receptors , do not mediate the melatonin protection against pentylenetetrazole induced seizures in rats. Neurobiology 2001(In press)

Tornheim PA, Liwnicz BH,Hirsh CS et al . Acute responses to blunt head trauma. J Neurosurg 1983; 59: 431-438.

Toulmond S, Duval D, Serrano A, Scatton B and Benavides J. Biochemical and histological alterations induced by fluid percussion brain injury in the rat. Brain Res.1993 Aug 20; 620(1): 24-31.

Virgili, M., Contestabile, A. Partial neuroprotection of in vivo excitotoxic brain damage by chronic administration of the red wine antioxidant agents, trans resveratrol in rats. Neurosci Lett. 2000, 281: 123-126

Willmore LJ, Sypert GW, Munson JB,. Recurrent seizures induced by cortical iron injection; A model of post traumatic epilepsy. Ann Neurol 4: 329-336.1978.

Willmore Lj, Triggs WJ, Gray JD. The role of iron induced hippocampal peroxidation in acute epileptogenesis. Brain Res 1986.382:422-426.

Willmore LJ, Triggs WJ. Effect of phenytoin and corticosteroids on seizures and lipid peroxidation in experimental post trauamtic epilepsy. J Neurosurg. 1984; 60: 467-472.

Gupta YK, Chaudhary G, Sinha K, Srivastava AK. Protective effect of resveratrol against intracortical $FeCl_3$ induced model of post traumatic seizures in rats.Methods and findings in experimental and clinical pharmacology 2001 23;8.

Yokoi I, Kabuto H, yamamoto, M, Mori A. Effect of ferric iron and active oxygen scavenger on monoamine release in the striatum of the rat. Jpn. J. Psychiatr. Neurol 44: 99-100. 1990.

Yokoi I, Toma J, Liu J et al. Adenosine scavenged hydroxy radicals and prevented post traumatic epilepsy. Free radic Biol Med 1995; 19: 473-9.

Young B, Rapp RP, Nortan JA, Haack D, Tibbs PA, Bean JR. Failure of prophylactically administered Phenytoin to prevent the late post traumatic seizures. J Neurosurgery 1983; 58: 236-241.

Young B, Rapp RP, Nortan JA, Haack D, Tibbs PA, Bean JR. Failure of prophylactically administered phe4nytoin to prevent early post traumatic seizures. J Neurosurgery 1983; 58:231-235.

Zhang, Z.H. Zuo, Q.H., Wu, X.R. Effect of lipid peroxidation on GABA uptake and release in iron induced seizures. Chienese Med J . !02:24-27.1989.

STRESS AND IMMUNITY : MECHANISMS AND MODULATION BY DRUGS

A. RAY, A. MASOOD, K. GULATI AND B.D. BANERJEE
Department of Pharmacology, V.P. Chest Institute, University of Delhi and Department of Biochemistry UCMS & GTB Hospital, Shahdara, Delhi

In 1936, Hans Selye first introduced the concept of 'stress' to biomedical research. He emphasized that non-specific agents called 'stressors' were able to induce a reaction which altered the normal physiological milieu. These agents could be physical (cold and heat), chemical or psychological. The system had to react to such forces in an attempt to 'adapt' to such demanding/challenging situations. Adaptation to such physical, psychological or environmental situation involved a chain of behavioral, autonomic, endocrinal and metabolic responses and these homeostatic 'stress' responses were controlled by complex brain mechanisms. It is implied, therefore, that adaptability or coping ability with such noxious, life threatening stimuli are basic perrequisites for life and survival.

Inspite of the multifaceted ongoing research in this field there appears to be little consensus about the definition of 'stress', Selye (1976) defined it as anything that disturbs the biological integrity/physiological homeostasis of the organism, either directly by physiological means or indirectly. In other words, it involves psychological situations which produce disorganization of behaviour a[illegible] induce physical and mental illness. Stress cannot be considered in isolation and the complexity of the pathways/mechanisms involved is a subject of considerable contemporary research. For example, the autonomic nervous system and the neuroendocrine system help to maintain the internal environment (homeostasis) during such aversive states. The central nervous system (CNS) is also a crucial mediator during stress and related responses and several brain areas have been implicated. The hypothalamus along with its connections with extrahypothalamic areas like some parts of the limbic system and brain stem autonomic nuclei regulate several stress responses. The amygdaloid complex in particular plays a crucial role (Henke, 1992; Henke and Ray, 1992). The hypothalamopituitary-adrenal (HPA) axis is important for the corticosterone response, as are other areas for the regulation of prolactin release. ACTH and b-endorphins are also important determinants of several stress related mainfestations (Amir et al., 1980). The CNS is also important for stress induced visceral/somatic reactions. Gastric ulcer formation in response to stress is an important visceral/emotional response to a variety of stressors and the brain-gut axis is involved (Szabo and Glavin, 1990; Glavin et al., 1991) . Several CNS areas like the cingulate cortex, the septo-hippocampal pathways and the amygdaloid complex are important neural substrates in this phenomenon. More recent data have shown the CNS may mediate the effects of stress on the immune system and a new discipline called 'psychoneuroimmunology' has come into being . Immune mechanisms form the basis of several psychosomatic disorders and the CNS is crucial in such interactions. Areas like the hypothalamus actually control immune reactions as shown is some experimental situations. Complex neurochemical mechanisms also regulate stress responses.

Biogenic amines (noradrenaline, acetylcholine, dopamine, histamine), amino acids (GABA, exicitatory amino acids), and more recently neuropeptides play important roles in some of the stress responses (Glavin, 1980; Pare and Glavin, 1986; Hernandez, 1986). The neuropeptides are particularly important since they are localized in areas which are densely populated with cell bodies, nerve terminals and receptors for these mediators. Thus, it is apparent that 'stress' cannot be considered in isolation and it is the complex interaction between different factors which ultimately decide the nature of a stress response. This could be aimed at adaptation to the environment to maintain a 'steady state' or homeostasis (neu stress) and to perform bodily functions (Selye, 1976). A favourable stress response culminating in improving physical / mental functioning is called 'eustress' (eu = good or healthy). An unfavourable or detrimental stress response is one which 'disease producing' potential and is labelled as 'distress' (dis = bad or negative). Such stressful situations have given rise to disease states like hypertension, gastric ulcers, anxiety neurosis etc. Based on the categorization of stress response it is evident that factors like personality and genetic predisposition, pre-existing disease, critical life events and psychosomatic states are key determinants of the stress reaction.

THE CENTRAL NERVOUS SYSTEM (CNS) AND STRESS

Stress is a result of interactions between the stressor and the organism. Hereditary and environmental factors determine the state of the organism and their susceptibility of various physical, psychosocial and emotional forces. Physical stress comprises of mainly external factors like temperature, radiation, noise, exercise and trauma, drugs and chemicals etc. Psychosocial stressors result from interactions with the environment and include social/reactive events like death, loss of a job or forced relocation. Pure psychological stressors results in chronic illness and most of them are self induced i.e. depends on one's emotional status and self control, like fear, anxiety, frustration, inferiority complex, etc. As is evident, there is apparently a reasonable degree of overlap amongst the so-called 'stressors' but some aspects are rather clear. For example, a purely physiological stimulus which occurs outside the knowledge of the individual is not a 'stressor'. Further, most of the conditions enumerated involve the perceptibility of the organism. A strong psychological or emotional component seems to be lurking in the background and thus the emotional status of the individual is an index of stress susceptibility. It is but obvious, therefore, that the CNS would play a crucial role in the stress response.

It has already been emphasised that psychological/ emotional factors play a key role in determining the impact of stress on health and disease. Accordingly, the CNS acts as an important mediator and several neural substrates are involved (Rees, 1980).

The Limbic System comprises of a group of structures (paleocorticol and subcorticol) that lie below the neocortex forming a ring or 'limbs' around the top of the brain stem. These structures include the preoptic area, the septohippocampal pathway, the amygdaloid complex, the anterior nucleus of the thalamus, some hypothalamic areas, the caudate nucleus and the reticular activating system. The paleocortical and related structures (the limbic cortex) surrounds the subcortical structures. The limbic cortex includes the entorrhinal cortex, the pyriform cortex, the cingulate cortex, the hippocampus, the olfactory bulb and tubercle. Apart from the limbic cortex, the principal functional element of the limbic system is the amygdaloid complex, the hippocampus (parts) and some other associated structures. The hypothalamus and the limbic system function in coordination, though the reticular formation, the limbic system and the autonomic nervous system are separate entities. The septum and the hippocampus, project by way of the fornix to the hypothalamus, The caudate nucleus receives fibres from the cingulate cortex and the thalamus.

The amygdaloid complex comprises of two groups of nuclciicorticomedial and basolateral, both of which play crucial roles in stress reactions (Ray and Henke, 1991). In addition, the hypothalamo-amygdala axis has been shown to participate in some endocrinal and visceral stress responses (Henke, 1979; 1982; 1988a; 1992). The amygdala is also involved in behavioral / emotional responses and acts as a centre where stress inputs are received, integrated and gated as efferent outputs to higher and lower areas in the brain. Functions like reward and punishment, fear/affect, rage and aggression are all important contributions of the amygdaloid complex. Stimulations and lesions, as well as, pharmacological manipulations in this area have reaffirmed the contentions mentioned above.

STRESS AND IMMUNITY

Concepts of natural and acquired immunity were reported in the traditional system of Indian medicine, Ayurveda about two thousand years ago, and psychological factors were one of the important determinants of disease susceptibility (Shukla et al., 1979). In the early 1960's, Salk (1962) indicated that genetic, behavioral, nervous and immune factors were related to disease states. Mirsky (1957) had already shown this in peptic ulcer patients. Studies have observed close relationship between stress and disease. Physiological stress like food and sleep deprivation was shown to effect immune mechanisms in man (Jasoo and Mckenzie, 1976). Changes in immunoglobulin levels with emotional fluctuations were seen in breast cancer patients and rheumatoid arthritis (Moos and Solomon, 1964). Bereavement was associated with depressed mitogen-induced T-cell proliferation (Bartrop et al., 1977). High stress susceptibility and poor coping was associated with a decline in natural killer (NK) cell activity (Glaser et al.,

1987). For many years, immunologists have studied the structure and function of the immune system. In these studies, the fact that was generally ignored was that the guardians of the defense system, i.e. lymphocytes and other cells like macrophages do not operate in isolation. Several studies have shown that they are linked with other physiological systems in the body. Interdisciplinary research flourished and focussed on the interaction between nervous, endocrine and immune systems. This emerging new discipline often referred to as 'psychoneuroimmunlogy', 'behavioral immunology' or 'neuroimmunology' has provided exciting data on the link between the brain and the immune system. A number of studies have shown that psychological factors like stress can alter immune reactivity (Croisset et al., 1987). A variety of stressors have been shown to influence immune functioning both in animals and man and in some studies the involvement of hormones and/or neuropeptides have been shown (Heijnen et al., 1989).

Studies in humans have shown that psychosocial factors alter the susceptibility to / recovery from several infections, allergic, autoimmune and neoplastic diseases. Experimental studies have indicated that the outcome of a stress stimulation depends on the stressor and the pathophysiological processes in the organ. This implies that the same stressor may effect different pathophysiological states differently. The acute or chronic nature of the stressor may also be a determining factor. However, a clearer understanding is still required in this respect and although most studies provide correlative evidence, direct evidence for psychosocially altered immune function is yet to be shown.

Quantification of immune responses during stress has received considerable attention in recent years. Stressful life events like bereavement, for example, is associated with depression and an increased morbidity and mortality in various diseases - many of which involve immune functioning. Thus changes in immune function provide a strong link between psychosocial factors and altered susceptibility to disease. Some features link reduced lymphoproliferative response to mitogens and impaired natural killer (NK) cell activity have been observed among the bereaved (Bartrop et al., 1977; Scheifer et al., 1983: Irwin et al., 1987). Similar changes in immune reactivity and effective responses have also been seen after marital separation, impending examinations and fotball games (Kiecolt-Glaser and Glaser, 1986; Ader et al., 1990)

.Of related interest and importance is the rapidly growing literature concerning immunomodulatory effects of psychotropic drugs - drugs of abuse as well as these used for therapeutic purposes (Ader et al., 1990). Immunological effects of such agents are reported to depend on species, the type of in vitro or in vivo immune response studied, the does and duration of treatment and in experimental studies, the timing of the treatment after antigen injection. Psychotropic drug action depends on the psychophysiological state of the organism. For example, the dopamine blocker, haloperidol, suppresses antibody responses in normal mice, but attenuates stress-induced changes in the humoral immune response.

THE CNS - IMMUNE INTERACTIONS

Considerable evidence has accumulated to indicate that a functional connection between the CNS and the immune system may exist. This is particularly evident from the fact that stress induced pathophysiological states have strong emotional components and immune functioning is modulated during several such psychosomatic states. Basically, the main routes exist which make such CNS-interactions possible : (a) the nervous 'wiring' system innervating lymphoid tissue, and (b) the 'soluble' connection via the neurecndocrine axis. Although, the above appear to have been accepted as fundamental pathways, the complex mechanisms underlying neuroimmunomodulation are largely unknown (Ballieux and Heijnen, 1989).

One of the early key observations concerning stress and disease was the association of immunocompetence and stress. Specifically, depending on the type and duration of stress, dramatic alterations in immune homeostasis can occur. A subsequent observation led to neuroendocrine and immune interaction concepts and this showed that hypothalamic lesions altered the immune status of the organizm. Conversely, it was also noted that at the peak of an immune response, the rate of firing of hypothalamic neurons was altered, as was the hypothalamic noradrenaline content. These preliminary observations revealed a direct link between the brain and the immune system and further suggested that afferent-efferent pathways brought about changes in both systems (Stein et al., 1976; Carr, 1991).

Another direct interaction between the CNS and the immune system is splenic innervation. The adrenergic innervation of the periarteriolar lymphatic sheath suggested that (a) circulatory flow into and out of the spleen, (b) convergence of antigen to antigen presenting cells within the spleen and (c) trafficking of lymphocytes - would all be regulated by the CNS. The link between the hypophysis and the thymus further strengthened the CNS-immune link hypothesis. Injection of anti-hypophysis serum in mice caused atrophy of the thymus and resulted in wasting disease. In interaction between the thymus (the principal immune organ) and the pituitary was suggested. The next experiments showed that hormones classically associated with neuroendocrine function could restore antibody production in immunodeficient mice and more recent studies showed that hormones could directly participate in immune modulation. Thus neuroendocrine peptide hormones could, besides acting on their 'classical' target organs, also influence immunocompetence. Conditioning experiments provided the next development in this field. Ader and Cohen (1975) used taste aversion paradigm with saccharin and cyclophosphamide and showed that rats could be conditioned to an immunosuppressive state. The pathways of this type of Pavlovian conditioning is still being elucidated. Most recent findings have shown that immune cells produce hormones that are restricted to the erstwhile neuroenodocrine axis. These studies showed do novo synthesis of ACTH and endorphin - like - molecules by lymphocytes. These hormones were biologically and antigenically similar to their neuroendocrine counterparts (Ballieux and Heijnen, 1989).

Thus immune cells could be conceived of as mobile endocrine units that perceive 'non-congnitive' stimuli and inform the brain.

STRESS, BEHAVIOR AND IMMUNITY

Stress is known to disrupt the biological homeostasis and induce a complexly interactive variety of responses in experimental animals. In this study, emotional stress was induced in rats by exposing them to restraint (immobilization) procedure in plexiglas restrainers for specific periods of time. This is a standard technique and is practiced globally in stress research laboratories and effectively utilised in our laboratory as well. (Ray et al., 1991; 1992a; 1992b) Restraint stress (RS) of different durations (1h, 6h, 24h and CRS) induced differential degrees of responses. The open-field test is a standard method for evaluating anxiety/stress related behvior (Bhattacharya & Satyan, 1997). All forms of RS induced neurobehavioral, visceral and immunological responses. Exposures of rats to 1h and 6h of RS induced primarily inhibited behavioral responses in the openfield test. There was increased latency of entry and defecation, whereas, ambulation and rearing were inhibited. On the other hand, gastric lesions were more consistently seen in the 24h RS and CRS models of stress. Both number and severity of gastric lesions were enhanced when compared to no-RS controls. In rats immunized with sheep RBC (SRBC) exposure to longer durations of RS inhibited both humoral and cell-mediated immune responses. In tests for humoral immunity different forms of RS supressed (a) the anti-SRBC antibody resforms as measured by the IHA technique, and (b) plaque forming cells count in the spleen as measured by the PFC assay. In tests for cell-mediated immunity, SRBC challenge induced increase footpad thickness (DTH response) was also markedly attenuated ($P<0.05$) after exposure to different RS treatments as measured by the fluid displacement technique. Repeated exposure to shorter durations of RS (1h RS and CRS) also inhibited humoral and cell-mediated immune responses, without markedly influencing the immune responses when compared to those of single RS exposures.

Earlier studies had shown that behavioral factors could predict the susceptibility to stress responses and that the gastric ulcerogenic effect had a strong behavioral component involved in its genesis. Further, there could be or close relationship between emotionality and strees susceptibility (Henke and Ray, 1992). The present study evaluated any possible relationship between behavioral and immunological factors during stress. Rats were screened as *"high emotional"* and *"low emotional"* groups by observing their activity in the open-field. This is a standard adn widely accepted technique with researchers in the area. After immunization with SRBC, the anti-SRBC antibody titres were measured in both groups and it was observed that the suppression in the antibody response were markedly greater in the "high emotional" group of rats. As has been observed earlier, our study also showed that gastric ulcer formation was more severe in the "high emotional" rats as compared to the other group. In both groups of rats, diazepam attenuated RS effects on immune and gastric parameters, the effects being more apparent in the "high emotional" group. Interestingly, plasma corticosterone, which is a known physiological marker for stress, was differentially elevated in all the forms of RS used in our experiments. The most marked elevations were seen after CRS and 24h RS exposure and these effects were attenuated after diazepam and buspirone treatments. RS-induced activation of the HPA-axis (as is evidency by increased corticosterone) was not consistently associated with immune and gastric responses - the most consistent association of the three responses (viz. Immune, gastric and endocrinal) was seen only with the 24h RS paradigm. Diazepam pretreatment reversed the RS-induced changes in all three above mentioned parameters in the 24h RS experimental schedule. Thus, behavioral factors and to a certain extent neuroendocrinal factors could influence the impact of stress on immune parameters.

NEUROACTIVE DRUGS, STRESS AND IMMUNITY

The effects of some anti-stress agents (both typical and atypical) were tested on the stress parameters tested above. The classical anti-stress agent, diazepam (1 mg/kg) produced a consistent attenuating influence on the behavioral effects of stress. The entry latency (see) into the open-field was reduced, as was the number of defecations (pellets). The ambulatory score and the number of rearings were increased, as compared to the RS exposed conditions. Stress ulcer formation was also attenuated after diazepam pretreatment and both ulcer number and severity were reduced. Similar stress ulcer attenuating effects and stress-induced neurobehavioral modulations were seen after the atypical anti-stress/anti-anxiety agent buspirone and the novel agent, ondansetron. Both stress-induced behavioral and gastric effects were more or less similarly influenced by the three anti-stress agents, with minor differences. In rats immunized with SRBC, RS of different durations/intensities suppressed both humoral and cell-mediated immune responses.

Pretreatment with diazepam attenuated stress-induced suppression of anti-SRBC antibody (Ray et al., 1991) titres and also neutralized the RS-induced suppression of SRBC challenge-induced increased footpad thickness as measured by the fluid displacement technique. Similarly, buspirone and ondansetron also reversed the RS-induced suppression of both humoral and cell-mediated immune responses in rats. However, the effects of diazepam were more consistent on the immune parameters as compared to the other agents.

Central neural pathways play a crucial role in the regulation of stress responses and cathecholaminergic neurotransmission is important in this regard. Both noradrenaline (NA) and dopamine (DA) are extensively distributed in the CNS and thus the study investigated the possible involvement of central catecholaminergic neurons in stress-induced immune and related responses in rats. Intracerebroventricular cannulae were implanted streotactically into the rat brain for injection of drugs for this purpose. Centrally acting neurotoxins, which deplated central catecholaminergic neurons of the transmitter were administred and their effects on stress-induced immune and visceral responses were seen. Intraperitoneal administration of the NA-ergic neurotoxin, DSP-4 (50mg/kg), which is known to deplete brain NA, was shown to further aggravate the RS-induced humoral immune suppression. Similar effects on RS-induced anti-SRBC antibody titres were seen after central (icv) injections of DSP-4, (50 ug), and the catecholamine synthesis inhibitor, o-methyltyrosine. The beta-blocker, propranolol, which has good CNS penetration, also induced nearly similar changes in SR-induced immune responsiveness through to a lesser extent. DSP-4 pretreatment also injluence RS-induced behavioral and gastric changes in that neurobehavioral suppression and gastric ulceration were significantly aggravated after neurotoxin treatment by both peripheral (i.p.) and central (i.c.v.) routes.

Intraventricular administration of the DA-ergic neurotoxin, 6-hydroxydopamine (6-OH DA)in desipramine pretreated (to prevent neurotoxin uptake into the NA-ergic neurons) rats, clearly aggravated the RS effects on the immune parameters in a manner similar to DSP-4. Similar effects were seen after administration of the DA-blockers, haloperidol and sulpiride. The effects of disruption of DA-ergic transmission in the CNS were, however, more clearcut on the visceral parameter i.e. gastric ulcerogenesis and the DA-blockers induced greater severity of stress ulcers (Ray et al., 1987; Ray and Henke, 1991). These results suggest that central catecholaminergic pathways play a crucial role in the neural modulation of immunity as well as other responses during stress.

The amygdalod complex is knwon to play a crucial role during the central regulation of stress responses (Ray et al. 1987; 1988; 1990; 1993; Henke et al., 1988a), and these experiments were designed to explore the possible role of this limbic area in the regulation of stress-induced immune modulation in rats. For this purpose, stainless steel cannulae were implanted stereotactically into the amygdaloid complex of rats. After a one week recovery period from surgery, rats were injected with intra-amygdalar (i/am) doses of ibotenic acid, DSP-4 and 6 - OH DA. In rats immunized with SRBC, ibotenate lesioned animals showed some protection against RS-induced immune responsivenes, particularly on humoral immunity, and also partrally attenuated stress ulcer formation. On the other hand, DSP-4 or 6- OH DA (i/am) did not induce such effects and further aggravated RS-induced immune suppression and gastric ulcer formation. Histological studies indicated that the intra-amygdalar injection cannulae were located appropriately and did not induce any structural damage in the area concerned site (Paxinos and Watson, 1982). These studies indicate that the amygdaloid complex may also play an important role in the regulation of stress-induced immune responses, and neurohumoral mechnisms at this level could be involved.

EMOTIONAL AND ENVIRONMENTAL STRESSORS AND IMMUNE RESPONSES

Environmental factors also exert a stressful influence on the biological system and thus the present set of experiments were designed to explore the effecs of environmental stress factgors like xenobiotic exposure on humoral and cellular immune responses and compare them with emotional (restraint) stress. Insecticides like organochlorine compounds are known to enter the system through the food chain, and compounds like DDT and lindane are known to exist in the body/system for appreciable periods of time. Exposure to DDT or lindane for 4/6 weeks exerted duration dependent effects on the humoral immune response and also cell-mediated immunity. Higher doses eg. 200 ppm of DDT and 80 ppm of lindane required shorter durations of exposure to inlufence the immune responses. For this purpose, rats were immunized with tetanus toxoid and complete Freund's Adjuvant. The effects of DDT/lindane appeared to be more consistent on both humoral and cellular immunity. Both forms of stress (Xenobiotic) exposure were seen to be associated with two important biochemical markers, viz. (a) reductions in gammaglutamyl transpeptidase (GGT) activity in the lymphoid tissue (Koner, et al., 1997), and (b) enhancements in malondialdehyde (MDA) levesl in the blood. Both these biochemical markers were significantly affected by both RS and xenobiotic exposure, and diazepam attenunated these biochemical and immunological effects. Further, subthreshold exposure levels of both emotional and xenobiotic stressors seemed to compliment each other in the immunosuppressive effects as seen in tests for humoral and cellular immunity in our present experiments. In the presence of low does levels of DDT/lindane exposure, shorter durations of RS (1h) significantly suppressed immune responses, and these changes were also attenuated by anti-stress agents (diazepam). Further, pretreatment with the antioxidant, ascorbic acid attenuated RS and lindane induced suppression of humoral immunity as measured by the anti-SRBC antibody response. The studies thus highlight the interactions between different forms of stressors and the probable biological mechanisms involved in immune regulation.

In summary, it appears that emotional stress could result in differential degrees of behavioral and immune modulation in experimental animals. Anti-stress agents attenuated these stress responses and their effects were comparable. The central nervous system played an important role in the mediation of these stress effects and neural pathways like catecholaminergic mechanisms could be involved. Behavioral and physiological factors could also inlfuence stress susceptibility and these were reflected in immune and gastric responses. The amygdalad complex in particular plays a crucial rule in such neurobehavioral and immunological response during stress via its nural pathways (catecholaminergic and GABA). Like emotional stress enviornmental stressors like xenobiotic (DDT, Lindane) exposure also influence specific immunity in a comparable and complimentary manner. Biochemical markers like GGT and MDA (lipid peroxidation index) were altered during both forms of stress and anti-stress agents/antioxidants attenuated these stress-induced changes. These observations provide a new neurobiological dimension to stress research and could be of considerable applied significance.

REFERENCES

1. Ader, R. and Cohen, N. Behaviorally conditioned immunosuppression. *Psychosom. Med.* 37 : 333-340, 1975.

2. Ader, R., Fellen, D. and Cohen, N. Interactions between the brain and the immune system. *Annu. Rev. Pharmacol. Toxicol.* 30 (1990) 561-602.

3. Amir, S., Brown, Z.W. and Amit, Z. The role of endorphins in stress : evidence and speculations. *Neurosci. Biobehav. Rev.* 4 : 77-86, 1980.

4. Ballieux, R.E. and Heijnen, C.J. Stress and immune response. *In : Frontiers of Strees Research.* H. Weiner, I. Horin, R. Murison, D. Hellhammer (Eds) Hans Huber, Toronto, 1989, pp. 51-55.

5. Bartrop, R.W., Luckhurst, E., Lazarus, L., Kiloh, L.G. and Penny, R. Depressed lymphocyte function after bereavement. *Lancet,* 1 : 834-836, 1977.

6. Bhattacharya, S.K., Satyan, K.S.. Experimental methods for the evaluation of psychotropic agents. *Ind. J. Exp. Biol.* 35:565-575, 1997.

7. Carr, D.J.J., Muller, R.M., Macleod. Intersystem communication by the immune and neuroendocrine system *In : Neuroendocrine Perspectives,* Vol. 9, EE. Muller, R.M. Macleod (Eds.) Springer Verlag, New York, 1991, pp. 163-206.

8. Croisset, G., Heijnen, C.J., Veldhuis, H.D., Deweid, D. and Ballieux, R.E. Modulation of the immune response by emotional stress. *Life Sci.* 40 (1987) 775-782.

9. Glaser, R., Rice, J., Sheridian, J., Fertel, R., Stout, J. et al. Stress related immune suppression : Health implications. *Brain Behav. Immun.* 1: 7-20, 1987.

10. Glavin, G.B., Restraint ulcer : history, curreent research and future implications. *Brain Res. Bull* 5 (Suppl. 1) : 51-58, 1980.

11. Glavin, G.B., Murison, R., Overmeir, J.B., Pare, W.P., Henke, P.G and Hernandez, D.E The nurobiology of stress ulcers. *Brain Res .Rev* .16: 301-343, 1991.

12 Heijnen, C.J. Kavelaars, A. and Ballieux, R.E. Brain hormones and immune system. *In : Neuroendorinal perspectives.* Vol. 6. E.E. Muller and R.M. Macleod (Eds.) Springer-Verlag, New York, 1989, pp. 53-64.

13. Henke, P.G. The hypothalamus - amygdala axis and experimental gastric ulcers. *Neurosic. Biobehav. Rev.* 3 : 75-82, 1979.

14 Henke, P.G. The telecephalic limbic systems and experimental gastric pathology : a review. *Neurosci. Biobehav. Rev.* 6 : 381-390, 1982.

15. Henke, P.G. Recent studies of the central nucleus of of the amygdala and strees unclers. *Neurosci, Biobehav. Rev.* 12: 143-150; 1988a.

16. Henke, P.G. Stomach pathology and the amygdala. *In : The Amygdala,* J.P. Aggleton (Ed.) Wiley Liss, New York, 1992, PP. 323-338.

17. Henke, P.G. and Ray A. The limbic brain, emotions and strees unclers. *Exp. Clin. Gestroenterol.* 1(4) : 287-292, 1992.

18. Henke, P.G., Sullivan, R.M. and Ray, A. Interactions of TRH with neurotensin and dopamine in the central amygdalar nucleus during gastric stress ulcer formation. *Neurosci. Lett.* 91 : 95-100, 1988b.

19. Hernandez, D.E. Neuroendocrine mechanisms of stress ulceration : focus on thyrotyopin relasing hormone. *Life Sci.* 39: 279-296, 1986.

20. Irwin, M., Daniels, M., Smith, T.L., Bloom, E. and Weiner, H. Imparied natural killer cell activity during bereavement. *Brain Behav. Immun.* 1: 98-104, 1987.

21. Jasoo, A. and Mckenzi, J.M. Strees and immune responses in rats *Int. Arch. Allergy. Appl. Immunol.* 50 : 659-663, 1976.

22. Kiecolt-Glaser, J.K. and Glaser, R. Psychological influences on immunity. *Psychosomatics.* 27 : 621-624, 1986.

23. Koner, B.C., Banerjee, B.D., Ray, A. Effects of stress an gamma glutamyl transpeptidase (GGT) activity in lymphoid system in rats : Modulation by drugs. *Indian. J. Exp. Biol.* 35 : 222-224, 1997.

24. Mirsky I.A. The psychosomatic approach to the etiology of clinical disorders. *Psychosom. Med.* 19 : 429-430, 1957.

25. Moos, R.H. and Solomon, G.F. Personality correlates of rapidity of progression of rheumatiod arthritis. *Ann. Rheum. Dis.* 23 : 145-151, 1964.

26 Pare, W.P. and Glavin, G.B. Restraint stress in biomedical research : a review. *Neurosci. Biobehav. Rev.* 10 : 339-370, 1986.

27. Paxinos, G. and Watson, C. *The Rat Brain in Stereotaxic Coordinates.* Academic Press, New York 1982

28. Ray, A., Puri, S., Chakravarty, A.K., Sen, P. Central Histaminergic involvement during stress in rats. *Indian. J. Exp. Biol.* 30:724-728, 1992.

29. Ray. A, Gulati, K, Henke, P.G. and Sen P. The amygdaloid complex, corticotropin relasing factory and stress ulcer formation in rats. *Brain Res.* 624: 286-290, 1993.

30. Ray. A, Henke, P.G. and Sullivan, R.M. Effects of intra amygdalar TRH and its antagonism by atropine and benzodiazapines during stress ulcer formation in rats. *Pharmacol Biochem. Behav.* 36 : 597-601, 1990.

31. Ray. A, Henke, P.G., and Sullivan R.M. Opiate mechanisms in the central amygdola and gastric strees pathology in rats. *Brain Res* 442: 195-198, 1988.

32. Ray. A, Mediratta, P.K. and Sen P.Modulation by naltrexone of stress - induced chages in humoral immune responsiveness and gastric mucosal integrity in rats. *Physiol. Behav.* 51 : 293-296, 1992.

33. Ray.A, and Henke, P.G. The posterior basolateral amygdala, dopamine and stress ulcer formation in rats. *Brain Res.* 558 :335-338, 1991.

34. Ray.A, Henke, P.G. and Sullivan, R.M. The central amygala and immobilization stress induced gastric pathology in rats : neurotension and dopamine. *Brain Res.* 409 : 398-402, 1987.

35. Ray. A, Mediratta, P.K., Puri, S and Sen P. Effects of stress on immune responsivenss, gastric uncerogenesis and plasma corticosterone : Modulation by diazepam and naltrexone. *Indian J.Exp Biol.* 29: 233-236, 1991.

36. Rees, W.L. *A short textbook of psychiatry*, ELBS, 2nd Edition, 1980.

37. Salk, J. Biological basis of disease and behavior. *Perspect. Biol. Med.* 5: 198-206, 1962.

38. Schleifer, S.J., Keller, S.E. Camerino, M., Thornton, J.C. and Stein, M. Suppression of lymphocyte stimulation following bereavement. *J.Am. Med. Assoc.* 250 : 374-377, 1983.

39. Selye, H. *Stress in health and disease.* Butterworths, London, 1976.

40. Skukla, H.C., Solomon, G.F. and Doshi, R.P. The relevance of some Ayurvedic (Traditional Indian Medical) concepts to modern holistic health. *J. Holistic Health.* 4 : 125-131, 1979.

41. Stein, M., Schevaci, R.C. and Camerino, M. Influence of brain and behaviour on the immune system. *Science,* 191: 435-441, 1976.

42. Szabo, S. and Glavin, G.B. Hans Selye and the concept of biologic stress. *Ann. N.Y. Acad. Sci* 597 : 14-16, 1990.

